REMEMBERING
SATAN

Lawrence Wright

—

REMEMBERING
SATAN

Alfred A. Knopf   New York   1994

THIS IS A BORZOI BOOK
PUBLISHED BY ALFRED A. KNOPF, INC.

Copyright © 1994 by Lawrence Wright

Portions of this work were originally published in *The New Yorker*.

Library of Congress Cataloging-in-Publication Data
Wright, Lawrence.
Remembering Satan / by Lawrence Wright. — 1st ed.
p.   cm.
ISBN 0-679-43155-1
1. False memory syndrome—United States—Case studies.
2. Ritual abuse victims—United States—Case studies.
3. Adult child sexual abuse victims—United States—
Case studies. 4. Ingram, Paul R.—Family. I. Title.
RC569.5.R59W75 1994
364.1′536—dc20   93-23561
CIP

Manufactured in the United States of America
First Edition

For Tina Brown
lucky star

Acknowledgments

This book first appeared, in large part, in *The New Yorker* magazine, and I am grateful for the wise counsel of my editor, Kim Heron, and the tireless assistance of fact checker Peter Wells. I also would like to thank the investigators in Olympia—Joe Vukich, Brian Schoening, Neil McClanahan, and Loreli Thompson—who were generous with their time and always helpful. Prosecutor Gary Tabor was always accommodating, and I thank him for his courtesy.

Elizabeth F. Loftus, at the University of Washington, has done much of the groundbreaking work on memory, and she afforded me a considerable amount of her valuable time and insight. Richard Ofshe, who has written about the Ingram case himself, was extremely helpful and insightful.

I owe a particular debt to Ethan Watters, a fine journalist who wrote about the Ingram case in *Mother Jones*. His research and perceptions about this case are reflected throughout this book. Thanks also to Cheryl Smith, who helped me decipher the workings of the polygraph, and Jan McInroy for combing through the manuscript with her careful eye.

Ann Close, my editor, and Wendy Weil, my agent, have been my invaluable companions and supporters for many happy years, and once again I acknowledge my gratitude for their advice and friendship.

REMEMBERING
SATAN

1

On the morning of Monday, November 28, 1988, the day that Paul R. Ingram was to be arrested, he dressed for his job, at the Thurston County Sheriff's Office, where he had worked for nearly seventeen years, went downstairs and ate breakfast, and then, to his surprise, suddenly vomited. He thought at first it must be the flu; then he realized that it was simply fear.

Ingram, who was forty-three, was already a familiar figure to most citizens of Olympia, Washington. Until that day, he had served as the chief civil deputy of the sheriff's department and the chairman of the local Republican party. He had been active in the deputy sheriffs' association and in the Church of Living Water, a Protestant fundamentalist congregation. He was the father of five living children. (A retarded daughter had recently died in a state institution.) As a politician, he was seen as a bridge between moderate conservatives and the Christian Right. As a police officer, he was more highly regarded by the public than by other police officers. Tall and square-jawed, with oversized glasses and a brown mustache, Ingram was known in his department for being a hard-ass type who enjoyed traffic patrol. Although Ingram claimed that he gave as many as five warnings for every ticket he issued, it is also true that he routinely made more stops than most officers. He developed a reputation for handing out speeding tickets for driving just five miles over the limit, and yet his personnel file contained not a single complaint; instead it was filled with commendations from citizens who wished to thank him for the courtesy he had shown while issuing their citations.

At eight o'clock that Monday morning, Ingram drove into the parking lot of the courthouse complex, which sits atop a hill beside Capitol Lake. Across the way, the white marble capitol looms, ghostlike, above the low-lying town, and beyond it one can see Budd Inlet, the farthest-reaching finger of Puget Sound. The briny air is full of the calls of seagulls, and the northern light is thin, even on a sunny day when the brooding Olympic Mountains are visible to the northwest and Mount Rainier shows off its snow-capped splendor fifty miles to the east. One can look at a map and imagine that the city is more vibrant than it actually is. The main highway on the western side of the state, Interstate 5, strings together Seattle and Tacoma, then reaches over to include Olympia before heading to Portland on its way to California. Olympia was once the largest port in the state, but with the decline of the timber industry the South Sound is virtually empty of maritime commerce. Neither the ferries nor the hydrofoils which course through the North Sound make a stop in Olympia. The city achieved a measure of regional fame through two local products that bear its name: the pale beer that is manufactured at the Olympia Brewery Company above the falls at the mouth of the Deschutes River, and the sweet, thumbnail-size oysters that grow in the bay. The brewery has long since sold out to Milwaukee interests; and as for the oysters, pollution and overharvesting have reduced them to an occasional, expensive delicacy.

Olympia became the capital of Washington Territory in 1853, when it was a bustling frontier outpost; now it is made up largely of bureaucrats, and the city bustles only when the legislature is in session. St. Peter's Hospital and a cardboard-box plant operated by Georgia Pacific are the other leading employers. Olympia is bordered by the townships of Tumwater and Lacey, making up what is known as the Tri-Cities, with a population of 68,000—Olympia proper accounting for just over half of that number. There are no skyscrapers, and parking is rarely a problem. Most people who live here like the slow pace, the modest scale, and the cozy society of small-town life. For many of them, the failure of the city to realize its early promise of becoming an industrial port like Tacoma or a sophisticated, international urban center like Seattle is a blessing that has allowed Olympia to stay charming and humane, if somewhat dull and self-satisfied.

Perhaps because of its beauty, its classical name, and a shroud of mystery that hangs over it—in the form of frequent fog or drizzle—Olympia has acquired a reputation as a spiritual center. J. Z. Knight, a well-known New Age channeler who owns a large estate off the Yelm Highway, is widely regarded as the richest woman in the county; the local lore is that her horse stables have chandeliers in every stall. Celebrity acolytes such as Shirley MacLaine and Linda Evans have sometimes passed through Olympia on their way to visit Knight. A small coven of witches runs a local herb shop. Like most Washingtonians, Olympians pride themselves on their tolerance in such matters, and it would be fair to say that the town is better known for its New Age believers than for its fundamentalist Christians; but both elements are deeply entwined with the life of the town, and are sometimes loudly at odds.

Fifteen minutes after Ingram arrived at work, he was summoned to the office of his boss, Sheriff Gary Edwards. An affable man with few enemies, Edwards was a rare Republican officeholder in a county long regarded as a stronghold of liberal Democratic politics. Ingram was not just an employee; he was an important political ally of Edwards and a friend for nearly a decade. In 1986 Edwards had appointed Ingram to be his chief civil deputy, causing some grousing on the part of those who had been leapfrogged by the junior officer; but Ingram had performed well in that position. He was better suited to administrative work than to investigations. Like Edwards, Ingram seldom gave offense; he seemed cheerful and unflappable—qualities Edwards had in abundance and which he apparently sought in his staff. With his earnest, friendly manner, Ingram was the kind of cop who was tailor-made for public appearances. He spent much of his time in schools talking to kids about the dangers of drug use, although he continued to do traffic patrol as he commuted to and from work.

Joining Edwards and Ingram in that meeting was the number two man in the department, Undersheriff Neil McClanahan. Intense and ambitious, McClanahan had risen through the ranks even more quickly than Ingram. They had known each other well since 1972, when both were young deputies and shared a county car. McClanahan wore glasses and a trim brown mustache, and when he put on his tweedy rain hat he bore a certain resemblance to Peter Sellers in the role of Inspector Clouseau—a point McClanahan would jokingly make about himself. It wasn't surprising that the careers of Paul Ingram and Neil McClanahan paralleled each other, since their skills and interests were similar; and although they were friends, they were also competitors in the small but still quite political hierarchy of the Thurston County Sheriff's Office. McClanahan's first action when he joined the other two men that morning was to relieve Ingram of the automatic pistol that he habitually wore in an ankle holster.

"Paul, there's a problem," Edwards said. He asked if Ingram knew about the charges of sexual molestation that his two daughters, Ericka and Julie, had made. (Ericka and Julie were then twenty-two and eighteen, respectively.) Ingram said that he did; however, he said he could not remember having ever molested his daughters. "If this did happen, we need to take care of it," Ingram said, but he added, "I can't see myself doing this." If he did molest the girls, then "there must be a dark side of me that I don't know about." These responses were disturbingly equivocal—a variation on the "maybe I did and maybe I didn't" theme that police often hear from suspects who are bargaining for a plea. But Ingram went on to say that if the charges were true, then not only his daughters but also his sons would need help. "I've never thought about suicide before, but if it turns out that I have done something, I want you to get all my guns out of the house, just in case," Ingram said, in a voice that sounded more puzzled than despairing. He requested a lie detector test, so he could "get to the bottom of this."

"I hope you're not going to make these girls go through a trial," Edwards said. The sheriff may also have been thinking of the reputation of his department, although at this very early stage in the investigation the prospect of a trial seemed remote. In fact, until this point, Edwards had confined the investigation to an administrative proceeding, such as might occur when citizens complain about an officer's erratic driving. An administrative inquiry might lead to a disciplinary hearing, which itself could result in a suspension or the loss of a job. It could all be handled very quietly.

Ingram willingly agreed to talk to investigators without a lawyer present, and so at nine a.m. McClanahan escorted him to the office of detectives Joe Vukich and Brian Schoening, who handled sex offenses. Both men knew Ingram well; in fact, his office was directly across the hall. Brian Schoening was a pale, sandy-haired veteran, a gravel-voiced grandfather with gray, unsurprised eyes. Ingram was the last man in the department that Schoening would have suspected of sexual abuse, but he had seen enough of the kinky underside of human nature to know that pleasant faces can hide appalling desires. Joe Vukich had met Ingram in 1976, even before joining the force;

after that they worked the same district, and Ingram had often invited the baby-faced rookie over to his house for barbecue and card games. As far as Vukich could tell, Ingram was a decent, easygoing family man and all-American husband. Ingram was both men's superior in the department; so from the beginning the interrogation was uncomfortable and conflicted for everyone, including the suspect.

Several hours into the questioning, Vukich turned on a tape recorder to take Ingram's official statement. Ingram now said, "I really believe that the allegations did occur and that I did violate them and probably for a long period of time. I've repressed it."

Vukich asked Ingram why he was confessing if he couldn't remember the violations, and Ingram replied, "Well, number one, my girls know me. They wouldn't lie about something like this. And, uh, there's other evidence."

"And what, in your mind, would that evidence be?" one of the detectives asked.

"The way they've been acting for at least the last couple years and the fact that I've not been able to be affectionate with them, uh, even though I want to be," Ingram said. "I have a hard time hugging them, or even telling them that I love them, and I just know that's not natural."

"Besides having a hard time being close to them, do you recall anything of a physical nature you may have done that could have been abusive, such as striking them?"

"Whew . . . I don't recall, uh, striking the girls," Ingram responded. "I don't lose my temper very often, but occasionally I do, or—or they may think that I'm, you know, arguing rather than, uh, conversing with them. Those may be looked at by them as abuse."

"If I asked you if you—and this is a yes-or-no answer—touched Julie inappropriately sexually, what would you say?"

"I'd have to say yes."

"And how about Ericka?"

"Again, I would have to say yes."

"What would you think the age of Ericka would've been when these things first started happening between you and her?"

"I can't recall myself, but I know that the age of five has come up in a couple of conversations." Ingram had first heard about the charges a week before.

"What do you remember?" the detectives pressed him.

"I don't remember anything."

It's not unusual in a police investigation for a suspect to say that he doesn't remember having committed a crime, especially if the crime is a sex offense. Oftentimes, the explanation involves the use of alcohol or drugs, but the claim of a faulty memory can also be a ploy on the part of the suspect to flesh out the charges—to see what evidence, if any, the police have. It was the experience of Schoening and Vukich that a suspect who said he didn't remember anything was either avoiding the truth or standing on the threshold of a confession; so at this point guilt was the tacit assumption that underlay the interrogation. Ingram wasn't saying "I didn't do it"; he was saying he couldn't *see* himself doing it.

Vukich turned off the tape recorder while he and Schoening attempted to move Ingram to accept his guilt. During the next twenty minutes, they told him that his daughters were shattered by his abuse, and provided him with some of the details that the girls had included in their statements. Ingram continued to be suspended between his statement that his daughters wouldn't lie and his assertion that he couldn't remember the abuse. He would later assert that Vukich assured him that the memories would return if he did confess (although there's no way to know if that assertion is true). According to notes that Schoening took during the interrogation, Ingram began praying feverishly. When the detectives turned on the tape recorder again, Schoening noted that Ingram was staring at the wall, clutching his hands, and that he then went into a "trance-type thing." Ingram began describing a scene in which he came into his older daughter's bedroom and removed his bathrobe. Then, he said, "I would've removed her underpants or bottoms to the nightgown."

"O.K., you say 'would've,' " one of the detectives said. "Now, do you mean 'would've,' or did you?"

"I did," said Ingram.

"After you pulled down her bottom, where did you touch her?"

"I touched her on her breasts and I touched her on her vagina. . . ."

"What did you say to her when she woke up?"

"I would've told her to be quiet and, uh, not say anything to anybody and threatened to her to say that I would kill her if she told anybody about this," Ingram said.

"O.K., you say you 'would've.' Is that 'would've,' or did you?"

"Uh, I did. . . ."

"And where did you go when you left her room?"

"I would've gone back to bed with my wife."

By the time the interview ended, many hours later, Paul Ingram had confessed to having sex with both his daughters on numerous occasions, beginning when Ericka was five years old. He had also talked about having impregnated his younger daughter, Julie, and taken her to have an abortion in the nearby town of Shelton when she was fifteen. All of these statements accorded in a general way with the charges his daughters had made, although Ingram's confessions were still maddeningly mired in conditional phrases. Brian Schoening, who is a talkative and emotional man despite his hard-bitten exterior, said later that he was deeply affected by Ingram's detachment in describing the sexual abuse of his daughters. Schoening had never seen such apparent remorselessness on the part of an offender, and it was even more galling to him because Ingram wore the same uniform that he did. Still, there was nothing very unusual about a community leader's being caught in a disgraceful act. If the case had ended that Monday, with Ingram's tentative confession, it doubtless would have caused only a brief sensation at most. In the ordinary course of things, he probably would have been spared a prison sentence and assigned instead to psychological counseling. His case would long since have been forgotten. But no one realized then where the hole in Ingram's memory would lead.

At four-thirty that afternoon, Ingram changed into the Thurston County jail's high-visibility orange coveralls and entered an isolation cell, subject to a twenty-four-hour suicide watch. Detective Schoening and Sheriff Edwards then made the dismal trip to Ingram's house in East Olympia to tell his wife, Sandy, the news.

2

————

The Ingrams owned ten acres off Fir Tree Road, near the Union Pacific Railroad tracks. Here the brief suburbs have grown ragged as the town turns into the country. There are rough houses and trailers and an abundance of powerboats and four-wheel-drive vehicles in the driveways. Scarcely a mile away is a corner of the immense Fort Lewis military reservation, which occupies much of the southeastern portion of the county. Occasionally, during maneuvers, one can hear the sounds of a mock war, with explosions and machine-gun fire. The house, which the Ingrams built in 1978, was not visible from the road. Although later it would be laden with spooky associations (McClanahan would compare it with the house in *The Amityville Horror*), on that November evening it was nothing more than an attractive barn-shaped structure, nicer than most homes in the area. It had the makings of a small estate. Both Paul and Sandy had developed a fetish for self-sufficiency. Paul raised chickens, rabbits, a couple of cows, and even ducks in a pond behind the house. A small herd of goats kept the lawn trim. Sandy maintained a year-round vegetable garden. A neighbor described the property as "well used," and it was indeed crowded with animal hutches and tools and a number of cars and trucks. For years Sandy had operated a day-care center in the house, so in addition to the normal clutter of family life the yard accommodated a swing set and a sandbox, and the house was full of plastic toys and rest mats.

Until that Monday, Sandy had thought of her marriage as happy, stable, and old-fashioned in a good sense. Paul's word was law, but because Sandy seldom disagreed with him, they almost never quarreled. She had her own life outside of the family—besides her day-care business, she had done a turn at public service, having spent one term on the county school board (in that sense, she was a more successful politician than Paul)—but for the most part her life was anchored in the home and the church.

Paul and Sandy had met in 1964, at Spokane Community College. Both were putting themselves through school, Sandy as a part-time maid and Paul as a janitor in a dairy plant. Both came from large and devout Catholic families. Sandy had spent two years in a convent school and had seriously considered becoming a nun. Paul had always attended Catholic schools and spent three years in a seminary, but he later decided that his priestly aspiration had largely been to please his mother. In any case, whatever clerical vocation he might have had melted away on the day he gave Sandy a lift to work. She was outgoing and full of fun, and they had so much in common. Paul was impressed that she was such a hard worker. Sandy also proved to be something of a tomboy; once, on a group outing, they went bobsledding down Mount Spokane on the hood of a '48 Buick, and Sandy laughed at the wild recklessness of it. Paul had practically no experience with girls; he rarely dated, and was a virgin when he met Sandy. They soon decided to marry, though both sets of parents were alarmed and thought they should wait. On their wedding day, in February 1965, both were nineteen years old. They had known each other for less than five months.

Paul's father, Sylvester, was a carpenter, an accountant, and a jack-of-all-trades who suffered from chronic ill health. His mother, Elizabeth, was a dietitian who held the family together during the hard times that followed a back injury to Sylvester in 1954. The children always had shoes and food, but little else. As the oldest of seven, Paul became the official babysitter and a virtual parent. His sister Robin recalls him as caring and self-sacrificing, and says he never expressed resentment at the extra burden he carried.

The family that Paul would help create resembled in many ways the family in which he grew up. Both of his parents were strict disciplinarians. Paul always felt that they showed much more love for each other than they showed for their children— a bitter observation that his own children came to echo. And however attentive and protective he may have been as an older brother, as a father Paul was a martinet, full of rules and prohibitions.

Sandy had been the youngest of four children and very much the family pet. She had a sweet, spunky disposition, and a stubborn streak that kept Paul from running over her. Although there had been a history of mental illness in her family, neither Sandy nor Paul worried about the possibility of a hereditary problem. Sandy, especially, wanted a large family; Paul wasn't so sure, but he didn't resist the idea. They set up housekeeping in a two-bedroom rented house in Spokane.

Paul Jr., also called Paul Ross by the family, was born in September of 1965, seven months after the wedding. With this new responsibility on his shoulders, Paul took a job as a building supervisor at a medical center. Months after Paul Ross's birth, Sandy learned she was pregnant again, this time with twins. Ericka and Andrea were born in September of 1966. Andrea, the firstborn, was underweight and sickly; Ericka was plump and healthy. Sandy took the younger twin home after a few days, but Andrea remained in the hospital for a week, and when she finally did come home she remained listless. The doctors assured Sandy that there was nothing wrong, Andrea was merely small; but a few days later she seemed to stop breathing. The panicked young parents rushed to the hospital with their gasping infant, who had turned blue as she struggled to breathe. Tests determined that she had spinal meningitis. A priest came to baptize her and administer the last rites, but Andrea confounded the doctors' expectations and survived. The meningitis, however, caused her brain to swell, with the result that her mental faculties were severely damaged and her skull was permanently enlarged.

The Ingrams quickly outgrew their little house. In early 1967 they bought, for $6,900, a three-bedroom house that had been repossessed by the Veterans Administration. The house was surrounded by a four-foot-high cyclone fence, which Paul Ross managed to scale while he was still in diapers. Sandy usually found him in the neighborhood, playing with other children, although twice she had to call in the police to locate him. From then on, he was kept on a leash when he played outdoors.

Paul hit the road, selling cameras door-to-door. It was his first real chance to travel, and he loved it, but the income never really covered their expenses. Sandy started looking after other people's children to take up the slack. Meanwhile, Andrea was in and out of the hospital with chronic attacks of pneumonia, and her needs became too great for the couple to handle. When she was still a baby, they sent her to a state institution, where she spent the rest of her life.

Sandy gave birth to a second son, Chad, in 1968. Paul, bowing to reality, took a more reliable job, as a field investigator with the Retail Credit Company. Later that same year, the company offered openings in several other cities. Moving would bring a pay raise and a chance for advancement. Paul and Sandy decided on Olympia, because it was small and semirural and appealed to their back-to-nature ideals. They bought a house trailer and moved it to the Flying Carpet mobile home park, in East Olympia. Soon Sandy was getting paid to look after other children in the camp. The income she provided was essential for the family, especially in those early days, but her own children came to feel that she paid more attention to the day-care children than to them.

Before long the expanding Ingram family was eager to move to larger quarters. When their fifth child, Julie, was born, in 1970, they secured a bank loan of $17,500 and built a three-bedroom house on a wooded lot in East Olympia. The boys shared one bedroom, and the girls shared another. Later they finished the basement, adding another bedroom and a recreation room. At last they had room for Sandy's garden and for the farm animals that Paul hoped would make them self-sufficient. He sold Amway products and a brand of dehydrated foods on the side. Shadowed by need throughout his own childhood, he was relentless in his drive to create security. From his point of view, he was being a good provider and giving his children an opportunity he had never had. But they began to feel that he valued them more as workers than as sons and daughters. "The old man didn't give a shit about anybody as long as you did your chores," Paul Ross later complained.

In 1969, almost as a lark, Paul applied to the reserve corps of the police department in Lacey, a small (there were only eight stoplights) adjoining township. He was accepted and began driving around in the evenings and on weekends with a borrowed pistol, doing traffic duty and handling domestic disputes. Within a few months he had learned enough about police work that he qualified to drive patrol on his own. Never in his life had he enjoyed anything so much. Paul thought of his police work as a hobby that brought in some additional money, but it also meant that he was spending almost no time at home with Sandy and the children. Chad had to teach himself how to ride a bike; later, he taught himself to drive a car as well.

In 1971, Paul moved from the Lacey Police Department to the Thurston County Sheriff's Office, and a year later the sheriff asked him to join the staff full-time. That meant a pay cut of a hundred dollars a month, which the family could scarcely afford; but Sandy supported Paul because he so obviously enjoyed the work. For the most part, Paul did well, although once in training class he made the mistake of offering his opinion that sheriffs should be appointed, not elected; the following morning he was invited into the chief deputy's office and thoroughly chewed out. The experience put him on guard about the politics of the office.

Paul quickly made friends in the department. He and Neil McClanahan, then another rookie, spent a lot of time together carpooling in the county car they shared. They often talked about religion, a subject of interest to both of them. At the time, Paul was still a Catholic, although he would eventually convert to a Protestant denomination; Neil was headed in the opposite direction. A deeply religious man, McClanahan was studying the catechism of the Catholic church and preparing for his own conversion.

Their spiritual pursuits and interest in civic service set them apart from most police officers, but neither man wanted to come across as a prude. Both joined a rotating poker game, along with several other deputies. Sometimes the game took place at the Ingrams' house. These games became so important to Paul that he installed a refrigerator in the basement recreation room to hold a keg of beer. No doubt, being a host to other members of the department, including the sheriff himself, enhanced Paul's standing and made him one of the guys. The morning after a poker party, the children would scour the floor under the table for loose change.

In 1972, Paul began having an affair with an older, divorced woman. Paul felt that he could discuss with her matters other than child rearing and the routine details of domestic life. His lover was a Lutheran, and she talked about her personal relationship with Jesus in terms that Paul had never heard in seminary. The affair foundered when it became clear that Paul would never leave Sandy. Although he was going to Mass less and less often, he was still enough of a Catholic not to believe in divorce.

Paul and Sandy's frugality, meanwhile, was paying off. They bought an old Ford pickup with a camper shell, and the family began spending summer vacations camping in Idaho. In 1976, they bought five acres of logged-off property on Fir Tree Road, with an option on an adjacent five acres. With characteristic energy, they began clearing the land in their spare time. Friends from the Olympia Police Department helped them put in a septic tank and grade a low spot into a pond. A nearby gravel pit provided material for a road at a bargain price. When carpenters finished the two-story house on the property, Paul and Sandy painted it together, inside and out. Jim Rabie, a detective in the Thurston County Sheriff's Office and a friend of Paul's, came to wire it, and Rabie's father built the kitchen cabinets.

At last, Paul and Sandy's dreams were realized. Their handsome home was surrounded by fir, alder, ash, cottonwood, cedar, and hemlock. In the spring, the dogwoods bloomed, and deer poked around in the bush. The woods were full of raccoons and possums and grouse, and there was an occasional red fox. There were ducks and herons in the pond. Sandy expanded her garden, making room for fruit trees and flowering plants. In addition to the chickens and rabbits that Paul raised, there was enough land to graze a few cows. It felt like paradise to Paul and Sandy, but not to their children, who thought of the place as remote and isolated.

The police investigators would interview many friends and neighbors of the Ingram family. Most described Paul and Sandy as ordinary folks who loved their children, even if they were strict. The most severe punishments meted out in the household included spanking for the younger children and being grounded for the older ones; usually it was a matter of withholding television or dessert. After the parents became devout fundamentalists, they didn't allow their children to participate in sports and rarely let them go to games or involve themselves in other extracurricular activities that might get in the way of chores or schoolwork. This was hardest on Chad, a natural athlete. "They weren't allowed to be kids," a neighbor observed, but the children always seemed well-mannered. Ericka and Julie were popular baby-sitters. One of the daughters' friends said that their dad was always yelling and that the brothers "goofed off and did weird things," although the only example of weirdness she could offer was that Chad had once tried to kiss her. A woman who had grazed a horse on the Ingram property said that Paul had called her and threatened to kill the animal if she didn't remove it right away. Every inch of his property had a purpose, he said; nothing was left for recreation.

The family doctor stated he had never seen any signs of abuse in the children. The Ingrams seemed healthy, for the most part. Ericka had a spate of heavy, irregular menstrual bleeding when she was sixteen, but that was common in the first three years of menstruation. Paul and Sandy belonged to a tennis club, and they played three times a week. At night, they all held hands and prayed before eating a big family dinner. The food was fresh, if somewhat rustic, although roasted rabbit and goat stew were not thought of as being terribly exotic in a region of the country where game was still a large part of the ordinary diet and self-sufficiency was held in high esteem. Sandy was always baking or stirring up something in the kitchen. She was a "perfect homemaker," said an admiring friend, who had once leased a trailer on the Ingram property. During that time the friend never observed anything unusual happening. Everyone who knew them described the Ingrams as a hardworking, Christian family; in fact, several people told the investigators that they had tried to model their own families on the Ingrams.

The previous year, Sandy had begun attending services at the Evergreen Christian Center, which is affiliated with the Assemblies of God. Paul was surprised, because Sandy had been deeply involved with their Catholic church, singing in the choir and teaching the catechism class. But he noticed a change in her right away—a softening, which he found very appealing. She began taking the children to the center on Sunday mornings and Wednesday nights. Eventually Paul went too, and he liked the open, welcoming atmosphere, although the hand waving and speaking in tongues put him off. A month later, however, Paul responded to an altar call and surrendered his life to Jesus. That fall, the entire family was baptized in the deep water.

The Ingrams were drawn to Pentecostalism in part because of its emphasis on the importance of the family. And yet, in the Ingram household, a troubling rift was developing between the parents and the children. Paul and Sandy were demonstrably affectionate with each other; indeed, there was a sexual charge between them that others could hardly miss. (They slept in the nude on a waterbed, and according to Paul they had sex nearly every other day.) With their children, however, they were stern and emotionally reserved. Sex was never discussed, except when the girls told Sandy that they intended to remain virgins until they married. There were few outlets for the children's emotional needs and youthful energy, however. Once the family joined the new congregation, Paul outlawed all sports activities and banned rock-and-roll music unless it was

Christian. Tensions worsened in 1978, when Sandy found herself pregnant again. After the child, a third son, named Mark, was born, Paul decided that he was going to make an effort to be a better father. Over time, the older children came to feel that Mark was their father's favorite; he was coddled rather than ordered around and put to work. Nearly every night, Paul read to Mark at bedtime—something that he had never done with the others—and later he bought the boy a computer and spent many evenings playing computer games with him. Ericka and Julie both complained that Mark was being spoiled.

The two older boys were rebellious and showed a disturbing tendency to live secret lives. In 1984, at the age of eighteen, Paul Ross turned down an appointment to West Point which his father had arranged, and then abruptly left home after wrecking his car for the third time in three months. He parked the car in a cemetery and left behind a note to Sandy saying that he had fallen in with a dangerous crowd. He warned his parents not to try to find him. "When you get this letter I'll probably be somewhere in South America," he wrote. Investigators later found the note in Sandy's desk. Their second son, Chad, whom Paul and Sandy considered the quietest and most even-tempered of their children, moved into an apartment in downtown Olympia for a short time during high school, and was arrested for shoplifting candy. Later, he went to Bible school in Tulsa, dropped out, and came back home to live.

Ericka and Julie, who shared a bedroom throughout their childhood, were often considered a pair, although Ericka was four years older than Julie and by far the more assertive. One can see a family resemblance: they inherited dark brown hair and eyes from both sides of the family, and have full, rounded faces, such as one might find in a portrait by Vermeer. What struck most people, however, was how different their personalities were. Ericka was moody and self-absorbed, Julie bubbly and outgoing, if somewhat in the shadow of her sister. Certainly Ericka was the beauty of the family, although she held herself apart and looked at life through eyes of cautious reserve. Her most striking feature was her mouth, which was small and sensual, with unusually high peaks on the arches of her upper lip; it was like the mouth of a Kewpie doll. She was still living at home when she turned twenty-two. Working as a tour guide at the capitol and intermittently attending college (she studied sign language and sometimes served as an interpreter for the deaf), Ericka always had her eye on the larger world. She bought stylish clothes and loved to travel. She had been to Greece, and in August of 1988 she had just returned from attending the Olympics in South Korea. Julie, on the other hand, was a homebody, like her mother. People thought she was the image of Sandy, and she dressed like her mother, in jeans and sweatshirts. Two years in a row, Julie had won the state championship in the Future Homemakers of America contest and had gone on to the nationals; that constituted most of her travel experience, except for the family vacations. The two girls were alike in one respect, though: they rarely went on dates—Ericka had been out only twice in the previous three years—and they were extremely shy around boys.

The Ingrams became a part of the extraordinary growth of Pentecostalism in America during the seventies and eighties. When the Evergreen Christian Center grew too large for the family's taste, they transferred to the Church of Living Water, an affiliate of the International Church of the Foursquare Gospel, which had been founded by the well-known evangelist Aimee Semple McPherson in the 1920s. The Church of Living Water was also growing quickly and soon moved from its modest quarters into an expansive campus with eight buildings that take up most of a city block. Like many congregations that once endured the stigma of being "Holy Rollers" on the poor side of town, the church projects an atmosphere that is intended to be informal and inviting. The sanctuary is a windowless theater called the Living Room, where the pastoral staff sit on a dais in easy chairs beside an artificial fireplace. It has the ambiance of the set of a daytime television talk show. There is a small gospel choir and a band.

Unlike the Catholic tradition that Paul and Sandy grew up in, the Pentecostal teachings of the Church of Living Water emphasized the truth of personal revelation, which sometimes appeared in dramatic forms. Here the congregation was often on its feet, waving its hands, shouting praise, instead of sitting in pews or kneeling silently at the altar rail. There was nothing rabid or fanatical about the services, as so many people still believed, but there was a powerful current of energy that could be shocking or thrilling, depending on what one thought about the message: that the Bible is the infallible word of God; that Jesus is His Son and will return to rapture the church and judge the world; that the only means of being cleansed from sin is through repentance and faith in Jesus; and that the gifts of the Holy Spirit—prophecy, healing, discernment, speaking or understanding strange tongues—are essential for personal salvation and available to all who believe.

The Ingrams were regulars at the church every Sunday morning and night and every Wednesday evening, and they also participated in the countless socials and study groups and retreats. Sandy started a food-and-clothing charity called Twelve Baskets, which became an important part of the church's community service. Frequently, Ericka would interpret sermons for deaf members of the congregation. She also persuaded her parents to take in two deaf girls as foster children, which proved to be an awkward arrangement for Paul and Sandy, because communication was so difficult.

The Church of Living Water sponsored an annual retreat for teenage girls called Heart to Heart, held at a camp on nearby

Black Lake. Julie and Ericka had attended for several years. Although she was really too old for the camp, Ericka returned in August of 1988 as a counselor. Five years earlier, during a fellowship discussion, Ericka had related an incident of what she characterized as attempted rape by a man she knew. The subject of sexual abuse sometimes arose during these sessions, and counselors took such revelations seriously. The authorities were alerted, and Jim Rabie, the sex-crime detective from the sheriff's office, followed up on Ericka's charge. He determined that there wasn't much substance to it—a married man had given Ericka a ride and put his hand on her knee—and the investigation was not pursued. Then, in 1985, during another Heart to Heart retreat, Julie said she had been sexually abused by a neighbor who lived on the Ingram property. When word of that charge got back to Paul, he took Julie to the county prosecutor and helped her file a complaint. Eventually, Ericka also accused the neighbor of improper sexual contact. Julie, however, became less and less able to speak about the alleged incident, to the point of becoming completely mute on the subject. Inconsistencies in her story began to surface, and the county prosecutor finally dropped the charges. Julie seemed relieved.

During the 1988 Heart to Heart, a woman from California named Karla Franko came to speak to the sixty girls in attendance. Franko is a charismatic Christian who believes she has been given the biblical gifts of healing and spiritual discernment. Before going to Bible college, she had been a dancer and a stand-up comic as well as an actress, and had parts in several sitcoms and TV commercials, which added a note of celebrity in the minds of the young girls in the audience. Often in speaking to youth groups such as this one, Franko would feel herself filled with the Holy Spirit and would make pronouncements that the Spirit urged upon her. Many extraordinary events took place at the 1988 retreat. At one point, Franko told the mesmerized group that she had a mental picture of a little girl hiding in a coat closet, and saw a crack of light under the door. Footsteps were approaching. There was the sound of a key locking the door. At that, a girl in the audience stood up, heaving with sobs, and cried out that she had been that little girl. Franko then had another vision. She said that someone in the audience had been molested as a young girl by a relative. Suddenly, a deaf girl rushed out of the room. A woman named Paula Davis, who, along with Ericka, was interpreting for the deaf campers, went after the girl and found her in the bathroom with her head in the toilet, trying to drown herself. In this charged atmosphere, a number of other girls came forward to say that they, too, had been abused. The counselors had their hands full.

Late in the afternoon of the last day of the retreat, the campers boarded buses to return to the church. Ericka remained in the conference center, sobbing disconsolately. She sat cross-legged on the floor of the stage with her head hanging between her knees. It was a dramatic, heartbreaking sight, but Ericka would not say what was wrong. The other counselors gave up trying to talk to her. They just gathered around her quietly to show their support. Finally, according to one of the counselors, she declared, "I have been abused sexually by my father."

"She seemed to be devastated just by having said those words," the counselor later told police.

Actually, that was only one version of the event—the version that the detectives placed in their files and later made available to defense attorneys. Another witness to the scene was Karla Franko, and she had a different account of what happened, which she claims she told investigators (there is no record of her statement in the files). Franko recalls that as she was getting ready to leave for the airport, a counselor came to her and asked her to pray over Ericka. "What does she need prayer for?'' Franko asked. The counselor shrugged. Franko went back to the stage, where Ericka was sitting Indian-style, a portrait in dejection. Franko stood over her and began praying aloud. Almost immediately, she felt the Lord prompting her with information. She stepped back and was silent as she listened to the Lord's urgings. The word ''molestation'' presented itself to her.

''You have been abused as a child, sexually abused,'' Franko announced. Ericka sat quietly weeping, unable to respond. Franko received another divine prompting, which told her, ''It's by her father, and it's been happening for years.'' When Franko said this aloud, Ericka began to sob hysterically. Franko prayed for the Lord to heal her. When Ericka's weeping eventually began to subside, Franko urged her to seek counseling, in order to get to the memories that were causing her so much pain. At no time, says Franko, did Ericka utter a word; she was so scathed and devastated by Franko's revelation that she could do little more than nod in acknowledgment.

Not long after the church retreat, both daughters abruptly moved out of the house. Ericka departed during the last week of September. She left the two deaf girls behind, in her parents' care. Julie left six weeks later. Both eventually moved in with friends, although Julie actually spent some nights sleeping in her car. Neither would say where they were or give any explanation for their actions. Paul and Sandy were distraught, especially about Julie. It was becoming a pattern in the Ingram household for the children to suddenly flee and hide, although Ericka, at twenty-two, had remained in the house longer than any of the others.

Ericka arranged to meet her mother after the evening church services the Sunday before Thanksgiving. That night there was an open house to dedicate the new sanctuary. Julie was there, and Paul took the opportunity to ask her to lunch. He said he wanted to talk about why she had moved out. Julie seemed to be in a cheerful mood and readily agreed. Paul then took ten-year-old Mark home, and Sandy went to meet Ericka at a nearby Denny's restaurant. She got there first, and sat at a table and ordered a cup of tea. For months, Sandy had sensed that Ericka was unhappy; but whenever she asked what was wrong, the only response Ericka had been able to give was a cryptic "You don't want to know." Now Ericka arrived in the company of her best friend, Paula Davis, who was to be her advocate in all that followed. Over the next two hours, Ericka talked of having been repeatedly molested by her father when she was young. In the last several years, she said, her brothers Paul Ross and Chad had molested her as well. Ericka linked her father's abuse to the poker parties in their old house. She said that the abuse had stopped when Paul was born again in the Pentecostal church, in 1975. As Ericka spoke, Sandy stared into her teacup. Finally she asked Ericka why she had never spoken about this before. "Mom, I did tell you," Ericka replied. "I tried to tell you, and you wouldn't listen."

"You're the only one in the family who didn't know," Davis added.

Sandy went home and confronted Paul. He said, "I never touched those girls." Chad was working late at the YMCA, and Sandy waited up for him. "You know I've always been a good boy, Mama," he said when she told him of Ericka's accusations against him. She called the associate pastor at her church, John Bratun, and learned that he already had heard about the allegations from the retreat counselors. According to Paul, Bratun told Sandy that the charges were probably true, because children didn't make up those kinds of things. Sandy and Paul had been planning to drive to the Oregon coast the next day for a week's vacation in a rented condominium, but that was now the last thing on Sandy's mind. In the morning, Sandy picked up Julie in the house where she was staying and drove her to school. On the way, Julie confirmed that her father and her oldest brother had molested her, too. She said that she had last been molested by her father five years earlier, when she was thirteen.

Against her better judgment, Sandy agreed to go ahead with the vacation, after her pastor said it would be good to get away. In her heart, Sandy felt that they should stay and deal with the accusations now, before they got out of hand; but Paul wanted to go—he needed to think. As soon as they left town, however, the investigation began in earnest. That very afternoon, a counselor from the local rape-crisis center took Julie to meet with police investigators, one of whom was Joe Vukich. The story she told them was somewhat different from the one she had told her mother that morning, and far more detailed. Julie said that the abuse had begun when she was in the fifth grade; her father was working the graveyard shift then, and sometimes he would sneak into the room where Ericka and Julie slept. He would be either naked or wearing shorts or sweats. He would get into bed with one of the girls and have vaginal or anal sex with her. As Julie told the story, she hid her face behind a curtain of brown hair. Each response came after a lengthy pause. Some questions she refused to answer. Because the investigators were concerned about the statute of limitations, which then extended for seven years in the case of assaults on minors, they concentrated on the most recent events. Julie told them that the last time her father had sexually abused her was three years before, when she was fifteen—not five years before, as she had told her mother. Detective Vukich asked Julie why she had never spoken to anyone about the assaults, and she replied that her mother had never wanted to listen.

That evening Vukich and Detective Paul Johnson, of the Olympia Police Department, interviewed Ericka at the home

of a friend of hers from church. Vukich was immediately struck
by how pretty Ericka was, and how vulnerable. She stated that
her father had begun sexually abusing her when she was five
years old. Vukich asked her to recall the last incident of abuse,
and Ericka said she thought that she must have been in the
fourth grade—well beyond the statute of limitations. Vukich
kept pressing for more details. "Once, I felt like I hurt all over
when I woke up—the bed was wet and yucky," Ericka said.
Suddenly she burst into tears and ran into the bathroom. The
detectives could hear her sobbing loudly for ten minutes. When
she came back into the room, she said, "I caught a disease
from my dad about a year ago. The doctor is in California, and
also there is a doctor in Olympia who treated me." She now
said that this 1987 incident was the last time she had sex with
her father.

The detectives left at about midnight. With the testimony
of two victims in hand, and with the promise of medical evidence, they already had a strong case to give to the county
prosecutor.

Ericka called Karla Franko in California, and Franko expressed surprise at hearing from her. Ericka repeated some of
the details she had given to Vukich and then informed Franko,
"It is all coming down. They have Julie's confession." When
Franko asked Ericka what she thought would happen to her
father, she said he was going to lose his job. Given the fact
that this was still an administrative proceeding, and not yet a
criminal one, Ericka may have had reason to believe that the
case would go no further than that.

Vukich interviewed Ericka again, during the Thanksgiving
weekend. This time she said that the last incident of abuse had
actually occurred during the final week of September, when
she awoke to find her father kneeling beside her bed, touching
her vagina. Vukich didn't question why she hadn't told him

of this incident sooner; it's not unusual for victims of sexual abuse to make partial disclosures. But it was notable that in the space of one week both girls had assigned several different dates to the last incidence of abuse. In Ericka's case the time frame had moved from a decade earlier to a year earlier and then to just two months earlier.

Sandy tried to talk to Paul about the allegations while they were on vacation, but he was extremely reticent. He spent a lot of time reading his Bible and walking on the beach, but he had trouble composing his thoughts. He said he felt as if there were a solid mass of fear in his stomach, as dense and impacted as a bowling ball. Sandy stayed in the condo and cried. Paul assured her that nothing had happened, and Sandy believed him, but she was filled with dread. At one point, Paul suggested that the girls were trying to split them up, but neither he nor Sandy could imagine why their daughters would want to do such a thing.

And so when Sheriff Edwards and Detective Schoening knocked on the Ingrams' door that afternoon of Monday, November 28, and told Sandy that Paul had confessed, she went into shock. Her knees buckled, and she nearly fainted. She wobbled into the dining room and sat down at the table. Edwards and Schoening were afraid to leave her alone; she was so distraught that they feared that she, too, might consider killing herself. They got in touch with the Ingrams' pastor, Ron Long, and waited until Long and his associate John Bratun arrived. The last image that Schoening recalls of that night is of Sandy still sitting at that table, pale and stricken, with her pastors standing on either side. His heart went out to her. He was glad that he already had gathered up the weapons in the house.

Schoening had not known Sandy well until then, having met her only occasionally, at the sheriff's office annual Christmas parties and summer picnics, and he was surprised at how deeply her agony affected him. The contrast between Sandy's emotional collapse and Paul's puzzled detachment was especially distressing. It had been a long and troubling day; but Schoening found that this, unlike most cases he had handled, was one he couldn't leave at the office. That night, he had the first of a series of nightmares.

3

COUNTY G.O.P. LEADER FACES
SEX-ASSAULT CHARGE," the front page of the *Olympian* pro-
claimed the next morning. The names of the victims were
withheld, in accordance with the newspaper's policy, but
Olympia is a small town, and anyone who wanted to know
the details had probably already heard them and had also heard
that the police were interviewing the children in Sandy's day-
care business, which she had immediately closed. In the chaos
of the moment, few who knew Sandy remembered that November 29 was her forty-third birthday.

Sheriff Edwards was well aware of the consequences of
seeming to protect one of his own—especially a political ap-
pointee whom he had jumped through the ranks and made
one of his chief deputies. Rather than turn the matter over to
another agency, however, Edwards decided to have his own
department conduct the investigation. He hoped to ward off
criticism by inviting a couple of detectives from other police
departments in the area to participate, while maintaining control in his own department. This decision would prove to be
the first of many mistakes. The Thurston County Sheriff's Office is a modest operation—at the time, 73 officers served a
county of 165,000 residents—and a personal crisis in one employee's family affected everyone else. No matter how objec-

tive Ingram's co-workers might try to be, their passions were instantly engaged. They felt surprised, embarrassed, and betrayed by their colleague. This was not merely one family's tragedy but a catastrophe for the morale of the whole department. To some extent, they, too, were victims in the case.

The investigative team Edwards put together included some of the best officers in the county. Every morning, and many afternoons, the team met in the conference room in the sheriff's office to discuss the case and divide up assignments. This room would become the scene of many agonizing debates. Seated around the table were Joe Vukich, dark and handsome but still baby-faced despite his mustache; Brian Schoening, who would fill the room with cigarette smoke and the washboard sound of his smoker's voice; Loreli Thompson, a detective who handled sex crimes for the Lacey Police Department; and, for a while, Detective Paul Johnson of the Olympia Police Department. As the investigation lengthened, Johnson dropped out; his department could not afford to lose him for months on end. Thurston County was small enough that every cop knew every other cop—by reputation, if not personally—and the detectives in this room represented the county's entire sex-crimes investigative force. They were used to cooperating with each other in special cases. An expert from the state patrol came in to help set up a computer program that could sort and classify the immense amount of data the detectives would eventually assemble. Overseeing the team was the most experienced investigator in the sheriff's office, Sergeant Tom Lynch, a tough and likable man who was head of detectives and would be the one person responsible for reading every bit of material and trying to make sense of it. Like Vukich and McClanahan—and Ingram, for that matter—Lynch had a dark mustache, the male cop's fashion statement.

Ordinarily, Lynch would have been in complete control of the investigation; but with the political implications of the Ingram case, and the public-relations problems posed by having a department investigate one of its own high-ranking officers, Undersheriff McClanahan unofficially took charge of the case. His usual duties were almost entirely administrative, so his active involvement was exceptional and seen by some in the room as unwanted meddling. McClanahan's perceptions of what occurred would shape and define the investigation, even though he only occasionally participated in the interrogations and rarely went into the field. He became the department's spokesman on the subject; and as the investigation deepened and broadened beyond what anyone could have imagined, he became more and more attached to the case. He had personal reasons for doing so: Ingram was a friend and a colleague (if also a rival), and McClanahan was perhaps closer to Ingram's family than anyone else on the force. He had felt a particular attachment to Julie when she was younger; he had always thought of her as his "little buddy." Ingram's revelations caused McClanahan to believe that his special relationship to Julie had filled a void in her life caused by her father's brutal breach of trust. (For her part, Julie did not remember having such a close relationship with McClanahan, but she came to accept that it must have been true.) Throughout the investigation, McClanahan saw his role on the team as being a voice for the victims.

On the morning after his arrest, Paul Ingram met with Richard Peterson, a Tacoma psychologist with a brusque, authoritative manner who often worked with the local police. Peterson would become an unofficial but highly significant member of the team. He first interviewed Ingram to determine his mental state and whether it was safe for him to be at large. As they talked about the case, Ingram asked why, if he had committed these heinous acts, he had no memory of them. Peterson told him that it was not uncommon for sexual offenders to bury the memories of their crimes because they were simply too horrible to consider. He went on to say that Ingram himself had probably been abused as a child. Peterson suggested that Ingram might recall being molested by an uncle, or even by his father. It would have happened when Paul was about five years of age, because that's how old his own children had been when he started to abuse them. Ingram said that the only sexual memory he could dredge up from his early childhood was his mother's cautioning him not to scratch his crotch in public. According to Ingram, Peterson then assured him that once he confessed, the repressed memories would come flooding back (although, once again, there's no way of establishing that as fact). But he had confessed already, Ingram said, and he didn't remember any more today than he had remembered yesterday. Peterson didn't have an answer for that; however, Ingram asked if he would attend the afternoon interrogation with Schoening and Vukich—perhaps Peterson could unblock whatever it was that was keeping him from remembering.

That day Vukich acquired two letters that Julie had written to a teacher, Kristi Webster, five or six weeks before. Webster had noticed a profound change in Julie's behavior in the fall of 1988. The eager, hardworking student Webster had known the previous semester had become morose and distracted, dragging through her classes with a haggard and blank face. Along with a friend, Julie had gotten in trouble for making long-distance calls from a school telephone. Julie had never broken a rule before, and so Webster asked her to write a note explaining why she was misbehaving. Julie wrote:

> My feelings about this whole ordeal are totally weird. Sometimes I feel good and sometime bad and then there are the day I feel totally confused and just wish I could move to a different state and start life all over w/ new friend and no one would have to know about my past. And I have time

mostly at night when I'm so scared. I don't sleep I just wait in my room for my *dad*. I hate it. I will never enjoy sex. It hurt so bad and it makes me feel very dirty.

Being a Christian I suppose to forgive *him* for what he did and still does to me, but Its very hard he also says thing to me like "if your a good girl God will take care of you." And if you tell you'll pay for it I promise you.

The significant statement in this part of the letter was that the abuse was still occurring at the time it was written. What followed, however, was even more explosive and changed the course of the investigation entirely. For Julie's memory now implicated people other than family members:

I can remember when I was 4 yr old he would have poker game at our house and alot of men would come over and play poker w/ my dad, and they would all get drunk and one or two at a time would come in to my room and have sex with me they would be in and out all night laughing and cursing. I was so scared I didn't know what to say or who to talk to. The wierd thing was Ericka & I shared a room and they never touch her because she would *say* something and also at night most the time she slept on the top bed. And I think my dad & all his friend were afriad the bed might break. And my dad was always said to them Stay away from her (Ericka). She is under special care of her doctor and he will find out.

A sex ring of pedophiles would in itself be earth-shaking news in Thurston County, but Vukich realized that the letter was even more incriminating than that. He knew about the poker games—Ericka had mentioned them in her confrontation with her mother—but he also knew that most of the poker players were colleagues of Ingram's at the sheriff's office. Tom Lynch, the chief of detectives, had been a regular at the games; so had Undersheriff McClanahan; even Vukich had sat in occasionally. The game had seemed to him completely innocent. Had it all been a charade, a front for a conspiracy of sex criminals operating out of the Thurston County Sheriff's Office?

Julie's second letter to Kristi Webster revealed the degree of her despair:

> I am so freaked out I can't even eat I have so much going through my head. It's very hard to understand. I'm really scared about this whole situation I don't know if I doing what is right I feel like this is all my fault that I cause this to happen I'm the problem and I wonder what going to happen to my family will my dad be lock up and my mom left behind w/ Mark or will this just blow over and no one will understand where I'm coming from. I'm at the edge of my rope.

Despite the fact that much of the department and key members of the investigative team had been implicated in the case, Vukich and Schoening renewed their interrogation of Paul Ingram that afternoon. The psychologist Richard Peterson joined them and quickly took control of the interview. He must have felt like a prophet; even before the interview officially began, Ingram confided that he was beginning to remember being abused by his uncle, as Peterson had suggested only that morning.

First, however, Ingram wanted to clear up the confusion he felt about being interrogated by his fellow officers. He had been crying and praying in his cell, and he expressed his anxiety that Schoening and Vukich doubted his sincerity. "I really want you to—to believe that I'm telling you the truth."

"Why is that important to you?" Peterson asked.

" 'Cuz I don't think Brian believes me," said Ingram.

"Their job is not to believe you," Peterson said bluntly. "It's to try and get as much information as possible."

"And I'm trying to—to prove that I am being coopera-tive," Ingram stuttered. "There's—I—I'm—I truly am."

Schoening responded in the same personal, emotional vein. "I guess what my feeling is . . . even this morning we gained some additional information, from Julie, okay, and I guess what I'm saying is . . . she has a good reason to suppress this crime—more than you do, Paul. I mean, this has really hap-pened to her."

What troubled Joe Vukich is that Ingram was a cop, "and as cops we have a very factual, very punctual, very data-minded frame of reference, if you will."

"Uh-huh," Ingram agreed.

"And that's what makes it hard for us at least to compre-hend that you can't recall this, because I'll bet you could go back and take a citation you wrote ten years ago . . . you'd pretty much remember what happened that day."

"Yeah, you're probably right. In a lot of cases I could do that."

"That's what confuses me about this," Vukich continued. "What happened with Julie happened just last month. It's—it's very real, it's very recent. Granted, it's very hard to talk about."

"I can't see it," Ingram protested. "I can't visualize it in my own mind."

"Your wife called this morning and tells me that Chad is really, really upset and shook about all this and he wants to talk to me as soon as he can," said Schoening. "What all he'll have to say I don't know, but it sounds to me like we're probably talkin' about all four of your kids, maybe all five of 'em. Your wife is sittin' there telling me how she can stand by ya and still love ya. I don't know why she should. . . . You're just tryin' to keep from tellin' any more than you have to tell. . . . It's kinda like a nonadmission admission."

Peterson began asking Ingram to describe his sex life with Sandy, which Ingram did with some enthusiasm.

"Did you ever use alcohol as part of your lovemaking?" Peterson asked.

"No, I—it would seem to me that alcohol would sting," Ingram said, surprised.

"It was pointed out that you used to drink quite a bit," Peterson said, making himself clear. "Someone said you used to have quite an appetite for beer."

"Oh," said Ingram, "what I would do . . . we got an old refrigerator and put a keg of beer [in it] and we used to have poker parties at the house and I did like to come home after I'd been workin' swing shift and sit down and have one, uh, maybe two beers."

Now that he had mentioned the poker parties, the questioning became more focused. "Would you drink more then?" asked Schoening.

"I can't say I never got intoxicated," said Ingram. "But I can remember, you know, some of the guys getting pretty wasted, and over a period of four or five hours I might have four beers."

"Where was your wife during the poker parties?" asked Peterson.

"As I recall, she would've gone to bed, 'cuz we'd stay up and play pretty late."

"So the poker buddies that you played with would be who?" asked Peterson. "Friends from the department, or—"

"Yeah, most of 'em were friends from the department, or friends of theirs," Ingram agreed. "We'd get, I don't know, five or eight guys together." He then named several men, most of whom were police officers. There were two names he failed to mention, a fact that would soon become significant.

"One night I won over a hundred dollars, and my wife

said, 'Hey, that's wrong,' and I said, 'Okay, I'll play next weekend and lose it all,' " Ingram related. "The next weekend we played and I couldn't lose for tryin'. It was unreal. I won about a hundred twenty-five dollars, and we just quit."

"Were the kids aware of the poker parties?" asked Peterson.

"Oh, yeah, 'cuz we played underneath their bedrooms."

"Anybody go up to see the kids?" asked Vukich.

"I just can't think of anything where anybody—"

"The reason I ask, Paul, is because Julie told me about a time or two where when there was a poker party she was molested."

"What we're talking about, Paul, is she was molested by somebody other than you," Schoening clarified in his rumbling voice. "She even remembers being—somebody tying her up on the bed and two people, at least, taking turns with her while somebody else watched, probably you."

Ingram gasped in surprise. "I just don't see anything," he said when Schoening pressed him. "Let me think about this for a minute. Let me see if I can get in there. Assuming it happened, she would've had to have had a bed, bedroom by herself . . . uh . . ."

The pauses in Ingram's statement sometimes lasted ten full minutes, intensifying the frustration on the part of the questioners. He would grab hold of his hair and lean forward, dead still, until his limbs went to sleep, while the investigators stood around, fuming with impatience. Schoening prodded Ingram by saying that even as they talked Julie was in fear for her life. "That person is still out on the street. That person is some friend of yours that worked or works for this department."

Schoening's remarks would have serious consequences, so it's important to note the assumptions buried in them. Julie's fears, insofar as she had expressed them, were about whether she was doing the right thing in coming forward with her story, and whether she would break up her family as a result. The only person she had seemed to be afraid of was her father. There was nothing in the record at this point that reflected her terror of being stalked by a potential killer. The extrapolations about her fear of someone else were only guesswork on Schoening's part. The terms of the investigation had been re-defined, however.

"We need to protect her, Paul," warned Vukich.

"She's terrified, Paul," Schoening added.

"I—I hear what you're sayin', but just be quiet and let me think," Ingram pleaded.

"Apparently, it's somebody that's still close to you, Paul," said Schoening, once again departing from the record. Was he guiding Ingram toward some private judgment of his own?

"Jim Rabie played poker with us. Jim and I have been fairly close," Ingram said helpfully. James L. Rabie, the man who had done the electrical work on the Ingrams' house as a favor, once worked sex crimes. As a matter of fact, he had been the one who had investigated Ericka's prior claim of attempted rape and had decided it wasn't worth pursuing. At that time, he held the job that Schoening had now, that of senior inves-tigator. Rabie and Schoening had a long-standing and well-known dislike of each other. Ingram had not mentioned his name in his original list of poker players.

"Is Jim the person she's talking about?" Vukich asked.

"Just—just don't put words in my mouth," Ingram re-sponded. "Jim has some—I guess I'd say—what I consider to be unnatural sexual attractions."

"What do you mean by that?"

"We went over to Yakima one time for something, and Jim bought some magazines, said to help him in his job when he was doing sex crimes. And he looked at 'em. I didn't. I just don't do that kind of thing. . . . Geez, I'd hate to think he'd had anything to do with my kids."

"How would you feel if he did?"

"Anger—uh, bitterness comes in. I just, gosh . . ." Ingram
went quiet for a moment. "I'm trying to get—to bring something up here. Uh . . . uh . . . Jim's the only one that comes
to mind. . . ."

"In this picture you have, Paul, do you see ropes?"

"Uh, you've put the ropes there, and I'm trying to figure
out what I've got," said Ingram. "It kind of looks to me like
she'd be lying facedown . . . kind of like she's hogtied."

"What else do you see? Who else do you see?"

"Maybe one other person, but I—I don't see a face, but
Jim Rabie stands out, boy, for some reason."

Schoening went out in the hall to collect himself. Sergeant
Lynch saw him there. Schoening appeared so agitated that
Lynch relieved him of his gun. "It's not Paul Ingram I want
to kill," Schoening told him. "It's Jim Rabie."

As Schoening walked back into the office where the interrogation was taking place, he passed Peterson coming out, his
eyes streaming with tears. Peterson, so gruff, so schooled in
the cruel twists of the criminal and the insane mind, had been
emotionally overpowered, not only by the scenes of bondage
that Ingram was describing but also by Ingram's infuriating
detachment. Vukich, too, had tears in his eyes. But Ingram
sat calmly, and he grinned in greeting when Schoening came
back in. Schoening had never seen anything like this mon-
strous equanimity.

"Paul, have you ever had any sexual relations with Jim
Rabie?" Schoening asked.

"I don't think so," Ingram said, in that same puzzled tone
that was becoming unbearable for the interrogators. "I'd just
hate to think of myself as a homosexual."

"Did I hear you say that you offered your wife to Jim?"
Peterson said as he came back in the room, apparently mis-
understanding the gist of the conversation.

"That I offered my wife?" Ingram asked. "No, I . . .

Number one, my wife would—I don't want to say she'd kill me, but she'd come close to it."

"Have you ever had any affairs at all, Paul? Extramarital affairs?" Schoening asked.

Ingram admitted that he had had an affair. "It was right about the time Julie was born."

This line of questioning had long since left the track of the original question of sex abuse. Without a lawyer present, the detectives and the psychologist were firing in all directions, hoping to hit some as yet unspecified target.

"Have you ever worn any of your wife's undergarments?" asked Schoening.

"I don't think so," Ingram replied. "I'd say no."

"Have you ever done any peeping?"

Ingram vividly recalled that, when he was working as a supervisor for a cleaning crew at Seattle First National Bank, every evening a woman across the street would undress in front of her window. "I'd stand up in the second-floor window and watch her," Ingram said. "She did a little dance. It got to the point that all the women were watchin' her, too. Finally somebody complained and the police made her close the blind."

"Why do you think you remember some of this stuff pretty well and . . . don't remember about your sons and daughters?" asked Schoening.

Ingram said he didn't know.

"Do you think it's because that involvement with your sons and daughters is illegal and it's hard for you to admit to that?" asked Vukich.

"More than illegal," said Ingram. "In my mind it's immoral and unnatural."

"Have you ever influenced or watched or had anything to do with your sons molesting your daughter?" asked Schoening.

"I don't have a picture, and that's the only way I can describe it to you."

That question would prove to be significant later in the case, as would one that soon followed, from Dr. Peterson, who asked, "Before your conversion to Christianity, were you ever involved in any kind of black magic?"

Ingram replied that there was a time when he had read his horoscope in the newspaper. "I don't know what you're driving at," he added.

"The Satan cult kind of thing," Schoening said.

This was the first mention of satanism in the Ingram case. Later, the detectives claimed that Ingram had previously brought the subject up himself, but it's obvious that in this exchange he did not pick up the theme—at least consciously. All Ingram could recall was that as a child, on Halloween, he had tied a cat in a sack and hung it from a telephone pole.

Over the next hour, Schoening, Vukich, and Peterson changed their strategy. They began to concentrate on Ingram's guilt. The mood began to change. "Do you know how badly damaged your daughter is?" asked Peterson, referring in this instance to Julie. "Eighteen years old, she's a senior in high school, and she can't look at wedding things. . . . She thinks she's responsible for destroying your family."

"That she's dirty," said Schoening.

"She shakes at the thought of having to talk about this stuff," Peterson continued. "She's frightened of you."

"And she's frightened of whoever this other person is," Schoening added, once again hypothesizing.

"She can't name the other person?" asked Ingram. "I don't want to put her through this, don't get me wrong."

"You're putting her through it by not recalling," said Peterson.

"Yeah, you are, Paul, 'cuz right now she's havin' a difficult time talkin' about it," said Schoening. "You gotta help if you want this stopped or you may have either a suicidal daughter or a dead daughter. . . . She can't take much more of this,

Paul. I mean, it's all comin' back to her and she's havin' a real difficult time.''

"Oh, Lord.''

"I've got some notes here,'' said Peterson. "When she was having her period, she says you put your penis in her butt. Did you hear that? Anal sex with your daughter.''

"My kids always tell the truth,'' Ingram replied.

"Why don't you listen to what she wrote here, Paul,'' said Vukich. "She says, 'I was four years old, he would have poker game at our house and a lot of men would come over and play poker with my dad and they would all get drunk and one or two at a time would come into my room and have sex with me.' Now, your daughter wrote that.''

"This is her writing, Paul,'' echoed Schoening.

"And you told us that she's honest,'' said Vukich.

"Oh, yes, my kids are honest.'' Ingram was sobbing now.

"So it's time, Paul,'' said Schoening. "Quit beatin' around the bush and let's get this out.''

Everyone in the room sensed that they were on the edge of a breakthrough. Between the tears, Ingram prayed aloud. He asked that his pastor be called.

"It goes back to the poker games, Paul,'' Vukich reminded him as Ingram closed his eyes and began rocking violently back and forth.

"Choose life over living death,'' Peterson exhorted, lapsing into the religious language that seemed to reach Ingram. "You are as alone as Jesus was in the desert when he was comforted.''

"God's given you the tools to do this,'' Vukich said. "You've got to show him by what you do and what you say as to whether or not you're worthy of his love and redemption and salvation.''

"Oh, Jesus!'' Ingram cried in a frenzy. "Help me, Lord! Help me, Lord!''

"One of the things that would help you, Paul, is if you'd stop asking for help and just let yourself sit back, not try to think about anything," Peterson said, in a tone that was suddenly quiet and calming. "Just let yourself go and relax. No one's going to hurt you. We want to help. Just relax."

In response, Ingram instantly went limp. He hunched over and put his face in his hands.

"Why don't you tell us what happened to Julie, Paul?" Vukich said. "What happened at that poker game?"

"I see Julie lying on the floor on a sheet. Her hands are tied to her feet. She's on her stomach," Ingram said. His voice was high and faint. There was no doubt in anyone's mind that he was in a trance. "I'm standing there looking at her. Somebody else is on my left."

"Who is that?"

"The only person that keeps coming back is Jim Rabie."

"Turn and look at that person," Schoening said.

"He's standing right next to you, Paul," Vukich said. "All you have to do is look to your left and there he is."

"He's—he's standing up," Ingram said. "I see his penis sticking up in the air."

"Does he have any clothes on?"

"I don't think so," said Ingram. He then mentioned the name of another sheriff's deputy who might also be in the room. For some reason, the investigators had no interest in this other man.

"Go back to that person who's standing there with his penis sticking up in the air, Paul," said Schoening. "What's he doing to your daughter?"

"Getting down on his knees," said Ingram. "He's behind my daughter."

"Is he puttin' his penis in her?"

"Uh, her legs are close together, but maybe she's being rolled over onto her side."

"What she saying, Paul?"

"She's saying no. . . ."

"He's rolling her over," said Vukich. "What's happening next?"

"She can't go over on her back 'cuz her legs and her hands are there. It looks like she might have something around her mouth."

"A gag?"

"Like a gag," Ingram agreed.

"Who put that on her?"

"I might have. I—I don't know. . . ."

"Is she clothed or unclothed?" Peterson asked.

"Unclothed, I believe. . . ."

"What's this person doing?"

"He's kneeling. His penis is by her stomach. Uh, he's big. I mean, broad-shouldered, big person."

"Any marks on his back?"

"He's hairy."

"Does he have any jewelry on?" Vukich asked.

"May have a watch on his right hand." Rabie is left-handed and wears his watch on his right hand.

"What time does it say?"

"Uh, two o'clock."

"How close are you to him?" asked Peterson.

"I'm pretty close."

"How are you dressed?"

"I don't think I've got anything on."

"Do you have an erection?"

"I think so. . . ."

"Are you rubbing yourself against her?"

"Uh, yes. . . ."

"Is somebody taking pictures?" Vukich asked.

"Uh, pictures—is there somebody off to the right of me? Uh, it's possible, let me look. I see—I see a camera."

"Who's taking the pictures?"

"I don't know. I don't see a person behind the camera."

"That person's very important," Peterson said. "He's the one that holds the key. . . ."

"Well, the person that I think I see is Ray Risch," Ingram said. Raymond L. Risch, Jr., was a mechanic who worked for the Washington State Patrol.

This interview lasted until late in the evening. John Bratun, the associate pastor of the Church of Living Water, arrived after dinner in response to Ingram's request, as did Gary Preble, an attorney, whom Ingram had also asked for. Ingram knew Preble through the local Republican party. Preble was a devout charismatic Christian, but he had practically no criminal experience and certainly had no idea that he was about to take on the biggest case in Thurston County history.

The little office where the interrogation took place became stale and overheated from the press of so many bodies. "Boy, it's almost like I'm making it up, but I'm not," Ingram said as the interview drew to a close. He had now implicated several people in addition to Jim Rabie and Ray Risch. He had produced several new memories of sexual abuse, one occasion as recent as the week before he left on vacation. He had also begun to see "weird shadows" and tombstones. "It's like I'm watching a movie," he told the detectives. "Like a horror movie."

4

Thursday, December 1, was a busy day for Jim Rabie. For the past year he had been working as a lobbyist for the Washington State Law Enforcement Association and serving as the lieutenant governor of the state Kiwanis organization. That day Rabie had three Kiwanis meetings in three different cities, beginning early in the morning and not finishing until late that night. By mid-afternoon he was exhausted. He suffers from narcolepsy and usually requires two naps a day to keep himself going; in fact, that disease, and his tendency to fall asleep at inopportune moments, had caused him to retire from the sheriff's office in 1987, after fourteen years in the department.

Rabie was a sociable type with a plump face and sleepy eyes. At the age of forty-five, he still had dark and curly hair. Although it was not really detectable, one leg was an inch and a half shorter than the other one, the result of a car wreck when he was a child, and he wore a built-up shoe. He didn't limp, but he couldn't move around very quickly. Most people who knew him thought of Rabie as a pleasant, decent fellow who liked a joke and usually wore a smile.

At three o'clock he stopped by the office of his insurance agent to pay off a bill. He asked the agent, who was a friend, if he had heard about the arrest of Paul Ingram. Rabie himself had gotten the news from a source in the department. He was dumbfounded, he told the agent, because Paul was such a close friend—Ingram had been Rabie's best man at his wedding, and Rabie had been Ingram's campaign manager when he made a losing bid for the state legislature, in 1984. "It just goes to show you, child abuse can happen anywhere," Rabie said.

The agent remarked that it must be frightening for a cop to face prison. Rabie said that the machinery of law enforcement had to be very careful when arresting a police officer, and for that reason he thought that the case against Ingram must be compelling. But he was puzzled by the fact that Paul seemed to be "playing games" with the investigators. When Rabie himself was investigating sexual abuse, a suspect who confessed was usually given a "safe to be at large" evaluation and let out of jail after a day or two. A suspect who was not cooperative was probably "in denial," Rabie said. Such a person would be sent to a state institution for evaluation and faced a likely prison sentence. As a cop, Ingram would know this.

The two men then talked about other cases of abuse and agreed that in most such cases the perpetrators were people who themselves had been abused as children. Often the abuse was completely blocked out of active memory and would come to light only when a person entered therapy later in life for some sexual concern, such as frigidity. It was for that very reason, said Rabie, that he lobbied successfully to get the statute of limitations changed in the state of Washington so that the perpetrator of a sex crime against a minor could be held liable for seven years, rather than three. (Later, the law was amended again, to allow charges to be brought for three years after a victim *remembers* a crime. It was a pioneering statute and has since been replicated by twenty-two other states.)

The agent decided to take a break and smoke a cigarette, so he walked outside with Rabie. The two men stood on the sidewalk shooting the breeze. Later, the agent would try to reconstruct the conversation, which at the time seemed interesting but certainly not consequential. He remembered that Rabie said that Joe Vukich was the investigating officer and that Vukich might "go too deep." It was a mistake to try to get all the details of a crime, many of which wouldn't be needed to gain a conviction. Rabie also mentioned that he had "an affinity" for abusers. He understood how they felt. It was that very quality, Rabie believed, that had helped him elicit confessions.

When the agent finished his cigarette, he went back to work, and Rabie drove over to the County Seat Deli, a cozy spot across the street from the courthouse complex that was always full of lawyers, judges, deputies, clerks, and secretaries who work at the county offices. At five o'clock he was meeting his wife, Ruth, and his friend Ray Risch for a bite to eat.

Risch, who was forty-one in 1988, was six feet four and thin, with a dark beard. He wore tortoiseshell glasses that were always sliding down his nose, and he had a shy habit of laughing and looking up and away—an oddly demure gesture in such a large man. He never seemed to know what to do with his long limbs, so when he was relaxing he had a way of crossing his arms and wrapping his legs around each other at the knee and ankle, like vines. When round Jim Rabie and gangly Ray Risch were together, one couldn't help thinking of Laurel and Hardy. Everyone who knew them would remark that Rabie and Risch were pals; they met for lunch nearly every day and often got together for dinner with their wives. Both were avid readers and like to work on cars. Rabie was the talker. Risch liked to listen and laugh.

The table talk, of course, was about their friend Paul Ingram. Ruth Rabie was a corrections officer in the Thurston County jail, where Ingram was being held. A firm, quiet grandmother who was looking forward to retirement, Ruth had been married to Jim for nearly twelve years. They had met when she joined the women's reserves in the sheriff's department. As a jailer, Ruth privately worried that Ingram was going to do something crazy that would cause him to be killed. This was just a wild and irrational thought, since Ingram was on suicide watch and being carefully monitored, but it was so strange having a friend and a high official in the sheriff's office suddenly behind bars.

Jim said that earlier he had called Sandy to ask if there was anything he could do. "How could this have been going on and me not know it?" she had asked him plaintively. He didn't know what to say. In his experience, he had found that many awful things could go on in a family without being acknowledged, even by the victims.

"There are two Paul Ingrams," Ray Risch said enigmatically. Jim asked what he meant by that. Ray said that every police officer has two personalities: one the ordinary civilian guy, the other the authoritative person behind the badge. The same was true of Jim when he was in the department, Ray observed.

Rabie and Risch didn't know at the time that either of them was under suspicion; but even as they were talking, Ingram was across the street in the interview room producing new memories of their having molested his children. That very morning, Julie had picked their faces out of a photo lineup and had described an incident in which, during one of the poker games, Rabie came into her room, raped her, and cut her with a knife.

When they finished chatting at the deli, Rabie went to another of his Kiwanis meetings and then drove across the street to return a slide projector to the sheriff's office; he had borrowed it from the crime-prevention department, which Paul Ingram headed. Since no one had ever asked Rabie to return his office key when he retired, he simply unlocked the back door and walked in. It was after seven. Rabie was wearing his red Kiwanis blazer. In the hallway, he saw Tom Lynch walking into the small room that Schoening and Vukich shared. Rabie stuck his head in to say hello. The detectives looked startled.

"What are you doing here?" Lynch asked.

"Returning this," said Rabie. "I'm a little surprised to see you here this late."

He wasn't nearly as surprised as they were.

"Can I ask a question?" Rabie continued earnestly, taking a seat in the same chair that many suspects had sat in when Jim Rabie was a detective in this very office. "I know that possibly you guys can't answer it, but has Paul been honest? I mean totally honest, because unless he is he will not be amenable to treatment." Obviously, Rabie was presuming Ingram's guilt. According to Lynch's notes, Rabie then said, "Paul and I have been very close for a long time, and maybe it would help if I talked to him."

There was a long, awkward pause. It was so bizarre, having a suspect breeze right into the sheriff's office, although weirdness had been a part of this case from the very beginning. The sense of unreality was heightened because Ingram and Rabie were so well known in the department. An unsettling feeling of identity tied the detectives to the suspects. Indeed, if Rabie had not retired, he would have been in charge of the case, so there was an odd, mirrored quality of investigators investigating the investigators. Finally, Schoening broke the silence and told Rabie, "You've been named."

Instead of immediately and adamantly denying the charge, Rabie undid his tie and sat back in the chair with an immense sigh. Vukich and Schoening exchanged a look. They identified this as the "Oh, no, I've been caught" reaction.

Rabie's initial response seemed to them eerily similar to Ingram's. He said that he couldn't remember the events he was being charged with, and he speculated that perhaps he had a "dark side." Also like Ingram, Rabie asked several times to take a polygraph exam. At nine-thirty that evening, Schoening turned on a tape and read Rabie his rights. Rabie also agreed to talk without a lawyer present. "I am completely baffled by what in the devil is going on," Rabie said.

"Jim, you're doin' the same exact thing to us tonight that you have seen with probably hundreds of pedophiles," Schoening said impatiently. "They want to minimize; they want to deny."

"I agree," said Vukich.

"Individual people, separately, have corroborated that you masturbated in front of and on Julie. Julie tells us that; so does Paul Ingram tell us that," Schoening continued, selecting one of various conflicting stories. "Don't you think you're in a denial stage?"

"I must be, because I honestly do not have any recollection of that happening, and I do not believe that I could've done it and blocked it out."

"How do you feel right now?"

"In a daze," said Rabie. "Scared."

"What're you scared of?"

"Because I know from your end of it that if you've got what you tell me you have, that I'm not leaving here. I'm gonna be in custody. And I have a firm belief that any cop that's charged is guilty until proven otherwise."

Vukich asked what Rabie would think if he were sitting on the other side of the desk with the same information. "What would be your honest evaluation?"

"Same things you're thinking," Rabie admitted. "That I must be guilty, and that I must be in a denial state." The significance of his plight swiftly settled in on him. "An ex-cop in prison is almost a sign of death," he observed. Even if he got off, the mere fact that he had been charged would mean that his reputation was destroyed, his lobbying career was finished, his Kiwanis work was over, his marriage was placed in peril, and he might not be allowed ever to see his granddaughters again, because suspicion that he was a child molester would always hover around him. In short, his life was ruined.

"I can't figure out why, if I did this, I wouldn't remember it happening," Rabie said, echoing Paul's complaint.

"You can't admit it to yourself, Jim, that's the problem," said Schoening. "You're like Paul was. You can't convince yourself that you really could have been part of this."

"I can't even picture someone masturbating on a small child," said Rabie.

"There's photographs of it, Jim," Schoening said, although he actually did not have such evidence in hand. "How about a picture of you lying on the floor, nude, next to Julie?"

"If I saw a picture of that I would have to believe it occurred," Rabie said.

While Rabie was being interrogated, Detective Paul Johnson and Detective Loreli Thompson had been assigned to question Ray Risch. They drove out to the trailer on a dead-end street where he lived with his wife, Jodie. Risch was feeling ill that night; that day he had been painting a car in the shop where he worked, and the fumes always left him feeling like he had the flu. He was lying on the couch watching TV at ten-fifteen when he heard the squad car turn into the dark cul-de-sac. For the detectives, the fact that Risch was looking out the window as they approached the house seemed suspicious, as did his first remark when he answered the door: "Is this about Paul?" Risch immediately agreed to go to the station. He didn't think it was surprising that he would be questioned, even at this hour at night; but he did notice that when he went to get his jacket and shoes, one of the detectives followed him into the bedroom.

As they arrived at the Thurston County Sheriff's Office, Risch noticed Rabie's El Camino in the parking lot. A moment later, Risch was sitting in another interrogation room having his rights read to him. Until this point, he maintains, he still thought the detectives were interested only in Ingram. He never dreamed he was also a suspect.

"I noted that Risch's legs were crossed both at the knee and at the ankle," wrote Detective Thompson in her report. In her opinion, Risch's body language indicated that he was protecting something. "I also noted that when questioning would become intense at points, his arms would cross tightly across his chest."

On being confronted with what appeared to be overwhelming evidence against him, Risch offered the same sort of equivocal statements about memory that both Ingram and Rabie had. "I wasn't present that I know of, unless I blocked it out of my head," he said.

The interrogations went on into the early morning—Rabie in one room, Risch in another, and Peterson, the ubiquitous psychologist, shuttling back and forth. "We're talking about a situation here, Jim, where you have, if you will, a cult," Vukich told Rabie, offering what was becoming the official theory. "A cultist-type attraction and activity between these . . . individuals that has continued over a prolonged period of time."

Eventually each man was told that his friend had broken down and was implicating him, although this was not true. "This has gone far enough!" Risch cried.

"Paul said you guys bullied him and you made him do this and he didn't want to," Schoening told Rabie. "Ray is saying basically the same thing. Only, he's saying that he was the one who was the weakling, and he's saying you and Paul were the worst two."

Rabie realized that this could be a bluff, but he was also aware that in a case like this, which had multiple suspects, one person could be offered a certain degree of immunity to provide testimony against the others—and that often it was a scramble to pin the ringleader tag on another suspect. "Give me the responsibility, because I've blocked it out enough—I must be the worst one," Rabie said glumly. "The only option is to lock me up, and you're going to have to throw away the key, because if I can't remember this, then I am so damn dangerous I do not deserve to be loose."

5

The next day, December 2, In-
gram met in Vukich and Schoening's office with Pastor Bratun. "I know I have a demon in me," Ingram said, and he
asked Bratun to perform an exorcism.

"You don't have a demon, but you've got several spirits,"
Bratun told him. Bratun had spent some time in Southern
California, where he had had some experience with people who
were in bondage to spirits. He set a wastebasket in the middle
of the floor and called out from Ingram the spirits of sexual
immorality and gluttony, among others. As he did, Ingram
attempted to regurgitate into the wastebasket, with little success. Still, he felt "delivered," he said, and when he went back
into the interrogation room he produced a new memory. In
this memory, Rabie, who is five feet eight inches tall, pushed
Ingram, who is six feet two, down the stairs. "He wanted to
do something that I didn't want him to do," Ingram told the
detectives. "He said he wanted Chad." Rabie shoved his way
into Chad's room. "Chad was on the bed and cowering. He
went over and ripped his pants off and made him kneel on the
floor and I was powerless to do anything. . . . He forced Chad
down and had anal sex with him." Chad was thirteen or fourteen at the time. "When Jim was done, he got up, put his
pants back on. He said he'd do that any time he wanted to,"

Ingram related. "He'd kill us if we said anything. He had control."

That afternoon, Detective Loreli Thompson interviewed Chad, then twenty years old. The young man said that he had never been abused, sexually or in any other physical manner, by his father or anyone else. "He said he had never really talked with Rabie beyond a casual hello," Thompson noted. Chad admitted that his father sometimes lost control and yelled at the children, but otherwise their relationship was "O.K." The young man was beginning to have doubts about the veracity of his own recollections, though. Recently, he and his mother had been looking through family photographs and other household items in an effort to prompt their memories. So far, neither of them was able to remember anything extraordinary.

Paul's memory, however, was becoming more and more active and intricately detailed, aided by the visualizations that Peterson and the detectives encouraged and by constant prayer and assurances from Pastor Bratun that God would not allow thoughts other than those which were true to come into his memory. Ingram began seeing people in robes kneeling around a fire. He thought he saw a corpse. There was a person on his left in a red robe who was wearing a helmet of cloth. "Maybe the Devil," he suggested. People were wailing. Ingram remembered standing on a platform and looking down into the fire. He had been given a large knife and was expected to sacrifice a live black cat. He cut out the beating heart and held it aloft on the tip of the knife. "At one point, Ingram said that the cat might have been a human doll," Schoening wrote in his report. "This was related by Ingram as a third party looking at the scenario, i.e., I see; I feel; reminds me of; I hear, etc." Ingram also produced a memory of himself and Jim Rabie murdering a prostitute in Seattle in 1983, thereby implicating both of them in an infamous unsolved murder spree known as the Green River killings. The bodies of at least forty women had been found in Washington and Oregon between 1982 and 1984, and the authorities believed it was the work of a serial killer. At Schoening's request, the Green River task force looked into Ingram's memories of the slaying but could find nothing that corresponded with any of the victims.

Where were all these memories coming from? Were they real or were they fantasies? If they were real, why couldn't any two people agree on them? The Ingram daughters had said nothing about satanic rituals, but through the church grapevine they were getting the gist of their father's latest revelations, which Pastor Bratun often knew about before the detectives heard them. Ericka confided to a friend that her father was talking too much and giving too many details—that he was saying things she didn't want to remember, and she wished he would just be quiet.

Ericka herself was now saying that her father had sexually abused her on almost every night of the last week she lived at home. Detective Thompson interviewed one of the deaf girls who had been living with the Ingrams (and had since moved to another foster home). The girl said that the Ingram house was full of hate. "I don't want—angry—ignore—don't talk with me anymore," she said through her interpreter. She remembered that Sandy and Ericka had bickered because Ericka wanted to leave, and that Ericka had been grounded. That was the most dramatic incident she could recall. She told Thompson that she had not observed any abuse.

On December 8, Chad went to see his father in jail. It was a shattering experience for him. Paul, who had always been so aloof from his children, was sobbing so hard that he could speak only in gasps. He managed to say that Chad had been a victim, and pleaded with him to try to remember the abuse. "You have to get it out," he cried.

"I've never seen him like that," Chad later told Schoening. "It's like it was a different person. It wasn't my dad there.

That wasn't my dad there. That wasn't my dad. . . . It didn't even feel like him when I hugged him."

Chad accompanied Schoening to the interview room, where Dr. Peterson was waiting. Before Peterson turned on the tape, Schoening advised Chad that he might be arrested because of Ericka's accusations against him, so from the beginning of this interrogation, which stretched over most of two days, there was an incentive for Chad to paint himself as a victim. He began, however, by once again denying that he had ever been molested. His main grievance in the family was that he had to do more chores than the other children. He did admit to attempting suicide three years before, when he was seventeen. "Probably something my dad said. I can't remember the specifics," he said. There was a pale trace of a razor cut on his wrist, or seemed to be. "Where is it?" Chad asked himself aloud, as he attempted to point it out to the detectives. "It's right here, right along the crease." The detectives did not indicate whether or not the scar was visible to them.

"It was something very traumatic to you that your dad said that really hurt you," Schoening said, theorizing. "Maybe it hurt your manhood."

Chad tentatively replied that his father might have called him a loser. "But I don't think he said that. I can't remember."

"You can remember what happened," Peterson admonished him. "You can choose to remember that if you want to."

"Like what?" said Chad, obviously confused. "What do you mean, 'remember'?"

"What he's sayin' is, it's there," said Schoening. "The memories are there. We're just tryin' to help you."

"I know, I know," said Chad. "They're there. I just can't—I just can't put the dot on it, though."

"Well, I'm not surprised," Peterson said. "It's not unusual with kids who've been through what you've been through to not be able to remember. Number one, they don't want to remember. Number two, they've been programmed not to remember."

"Mm-hm."

Some time later, Peterson said, "I can tell you that the way to being what you want to become—a healthy adult—is to deal with those memories."

"Mm-hm."

"Because they have—they—I say 'they' because I believe that there's a 'they' who have done this to you."

"Mm-hm."

At moments, the conversation lurched into therapy or instant psychoanalysis, as Chad was urged to reveal his thoughts about his family and his rather limited sexual experience. Eventually, the interrogators prodded the young man into talking about his mental problems. He admitted that he had heard voices inside his head. Then, in a painfully halting manner that reminded the detectives of his father's interminable pauses, Chad described vivid dreams he had had as a child: "People outside my window, looking in, but I knew that wasn't possible, because . . . we were on two floors and I would . . . I would have dreams of, uh, little people . . . short people coming and walking on me . . . walking on my bed . . . uh, I would look outside and . . . out of my door." The little people reminded him of the Seven Dwarfs, he said.

"Those are dreams of being invaded," Peterson declared.

"Yeah, and I would look out my door and I would see . . . a house of mirrors and . . . and no way of getting out."

"Of being violated, trapped in an inescapable situation," Peterson said, interpreting. "What happened to you was so horrible."

"Right."

"You want to believe it's dreams," Schoening said. "You don't want to believe it's real. It was real. It was real, Chad."

"No, this was outside my window, though," Chad protested, pointing out that his bedroom had been on the second floor. Also, his older brother had slept in the same room—why hadn't he ever seen anything?

"What you saw was real," Schoening insisted. "This same type of stuff has come out of your dad, too."

"Were you shaking in your boots or did you pee on the floor? Were you that scared?" asked Peterson.

"No, no," said Chad. He claimed he had no strong feelings about the dream, just a leaden sensation, as if he were stuck in concrete. "I couldn't talk. I couldn't move except to close the curtain," Chad went on. "The only thing I could feel was pressure on my chest."

"What was on your chest?" Peterson asked.

"Well, this is a different dream," Chad said, recalling a recurring nightmare of his adolescence. "Every time a train came by, a whistle would blow and a witch would come in my window. . . . I would wake up, but I couldn't move. It was like the blankets were tucked under and . . . I couldn't move my arms."

"You were being restrained?" Peterson asked.

"Right, and there was somebody on top of me."

"That's exactly real," Schoening said excitedly. "That's the key, Chad. That's what was really going on."

"Chad, these things happened to you," Peterson insisted. "They assaulted your ability to know what was real."

"O.K."

"Pretty hard to remember this?"

"No, it was like it was yesterday." Chad then recalled that when the train whistle blew, he would find himself on the floor, and a fat witch with long black hair and a black robe would be sitting on top of him.

"Look at her face," Schoening said. "Who is this person? Somebody who is a friend of your family's?"

"It was usually dark," said Chad. He said the witch's visits occurred once or twice a week, lasting for half an hour, until they moved out of the old house. "I would hear the whistle; I would feel the pressure on my chest; I would be on the floor; but I would never feel myself getting out of bed, moving to the floor, and then I would be on the floor and then I would be back in bed, but never feel myself going from the floor back to the bed." As for his brother, Chad recalled that when the witch was in the room, Paul Ross would be gone, "but then when I would wake up, I would look and he would be there."

"Who does this person remind you of?"

"I don't know."

"You don't want to know or you don't know?" Peterson asked.

"Probably I don't want to know."

"Somebody you respect?"

"Right."

"Is there something there physically to keep your mouth from making noise?" Schoening asked.

"No, because I remember breathing."

"What's in your mouth?"

"I don't know. A cloth, maybe."

"It's very important, Chad. What's it feel like in your mouth?"

"Uh, it's not hard."

"Just let the memory come," Peterson advised. "It's not what you think about, it's what you're trying *not* to think about." When Chad resisted being steered any further, Peterson and Schoening told him that he had been programmed not to remember anything. "Why'd you have to run away from it?" Peterson demanded.

And Schoening added, "You wanted to go somewhere safe, right?"

"No, it was safe here," said Chad. "I always felt safe."

"Even when all this was going on?" Schoening asked.

"Except for the dreams," Chad said, obviously bewildered. "I—Because I thought they were—I put them off as dreams."

"Destruction of his sense of reality," Peterson said authoritatively. "Destruction of any ability to feel. Total, absolute obedience and subservience to the group."

A few minutes later, Schoening said, "Let's go back to when you were fourteen to sixteen and this person's sitting on you." How much room did Chad think there had been between the witch's pelvic area and Chad's chin? Chad supposed there had been a foot or so. "They would sit there real high," Schoening reminded him. "And you got something in your mouth."

"Yeah."

"And it's not cloth."

"Right."

"It's not hard, like a piece of wood."

"Right."

"What is it?"

Chad thought a moment about this riddle and then began to laugh nervously. "You just made me think—oh, golly."

"What is it?" Schoening insisted.

"I don't know. I don't know."

"What were you thinkin'? C'mon."

"I thought it was a penis, O.K.? I—it could be."

"O.K., don't be embarrassed. It could be," Schoening said. "Let it out. It's O.K."

"I don't know what's happening to me," Chad said miserably.

Once the interrogators had been able to translate the nightmares into reality, the rest followed easily. The witch underwent a sex change, and Chad's initial certainty that he had never been abused was completely overturned. The little people of Chad's first dream, who had reminded him of the Seven Dwarfs, were reinterpreted as being members of a cult who regularly abused him over most of his life. But Chad had forgotten all of it, the interrogators told him. He had been conditioned to accept the abuse and then to repress the memories.

"By God, those who've done this to you ought to pay for what they've done," Peterson said. "And I'll tell you something—you have the right to sue those fuckers and get as much as you want from them."

"That'd be nice," Chad said.

"You're damn right it'd be nice. Pay for a college education."

"Yeah."

"Pay for a nice car. Get you started in life."

"Well, I've already got a nice car."

"Yeah, but do you have a BMW?"

When he came to the interview, Chad had been threatened with arrest. Now that he had accepted his status as victim, he was being offered a view of the rewards he might claim. Peterson urged him to "go public" with his new discovery. "Wouldn't it feel great to say this was real—it's not a dream?" said Peterson.

"That's why I want to see the faces, so I can . . . say these are the ones that did it to me," Chad concluded. "I have to put a face to it."

At this point the detectives turned off the tape.

Earlier, Chad had examined the same photo lineup that his sisters had seen, including some twenty driver's-license pictures, mostly of former employees of the sheriff's office. Of those pictured, Rabie and Risch had been the closest friends of Paul Ingram and the ones most likely to be recognized by the children. Chad knew both men well; in fact, he had done odd jobs for them on several occasions. But when he was first presented with the lineup, he couldn't identify any abusers. During the interval while the tape was off, Chad examined the pictures again.

"Who's the face in the dream?" asked Vukich, when the tape was turned back on.

"Jim Rabie," Chad answered.

The following day, Chad produced a memory of being assaulted by Ray Risch in the basement of the Ingrams' house when he was ten or twelve years old. At this point, Chad leaned forward and stared at the floor "in a trance-like state," Schoening's notes record. "Sometimes he would go for 5–10 minutes without saying anything and at one point, drool came out of his mouth and onto the floor."

6

Loreli Thompson has a playful manner, but she hides her eyes behind dark, silver-rimmed aviator glasses. As a young girl, growing up in Olympia, Thompson had been drawn to puzzles of every kind—codes, crosswords, mysteries—and by junior high she had decided she wanted to be a detective. When she finally achieved her goal, in November of 1984, she was the first female detective in the county. While she was still a rookie, she encountered her first pedophile, a man who had molested several young girls in an apartment complex. Thompson persuaded him to confess. She discovered that she had an instinct for sex crimes, one of the most puzzling departments of criminal behavior. In order to better understand the motivations of sexual offenders, Thompson got a master's degree in clinical psychology, which was added to her master's in criminal justice. Her reports are full of telling psychological observations.

She saw every kind of sexual offender, from sadistic rapists to exhibitionists and voyeurs. In many cases she found that an understanding pat on the hand would help lead the perpetrator to her ultimate goal, which was to persuade him to confess. Thompson tries to keep her cases out of the courtroom. It was often difficult for juries to make sense of sex crimes or sometimes even to believe that crimes had taken place, especially when there was little evidence other than an accusation. When the accusation came from a child, juries tended to be even more skeptical. Thompson had seen how easily confused children could become in the presence of a forceful defense attorney; moreover, most sexual offenses against very young children are digital or oral, which means that there is characteristically very little evidence, no sperm or scarring. In Washington State, there are three categories of what is still informally called statutory rape. First-degree rape or molestation of a child pertains to children under twelve and a perpetrator who is more than twenty-four months older than the victim—for example, an eleven-year-old girl who engages in sex with a fourteen-year-old boy. Second-degree rape involves children who are twelve and thirteen. Third-degree rape (the offense Paul Ingram was charged with, because these alleged offenses are ones that took place within the statute of limitations) occurs in the case of an underaged victim and a perpetrator who is more than four years older; a fifteen-year-old and a twenty-year-old cannot legally have sex in Washington, although two fifteen-year-olds can.

After Jim Rabie's retirement, Loreli Thompson came to be regarded as the best sex-crimes investigator in the county. Other departments would sometimes consult her, especially in crimes against children, and by the time the Ingram case came into her life, she had already seen perhaps three hundred child victims in Thurston County. Some were as young as two years old. Many had been repeatedly molested for years. Because of her reputation and skill, Thompson was given the delicate task of interviewing Julie. In her experience, there was nothing very unusual about two little girls growing up in a house with a pedophile. She witnessed the effects of child abuse every day. Paul Ingram's emerging satanic memories did sound a jarring note to Thompson, but then what else could explain the wreck of a girl who sat in her office, practically mute, idly shredding her clothing and pulling her hair? Julie was the most trauma-

tized victim that Thompson had ever seen. She had more success in getting statements out of four-year-old children who
had been raped and beaten. Julie would sometimes write about
the abuse in her upright, legible script, but she simply could
not speak about it aloud. Early on, Thompson came to believe
that Julie had been tortured.

All the familiar road signs of a typical police investigation
had been turned about. The detectives were groping to understand what was going on in their community—and, indeed,
in their own department. The alleged central perpetrator was
admitting to more depraved crimes than the victims were
charging (until this point, neither of the Ingram daughters had
said anything about satanic abuse). It seemed nearly impossible
to coordinate all the accusations into a coherent set of charges.
The investigators realized that they were probing into strange
and unsettling territory. Jaded cops who regularly visited the
worst precincts of the human psyche were thoroughly shaken
by the emerging revelations of the Ingram case. The memories
that Paul Ingram was producing were at once disjointed and
intricately detailed, like shards of a shattered vase. Ingram could
describe the ornate fragments, but he seemed to have no way
of piecing them back together. Even more disquieting to the
investigators was a growing conviction that the Ingram case
was, as they frequently said to each other, "the tip of the
iceberg"—the iceberg being the nationwide satanic conspiracy.

Brian Schoening took to sleeping with the lights on. The
interviews with Ingram went on for hours and hours, sometimes from early morning until nearly seven at night. Schoening began to dread the daily gamut of emotions, which at
night would be replayed in his mind as grisly nightmares. One
scene in particular haunted him. It was based on the image of
Julie being hogtied on the floor, although in Schoening's recurring dream the victim was his beloved granddaughter. He
would try to reach her, but for some reason he never could.

In the dream, she always looked terrified, and she would call out her pet name for him, "Boppa." Sometimes the dream would come before Schoening could even get to sleep. He would often awaken crying or shouting out loud. In the morning he would return to a world where nothing was normal.

Any extensive police investigation is freighted with suggestive details that color the detectives' judgments about the suspects and the defendants. Thompson, for instance, interviewed the former wives of Rabie and Risch. Rabie's ex described him as insecure and claimed that in the latter part of their eleven-year marriage, which ended in 1977, he developed a taste for pornographic books and movies. He was never interested in the occult, however. He had a passion for Louis L'Amour westerns, and the only quirk in his personality that she could recall was his irrational fear of birds. The former Mrs. Risch said that her husband "walked out and left us on the first of June in 'seventy-six." She also alleged that Risch was a liar. What she meant by that, she said, was "it was difficult for Ray to face reality. He would take the situation such as in the area of jobs, he always had a fantastic prospect coming up and he was gonna get this great job—you know, lots of money. There were many times when he would tell me one thing and I would find out that it was not the truth. So I got to the point where I did not really trust his words on a lot of things." Risch never abused the children, the woman said, but her son once told her about a strange incident concerning Paul Ingram. "It sounded too fantastic, but now that this has come up . . ."

"What'd he say?" Thompson asked.

"He said something about one time when his dad had scared him, that he made him lay down in the driveway and Paul had driven the car over the top of him . . . and it scared him really bad. . . . This has got to be the imagin—" She suddenly broke off, then declared: "You know, no sane adult is going to frighten a little four- or five-year-old and make him lay down . . . but then again . . ." She didn't know what to make of it.

The psychologist, Richard Peterson, had never been involved in a police interrogation before, and he had no official role in this one beyond determining whether it was safe for the suspects to be at large. A former assistant professor of psychology at Oberlin College in Ohio, Peterson had come to Washington in 1982 to work for the Mentally Ill Offender program, which he did for two years before going into private practice in Tacoma, specializing in forensic and clinical psychology. Since that time, he had worked with as many as three thousand sexual offenders. He was a familiar presence in the jails and courtrooms of Washington State, where he was often called upon to testify about a suspect's mental condition. His active presence and that of Pastor Bratun at several key interviews would later become a subject of controversy in the defense of Rabie and Risch. At the time, however, the detectives were grateful for Peterson's participation. Peterson at least had some familiarity with these matters—the year before, he had had the unnerving experience of encountering patients who remembered being victims of satanic abuse.

Thousands of therapists have reported similar cases in recent years; but to Peterson, in 1987, it was still rare enough to be surprising. "Survivor" stories began to surface with the publication, in 1980, of a book called *Michelle Remembers*, written by a thirty-year-old Canadian named Michelle Smith and her psychiatrist, Lawrence Pazder (who later became her husband). The book describes Smith's memories of black-magic ceremonies and of atrocities she was subjected to by a satanic coven, which purportedly counted among its members Smith's mother. Smith recovered these memories while she was undergoing therapy, following a miscarriage. Usually the memories surfaced when Smith was in a hypnotic trance. Her account became a model for the many survivor stories that would follow, although, typically, there was no evidence that any of her story was true. Indeed, her sisters (unmentioned in the book) and her father deny that these fantastic events occurred, and police in her native Victoria, British Columbia, were unable to substantiate any of the baby sacrifices that Smith remembered. Smith's mother is deceased.

Most accusations of satanic-ritual abuse in the early eighties were attached to allegations of sexual molestation in day-care centers. In January 1988, Memphis's daily paper, the *Commercial Appeal*, published the results of an investigation into thirty-six such cases around the country. It was one of the first skeptical examinations of the ritual-abuse phenomenon. The reporters, Tom Charlier and Shirley Downing, found that most cases evolved out of a single incident involving one child; but through publicity and runaway police inquiries, the investigations spread, and subsequent accusations were made against police officers, defense lawyers, and even the social service workers investigating the complaints. In the thirty-six cases examined, ninety-one people were arrested and charged with abusing children or endangering them; and of the seventy-nine defendants whose cases had been settled, twenty-three had been convicted, most on lesser charges that had nothing to do with ritual abuse. There was virtually no evidence in any of these cases except for the uncorroborated stories of the very young children. Prosecutors in the day-care cases often used *Michelle Remembers* as a reference guide.

The best-known of these cases involved the Virginia McMartin Preschool, in Manhattan Beach, California, and it engendered the longest and most expensive ($15 million) criminal-court case in American history. Peggy McMartin Buckey and her son, Raymond Buckey, along with five other child-care workers, were charged with molesting 360 children over a ten-year period. It began in 1983 when a housewife, who had a history of mental illness, claimed that Raymond Buckey had sexually assaulted her son, who was two and a half at the time. She said that her child described airplane flights, animal sacrifice, and sex rituals inside churches. The Manhattan Beach Police Department then sent a letter to two hundred families whose children attended the preschool, saying that the police were investigating possible criminal acts, including oral sex, fondling of genitals, sodomy ("possibly committed under the pretense of 'taking the child's temperature' "), and the photographing of naked children. The panicked parents, who until then had not noticed any signs of abuse, were referred to the Children's Institute International. A nonprofit sex-abuse center, CII was run by a woman who interviewed children while wearing a clown outfit and who later testified before Congress that she believed in a network of "child predators" who were operating day-care centers as covers for child pornography. Soon children who initially had denied that any abuse had taken place remembered going to the cemetery on buses with shovels and pickaxes to dig up coffins. They told about teachers flying through the air and seeing naked nuns and priests frolicking in secret tunnels under the school (no such tunnels were ever found). Glenn E. Stevens, who was a co-prosecutor in the McMartin case, quit in disgust, denouncing the prosecution as a massive hoax. "If a child said no, nothing ever happened to them, the interviewer would then say, 'You're not being a very bright boy. Your friends have come in and told us they were touched. Don't you want to be as smart as them?' " Stevens said. Michelle Smith and other "survivors" met with some of the children and the parents in the McMartin case. Eventually, most of the charges were dropped and the others resulted in acquittal or mistrial; but by then there had been more than a hundred cases around the country in which children made accusations of fantastic abuse, usually involving details similar to those publicized in the McMartin case, such as devil worship, open graves, cannibalism, airplane trips, nude photography, being urinated or defecated on, and murdering babies. The McMartin parents formed a group called Believe the Children, which waged the campaign in the media and provided support for parents who felt that their children had been similarly abused. Within a year in the Los Angeles area alone, allegations of ritual abuse arose at sixty-three other day-care centers. One sensational case appeared in 1986 in Sequim, Washington, not far from Olympia, after a woman noticed a rash on her granddaughter's vagina. Five children later stated that they had been taken to graveyards and assaulted by adults in hooded robes. Charges against the preschool operator in Sequim and her son were later dropped because of insufficient evidence.

Peterson became sufficiently interested in the subject to conduct a survey of Tacoma and Seattle therapists in early 1988, and he found that a quarter of the respondents had treated victims of satanic-ritual abuse, or SRA, as it was coming to be known in the rapidly developing literature of the phenomenon. That same year, an influential paper appeared, under the title "A New Clinical Syndrome: Patients Reporting Ritual Abuse in Childhood by Satanic Cults." The authors were two psychiatrists, Walter C. Young and Bennett G. Braun, and a psychologist, Roberta G. Sachs, who specialized in dissociative disorders. These are psychiatric maladies characterized by an unintegrated sense of identity, the best-known of which is multiple-personality disorder, or MPD. People who suffer from dissociative disorders also have disturbances of memory, which can range from dreamlike recall to partial memory lapses—or fugue states—to complete psychogenic amnesia and out-of-body sensations. The authors interviewed thirty-seven people undergoing treatment for dissociative disorders who also spoke of having been victims of SRA. They found an astonishing similarity in the stories of the patients they analyzed. The most common abuses reported were of being forcibly drugged during rituals; of being sexually abused, often with sexual devices;

of witnessing the abuse or torture of other people or the mutilation of animals; of being buried alive in coffins; of being forced to participate in the sacrifice of human adults or babies; of being ceremonially "married" to Satan; of being impregnated during a ritual and later having to sacrifice the fetus or infant to Satan; and of being made to eat human body parts. It was a virtual checklist of the atrocities originally described in *Michelle Remembers*. "The lack of independent verification of the reports of cult abuse presented in this paper prevents a definitive statement that the ritual cult abuse is true," the authors conceded, but they went on to say: "Despite the fact that some patients have discussed ritual abuse with other patients, and the fact that patients have had contact with referring therapists who may have provided information to them, it was our opinion that the ritual abuse was real." Many other therapists, counselors, and psychiatrists were also coming to that conclusion. Furthermore, Braun saw a link between multiple-personality disorder and SRA; he believed that of the two hundred thousand Americans that he estimated were suffering from MPD, up to one-fourth could be victims of SRA.

Dr. George K. Ganaway, who is the program director of the Ridgeview Center for Dissociative Disorders in Smyrna, Georgia, observed the same link but drew a different conclusion from it. Ganaway suggested that dissociative disorders might account for the SRA phenomenon, rather than vice versa, because the alleged victims were highly hypnotizable, suggestible, and fantasy-prone. In a 1991 speech before the American Psychological Association called "Alternative Hypotheses Regarding Satanic Ritual Abuse Memories," Ganaway warned: "When individuals are highly hypnotizable, they may spontaneously enter autohypnotic trance states, particularly during stressful interview situations. . . . Experimental hypnosis evidence indicates that memories retrieved in a hypnotic trance state are likely to contain a combination of both fact *and* fantasy in a mixture that cannot be accurately determined without external corroboration." Furthermore, hypnosis increases the subject's confidence in the veracity of both correct and *incorrect* recalled material. Highly hypnotizable individuals suspend critical judgment while in trance states and compulsively seek to comply with the suggestions of the interviewer, Ganaway said. There was thus an obvious danger that an unwary therapist might unconsciously guide patients to conclusions that already existed in the therapist's mind. That concern had caused lawmakers in a number of states, including Washington, to reject testimony that had been enhanced through hypnosis. In an earlier paper, "Historical Versus Narrative Truth: Clarifying the Role of Exogenous Trauma in the Etiology of MPD and Its Variants," Ganaway had proposed that much of what was being remembered as satanic-ritual abuse was in fact an invented "screen memory" masking more prosaically brutal forms of actual abuse, such as beatings, rapes, deprivations, or incarcerations. This paper became a touchstone for mental health workers who believed that something awful had happened to their anguished patients but that, whatever it was, it was something other than satanic-ritual abuse. *

---

*Ganaway has since become more circumspect in asserting that real abuse occurred. "I was perhaps being charitable and even overprotective of colleagues who were claiming to be uncovering spontaneous, allegedly uncontaminated cult-related material," he wrote in 1992. "Whereas the screen memory hypothesis has proven to be a likely possibility in a small number of cases I have seen since then, regrettably the most common likely cause of cult-related memories may very well turn out to be a mutual deception between the patient and the therapist. . . . Once reinforced by the therapist, this belief system may become fixed and highly elaborated, sometimes with tragic consequences. In these cases the common denominator in the satanic ritual abuse phenomenon may very well turn out to be the therapists themselves." (Ganaway, "On the Nature of Memories: Response to 'A Reply to Ganaway,'" *Dissociation* 5, no. 2 [June 1992].)

A 1991 survey of members of the American Psychological Association found that 30 percent of the respondents had treated at least one client who claimed to have suffered from satanic-ritual abuse, and 93 percent of those who completed a second survey believed their clients' claims to be true. Another poll addressed the opinions of social workers in California. Nearly half of those interviewed accepted the idea that SRA involved a national conspiracy of multigenerational abusers and baby-killers and that many of these people were prominent in their communities and appeared to live completely exemplary lives. A majority of those polled believed that victims of such extreme abuse were likely to have repressed the memories of it and that (contrary to scientific evidence) hypnosis increased the likelihood of accurately recalling what had happened.

The question of whether SRA is real has riven the mental-health field. On the one hand, there are those who compare survivors of satanic-ritual abuse to people who claim to remember past lives or to have been abducted by aliens: the evidence—or lack of it—is about the same in each instance. On the other hand, there are those who compare survivors of SRA to the survivors of less spectacular forms of child abuse. They point out that in many cases memories of what one might call ordinary abuse are forgotten, and are recovered only in therapy, through exactly the same process that produces memories of ritual abuse. If some recovered memories are deemed authentic, they ask, then why not others? Where does one draw the line in deciding what to believe?

How delicate this argument has become was apparent at the August 1992 meeting of the American Psychological Association, in Washington, D.C. Michael Nash, an associate professor of psychology at the University of Tennessee, presented a clinical account of a patient who had reported remembering an abduction by aliens. "I successfully treated this highly hypnotizable man over a period of three months, using standard uncovering techniques and employing hypnosis on two occasions," reported Nash. He took the position that the abduction story was relevant therapeutic material but not literally true. "About two months into this therapy, his symptoms abated, he was sleeping normally again, his ruminations and flashbacks had resolved, he returned to his usual level of interpersonal engagement, and his productivity at work improved. What we did worked. Nevertheless, let me underscore this: he walked out of my office as utterly convinced that he had been abducted as when he walked in. As a matter of fact he thanked me for helping him 'fill in the gaps of my memory.' I suppose I need not tell you how unhappy I was about his particular choice of words." Nash went on: "Here we have a stark example of a tenaciously believed-in fantasy which is almost certainly not true, but which, nonetheless, has all the signs of a previously repressed traumatic memory. I work routinely with adult women who have been sexually abused, and I could discern no difference between this patient's clinical presentation around the trauma and that of my sexually abused patients. Worse yet, the patient seemed to get better as he was able to elaborate on the report of trauma and integrate it into his own view of the world."

The conclusion that Nash drew from this experience was that "in terms of clinical utility, it may not really matter whether the event actually happened or not. . . . In the end, we (as clinicians) cannot tell the difference between believed-in fantasy about the past and viable memory of the past. Indeed there may be no structural difference between the two." In reaction to Nash's speech, someone in the audience asked if he had ever considered another hypothesis in his treatment of the young man, which would explain everything: that the alien abduction had actually occurred.

Therapists were not the only source of information on SRA in 1988, a seminal year in the spread of the phenomenon. On

October 25, just before Julie wrote the second note to her teacher, disclosing the abuse by her father and the poker players, the Ingram family sat down together and watched a prime-time Geraldo Rivera special on NBC entitled "Devil Worship: Exposing Satan's Underground." It was one of the most widely watched documentaries in television history, although it was only one of many such shows. (The day before, the subject of Rivera's daily program had been "Satanic Breeders: Babies for Sacrifice." Daytime talk shows had become obsessed with satanic abuse since the McMartin case.) "No region in this country is beyond the reach of the Devil worshipers," Rivera said on location in Nebraska. "Even here in the heartland of America, stories of ritual abuse crop up. The children you're about to meet were born into it. They say their parents forced them to witness bloody rituals and even, they say, to participate in ritual murder." Then he showed a clip of a young girl who testified, "My dad was involved in a lot of it. He's, like, one of the main guys; he's a leader or something. He made us have sex with him and with other guys and with other people."

That year also saw the publication of several books that discussed SRA, including *The Courage to Heal: A Guide for Women Survivors of Child Sexual Abuse*, by Ellen Bass and Laura Davis. Although this book is only one of many "survivor" books, it is by far the most successful, having sold more than 750,000 copies. It is sometimes called "the bible of the incest-recovery movement," and in terms of its consequences, it would have to be considered one of the most significant publications of the century. Neither of the authors is a trained therapist; Ellen Bass is a poet, and Laura Davis is a short-story writer, and both lead workshops on recovery. They make a number of assertions that have become commonplace in such books, such as the notion that childhood abuse is frequently forgotten and can be recovered in therapy. Much of *The Courage to Heal* is in the form of survivors' stories, including that of

"Annette," who grew up in an upper-middle-class home in the Midwest. Annette's parents were active in their church and leaders in their community, but they were also secret satanists—along with other prominent members of the town. Before she was twelve, Annette was impregnated, then forced to watch as her babies were sacrificed. "I completely blocked out the abuse," she writes. "I couldn't believe my parents had done such heinous things to me. My family had been so proper and clean, they squeaked."

According to one of Julie Ingram's friends, who talked to Loreli Thompson, Julie read a book about incest and then lent it to the friend. The friend could not remember the title. Julie admitted that "she cried the whole time she read the book," the friend recalled. "I was thinkin': 'The whole entire time?' I mean, I can understand at the really, really sad parts. . . . Well, Julie's really sensitive and she really cares about those kind of things. I guess that's Julie for you."

Another influential book that appeared in 1988 was *Satan's Underground*, by a woman writing under the pseudonym Lauren Stratford, which purported to be a true account of the abuse and sexual slavery she endured as a child. *Satan's Underground* became a paperback best-seller, and it was widely read in fundamentalist Christian congregations. For many religious believers, stories of satanic-ritual abuse merely confirmed a worldview they already strongly held. Hal Lindsey and Johanna Michaelsen, two other very popular Christian authors, endorsed *Satan's Underground* and thereby added considerably to its credibility. "If there is one thing that cult satanists do well, it's cover their tracks in such a way as to thoroughly discredit witnesses who might seek to come against them," Michaelsen wrote in the foreword. She elaborated what has become the standard explanation for the lack of evidence in cult crimes: "Animals are indeed killed and buried, but are later dug up and disposed of elsewhere. The children are fre-

quently given a stupefying drug before the rituals so that their
senses and perceptions are easily manipulated in the dim candlelight of the ritual scene. The pornographic photographs
taken of the children don't show up because they're carefully
kept in vaults of private collectors." Stratford first began to
recall memories of her abused childhood when she was hospitalized for an unspecified "life-threatening disorder." In order
to deal with the physical pain, the author underwent "guided
imagery," which is similar to hypnosis, with a therapist. In the
process, she recovered horrifying memories of being pressed
into pornography by her mother, becoming a child prostitute,
and joining a satanic cult. In one vivid scene, she describes
being placed in a barrel as the mutilated bodies of sacrificed
babies were dropped on top of her. Eventually, however, the
original publisher decided to withdraw *Satan's Underground* after a well-researched article in *Cornerstone*, a Christian magazine, attacked the book as a hoax, and portrayed the author as
a deluded and unfortunate woman—as it happens, from a rigid,
fundamentalist Christian family like the Ingrams, from Tacoma, just north of Olympia—who had a history of self-
mutilation and of making sexual accusations that were never
verified. (The book has since been reissued by another publisher, with few changes.)

It chanced that in the summer of 1988 Ericka Ingram had
noticed a copy of *Satan's Underground* on the coffee table of a
house where she was baby-sitting and had asked if she could
borrow it. When she returned the book, she said that she had
read it all the way through. Later she told police that she had
read only a few chapters, then tossed the book into the backseat of her car, because the shock of recognition had been too
great to bear.

Thus two communities that normally have little to do with
each other—fundamentalist Christians and a particular set of
mental health professionals—found common ground in the

question dominating any consideration of satanic-ritual abuse: whether to believe it actually exists. In the absence of evidence that these stories or memories of satanic-ritual abuse were real, one could either reject them as absurd, withhold judgment until evidence appeared, or accept them on faith. The middle ground was rapidly shrinking as the proselytizers for both groups spread the word that SRA was real and anyone who doubted it either was "in denial" or was part of the satanic underground. (Interestingly, the rise in reports of SRA coincided with the collapse of international communism, suggesting that one external enemy was being replaced by another, closer to home. Bennett Braun made this connection explicit in a speech in 1988, describing the satanic conspiracy as "a national-international type organization that's got a structure somewhat similar to the communist cell structure, where it goes from . . . small groups, to local consuls [sic], regional consuls, district consuls, national consuls, and they have meetings at different times.")

The Los Angeles County Commission for Women formed a task force in 1988 to call attention to the purported rise in satanic-ritual abuse, thereby claiming SRA as a women's issue, ostensibly because women and children were the main victims of cult crimes. The commission issued a report that defined satanic-ritual abuse as "a brutal form of abuse of children, adolescents, and adults, consisting of physical, sexual, and psychological abuse, and involving the use of rituals," and continued:

> Ritual does not necessarily mean satanic. However, most survivors state that they were ritually abused as part of satanic worship for the purpose of indoctrinating them into satanic beliefs and practices.
> Ritual abuse is usually carried out by members of a cult. The purpose of the ritual elements of the abuse seems three-fold: (1) rituals in some groups are part of a shared belief or

worship system into which the victim is being indoctrinated; (2) rituals are used to intimidate victims into silence; (3) ritual elements (e.g., devil worship, animal or human sacrifice) seem so unbelievable to those unfamiliar with these crimes that these elements detract from the credibility of the victims and make prosecution of the crimes very difficult.

The report goes on to say that the central feature of ritual abuse is mind control, which is achieved through the sophisticated use of brainwashing, drugs, and hypnosis: "The purpose of the mind control is to compel ritual abuse victims to keep the secret of their abuse, to conform to the beliefs and behaviors of the cult, and to become functioning members who serve the cult by carrying out the directives of its leaders without being detected within society at large."

Elizabeth S. Rose (the pseudonym of a free-lance writer who says she herself is an SRA survivor) wrote in a cover story for the January/February 1993 *Ms.*, "People would rather believe that survivors—particularly women survivors—are crazy. This keeps many survivors from coming forward." The cover line read, "BELIEVE IT! CULT RITUAL ABUSE EXISTS." The frequent reference to the need to believe in ritual abuse arises from the long-standing cultural resistance to the reality of child abuse, but it also points to the quasi-religious nature of the SRA campaign. At Safeplace, the rape-crisis center where Julie Ingram sought refuge after leaving home, counselors say that the disbelief that usually greets such charges parallels the incredulity that often greeted bona fide allegations of incest and sexual abuse only a few years ago. Nevertheless, the counselors have frequent internal debates about whether the increasing numbers of women who come to them talking about satanic-ritual abuse and human sacrifice are telling the truth. "Here's my dilemma," Tyra Lindquist, the administrative coordinator of the center, said. "We are already struggling against a tidal wave of disbelief—it's a tidal wave! Nobody wants to believe how bad it really is for women and children. Whoever walks in or calls us on the phone will tell us what she needs to survive this minute, this day. Our job is to help her survive through recovery. It's not our role to believe or disbelieve."

A fourth group to become concerned with the SRA phenomenon was the police detectives charged with looking into the crimes of the alleged cults. Joe Vukich recalls going to a homicide seminar in Portland, Oregon, where a detective from Boise, Idaho, gave a presentation on cult crimes. "Folks, I'm here to tell you this stuff is going on!" the detective said. Vukich turned to an officer sitting next to him and remarked, "Not in my department. I'd know about it." Soon dozens of police workshops around the country were discussing the phenomenon. Michelle Smith and Lawrence Pazder were often featured speakers, along with specialist "cult cops," who were likely to be fundamentalist Christians.

On the Ingram investigative team, only Neil McClanahan, who had come from a mainstream Protestant tradition but had converted to Catholicism, would describe himself as a devout Christian. All three of the detectives—Brian Schoening, Joe Vukich, and Loreli Thompson—were born and raised Catholic, although Schoening and Thompson were no longer practicing.

During the investigation Schoening and Vukich traveled to Canada to participate in an SRA workshop. They listened to speakers discuss teen satanism and role-playing games such as Dungeons and Dragons. They were given an overview of the history of satanism, from the "magic theater" of eighth-century Greece to its sway in Hitler's Third Reich. They were presented with the modern occult teachings of Anton LaVey, the author of *The Satanic Bible* and founder of the Church of Satan. They were instructed in such esoterica as cult holidays and the protocols of a black mass. They were shown magical symbols, runes, and glyphs. It was an amazing experience for the two detectives, but most shocking to them was the fact that they were greeted as experts on the subject. Before long, Schoening and Vukich and other Olympia detectives were besieged by calls from police officers around the country who were also engaged in investigating recovered memories of satanic-ritual abuse.

Early in the Ingram case, Undersheriff McClanahan telephoned Supervisory Special Agent Kenneth V. Lanning at the behavioral-sciences unit of the Federal Bureau of Investigation Academy in Quantico, Virginia. Lanning, the FBI's research expert on the sexual victimization of children, had been hearing stories of sexual abuse with occult overtones since 1983. At first he had tended to believe the stories; but as the number of alleged cases skyrocketed, he had grown skeptical. Soon hundreds of victims were accusing thousands of offenders. By the mid-eighties, the annual number of alleged satanic murders had reached the tens of thousands. As a result of information provided by a prison official in Utah, word circulated in the police workshops that satanic cults were sacrificing between fifty and sixty thousand people every year in the United States, although the annual national total of homicides averaged less than twenty-five thousand. Believers contend that no bodies are found because satanists often eat their victims and have access to sophisticated methods of disposal. It amazed Lanning that police officers, who regularly complained about inaccuracies in the media and often joked about tabloid-television accounts of "true" crimes, were susceptible to such material when it involved satanism. Yes, there were psychotic killers who heard the voice of Satan, just as there were psychotic killers who heard the voice of Jesus, but that didn't mean that they were members of an organized religious cult, Lanning argued. If satanic-ritual murder was defined simply as a killing that was committed by two or more people whose primary motive was to fulfill a prescribed satanic ritual, then Lanning could not find a single documented case of the phenomenon in the United States. He worried that many officers were allowing their personal religious beliefs to affect their judgment.

Lanning told McClanahan that after looking into hundreds of similar stories, he had come to the conclusion that they were merely a symptom of modern hysteria. McClanahan replied that the Ingram case was different: he had a perpetrator who was confessing to the crimes and implicating other members of the cult, and there was a likelihood that he would obtain other evidence, such as scars and photographs. "Well, you've got more than anybody else," Lanning conceded. When McClanahan hung up, it struck him that the Ingram case was much more important than anyone had realized—that it was the one case in America that could prove, finally, that satanic-ritual abuse was real.

7

Q uestions to Ask God,"
Sandy Ingram wrote on a scratch pad next to a grocery list in
December 1988. "Has my life been a lie—Have I hidden or
suppressed things bad things that have happened in the
past. . . . Have I been brainwashed, oppressed, depressed—
controlled—without knowing it." What had once seemed to
her a happy, normal life was no longer recognizable. Her husband and three of her five children were describing an existence
she could hardly imagine. The police were still trying to find
and interview Paul Ross, and how could she guess any longer
what he might say? Her day-care license had been suspended,
so she couldn't reopen her center even if she chose to. How
was she going to support herself and the one child still at home,
her nine-year-old son, Mark? "What I would like to do for a
job," she wrote. "Chore work, go to school, pediatrick nurse,
art teacher."

Two days after Paul's arrest, Sandy had gone to see him in
jail. She sat facing a milky sheet of Plexiglas. Paul came into
the room beyond, wearing orange coveralls and looking pale
and thin. He picked up the phone on his side of the divider.
She realized that they would never touch each other again. It
was as if Paul were in some other, unreachable realm of reality.
They talked in generalities about the case, awkwardly trying to

keep the conversation alive. Paul reminded Sandy to get her driver's license renewed. Then he said that Pastor John Bratun had instructed him to make a confession to her that had nothing to do with his arrest: he told Sandy about the affair he had had, which had been over for thirteen years. Sandy was devastated. If she hadn't known about the affair, she found herself thinking, then what else might she not have known about?

The house on Fir Tree Road was so empty. During the day, Mark was in school, and for the first time in her life Sandy was alone: no day-care children, no husband coming home for lunch, no enormous loads of laundry to be done, no family dinners. There was so much silence and time. Sandy went to the mall and got her ears pierced.

That empty period was about to change, however. During the first couple of weeks in December, concerns arose on the part of the investigators about Sandy's role in the abuse. Both Ericka and Julie had initially denied that their mother was involved, but as the investigators and others repeatedly questioned how so many dreadful things could have been going on in the house without Sandy's knowledge, her daughters began making small disclosures.

Ericka told a friend about the poker games, when the men came into her room. Her mother would sit on the bed and watch, Ericka said.

"Your mother was a cheering section?" the friend asked.

"Well, she wouldn't do anything," Ericka explained. "She wouldn't say anything. She'd just watch."

"We're talking about your mother!" exclaimed her friend, who was a mother herself and simply couldn't imagine such a scene.

"It was strange," Ericka agreed.

The troubled friend reported the conversation to the police.

Detective Vukich interviewed another friend of Ericka's, who had heard a similar account. Sandy would come in before the men arrived and "get her ready," the woman told Vukich. "She said that her mother would be touching her vagina at times."

"Did she say if that was strictly for the purpose of getting her ready or her mother was, in fact, sexually abusing her?"

"She used the words 'sexually abused.' "

"And how recent was that?" Vukich asked.

"She said it happened two times in the month of September," the woman answered.

The woman also related that Ericka had wondered whether her parents had given her drugs that affected her memory. "She said sometimes she had a hard time remembering what happened, and then all of a sudden it'd come back to her, but she didn't realize why she couldn't remember in the first place."

Vukich and Thompson met with Ericka on December 8. She was cheerful and talkative, according to Thompson's notes, until they asked again about her mother's role; then she became withdrawn and communicated only with a few words or by shakes of the head. She recalled an evening, when she was nine or ten years old, on which her mother had entered her room, followed by her father, Rabie, and Risch. Rabie had stripped her and made her pose while he took photographs. Risch had held a gun. There had been many other photo sessions. Her mother had watched while this happened but had not participated.

Loreli Thompson left in the middle of the interview to meet with Ericka's younger sister. One of the discordant features of the investigation was that each girl's story tended to leave out the other, although they had been roommates for most of their lives. There were other discrepancies. Julie had never mentioned anything about Sandy's being involved, nor had she spoken about pornographic photographs taken by Rabie or Risch. Unlike Ericka, Julie had not been able to say the names of these two men; whenever either Julie or Detective

Thompson referred to them, Rabie was called Number Twelve and Risch Number Fourteen, which is the way they were identified in the photo lineup.

When Thompson asked Julie if her mother knew about the abuse, Julie responded, "I do. I think she does." Had Sandy ever been in the room when "bad things" happened? Julie replied, "I don't think so." Thompson then asked when the last time had been that Twelve or Fourteen had photographed her. Julie slumped in her chair, drew her knees up to her chest, and wrote on a piece of paper, "Six years old." Where? "My bedroom," she wrote. Where was Ericka while this was happening? Julie shrugged. Where was her mother? No response. Then Julie wrote that Twelve and Fourteen had put their hands all over her body and told her she was special. Was anybody else in the room? Thompson asked again. Finally, Julie wrote, "My mom." She began to shake. Thompson asked if her mother had said anything to her. "She told me to be a good girl and that no one was hurting me." Then Julie began sobbing. Thompson ended the interview.

That Sunday Julie went to church, and while she was praying at the altar her mother came and knelt beside her. The eyes of everyone in the church were on them. Sandy had not seen either of her daughters for a month, since this catastrophe in their family began to unfurl itself in such a frightfully public manner. This was the only way she could arrange to see Julie, so she leaned over and whispered that she loved her and that she would not have let anyone hurt her. She said that she did not know what had been going on. Julie got up and left without a word.

Sandy was sitting at home when police investigators arrived with a warrant to examine the Ingram house once again. The detectives advised Sandy of her rights and said that they were investigating her involvement in photographing and sexually touching Ericka. They were hoping that their search would uncover the photographs of sexual abuse. Richard Peterson came along for the ride. While the investigators combed through the bedrooms, Peterson poked around. He said he hadn't noticed any family pictures in the house, so Sandy took him to the hallway, where they kept framed photos on the wall. Some of the trim was missing from the doorways, he observed. That seemed odd, although Peterson didn't realize that the Ingrams had done much of the work on the house themselves, and it was still partly unfinished. Indeed, their way of living seemed foreign to him. Sandy's canning closet was full of vegetables and fruits from her garden. She was so proud to be able to provide for her family; she even entered her canning into competitions at the county fair. But to Peterson, the fruit jellies and pickled okra and tomato sauces were evidence that the Ingrams were on the edge of destitution. Otherwise, why couldn't they buy their food at the grocery store? They even slaughtered rabbits, although, as one of the detectives noted in his report, it wasn't Paul who did the butchering, it was Sandy. She enjoyed it, she said.

Sandy was knitting at the dining room table, trying to stay calm as the detectives turned her house upside down. Accusation hung in the air. One of the men remarked that either Sandy knew what was going on and ignored it, or else she must have participated.

"I haven't done either," Sandy said. "I didn't know anything."

The detective responded by saying that Sandy should have known through her sex life with Paul that he had been fooling around with the kids and other people. But in Sandy's opinion, there had never been anything forced or weird in her sex life. It was "very normal, very fun, very dear, and very satisfying." She was completely stunned when one of the detectives told her that Paul had been a homosexual for most of his life.

The search uncovered nothing incriminating, although several items were collected for evidence. There were four plastic boxes containing old datebooks; the letter Paul Ross had written to Sandy when he left home; and two books, *The Pleasure Bond* and *Devil's Gamble*. The detectives also took a broken lock from Julie's door. Julie had stated that she had installed the lock to keep her father from coming into her room and raping her. She said he had broken in anyway. At the time, however, Julie had told her mother that she had put a new doorknob on her door while she was baby-sitting, but she had installed it incorrectly and managed to get locked into her own room with the little children. Finally Chad had kicked the door open to rescue them. Sandy had been sympathetic. She remembered telling Julie, "It's all right, we'll fix it. If you need a new doorknob, Dad'll be happy to put it on." Now Paul was remembering that, indeed, he had been the one to break the lock in order to get to Julie. Sandy didn't know what to believe anymore.

"Who are you most afraid of, Rabie or Risch?" one of the detectives demanded.

"I'm not afraid of anybody," Sandy said boldly, although at that moment she was close to panic. The detectives finally left when Sandy decided to call a lawyer.

Everything in Sandy's life was flying to pieces. The marriage that she had once considered secure and happy had been publicly exposed as a sham. Now her own daughters were accusing her of sexual abuse. Could such things really have happened without her remembering them? Was there a "dark side" to Sandy, as there must have been to Paul?

What terrified Sandy most was the likelihood that she would lose Mark. Someone had called the state's Child Protective Services and said that Mark had to be taken away from Sandy before the same things happened to him. The police knew that the anonymous caller was Ericka; she had been demanding custody of Mark. Sandy was afraid that unless she admitted that abuse had taken place in her home, she would be declared to be "in denial" and therefore an unfit parent. When Sandy spoke to Paul about her dilemma, in early December, he said that maybe it was a good idea to surrender Mark. At that moment, Sandy stopped defending her husband. "The house is very cold—and my heart is broken over & over," she wrote on a scrap of paper. "Things will not ever be the same."

On December 16, Sandy went to see Pastor John Bratun in his office at the Church of Living Water. Bratun was a kind-looking man, forty-three years old, with a long face and a mustache; he reminded Sandy of Tennessee Ernie Ford. He had been in Olympia for a little over three years; before that, he had served as assistant pastor for several Foursquare churches in Southern California. From the night of Paul's arrest, when Bratun went with Pastor Ron Long to comfort Sandy at the house, and then visited Paul in his cell, Bratun had been intensely involved in the Ingram case. Another church member, Paula Davis, who was Ericka's advocate, was present at most of her interviews. Information passed freely among the police, the church, and the victims.

Sandy would later say that she had always felt she could trust Pastor John, as she called him; and so she felt stung when he told her now that she was "eighty percent evil." He reiterated the speech that she had heard from the detectives: either she had known what was going on in her house and ignored it, or she had participated in it. She was probably going to go to jail unless she made a confession. Sandy bridled at the threat. "That may work with some people, but it won't work with me," she said defiantly. Still, she left Bratun's office feeling hurt and confused and even more afraid.

She was now almost completely alone; even her church had turned against her, and she could sense the relentless mechanism of the investigation bearing down upon her, ready to snatch her youngest child out of her hands and to grind away the small core of dignity that was left her in this sensational scandal. When she got home, she bundled Mark into the car and fled, forgetting to turn off the television in her haste. In a way, she felt, the escape was exhilarating. She had never driven even the short distance to Tacoma on her own, and now she was driving all the way across the state, through a snowstorm, to take refuge with relatives. She had never driven in snow before.

Paul, meanwhile, had produced another memory, this one involving Sandy. "It was late 1975 or early 1976," he told Schoening and Vukich. "I was at home with Paul Jr. and Chad while Sandy had gone shopping with the girls. It was about seven or eight at night. It was dark out and Jim Rabie, Ray Risch, and [another man] came over to the house. . . . Knowing that Sandy was gone, they wanted to have sex with the boys. We all went up to the main floor of the house to the first bedroom on the right and the boys undressed. I don't remember if they undressed themselves or we undressed them, but they did get undressed. Ray had on work clothes—clean coveralls and work boots. He and Jim undressed. I don't remember what Jim had on. Ray knelt on the floor and Paul Jr. sat on the bottom bunk of the bunk bed and leaned over and orally stimulated Ray's penis. At the same time, Ray was fondling Paul Jr. Jim Rabie also undressed and had laid Chad on the floor on his stomach, so that he could have anal intercourse with him. . . . Chad would have been seven to eight and Paul would have been eleven to twelve. . . .

"At this time, Sandy came home. All of a sudden. I don't know if the dog barked or whatever, but she came home. . . . I think she was early. . . . She had on a coat and she was carrying a package or a sack and the girls were behind her and our little dachshund came in with them. She kinda said hi as she came up and then when she saw what was happening, uh,

I suppose she dropped the sack and, you know, got very angry. I don't recall the words that were said. I do recall that she was very upset and very angry. Jim Rabie grabbed her by the hair and very forceful, very angrily, almost vicious, said, 'You can't do anything to us. If you say anything, Paul will go to prison and your family will be embarrassed.' And then he told her, he said: 'I'll kill the kids.' " This was a side of Rabie that Ingram had never seen before. Until now Rabie had always seemed a very gentle person.

"How were the boys reacting while all this was going on?" asked Schoening.

"I don't recall," said Ingram. "I can kinda see the girls running when they saw what was happening, when they saw the viciousness with which Jim grabbed Sandy by the hair and started screaming at her. They ran into the living room and hid. I believe I was kind of outside the room when all this was going on, and I don't know what the boys did."

Rabie and Risch and the other man took Sandy downstairs, Ingram said. They stripped her and ripped up a sheet and tied her to the bed frame. "She was spread-eagle on the bed," said Ingram. "Jim Rabie raped her first, and I recall it was vicious—you know, he wasn't nice at all about it. And then Ray Risch raped her." Rabie again threatened to kill the children if Sandy told.

"After they left, I untied her and she put something over her and sat on the end of the bed," said Ingram. "She said, 'Why?' " Ingram had told her that he had gotten involved in a witchcraft ritual. "I signed a contract with them where I promised secrecy and said I wouldn't reveal anything about the group or what they did." It was hopeless to resist, he believed. The only way out of the cult was by death.

"My memory is becoming clearer as I go through all this," Ingram said at the end of the session. "It's getting clearer as more things come out."

As Paul was giving his statement to detectives, Sandy was writing in her diary. "It is now Dec. 17th—I am in Spokane. Brought Mark here in case I get arrested," she wrote. "So much has happened I don't know if I can say it all—Jesus you know me better than I know myself—You know if all this is true. You know the truth—Please Jesus answer my hearts cry. Help me to get in touch with the truth with reality. I am afraid Jesus. I am afraid. Sometimes I am numb—sometimes I am excited about a new future. . . . Where have my children gone, my precious babies that I love—Forgive me Forgive me for not seeing—Oh Lord I do not understand. Help me to understand. Help! I took off my wedding ring Dec. 16th in Ellenburg."

8

On December 18, Detectives Brian Schoening and Joe Vukich finally located Paul Ross, the eldest of the Ingram children. His flight from home had led him to Reno, Nevada, where he was working in a warehouse. They went by his apartment; he wasn't home. Schoening left a note on the door asking him to call them at the motel where they were staying. He called at eight-fifteen the next morning. There was a warrant outstanding for him in Thurston County for malicious mischief—he was accused of having battered someone's car with a baseball bat—and he wanted to know if that was why the officers had come. No, Schoening told him, there was a problem in his family. His father and two other men, whom Schoening didn't name, were in jail, and his sisters were in protective custody. The rest of his family was safe. Schoening didn't reveal what the charges were, but when Paul Ross met with the detectives several hours later he guessed that his father had been charged with a sexual offense.

There are no recordings of Schoening and Vukich's interview with Paul Ross, only notes made by Schoening and the boy's own statements later. The detectives found Paul Ross to be hostile, bitter, and evasive. "I'd like to shoot my dad," he admitted. "I've always hated him." He said he wasn't surprised that his father was in jail, because his father had physically abused him. Specifically, the young man recalled an incident several years before in which his father had thrown an axe at him. Ingram had been standing on a deck behind the house, and Paul Ross and Chad had been in the backyard, below him. Angry because the blade was dulled, their father had thrown the axe from the deck, and if Paul Ross hadn't moved it would have struck him. What was significant about this memory was that, unlike so many others the detectives had heard, two other people had remembered it, and remembered it more or less the same way. Chad had said that it was a roofing axe that the boys had lent to a neighbor. It had gotten dull, which upset their father. He wanted the boys to sharpen it. Paul's account was that he had only meant to toss the axe down to his sons and had been surprised when it landed right at the boys' feet. He had always felt bad about the incident, he said, and supposed that this was the reason his eldest child had left home. The axe story had the feel of a normal memory; it was practically the only one in the case.

As the one person in the family who had not been exposed to the church grapevine and who claimed not to have heard about his father's arrest until that morning, Paul Ross was the least contaminated source the detectives had encountered. As they spoke to him, however, a now familiar fixated expression came over his face. He sat in the detectives' motel room, staring out at the foothills of the Sierra Nevada, and his voice took on the monotonous quality of a trancelike state. Schoening was incredulous. It seemed as if everyone he talked to on this case fell into a trance. For him, these interviews were an emotional seesaw; whenever one of the Ingrams went robotic, Schoening would start chewing the furniture. What was driving him crazy was the absence of feeling. He was filling in the pain, the outrage, the humiliation, the horror, from his own emotional palette.

Because the interview with Paul Ross was not recorded,

one cannot know how much information the detectives fed to him, or what might have been suggested while the young man was entranced. Vukich asked what he remembered about sexual abuse from his childhood. Nothing came to mind at first. He did recall the poker parties, and he mentioned the names of several of the players, including Rabie and Risch; then he picked out their photographs and those of several others. He said that he hated Rabie. He called Risch "a gay guy." When the detectives asked him to explain, Paul Ross recalled an evening when he was ten or eleven years old. He heard "a muffled cry, a yelp, almost like somebody stepping on a dog's tail." He crept downstairs to investigate. The door to his parents' bedroom was open just a crack. Peeking in, he saw his mother tied to the bed, "spread eagle," with belts around her feet and what appeared to be stockings lashing her arms to the posts. "Jim Rabie was 'screwing' her," Schoening's report related, "and his dad had his 'dick' in her mouth." Ray Risch and another man were "to the left, 'jacking each other off.' His dad came over and hit him so hard it almost knocked him out, yelled at him to leave them alone, and closed the door." Paul Ross then got a fifth of whiskey and retreated to his room. He became an alcoholic that very night, he said.

This story was so close to the memory that Paul had produced only a few days before. The detail about Sandy being tied to the bed was a match, almost like the axe story. And yet, if Sandy was a victim of such a brutal rape, why couldn't she remember it? Why couldn't Paul Ross remember his own abuse by Rabie and Risch the same night they raped his mother? What about the years of abuse his sisters endured—why didn't he know about or remember that? He did mention one occasion when his father came into the bedroom he shared with Chad and took his younger brother out of the room in the middle of the night. The boy was crying. That was all that came to mind.

In fact, there wasn't a single bit of Paul Ross's statement that the detectives could use. It was so tantalizing, so frustrating. They couldn't charge suspects for crimes the victims couldn't recall. If only Paul Ross could remember more, or admit that he also had been abused! As it was, Paul Ross was more of a liability than an asset to the prosecution. At one point, Schoening became so upset he backed the young man against a wall. "We know you're a victim!" he insisted. The young man demanded a break. He said he needed to be alone. He promised that he would be back in thirty minutes. He walked out and didn't come back.

He did locate his mother, however, and telephoned her for the first time in two years. "Mom, I know everything that happened," he told her, according to Sandy's later statement. She said he related what he had said to the detectives, including the rape scene. Sandy asked Paul Ross if he had repressed these memories and then suddenly recovered them. No, her son told her, he had always remembered them, but lately he had been going to a hypnotist who was helping him remember even more.

Sandy recalled the remark that Ericka's friend Paula Davis had made to her that night at Denny's when Ericka had first disclosed the abuse to her. "You're the only one in the family who didn't know," Davis had said. That must have been true, Sandy realized. Now the only person in her family, except herself, who maintained that he had never been abused was nine-year-old Mark.

On December 20, back in Olympia, Joe Vukich and Loreli Thompson met with Ericka and her advocate, Paula Davis, at the sheriff's office. Davis, twenty-nine, was a schoolteacher who described herself as Ericka's best friend. Under Washington state law, victims of violent or sexual crimes are entitled to have a spokesperson present at any interview. Given the victim's state of mind, the investigators thought it appropriate to conduct the session in a special room that had been set up—ironically, by Jim Rabie—for interviews with abused children. Ericka and Paula sat in miniature chairs, amid the plastic toys and security blankets.

Vukich asked Ericka if her brothers or her sister had ever discussed their abuse with her. "No." Ericka was monosyllabic. Sometimes it seemed that she didn't even hear the questions. Vukich managed to get her to say that the last time Rabie had molested her was three months earlier, in September.

"Was your sister in the room with you?" asked Vukich.

"No."

After a while, she whispered that she needed to stop for a moment. The detectives left her in the room with Paula. When Vukich glanced in through a small window in the door, he saw the two women sitting on the floor. Ericka was cuddled up in Paula's lap, sobbing. His heart went out to her. He'd never seen a grown woman reduced to such a state.

"Do you remember what we asked you, Ericka, about what Mr. Rabie did when he came over to the bed?" Vukich said when the interview resumed.

Ericka sat mute, shifting in her chair and tugging at a thread on her jeans. A minute passed.

"And this was the last week of September," Thompson said to break the silence.

"What was it that he did, Ericka?" Vukich asked again. "Did he make you do something to him?"

"Yes." She hid her face in Paula's shoulder.

"Did he make you touch him somewhere? You're shaking your head. Is that yes or no?"

"Yes."

"What part of his body did you have to touch, Ericka?" Thompson asked.

"Can we stop for a minute? I have to go to the bathroom," Ericka suddenly announced, and she left the room.

The detectives could hear her retching in the toilet. Davis went after her. The two women were gone for some time. When they came back, Ericka handed the detectives a sheet of paper on which she had written a detailed statement. Vukich read it aloud for the record:

> I was asleep in my room in bed and heard Jim Rabie come in and that's when I looked up and saw him. He started touching me with his hands first on the outside of my sweats, then underneath. He touched my chest and on my private parts, front and back. He inserted his fingers in my front and back private parts. He kept telling me to be quiet in a threatening voice. My mom and dad were awake someplace in the house. He forced my head to his front private part with his hands. He was very rough and hurt me with his hands. It seemed that this continued for a long time. I was scared and didn't know what to do. He had previously threatened me that he would kill me and do worse things to me if I refused or if I told. He thrust his front private part into my mouth repeatedly for a long time. Then he ejaculated in my mouth. His pants were down, but not off. Then he started making grunting noises. Then he started touching me orally with his mouth on my chest and front and back private parts. This seemed to continue for a long time and he was very rough and hurt me. Then he stopped and said I knew what would happen if I told. Then he urinated all over my body in bed. He didn't defecate on me this time. Later, my father came in.

Vukich could barely control his emotions as he read this; he felt overwhelmed by the monstrousness of the scene Ericka had just described. "I think I'd like to start at the end, where you say 'He didn't defecate on me this time,' " Vukich said gently. "Were there other times when this same scenario happened where he did defecate on you?"

"Yes."

When Ericka left the interview room, Vukich took her handwritten statement down the hall and threw it on his lieutenant's desk. "The son of a bitch shit on her!" he cried. His voice was quaking. He had never felt this way about a victim before. His feelings were more those of a protective older brother, he believed, or the loving father she had apparently never had—even though he was not that much older than Ericka. When the other detectives observed how emotional Vukich became in speaking about her, they joked nervously that he was falling in love.

The same day that Ericka was making this statement, Sandy drove back to Olympia. She had decided to leave Mark in the care of her relatives in Spokane in order to keep him out of the grasp of the Child Protective Services. She knew, however, that she wouldn't be able to hide him forever.

Sandy went straight to Pastor Bratun's office. This time, Bratun was more understanding. He explained to her that when he had said she was eighty percent evil he was also saying there was a side to her that was twenty percent good. This was the side that had brought her back. This was the side that was trying to remember. To encourage her he revealed some of the new memories that Ingram was producing. Many of them concerned satanic scenes. One involved a former girlfriend of Ray Risch's, who Paul said was the high priestess of the cult. Paul had remembered having sex with her after a ritual in a barn. He had signed an oath in blood, pledging loyalty to the cult. If he tried to break away, his younger daughter would be killed. Sandy said she couldn't remember any such scenes. Paul had also recalled Sandy having sex with Risch, Bratun told her. He asked if that had ever happened. Sandy said no, then hesitated. "Oh, no!" she cried, and fell forward, burying her head between her knees.

The first memory Sandy produced resembled the scene her

eldest child had described. She was not tied to the bed, how-ever, and it was Risch having sex with her, not Rabie. Paul stood to one side, guarding the door. Then another memory surfaced. This time she was tied up, but she was on the living room floor. Rabie was there, naked, and for some reason he was on all fours, howling like a dog. Sandy then saw herself in a closet with Paul. He had hold of her hair and was hitting her with a stick of kindling. The others were in the living room, laughing at her, calling her fat. Paul pulled her out of the closet and hurled her on the bed, where Rabie and Risch had anal intercourse with her. It seemed to Sandy that these events must have happened sometime before 1978.

After leaving Bratun's office, Sandy returned to Spokane to spend Christmas with Mark.

Paul Ingram had just been transferred to a jail in another county. His bail was set at $200,000. Once he was away from the daily interrogations and the constant reinforcement of the detectives and the urgings of his pastor, he began to have renewed doubts about the accuracy of some of his memories. A Christian counselor hired by Ingram's attorney adminis-tered a series of diagnostic tests. On the Minnesota Multi-phasic Personality Inventory (MMPI), Ingram showed himself to be adaptable, resourceful, and self-reliant, if also restless, nonconforming, and easily bored. "Individuals who have this MMPI profile often perceive the world in different and original ways," wrote the counselor in his report. "They may be per-ceived as somewhat eccentric, unpredictable, or imaginative. They tend to think differently, at times negatively, and fre-quently are perceived as aloof, touchy, emotionally distant or apart, and preoccupied." The Millon Clinical Multiaxial In-ventory (MCMI) revealed a person with an exaggerated need to be liked. Ingram showed a "rigid and tense compliance to social convention." He was the kind of person who was prone to follow orders. People such as Ingram "tend to show a perfectionist element, and condemnation causes them considerable tension, especially if conveyed by persons in authority. . . . This overall cooperativeness may hide strong rebellious feelings that may occasionally break through the front of propriety and restraint. These individuals lack insight, are often indecisive, and are easily upset by deviations from their daily routine. A pattern of rigid self-control is typical, and individuals with this profile only occasionally relax the edgy tension and guarded defensiveness that conceal their anxious feelings." The Rorschach test described a person who "has difficulty getting the whole picture." In the opinion of the counselor, Ingram "distorts data to meet his own needs rather than showing an outright thought disorder."

Ingram insisted on taking the Sexual Addiction Screening Test three times—once giving answers based on his state of mind before his arrest, once for the period before Pastor Bratun came and delivered him of demon spirits, and once for his current state. The first exam showed him to have no sexual deviations at all; however, on the basis of Ingram's responses in the two other exams, the counselor diagnosed him as a pedophile and a "walking time bomb."

The counselor also talked to Dr. Peterson and Pastor Bratun about Ingram. Peterson described Ingram as highly manipulative and completely separated ("dissociated") from his feelings, so much so that Peterson believed that Ingram had two ego states—a split personality, in layman's terms. He also recognized the effects of cult programming on Ingram. Bratun agreed with Peterson's observations. He saw the two ego states consisting of, on the one hand, a hardworking, civic-minded, loving father, who was so priggish he "wouldn't let his daughter come downstairs in a nightgown," and, on the other hand, an angry, violent, and manipulative individual who was the polar opposite in every respect of the Paul Ingram most people knew and respected. In Bratun's opinion, the exorcism in the jail cell had been the key moment in integrating these two opposing halves.

"He speaks with very flat responses, and no affect," the counselor reported. "It appears that he gives himself permission to 'get a memory' when this is done in a Christian context. Mr. Ingram appears to be a product of a dissociative disorder in which there is more than one personality that is capable of assuming control. He does not, however, appear to fit the criteria of multiple-personality disorder. Mr. Ingram does appear to have been affected by periods of intense indoctrination around cult issues. . . . In a sense, the longer his secret life remained separated, and the more pressure was brought by external forces to do more and more deviant sexual acting out, the more tightly he bound the walls of his separate, dissociative life." The Christian counselor added that, as Ingram was prayed for, "he began to make the tightly bound compartments mentioned above (separate ego states) porous and allowed some of the memories to begin to return." This defense counselor would eventually testify for the prosecution.

It was a stark Christmas for many families. The detectives found that the Ingram case was following them home, when they had the chance to be home at all. They certainly weren't in a holiday mood. To cheer them up, Ericka brought in a plate of Christmas cookies. Undersheriff McClanahan was so worried about the mental health of his investigative team that he assembled a team of psychologists to debrief them. The detectives were encouraged to express their feelings candidly, but they reacted so furiously that the psychologists beat a retreat and diagnosed the whole bunch as suffering from post-traumatic stress disorder.

Rabie and Risch were both in solitary confinement. Rabie was still pleading for a lie detector test. He refused to take his medication for narcolepsy and spent much of his time sleeping; it was the only time he had ever felt grateful for his affliction. During his waking moments, the former detective pored obsessively over the police reports of his case, which his attorney had secured. Risch lost forty pounds in solitary, and his hair, which had been jet black, turned completely white. His wife worried that he might have suffered a stroke; one day, he suddenly seemed unable to complete a sentence. His thoughts wandered, and he had difficulty hearing.

On the day after Christmas, Sandy returned, again alone, to the house on Fir Tree Road. "Dear Paul," she wrote that day, "I am praying for you that you can be totally and wholly restored. . . . Sometimes I am very afraid. Afraid because of what has happened in the past. . . . Sometimes I am even afraid of you Paul mostly because I do not know the truth. Was I controlled by you." Apparently contradicting what she told Pastor Bratun, she continued, "I am not remembering anything, but with God's help I will remember. I was very tired after driving today. I was also very upset—and didn't want to come back here. I didn't want to leave Mark." Then she began to draw upon other memories, memories that she and Paul shared. "Do you remember Paul Ross he was such a good baby so smart—do remember Ericka so beautiful, so tiny a diaper just wouldn't fit. And Andrea—How they would cry every night and I would sit & cry & hold them and as soon as you come home & took one of them they would quit crying—& Chad how badly you wanted another boy—He was a delight a quite delight always telling funny things He was hard to correct because everything he said would make you laugh—" Here the handwriting became skewed, and it spilled over the ruled lines of the stationery. "Paul, Do you remember how we meet—How shy you where? Do you rember that first drive in movie I remember but not the movie Do you rembere even before we married how we said or you said if we were unfaithful that was it Do you Remember—all the Ice Cream—when I was pregnant with Paul Ross—''

The last line ran off the bottom of the page.

9

On December 30, Ericka and Paula Davis returned for another interview session with Joe Vukich. Ericka wrote out a new statement:

Mom

She used to spank me at first when I came home from kindergarten. That was for doing nothing wrong. She would spank me very hard for a long time. Later she would spank me with wooden things or whatever she could get in her hands brushes things like that. Most of the time she was angry and would hit or kick or push. She never defended me or the other kids when our dad would come beat us. They had polls [poles] and she would use them as sexual devices to hurt me. The polls were like things used in a closet for hanging things on, made out of wood. She would do that when my father was also not there. Other people also saw these polls. She just told me not to talk about things that were happening or say I don't want to ever hear you say that again. From the time I was about 5 yrs old until the time I was about 12 yrs old. until we moved from 89th St. I remember being carried from my bed, by my father in the middle of the night. There were many people there waiting outside by the barn. Some of them were Jim Rabie, Ray Risch, Mom, Dad, High Priestess in a robe the people wore white, red & black.

There were many men there & some women. They chanted as I was carried out. It was cold out middle of the night and all I wore was a nightgown. My mother walked with us to the barn from the time I was taken from my bed until the time I we were in the barn. There was a table inside the barn. There was also a fire. All the people around the table including my mom & dad wore a gown & a hat resembling a viking hat with horns. There was a lot of blood everywhere. There was pitchforks in the ground—that was also used to threaten us with. The sacrifice. They would lay it first on the table then the high priestess would pick it up all the people would chant & the women would say words then the baby would be put on the table & all of the people including my mother & father circling the table would stab it with knives until it died. They continued to do this for a long time sometimes even after it was dead. Then they would all walk to the pit and chant and the high priestess would carry the baby and put the baby in something white then put it in the ground. Then they would bury it. The baby was a human baby about 6–8 months old. Sometimes they would use aborted babies. They would tell me this is what would happen to me also. They also would say you will not remember this. They would say it over & over again like a chant.

It was the first time that anyone in the Ingram family other than Paul had mentioned satanic rituals. His accounts had not included any mention of human sacrifice, however. Ericka then drew maps of the old house and the new one on Fir Tree Road, indicating where the ceremonies were held and where the babies were buried.

Loreli Thompson was beginning to get suspicious of some of Ericka's stories, which seemed to change with every telling. In the morning briefings she urged Vukich to be more confrontational. There were some other details that didn't add up, she insisted. Why did the daughters have to tell their mother about the abuse if, in fact, she was involved? Vukich was defensive; he believed Ericka was still too traumatized to respond to such close questioning. The truth was that all the detectives were turning into advocates for the victims they had been assigned. Schoening had become very protective of Sandy, just as Thompson had with her charge, Julie. Thompson worried that if she pushed too hard Julie might hurt herself. It wouldn't be easy to live with a suicide on her hands. But Thompson realized that if Julie was ever going to be able to testify, she would have to respond to the contradictions in her story. The next time Thompson met with Julie, she asked specifically why Sandy would have inquired about the abuse that morning in November, when she picked Julie up at school just before going on vacation with Paul. Julie wrote down, "I think she ask me to make it look like she didn't know." Julie looked exhausted; she said she had not slept well in days. Thompson asked Julie if she had been in communication with her sister about the case. "She called me and told me about satanic stuff," Julie acknowledged. Did she remember anything like that? "I remember burying animals," she said. "Goats, cows, and chickens." Were these natural deaths? Julie didn't know. Did she ever go to parties where people were wearing costumes? Julie became thoughtful. "No," she finally answered. Any ceremonies besides church? She shook her head no.

When Thompson inquired about an abortion Julie said she had undergone, Julie wrote, "I was 15 year old. I remember driving for about 30–45 min. and the doctor office was very little and an orange color. The only thing I remember about the abortion was pain. I screamed it hurt so bad." Her father had taken her to the clinic. That was about all she could remember.

"I then asked if there were marks or cuts on her body from the abuse," Thompson wrote in her report. "She shook her head yes, radically. She showed me her forearms. I noted two light cuts on the right arm and two round marks on the left arm. These were small round marks similar to a burn mark. All of the injuries were on the forearms. I inquired about cuts on her upper arms, back and legs. She wrote down, 'Yes,' that there were injuries there. I asked how these wounds were inflicted. She wrote down, 'With knives.' . . . I asked who did this to her. She wrote down, 'Jim Rabie and my dad.' " Julie then put her head down on the table and began to cry. Thompson asked if she might let her see the scars, but Julie adamantly refused.

The sisters' inability to actually talk about their abuse was becoming a problem as the trial date of Rabie and Risch approached. Rabie was charged with seven counts of statutory rape in the second degree, rape in the second degree, and indecent liberties. The charges against Risch were three counts of statutory rape in the second degree and rape in the second degree. Gary Tabor, the chief prosecutor, met with Julie in Detective Thompson's presence. A conservative, deeply religious man who still speaks in the flat, nasal tones of his native Oklahoma, Tabor has a heavy-lidded gaze, a gap-toothed smile, and a reputation as the smartest prosecutor in the county. Even he was confounded by all the rabbit holes in the Ingram case, however. From the prosecution's point of view, this recent note of satanic-ritual abuse was more than troubling, because juries tend to disbelieve such allegations. Tabor longed to keep the case simple, but it went on metastasizing and invading new territory. He could easily imagine what a clever defense attorney might do with the mass of contradictory memories that constituted the case against Rabie and Risch so far. Moreover, the victims appeared to be so traumatized that it was an open question whether they could testify in court. Tabor was trying to size up Julie as a witness. What he saw was not encouraging. She could not make eye contact. She pulled chewing gum out of her mouth in long strands. Tabor asked her if she was having

trouble remembering the abuse. Julie replied that she just remembered things as she went along. She began tearing at the
rubber sole of her shoe. Tabor asked how her mother had
acted when she came into the room before the men came to
abuse her. Julie didn't answer. Tabor and Thompson then
watched as Julie peeled the sole off her shoe.

In a letter dated January 18, 1989, Sandy wrote:

> Dear Ericka and Julie,
> Mark is doing fine. . . . I call him everynight and see him
> every week. . . .
> Also I do have the house & 4 acres on the market to sale
> for 79,500 I still owe the bank about 48,000. Also have the
> other 6 acres for sale in two acres pieces. As soon as anything
> sales, I will be putting money into your savings accounts. I
> am hoping I can give each of you—Chad & Mark & Paul Ross
> also—enough money so that you can relocate, or go to college
> or do whatever you desire. . . .
> I am also planning to go to college and to relocate. Also I
> will be taking back my maiden name & start again.
> I am not talking with Paul because as I remember what
> has happened to me I am very much afaird. . . .
> If there is anything that you think you want from the
> house please let me know. Ericka I thought you might like
> your dishes from Greece. . . . I can put some things out like
> that & we can make arrangement for you to come & get
> them.
> I am paying your medical bills & your insurance & car
> payment & will continue to do so for a time—but I have no
> income until something sells. . . .
> Again I ask for your forgiveness. I trully did not know
> what was happening and I am just beginning to remember
> what did happen to me & I have remember something that
> have happened to you both. I do not understand it all or

remember it all yet. But I will and they are not above the law and you both do not have to fear any longer. . . .

Love Mom

The day after Sandy wrote to her daughters, Loreli Thompson drove Julie to Seattle. Both sisters had spoken of having had abortions, in addition to severe scarring from other abuse. The attorneys for Rabie and Risch had been pressuring the court to have them submit to a physical examination to verify that the abortions and scarring were authentic. Julie had finally agreed to see a female doctor who specialized in treating abuse victims. All the way to Seattle, Julie was quiet. Thompson knew how much she hated talking about the case, so it wasn't surprising that she'd be solemn. When they arrived, Julie insisted on going into the examining room alone.

Earlier, Julie had told Thompson that the scars on her body made her so self-conscious that she never changed clothes in the high-school locker room and never wore a bathing suit without a T-shirt to cover her. When Julie emerged, the doctor told Thompson that there was no lingering evidence of an abortion, but that its absence wasn't conclusive; often there would be no residual scarring, particularly in a very young woman. Repeated vaginal or anal abuse would not necessarily leave a mark, either; so the fact that the doctor found none was not unusual. The epidermis, however, is less forgiving—it would tend to reveal physical abuse. But the doctor had found no marks or scars anywhere on Julie's body.

Julie was unusually chatty on the ride back to Olympia. This time, it was Thompson who was quiet. There should have been scars, she kept thinking. Julie had said there were scars.

Later, the same doctor examined Ericka; except for mild acne her only scar was from an appendectomy.

"Would it be possible for someone to be cut superficially and for that to heal without making a scar?" Thompson asked. "I would think any significant cut would probably leave a scar," the doctor said.

As for evidence of Ericka's abortion, the doctor told Thompson that Ericka denied that she had ever been pregnant; in fact, she claimed that she had never been sexually active.

In every successful investigation, there is a point of coherence, where the mass of assembled facts takes on a pattern. The detectives can begin to draw inferences; they can recognize the probable truth and the probable lies. The Ingram case was moving in the opposite direction: what had seemed to make sense in the beginning was becoming ever more mysterious; the mass of facts grew enormous, but the patterns kept dissolving. Compounding the puzzlement and the general sense of panic was the fact that the case against Rabie and Risch was moving steadily toward trial, like a barrel approaching a waterfall.

Joe Vukich saw Ericka again on January 23. Ericka had new disclosures to make, and once again they were so painful that she had to make them in writing. She described being abused by her mother, her father, Rabie, and Risch with leather belts and various sexual toys and bondage devices while someone took photographs. Sometimes she was gagged or whipped. She remembered a thick wooden paddle with holes in it. She was threatened with guns and knives. When Vukich asked about her abortion, all Ericka would write was, "It was at night." He tried to press her to say more, but she indicated it was too hard to talk about. Then Paula Davis wrote this statement for her:

> My father made me perform sexual acts with animals including goats & dogs. My father made me fondle their genitals first. Sometimes I was on my hands & knees & sometimes I was lying down. He would bring the animals to me & have

them perform oral licking to my genitals. Sometimes I was on my period, sometimes not on my period. Then my father would force me to have vaginal intercourse with the animals, While he took photographs. My mother was also present & also had intercourse with the animals.

These events had taken place from the time Ericka was in kindergarten until she was in high school. While Davis took down the statement, Ericka doodled on another sheet of paper—little flowers and what appeared to be a frowning butterfly.

10

The trial date for Jim Rabie and Ray Risch had been set for February 1989, just a couple of weeks away. Although they had made statements that the investigators found equivocal, both men maintained their innocence. As the prosecution prepared its case, Gary Tabor continued to have doubts about whether Ericka and Julie could testify. Only recently had Sandy come forward to make statements implicating the defendants, but these had concerned her, not her daughters. The statement of Paul Ross might do more harm than good to the prosecution's case, since he was unable to verify the abuse to his sisters. Schoening and Vukich went back to Reno to try to talk to the eldest Ingram child again. After nearly two hours of pleading, the detectives thought they had persuaded him to give them another statement, but the young man didn't show up the next morning as promised. The detectives went to his apartment several times and left notes on his door. No one appeared to be home. The next day they went again. This time they heard the stereo playing inside the apartment and the sound of laughing. They knocked and called through the door, but no one would answer. Finally, they flew back to Washington State—only to find that Chad had begun to recant. He was now declaring that the entire scenario he had given to investigators was only a bad dream.

That left Paul Ingram as the sole reliable witness in the case. He had pleaded not guilty in his first court hearing, in December, but Tabor saw that as a routine plea. Ingram had always indicated his willingness to testify, although such testimony almost invariably comes about in exchange for a plea bargain; in fact, the prosecution had put together a deal in which Ingram would plead guilty to nine counts of third-degree rape, with the sentences to run concurrently. In return, the prison time would be minimal. There was even a chance that Ingram could walk out of the courtroom a free man once he had testified against his friends.

Ingram confounded everyone by agreeing to testify without making any deals. G. Saxon Rodgers, who was Jim Rabie's attorney, was incredulous—and dismayed. The situation had been a prosecutor's dream, since a jury will usually discount testimony that has been purchased with a plea bargain. Until then Rodgers's theory about the case was that Ingram really had abused his daughters, but in order to mitigate his sentence he had implicated Rabie and Risch, two innocent men. Again and again Ingram had described himself as being a helpless onlooker to the crimes of his friends. He thereby created a conspiracy case in which he would play the role of the key state witness. All this would fit in with the portrait of the cunning, politically sophisticated former deputy sheriff which Rodgers had intended to paint in court. In this rendering, Ingram had controlled the case from the beginning. But when Ingram agreed to testify for nothing, he took the brush out of Rodgers's hand.

On January 30, Sax Rodgers and Richard Cordes, who represented Ray Risch, were permitted to meet with one of the prosecution witnesses. It was Julie. The meeting took place at the Lacey Police Department. Once again, Julie said she hadn't slept in days, and she looked it. She cuddled a stuffed bear that Loreli Thompson had given her, and often didn't respond to questions from the attorneys about the abuse. She seemed to be in a fog. At one point, she crawled under the desk and hid there for ten minutes. When the questioning resumed, Rodgers took a more indirect tack. He asked Julie about Ericka's deceased twin, Andrea. Although they were not identical, they had looked very much alike, except for Andrea's swollen head and the cramped limbs that had confined her to a wheelchair. Julie remembered visiting her at the state institution in Spokane. Sometimes the family would pick up Andrea and take her on vacation to Deer Lake; she wasn't so retarded that she didn't know who they were. Julie remembered her singing the alphabet song and "Jesus Loves Me." Sometimes she had a pointer strapped to her forehead and would pick out tunes on the keyboard. Andrea had died in 1984, just before the twins' eighteenth birthday. Ericka had taken the news very hard; she shut herself up in her room for a month. "A part of me has died," Julie said Ericka had told her.

When the attorneys tried to resume talking about the case, Julie retreated to one-word replies. She spun the stuffed bear in the air. She described Jim Rabie as "Fat. Short. Dark hair. Ugly." She did not know if he had any marks or tattoos. (As it happens, Rabie's chest bears a ropelike, three-inch keloidal scar which was the result of a near-fatal electrocution two decades before. Neither Ingram nor any of the alleged victims had noticed it.) Finally, Cordes asked if Julie would just tell him what his client had done to her. She shrugged.

"Will you ever?" he asked.

"Maybe I will," she responded.

That was the end of the interview. It had taken three and a half hours, and she had said virtually nothing.

A week later, Rodgers and Cordes met with Ericka and the investigators at the sheriff's office. Ericka was far more talkative. She didn't know exactly what happened to Julie or her brothers; in fact, she said that she hadn't known about Julie's abuse or her pregnancy until learning of it from the detectives. She described severe sexual and physical abuse that she herself had suffered, but admitted that she had no permanent scars or marks. She said her mother had been sexually abusing her since she was ten years old; sometimes her father watched, and he would also do things to her when her mother was finished. The last time her mother abused her was in September 1988, when Sandy stuck a closet pole in her vagina. In response to the obvious question of why Ericka would need to reveal the abuse to her mother two months later, if Sandy had been a regular participant in the abuse for more than a decade, Ericka said that everyone had told her this was something she needed to do.

Rodgers finally asked about his client's involvement in these acts, and Ericka told him that Jim Rabie had assaulted her eight times in September alone, and many more times before that—perhaps fifty or a hundred, going back to when she was thirteen. The last time she was assaulted, her father began it, then it was Rabie, then her mother; afterward, each of them defecated on her. As for Risch, she couldn't remember him doing anything sexual to her, except for taking photographs. Usually he just came along to watch.

The prosecutor's attempts to keep the case simple vanished as Ericka elaborated on the satanic rituals before the amazed defense attorneys. She described orgies in the woods, in which babies were sacrificed and buried behind the Ingram house. Rabie and Risch were there, she said. Once, when she was a sophomore in high school, they held her down and tied her to a table. She was pregnant, she said, and someone aborted her baby with a coat hanger. That was very painful. Then the baby was cut up and rubbed all over her body. She had seen approximately twenty-five babies sacrificed over the years.

The defense attorneys could sense panic on the opposing side. The satanic-abuse accusations hadn't hit the press yet, but it was easy to imagine the public outcry when they did, and the pressure that the prosecution would be under to produce convictions. Perhaps all this could be avoided or, at least, contained. The prosecutor, Tabor, might be persuaded to drop the charges against Rabie and Risch if Ingram would quietly plead guilty and get treatment.

Before Tabor would agree to a deal, however, he would have to be persuaded that Rabie and Risch were really innocent men caught up in some kind of familial hysteria. Rabie was still asking for a polygraph test. He knew that polygraphs were not infallible and could not be admitted as evidence, but he had used them repeatedly in his own investigations. He also knew Tabor and the detectives: if Rabie had been in their place, he would have had to think very hard about continuing a prosecution against a man who had willingly taken a lie detector test and passed it.

Early on the morning of February 3, Rabie was taken from his cell in Mason County in chains. He was loaded into a police car and driven to the Olympia Police Department, where Maynard Midthun, an officer Rabie knew, administered the test. It lasted into the afternoon. Several of the investigators watched the procedure on a monitor in another room. They could not forget that Rabie was a former colleague, and that he had been in their place many times. Once again there was that sense of the universe being inverted, as if the entire situation would be revealed as a case of mistaken identity, or a folly of absurdly massive dimensions. It was exactly that rotten odor of comedy that made the Ingram investigation so gruesome, that drew everyone—the detectives, the suspects, the victims—deeper into the macabre.

"Here are the things that will happen here today," Midthun told Rabie. "Initially we're gonna talk about you. . . . Then we'll get into a discussion of the case. Following that, we'll work up some questions that you and I agree are valid questions that will resolve the issue." After that, Rabie would be hooked up to the polygraph and take the test. "This is just another workday for me," Midthun said. "It's your test. Perhaps one of the biggest days in your life."

"Could be," Rabie agreed. He was feeling anxious but confident.

Midthun asked whether Rabie was experiencing any discomfort, and Rabie said he had a toothache and had been suffering constant back pain since he was put in jail. He had taken a sinus pill and something for his digestion the night before, but nothing that should affect the test. The object of this portion of the examination was to put the subject at ease, so Midthun asked Rabie to tell him about his life, particularly his formative years.

"I was raised on a farm," Rabie said. It was a fifty-acre farm in the Yakima Valley, on which Rabie's father raised sugar beets, corn, and hops. The only notable feature of his ancestry was a grandfather who had been hanged for stealing sheep. "I was the eldest child and I had a sister that was eleven months younger than I, and when I was five and she was four we were in an auto wreck. My dad was driving and my sister was killed. My mother was permanently crippled from it. I had a broken leg and a concussion and some head injuries." The cast on the broken leg kept it from growing at the same rate as his good leg, so that limb remained an inch and a half shorter. For the next five years, Rabie was an only child, until his parents adopted another little girl, who was thirteen months old at the time.

It was a rather lonely childhood. The farm was two miles out of town, and there was little to do outside of chores and schoolwork. "I was always overweight and very self-conscious and had no real girlfriends or anything," he recalled. "I'd go to the library. That, to me, was the best thing I could do, and like I said, I didn't socialize much." He was once arrested for driving a car without a license when he was fifteen, but other than that he had never gotten into trouble.

"I really think I had a good childhood," Rabie said, somewhat defensively. He admitted that he didn't really get along with his father, who had a quick temper and had slapped his son on several occasions. The summer Jim graduated from high school, they had a falling out. Jim had complained about his father's coarse eating habits. "He said, 'If you don't like the way I do things, you can move out,' " Rabie recalled. Since he was going away to college anyway, that's exactly what he did.

For the next three and a half years, Jim studied economics and tried to support himself in school. He finally dropped out and began driving a tour bus in Seattle, which he found very satisfying. At the age of twenty-three, he married for the first time, to a schoolteacher. In the meantime, Jim's father had traded the family farm for a general store, which turned out to be a disaster. His father was never cut out for commerce. "It was killing my mother psychologically. She just couldn't stand it," Rabie said. "And so I took over the store and dad got out and I ran it for five years on a shoestring." Jim did everything from the meat cutting to the bookkeeping. Meanwhile, he was commuting forty-five miles every day, each way. "Probably that's what busted up my first marriage," he said. "I was never around."

It was while he was running the store that he electrocuted himself. "I was working on one of the compressor units," he said. He rolled over on an exposed 220-volt wire. He couldn't move off the wire; he couldn't breathe or call out. His body went into convulsions. He remembered hoping that the clerks would know to turn off the power before they touched his body. Then suddenly "it was like a hand picked me up off of there and I went and I passed out in back." In his opinion, it was the hand of God. "I'm not a Bible-pounder by any means," he said, but he did feel that he had been spared, although he didn't know why.

After that experience, Jim sold the store and applied to be in the sheriff's reserves. "I always thought I was too small to be a cop." He happened to be just tall enough. Unexpectedly, he had entered into what he soon decided was his life's calling, law enforcement.

He divorced his first wife in 1977 and started dating Ruth. They had a solid relationship, in his opinion. He depicted his life as being happy and fulfilled—until the Ingram case came along.

"You've painted the model pictures," Midthun said. "I'm challenging you, 'cause I'm also looking for the human side of Jim Rabie, and I'm gonna tell you why. A very important part of this test is 'Who is Jim Rabie?' In fact, it may make up about one-half of our conversation prior to the charts. The other half will be about the case. There, we're gonna talk about some allegations that are very serious, and they could only be accomplished by somebody who is, let us say, a victim himself." The paradigm he was referring to was the common assumption that children who were abused often grow up to be abusers themselves. Rabie would know all the symptoms from his police training, Midthun conceded. One would expect to see a person who has difficulty controlling his anger and who had been abusing other people since childhood. "I'm not doing this for any reason other than to make sure you're painting an accurate picture," said Midthun. "Now, I want the truth, O.K.? That model child was a model child, perhaps—very bright, very good grade point, good anger control—but we all have our transgressions. Tell me some of the dirt, Jim."

"I've thought about going into anger-control counseling," Rabie admitted. "In my normal life I have no problem with anger control. Those that are very close to me, I can get very angry with—verbally, not physically."

"Does it ever turn out to be malicious?" asked Midthun. "Have you found yourself to be vindictive?"

"When provoked, and my anger is really high, I can be vindictive, yes," Rabie agreed.

"Have you ever been a victim of abuse?"

"Never physical abuse, but I do feel that I was a bit of a victim of my father's mental abuse."

When Midthun asked him if he had ever been in a fistfight, Rabie said that he had gotten his nose bloodied by a school-mate back when he was in high school. "All I did was grab him, because I'm not a boxer, and he came up a couple days later and apologized to me, and we've been pretty good friends since then."

"What you just described to me is a textbook description of somebody who is normal," said Midthun. "Is it true?"

"Yeah, that's what happened."

"Somebody who is acting out, who is gonna place blame someplace other than where it belongs—like, on themselves—they're gonna blame others for their problems," Midthun observed. "I mean, they would retaliate. It would be one of those things where years after that fight they would still be holding a grudge. They would be still looking for a way to get even, and here you're telling me this guy has become a friend. . . . Doesn't it make sense that only somebody who is very comfortable with hurting other people could commit the type of crimes that you're accused of?"

"Yeah, I guess," Rabie said. "I hadn't looked at it that way in the whole case."

"In those formative years, was there ever any sexual acting out?" Midthun asked. "I'm looking at sexual deviancy. . . . I'm not talking about getting your hands on a *Playboy* magazine when you're thirteen years old."

Rabie admitted that he had masturbated frequently, but otherwise his lifetime sexual experience was confined to five women. He said he was once tempted by a prostitute, but he was broke at the time.

This all seemed so normal—bland even, almost Victorian. "The person that was just described to me has no ties to these deplorable acts," Midthun said. Why, then, did Rabie think he had been charged with these crimes?

"Because Brian has a big hard-on for me."

"Brian?"

"Schoening. Brian brought my name into this. Paul was searching for the individual to hang it on," Rabie explained, giving his version of events. Having studied the police reports and transcripts of some of the interviews, and having heard some of the department gossip, Rabie pointed out that Julie initially had implicated her father, an uncle, and a friend of her father's. "She was asked if the friend was still around, and her response was, 'Probably,' which would exclude me, 'cause she knew I was around, and it would exclude Ray Risch, which is my closest friend, 'cause she had ridden with him less than a month before that." When Paul was first questioned and started naming friends who might be involved, he kept visualizing someone big. All the other men he named were over six feet, but for some reason Schoening kept bringing Rabie's name back into the discussion. Then, when Julie was shown the photo lineup, the only ones she knew by name were Rabie and Risch. "I think Paul is really enjoying that he is running the sheriff's department ragged on a case that could've been over very quickly," said Rabie. "I actually have had almost minimal contact with the girls or the kids—any of the kids. I can't even tell you what Ericka looks like."

Then why was Rabie so ambivalent when he was first questioned about his involvement in the case? He claimed that the detectives had never hinted at the extent of the charges; he thought they were talking about a sexual molestation, such as inappropriate touching, that might even have been unintentional or have taken place while he was intoxicated. "They're talking about a molest that occurred in the seventies, and they're not very specific; they're telling some things about a picture and [being] nude, but they're not saying what I'm doing, exactly. . . . I do start doubting my own memory if you've got a whole string of people telling that I've been doing this, and you've got photographs." Since he learned the nature of the charges and the span of time they were supposed to have covered, he no longer believed that he could have blocked the events out of his mind.

At this point, Midthun began preparing the four questions that would make up the heart of the test. He reviewed some of the charges that Ericka and Julie had made against Rabie, which were clearly not accidental touching or incidental molestations but savage, chronic abuse. He would ask a question concerning each of the girls to determine whether Rabie had ever had sexual contact with them. Another question would be whether Rabie had threatened the Ingram children. "For the sake of the test, we don't care about Paul and we don't care about Sandy, because they're adults," said Midthun; in any case, Rabie had not been charged with any crimes concerning the parents. A final question, which Midthun said would enhance the reliability of the test, would be whether Rabie intended to respond truthfully. Midthun then took a bathroom break and came back to wire the suspect to the polygraph machine.

The lie detector is both a crude and a fragile instrument. It has been used by police departments since 1924 and has changed little since that time. Midthun strapped two corrugated rubber tubes around Rabie's midsection, one across his upper chest and one just above his stomach, over his diaphragm. These pneumatic tubes led to a bellows that recorded the expansion of the lungs with each breath. He then placed a cardiac cuff, such as medical technicians use to take blood pressure, around

Rabie's upper right arm, and inflated it to more than eighty pounds of pressure—somewhat higher than normal, to account for Rabie's moderate corpulence. Finally, he attached metal plates around Rabie's left index and ring fingers with Velcro straps. These tiny plates measured the galvanic skin response (GSR), which is, essentially, the reaction of the sweat glands to the minuscule amount of electric current running through the plates. Moisture coming into contact with the current would produce a measurable response.

The information gathered by these devices is recorded on a continuously moving graph. Normal breathing appears as a wavy line of gentle hills and valleys. The blood pressure is represented by a series of spikes reflecting the constrictions of the heart. The GSR is a narrower, undulating line. In each case, there is a commonsense understanding of the reaction that is being gauged: a person says, "I caught my breath," or "My heart pounded," or "I broke out in a cold sweat." It is exactly these kinds of stress responses that the polygraph records. Of the three, the GSR demonstrates the most dramatic reaction, sometimes producing wild swings across the graph that look like angry scribbles, but respiration is thought to be the most significant indicator. People who are trying to cheat the polygraph will sometimes hold their breath or take drugs that suppress their reactions. In fact, people can be trained to beat the polygraph through rather minute actions such as flexing one's toes or biting one's tongue. Coughing, sighing, or simply shifting one's weight in the chair can produce reactions, which is why the polygraph operator must constantly observe the subject and note on the chart each time the person swallows or takes a deep breath. The startled reaction to a ringing telephone looks like an earthquake on the graph.

What is actually being detected is not deception but anxiety. The philosophy behind the machine is that lying is inherently conflictual. That's not true for everyone, however;

sociopaths who don't appear to suffer the ordinary pangs of conscience may lie without registering measurable stress on the polygraph. Moreover, people who are genuinely deluded will appear to be telling the truth even if what they are saying is beyond possibility. Some studies have shown that polygraphs are accurate only 64 to 71 percent of the time when used in criminal investigations. The most common error is to mistake innocent subjects as guilty, rather than vice versa. For all of these reasons, polygraphs are generally not allowed in court, and limitations have been placed on their use by private employers.

Many law-enforcement officers, however, believe that in the hands of an experienced operator, such as Maynard Midthun, the polygraph is close to being infallible. Jim Rabie believed this when he was a cop. Midthun offered the example of two men accused of a bank robbery. One is guilty, the other innocent. Each has been identified by an eyewitness. Each convincingly denies his involvement. "We don't know if they're telling the truth," said Midthun. There is a difference between the two suspects, however. "The guy who really did it," Midthun explains, offering a commonplace understanding of the nature of memory, "he experiences distinct physiological changes that take place when he walks through the front door of that bank, and he pulls out that weapon and sticks it in the face of that teller. . . . It's as though somebody has turned on a video camera in his mind. . . . There is a permanent record there of the words spoken, the deeds done, the emotions felt—it's all there, recorded." The innocent man, on the other hand, hasn't had the experience. There's no tape playing in his head. Three years after the bank robbery, both men come in for polygraphs. The innocent man denies he robbed the bank. "What I see on the polygraph charts is general nervous tension, and it's that way throughout the entire chart. One question does not mean any more to him than any of the others, because it's the same. He has no frame of reference. He never spoke those words. He never did that deed." When the guilty man takes the same test, however, "at that point, the video camera clicks on. The camera's been off for three years, except when he wanted to reflect back on how fun it was and how cool he was for getting away with it. But when we go into the polygraph test, he cannot push the off switch. He cannot turn that son of a gun off. . . . I ask the question, 'Did you rob the bank?' The camera is playing and he sees an instant replay of himself entering the bank, sticking his nose in the teller's face, and watching her just totally lose control. He'll never forget that. . . . There's that adrenaline rush. Then he flunks the test."

Because of his experience in the use of the polygraph, Rabie may have realized that harboring secret guilty thoughts about one's past actions can cause false reactions; for instance, the innocent person who is accused of robbing the bank might register a highly anxious reaction if he had done something similar in the past. That's why polygraph operators spend several hours before the test trying to determine areas of conflict; it's also why the questions must be made as specific as possible. In any case, as he was being wired to the machine Rabie suddenly felt the need to clear his conscience. It turned out that his sexual life had not been unblemished, after all; he admitted to several indiscretions, the most serious being an incident that happened when he was thirteen and he was playing with a four-year-old girl. "I don't remember exactly the circumstances," Rabie said, fumbling over his words, "but I ended up—I know I had my penis between her legs—didn't try to enter her in any manner, but between her legs."

"Let's chalk that one up to one of life's experiences," Midthun said forgivingly. "What I would be interested in is if you went back for seconds, because that would begin to make a pattern, right? One time does not make a pattern. The true pedophile, the person who would do the horrible things that the Ingram family has complained about, has a pattern of unnatural acts."

To establish a controlled lie as a base for measurement, Midthun had Rabie write the numeral 7 on a piece of paper. He then instructed him to respond "No" when asked if he had written the numerals 4, 5, or 6, which was an honest response; then say "No" for 7, which was a lie; then "No" again for 8 and 9. Midthun would then have what he called "a perfect picture of a lie, much like the bank robber tells, surrounded by nervous truthful responses, much like the innocent person." Rabie's GSR barely registered when he lied about the 7, but his heartbeat jumped off the chart. Midthun had to adjust the pen to keep it on the graph.

Midthun then began the test, mixing in irrelevant questions with the four key questions that were designed to determine whether Rabie was guilty or innocent.

"Is your first name James?"

"Yes," said Rabie.

"You were born in the month of May?"

"Yes."

"Regarding sexual contact with the Ingram children, do you intend to answer truthfully?" This was Midthun's first key question.

"Yes!" Rabie said loudly.

"Is today Friday?"

"Yes."

"Have you ever had any sexual contact with Julie?" This was the second key question.

"No."

"Other than what you've told me about, between the ages of twelve and thirty, did you ever take part in an unnatural sex act?"

"No."

"Do you sometimes watch television?"

"Yes."

"Did you have any sexual contact with Ericka?" The third key question.

"No."

"Have you ever threatened any of the Ingram children?" The fourth key question.

"No."

"Before the age of thirty, did you ever intentionally hurt anyone?"

"No."

Midthun performed the test three times to make certain of Rabie's responses. In each of the four relevant questions, the graph showed that Rabie had lied.

11

$\mathbf{D}$etective Brian Schoening was waiting at the Seattle-Tacoma International Airport on the morning of February 2 to pick up Dr. Richard Ofshe, a social psychologist from the University of California at Berkeley. Ofshe had been recommended to the prosecution as an expert on cults and mind control. With his dark, owlish eyes and a luxuriant gray-white beard that lent him an air of Zeus-like authority, Ofshe certainly looked the part of a distinguished professor. Brainy, arrogant, long-winded, precise, insightful, prickly, and self-promoting, the forty-seven-year-old Ofshe had all the faults and virtues of the academic genius, as well as a taste for fine food, fast cars, and heated controversy. His credentials included a Pulitzer Prize, which he shared in 1979, for research and reporting on the Synanon cult in Southern California. He had written extensively about how the thought-control techniques developed in Communist China, the Soviet Union, and North Korea had come to be employed and refined by various religious cults in the United States. His research had caused him to become involved in a number of lawsuits against the Unification Church, the Church of Scientology, and est, to name a few. His critics called him an anti-cult extremist; they believed that his campaign against cults could as easily be turned against organized, established religions. But few cared to take on Richard Ofshe directly; his appetite for intellectual combat was matched only by his stubbornness.

Gary Tabor had been looking for some expert who could explain what appeared to be the mind-controlled behavior of virtually everyone in the Ingram case, suspects and victims alike. He had called Ofshe and asked if he had much experience with satanic cults. Ofshe had told him candidly that no one could really claim to be an expert, because so far such allegations were largely unproved. This is real, Tabor had assured him. Then I'm interested, Ofshe had replied.

As they drove to Olympia, Schoening briefed the professor on the case. Practically nothing that anyone was saying could be verified. All the stories were at war with each other. People weren't even talking normally, Schoening complained. Ofshe asked what he meant by that, and Schoening described Ingram's third-person confessions in which Ingram saw himself from the outside, as if the Ingram who was watching and the Ingram who was acting were two different people. He mentioned the "would've"s and "must have"s that characterized Ingram's language. As for the daughters, they talked little, if at all.

The problem everyone had was Paul's continuing inability to remember clearly. That struck a familiar chord with Ofshe. In addition to his work with cults, he had interested himself in coercive police interrogations. At that moment, he had a paper in press with the *Cultic Studies Journal* concerning innocent people who became convinced of their guilt and confessed. In each case that Ofshe had studied, the confession had come about when the police succeeded in persuading the suspect that the evidence against him was overwhelming and that if he couldn't remember committing the crime, there was a valid reason for his lack of memory, such as his having blocked it out or fallen into some kind of fugue state.

In the Ingram case, Ofshe was told, the reason the suspect couldn't remember raping his children repeatedly over seventeen years was that he had repressed the memories as soon as the abuse occurred. Even the prosecution was uncomfortable with that theory, and the notion of mind control had arisen as an alternative to it. Perhaps the cult had interfered with the ordinary process of memory formation, through drugs or chronic abuse. Perhaps the reputedly brilliant Dr. Ofshe could unlock the programming that had scrambled the circuitry of nearly everyone in the Ingram family.

Ofshe's first interview was with Paul Ingram, in the presence of Schoening and Vukich. He was impressed by Ingram's eagerness to help and his longing to understand his own confused state of mind. As Ofshe tried to get Ingram to lead him through the case, however, he decided that there was clearly something wrong. In Ofshe's opinion, it wasn't possible for the human memory to operate in the fashion that Ingram was describing. Either he was lying or he was deluded. When Ofshe asked him to describe more routine episodes in his life, Ingram demonstrated perfectly ordinary recall. Then where were those other memories coming from? Ingram described the manner in which he would get an image and then pray on it. He told Ofshe he had been practicing a relaxation technique he had read about in a magazine, in which he would imagine going into a warm white fog. Minutes would pass and then more images would come, he said, and he felt confident that they were real memories because Pastor Bratun had assured him that God would bring him only the truth. After a while, he would write his memories down. Ofshe wondered if Ingram was possibly taking a daydream and recoding it as a memory. He made a spontaneous decision to run what he later referred to as a "little experiment" to determine whether Ingram was lying or believed that what he was relating was genuine.

"I was talking to one of your sons and one of your daughters, and they told me about something that happened," Ofshe said to Ingram, giving a wink to Schoening and Vukich. The two detectives looked at him in complete dumbfounded surprise, since Ofshe had not yet met any other members of the Ingram family. "It was about a time when you made them have sex with each other while you watched. Do you remember that?"

No, Ingram didn't remember that. In fact, the detectives had posed a similar scenario to him in his first round of interviews, when he was confessing to a number of crimes, and he had not remembered it then, either. But Ofshe was not deterred. "This really did happen," he insisted. "Your children were there—they both remember it. Why can't you?"

Ingram wanted to know where it had happened.

"It happened in the new house," Schoening said, playing along.

Ingram closed his eyes and put his head in his hands, a familiar posture to the detectives. Several minutes passed.

"I can kind of see Ericka and Paul Ross," Ingram said.

Ofshe told him not to say any more. Go back to your cell and pray on it, he said.

When Ingram left the interview room, the detectives jumped down Ofshe's throat. What was he up to? Ofshe explained that he was simply testing the validity of Ingram's memories. In that case, they asked, why couldn't he have picked something a little further out of the realm of possibility? None of the investigators would have been surprised if Ingram had orchestrated sex among his children—that wasn't any more bizarre or depraved than the stories they had already heard.

Later that afternoon, Ofshe met Julie at the sheriff's office, in the company of Detective Thompson, Gary Tabor, and Julie's advocate from a local rape crisis center. Julie turned her chair around and faced the wall, communicating mainly through nods of her head.

Despite this awkward arrangement, Ofshe thought he detected a certain playfulness in Julie. He hoped he could use it
to draw her out. For the first time, Julie produced cult memories of her own. She wrote a brief description of people in
robes and a doll hanging from a tree. Ofshe asked if the members of the cult had told her they had magic powers. "No,
they didn't," Julie said. Did anyone ever tell her that the cult
knew what she was doing all the time? There was no answer.
Was that a question she didn't want to answer? The back of
Julie's head nodded. "That means it's true, then," Ofshe said.
He asked Julie to write down how they were able to spy on
her. Julie wrote, "They said that a high and mighty man spoke
to them and would tell them ever thing I said, or did. The
high & mighty man spoke to them threw other people." Was
that high and mighty man the Devil? Julie shrugged. Had she
ever seen any bad things done to animals? She shook her head
no. To babies? No. Dolls? Yes, Julie indicated, and wrote:
"They would hang dolls with blood on the trees and say the
white lady would kill them and who kill you if you told."
She didn't know who the white lady was, but she wrote that the
woman wore "a long white dress like a costume." Julie talked of
having gone to church frequently when she was a child and
having liked it "some." She believed in Satan but did not
know why. She described herself as being a weird and nervous
person. Ofshe asked her to write the names of any other children in the cult. She wrote down "Ericka, Chad, Paul," and
the names of three other children—names that had not previously come up. Then she listed the adults, again mentioning
new names. For the first time, the membership of the cult was
taking shape. As far as the investigators were concerned, it was
a highly productive interview. They were amazed at how much
information Ofshe had been able to get out of Julie.

The contrast between the sisters struck Ofshe strongly

when, the next day, he met Ericka. Julie was such a casual dresser—to the point, really, of being careless—whereas Ericka was heavily made up and wore her hair teased into a dramatic coif. Instead of shrinking from the spotlight, Ericka seemed eager to claim center stage. The sisters scarcely seemed related at all, except as opposites: Julie so shy, Ericka so bold; Julie so plain and naive, Ericka so attractive and shrewd.

Until now, the interrogation of the girls had focused on the commission of crimes. Ofshe chose another tack. He proposed to Ericka that he was like an anthropologist who had just dropped into her town and was interested in learning about her life in the cult. Tell me what the meetings were like, how they fitted into your ordinary life, he said. It was similar to the approach he had used in debriefing members of other cults. In such organizations there is a hierarchy of personalities; there are routines, taboos, maxims, legends, dogma, group history— a society, in other words. By her own estimate, Ericka had attended eight hundred and fifty rituals during her life and watched twenty-five babies sacrificed. What, exactly, went on during the rituals? Ofshe wanted to know. "They chant," Ericka said. What were the words? She couldn't remember. Did you sit or stand? he asked her. She couldn't remember that either. Who were the other people and what were they like? It was too stressful to talk about. Before concluding the interview, Ofshe asked if her father had ever forced her and one of her brothers to have sex while he watched. Ericka said that nothing like that had ever happened.

That day Ofshe visited Ingram again, in jail. Ingram said he had gotten some clear memories of Ericka and Paul Ross having sex. He had made some notes. Once again, Ofshe asked him to say no more, just go back to his cell and pray and visualize and write it down for him.

Ofshe also met with Sandy. She told him that she was beginning to retrieve more memories now, through the counseling of Pastor Bratun. She had also seen a psychiatrist and a psychologist.

"How does Pastor Bratun help?" Ofshe asked.

"He kind of prods," Sandy said. "When we start, initially he did describe a scene to me."

"One that Paul had given him?" asked Ofshe.

Sandy agreed that most of her memory sessions began this way.

Ofshe wanted to know if Sandy was afraid of her husband.

"No," she said. "I remember him hollering at me sometimes, in my normal memory, but it was never anything that seemed out of line. I remember him hitting me one time, in my normal memory, but I don't remember anything that would have given me a clue that something was wrong."

"Where did you get this idea of a normal memory and some other kind of memory?" Ofshe asked.

"There are things I remember, like birthday parties and how old the kids were in this particular year," Sandy said. "Then there are the things that I've remembered since then. It is different from what my other memories are."

Ofshe asked her to describe the memories she was getting with the help of Pastor Bratun. Sandy detailed several rape scenes with Rabie and Risch, and satanic rituals in the woods. She watched Paul having sex with the high priestess. "I remember being tied to a tree," she said. "There was water and fire. One time, Jim took the kids by their heels and dumped them in the water. And they wanted me to put on a white robe. . . . Ray's standing out there and he's holding all the robes, and when I first saw the scene it felt like an initiation."

"Do you 'see' the scene, or do you remember it?"

"No, I see it," Sandy said. "And, uh, everybody says this pledge of allegiance and we're all outside, and there's this book on the table and, uh, Jim is holding my shoulder and his nails are all painted black and they're real long and they go into my shoulder and this book is *bleeding*"—her voice broke, and she began to sob—"and Paul and [the high priestess]* and Jim touch it, and the blood runs all over Jim and up his arm and all over his head and then it runs all over me!"

"So the blood runs uphill?"

Sandy laughed despairingly. "Jim says I am ready, and they put me on the table, and there's like a leather strap around my neck and my arms and my legs and my ankles, and then [the high priestess] cuts my clothes off with the knife!"

By now Sandy was shaking. Everyone who had seen her when she was caught up in this state had been alarmed by her bobbing head, her rolling eyes, and her high, quaking voice. Her face became bizarrely contorted. When Sax Rodgers deposed her, it had been one of the most rattling experiences of his life. Even Loreli Thompson had been unnerved by the eerie spectacle that Sandy presented.

Ofshe now pulled her back by getting her to describe ordinary memories, such as family vacations. She immediately calmed down. She talked about trips to Deer Lake in eastern Washington, and picking up Andrea beforehand, and other times, when the kids were small and they would all go camping and take long walks together. "There was a little store there, and paddle boats, and the kids could fish off the dock and swim."

"Do you remember those things?" Ofshe asked.

"Yes."

"Can you remember them without 'seeing' them?"

---

*The name of the woman referred to as the high priestess, as well as the names of other persons who were implicated in the investigation but who were not charged, are not part of this account.

"Yes."

"Can you remember the other kinds of scenes without 'seeing' them?"

"I don't know. I just see 'em, that's all," Sandy said. "I can feel them touching me and holding me. I can smell things."

"So it's real for you."

Sandy agreed that it was very real.

"Would it surprise you if I told you that I think nothing happened?" Ofshe asked.

"Well, we've talked about that," Sandy admitted. "I've even thought about that myself—you know, that this was all a big lie and a hoax."

"Those aren't the words I would use," Ofshe said gently. "If I told you I thought this had all come about by mistake, would that surprise you?"

"Well," Sandy said, "everything that's happened has been very surprising and very strange, but I'd wonder why I was feeling them touching me, holding me, and I could smell them, feel them, and hear them."

"Do you have bad dreams like this?"

"No," Sandy said. "There'd have to be another explanation—or else you can just put me away! And I don't think I'm crazy."

To everyone's astonishment, Paul Ross had returned to Olympia for a spell, and Ofshe managed to interview him as well. Like the detectives, Ofshe was struck by the air of dangerousness that surrounded the young man. Paul Ross related the same story that he had told before, about his mother being tied to the bed while Rabie raped her, and his father hitting him. He described his father as a "Dr. Jekyll and Mr. Hyde" personality. His mother, on the other hand, "always seemed to be the loving, caring mom," but after what his sisters had said about her, Paul Ross supposed she must have been involved in the abuse. He guessed she too must have a separate personality.

Paul Ross said he didn't know anything about the satanic rites that had supposedly gone on in his family, except what he had read in the newspaper, and yet he was quite learned on the subject of demonology, a subject he had been studying for the past ten years. He had read Aleister Crowley, the Egyptian *Book of the Dead*, and many of the most significant books on witchcraft, satanism, magic, and voodoo. As a professor, Ofshe admired Paul Ross's scholarship, and he was frustrated that this angry but nonetheless quite studious young man was working in a warehouse. He several times took the opportunity to recommend that Paul Ross apply to college, and even offered to advise him.

"I would like to touch on whether or not anything at all was done to you," Ofshe then said cautiously, "and whether or not you were ever part of any group sessions that had any aspect of ritual."

"First of all, I don't know," Paul Ross responded. "And second, I don't remember anything." When Ofshe asked him to explain, the young man said he had no clear memories before he was eight years old, although after talking to detectives he recalled that he had fallen down the stairs a lot. "Either I was really clumsy, or somebody did a lot of pushing. I remember one time waking up in the hospital after they had shaved the back of my head. It seems like I should remember falling down the stairs." This happened when he was four or five years old. He still had a scar. But as for being present at satanic rituals all through his childhood, Paul Ross said, "I couldn't say yes or no. I don't remember anything."

Like everyone else in the case, Ofshe was perplexed by Paul Ross's story. It was so suggestive but also so unconfirming. Did the abuse happen? The young man believed it must have, but he couldn't remember it; nor could he remember the rituals. The only thing he clearly recalled was Rabie's assault on Sandy. And yet, Ofshe felt if that part of Paul Ross's story was actually true, then everything else the family remembered—even the most fantastic ritual scenes—must be true as well.

The next time Ofshe visited Ericka, she said she believed that her mother was still a member of the cult. She related a recent incident in which Sandy had come to visit her at the house of Pastor Ron Long and had given her the cult's "death kiss." Ofshe asked her to describe it. What made it different from an ordinary kiss? Ericka couldn't say. When Ofshe later asked the pastor and his wife if they had seen Sandy kiss Ericka, what they described was an ordinary peck on the cheek.

Ofshe now saw Paul Ingram for a third time. Schoening recognized the look on Ingram's face when he came into the interview room. He was beaming. Ingram was always proud of himself after he had come up with a new memory. He handed Ofshe a three-page written confession. Ofshe read it through. "Daytime: Probably Saturday or Sunday Afternoon," the confession began, very much like a movie script:

> In Ericka's Bedroom on Fir Tree. Bunk Beds set up. Ericka & Julie are sharing the room. I ask or tell Paul Jr. & Ericka to come upstairs & then we go into Ericka's room. I close the door and tell them we are going to play (a game?).
>
> I tell them to undress. Ericka says "But Dad", I say "Just get undressed and don't argue" From my tone or the way I say it, neither objects and they undress themselves. I'm probably blocking the door so they could not get out.
>
> Ericka is about 12–13. Body fairly well developed. Paul is 12–14. Both have some pubic hair.
>
> I tell Ericka to knell and to caress Paul's genitals. When erect I tell her to put the penis into her mouth and to orally stimulate him. I also tell her to continue using her fingers. I have her also run her tongue along his penis. When Paul has

his orgasm I have Ericka hold his penis in her mouth and continue stimulation. I tell her to swallow the sperm, but she runs to the bathroom and spits. I tell her to get back to the room & tell her the sperm is protein and won't hurt her.

I have Ericka lie on her back on the floor. I tell Paul to knell over her to rub her vagina gently with his fingers. I also tell him to caress and touch her breasts. When he has a full erection I tell him to enter Ericka and complete the sex act. When they are finished, I have Ericka clean up and tell her to come back to the bedroom.

I undress and tell Ericka to orally have sex with me. She does what I tell her to do. That is to stimulate me with her fingers, tongue and mouth until I come. I tell her to catch sperm in her mouth, and she can swallow or spit. I believe she spits in the bathroom.

I have her lie on the floor. I caress her vagina and breasts and probably orally caress her vagina. I have vaginal sex. Paul watches all of this. If she did not have an orgasm I would have stimulated her with my fingers until she did.

I may have told the children that they needed to learn the sex acts and how to do them right. That it is important that each participant have a pleasurable experience.

I may have anal sex with Paul, not real clear. At other times I have had anal and oral sex with him.

We all get dressed. I ask "Now you both enjoyed that didn't you?" Neither looks me in the eye, nor says anything. I say "You might as well enjoy it. We need each other, there's no reason to fight it."

Paul goes downstairs. I go to my bedroom, perhaps to clean up, Ericka stays in her room. I go downstairs. Sandy and the other children are down there. I go to Sandy in the kitchen and kiss her as if nothing has happened. Nothing is said about what just happened. I don't think Sandy is aware of what went on.

I'm not sure how often this type of activity occurred. I believe that I tell them to be gentle with each other.

I believe that when I tell Paul & Ericka to come upstairs, those on the main floor who heard me and Paul & Ericka, knew what was going on and not to interrupt us.

The ability to control Paul & Ericka may not come entirely from me. It seems there is a real fear of Jim or someone else. Someone may have told me to do this with the kids. This is a feeling I have.

Here was a detailed, explicit confession, complete with dialogue, of a scene that never happened. So far, Ofshe's little experiment had demonstrated just how much pressure it took to make Ingram comply with his demands to create a memory, and the answer was scarcely any. The next task was to determine whether Ingram now would admit that the confession was false. But in this, Paul was unshakable. "It's just as real to me as anything else," he maintained.

Ofshe now had serious doubts whether Ingram was guilty of anything, except of being a highly suggestible individual with a tendency to float in and out of trance states and a patent and rather dangerous eagerness to please authority. He suspected Ericka of being a habitual liar. Throughout the investigation, Julie's accusations had followed Ericka's lead. Ofshe doubted whether the sisters had ever intended their charges to be drawn into the legal arena. Once the charges had been filed, Ofshe believed, the sisters pasted over the inconsistencies in their original accusations with ever more fanciful claims. The whole misadventure was a kind of mass folly—something that would be suitable mainly for folklorists if it were not that innocent people's lives were being crushed. When Ofshe left Olympia, he was convinced that a new Salem was in the making. The witch trials, he believed, were about to begin.

12

Chris listens to his older brother, Jim, talk about how Chris was lost in a shopping mall when he was five years old. "It was 1981 or 1982. I remember that Chris was five. We had gone shopping at the University City shopping mall in Spokane. After some panic, we found Chris being led down the mall by a tall, oldish man (I think he was wearing a flannel shirt). Chris was crying and holding the man's hand. The man explained that he had found Chris walking around, crying his eyes out, just a few moments before and was trying to help him find his parents."

This scene comes from an experiment conducted by Elizabeth F. Loftus, a professor of psychology at the University of Washington in Seattle. It was part of a study to determine whether false memories can be implanted and come to be believed with the same assuredness with which one believes real memories. Chris, who is fourteen, has no memory of ever being lost in a shopping mall, but when he is told this story by a person he regards as an authority—his older brother—his usual resistance to influence falls away. Just two days later, when Chris is asked to recall being lost, he has already attached feelings to this nonevent: "That day, I was so scared that I would never see my family again. I knew that I was in trouble." The next day, he remembers that his mother told him never to do that again. On the fourth day, he recalls the old man's flannel shirt. By day five, he can see the stores in the mall. He can even recollect fragments of conversation with the old man. When Chris is finally told by his older brother that the lost-in-the-mall memory is false, he is shaken: "Really? I thought I remembered being lost . . . and looking around for you guys. I do remember that. And then crying, and Mom coming up and saying, 'Where were you? Don't you—don't you ever do that again.' "

Dr. George Ganaway, who has written extensively about the effect of hypnosis on memory, performed a related experiment that was inspired by Loftus's research. He asked a highly hypnotizable subject to allow him to make a suggestion to her while she was in a trance state. The suggestion was that between the time she left the shopping mall and arrived home there were five missing hours. Could she account for the time? The subject began to tell a story about driving past a ranch and stopping to help a cow deliver a calf. Ganaway, who admits he was looking for something more exotic, added the detail that there was a bright light overhead. At once the woman recalled that there was a great noise, and she looked up to see a UFO. Both the woman and the newly born calf were taken up by aliens.

"Did they experiment on you?" Ganaway asked.

"No."

"Try harder," he suggested.

"Oh, yes," she suddenly remembered, and then began to unfold an elaborate abduction drama, which spiraled back into an earlier time in her life when she had also been abducted. She then recalled a near-death experience and kept regressing until she entered a past life in eighteenth-century England, when she was living in a castle. All of this unfolded from the hypothesis that there was a gap in her day for which she needed to make an accounting.

When the subject came out of her trance, Ganaway asked what she recalled. She remembered only delivering the calf, which she knew didn't happen. She was shocked when he showed her a video of herself producing these statements, but upon reflection she was able to describe the daily experiences that formed the raw material of these fantasies. For instance, in the trance the subject said that the aliens had taken a tissue sample that had left a cloverleaf scar. As it happened, the day before she had been wrapping a clover leaf as a present. The eighteenth-century British lady complained of having to "sew, sew, sew," and the subject had just completed sewing a dress for her daughter.

Even stranger than these confabulated memories was the fact that during the next year the subject had repeated flashbacks of the images she had conjured up in the trance. Several days after the experiment, for instance, she was driving past a billboard advertising Bugle Boy jeans and suddenly had a vision of being in the alien spacecraft. These flashbacks happened despite the fact that she knew the images were fantasies and had been produced in an experiment; they still clung to her memory with the tenacity of real events.

Other experiments have demonstrated how unreliable memories are for things as trivial as whom people voted for in the last election or where they were when the shuttle *Challenger* exploded. After a sniper attack at an elementary school playground, children who were not at school when the attack occurred developed memories of witnessing the event. Loftus quotes one government study of 590 persons known to have been in an injury-producing automobile accident; approximately 14 percent had forgotten the event a year later. In another example, 1,500 people who had been discharged from a hospital during the preceding year were asked about the experience; more than a fourth did not remember being hospitalized.

The research that Loftus and others have been conducting on memory threatens many of the most deeply held convictions of psychology—most prominently, the concept of repression, "the cornerstone," as Sigmund Freud wrote in 1914, "on which the whole structure of psychoanalysis rests." The theory has it that, like denial—which pushes aside painful thoughts that are a part of the present—the act of repression blocks painful or conflictual memories of past events from gaining consciousness. These repressed memories, feelings, wishes, or desires lurk in the unconscious and may cause a person to act in an irrational and apparently self-defeating manner. If a child, for instance, is angry at his father but has repressed this feeling, he may express his rage by breaking the law. Thus, when Chad Ingram was caught clumsily trying to shoplift some Christmas candy when he was seventeen years old and went to jail in handcuffs, it was "the proudest moment of my life." The whole point of psychoanalysis is to bring repressed material into conscious awareness, where it can be identified and disarmed.

According to the repression theory, patients may be expected to recover memories of childhood trauma in therapy, although on occasion such memories may simply pop into consciousness as a result of being cued by something in the surroundings. A woman named Eileen Franklin was playing with her five-year-old daughter in San Mateo, California, in 1989 when she suddenly recalled the expression on the face of a childhood friend who had been murdered twenty years before. In therapy, more fragments of that memory returned. She remembered having seen her father sexually assaulting her friend in the back of a Volkswagen van and later crushing her friend's skull with a rock. This, at least, is the story she told on the witness stand. Franklin earlier had told her brother and mother that the memory had come to her while she was under hypnosis. The state of California does not admit hypnotically enhanced recollections. By the time she got to court, she had changed her account several times. She said that she had retrieved the image in a dream, then that it had come to her in therapy, and finally that it had come in the flashback she had while looking at her daughter. That is the statement she later told the jury. Based primarily on Franklin's description of the recovered memory, her father was convicted of murder in the first degree.* He is now serving a life sentence in San Quentin prison.

Similarly, when Frank Fitzpatrick, a thirty-eight-year-old insurance adjuster in Rhode Island, found himself in great mental pain and could not understand the cause of such anguish, he lay on his bed and began to remember the sound of heavy breathing. "Then I realized I had been sexually abused by someone I loved," Fitzpatrick later told the *New York Times*. Eventually, he was able to put a name to his abuser: Father James Porter, who had been his priest in North Attleboro, Massachusetts, three decades before. "Remember Father Porter?" Fitzpatrick asked in an ad he placed in newspapers in 1989, as part of a search for other victims. More than a hundred people have since come forward. Most of them had never forgotten the abuse; for a small number of others, there was a sudden realization, when they heard about the case on the radio or on television, that it had happened to them.†

Public awareness of recovered memories of abuse increased with the 1991 revelation by Roseanne Arnold that she remembered being sexually abused by her mother, from infancy to

---

*For an insightful account of this fascinating case, see *Once Upon a Time* by Harry N. MacLean (HarperCollins, 1993).

†Initial reports suggested that 20 percent of the Father Porter victims had repressed their memories of the event; however, Dr. Stuart Grassion, a psychiatrist who evaluated the victims, says that the figure is closer to 5 percent.

age seven. The same year, Marilyn Van Derbur, a former Miss America, said she had repressed memories of childhood sexual abuse by her father until she was twenty-four years old. Loreli Thompson has never had the experience of having repressed memories suddenly surface in her own mind, but she gets calls all the time from people, mainly women, who do remember abuse and want to know whether they can prosecute. In most cases, the statute of limitations for criminal proceedings has expired; however, changes in legislation in several states, Washington among them, have adjusted the statute of limitations for civil litigation, so that suits can be brought within three years of the date the abuse is *remembered*, regardless of when it was committed. A number of survivor self-help books, such as *The Courage to Heal*, advocate bringing suits against perpetrators, who are usually the victim's parents. Such actions can be very difficult to defend, given the passage of time, and terribly expensive, while the plaintiff can often obtain a lawyer on the promise of a contingency fee. Moreover, if the victim can't afford therapy, the state will pay for it, and this has led critics to charge that both therapists and clients have an incentive to search for memories of abuse that may not have happened.* In any case, recently there has been a flood of accusations based on recovered memories. Many of these memories are of satanic-ritual abuse.

The concept of repression is so deeply fixed in the culture that few question its factual basis. ''Remembering Incest &

---

*Washington was the first state to allow recovered memory claims under the crime victims' compensation program, in 1991. Since then, recovered memory claims have grown faster than any other kind of claim; moreover, the average recovered memory claim costs $9,127, compared with $1,997 for family sexual assault and $1,552 for a nonfamily sexual assault. See the series ''Buried Memories, Broken Families,'' by Stephanie Salter and Carol Ness, in the San Francisco *Examiner*, April 4–9, 1993.

Childhood Abuse Is the First Step to Healing," said a 1992 ad from Adult Survivors of Child Abuse, a California treatment center, and that statement fairly characterizes the premise of the survivor movement. Along with an 800 number for counseling, the ad lists symptoms of repressed, as-yet-unrecovered memories of abuse: "mood swings, panic disorder, substance abuse, rage, flashbacks, depression, hopelessness, anxiety, paranoia, low self-esteem, relapse, relationship problems, sexual fear, sexual compulsion, self-mutilation, borderline personality, irritable bowel, migraine, P.M.S., post-traumatic stress, bulimia, anorexia, A.C.O.A. [adult child of an alcoholic], obesity, multiple personality, hallucinations, religious addiction, parenting problems, and suicidal feelings." This broad list parallels other checklists, in survivor books and workshops, where people are often told that the absence of memories of abuse is no indication that the abuse did not take place.

"Children often cope with abuse by forgetting it ever happened," write Bass and Davis in *The Courage to Heal*:

As a result, you may have no conscious memory of being abused. You may have forgotten large chunks of your childhood. Yet there are things you do remember. When you are touched in a certain way, you feel nauseated. Certain words or facial expressions scare you. You know you never liked your mother to touch you. You slept with your clothes on in junior high school. You were taken to the doctor repeatedly for vaginal infections.

You may think you don't have memories, but often as you begin to talk about what you do remember, there emerges a constellation of feelings, reactions, and recollections that add up to substantial information. To say "I was abused," you don't need the kind of recall that would stand up in a court of law.

Often, the knowledge that you were abused starts with a tiny feeling, an intuition. It's important to trust that inner voice and work from there. Assume your feelings are valid. So far, no one we've talked to thought she might have been abused, and then later discovered that she hadn't been. The progression always goes the other way, from suspicion to confirmation. If you think you were abused and your life shows the symptoms, then you were.

This argument is strikingly similar to the one advanced by Sigmund Freud in his paper "The Etiology of Hysteria," which he read to the Society for Psychiatry and Neurology in Vienna in the spring of 1896. At the beginning of his practice, Freud saw a number of patients, mostly women, who manifested the neurotic behavior of a then-popular diagnosis, hysteria. Bodily symptoms ranged from paralysis, tremors, hallucinations, blindness, deafness, chills, choking, vomiting, hiccuping, and a painful need to urinate, to name but a few. Linking this bewildering variety of symptoms was the fact that they were psychological in origin, although they masqueraded as physical disease. An example is a patient whose hand has gone numb. As a mental concept, the hand is a distinct entity, but from a neurological perspective it is a complex of nerves running from the fingers through the wrist and arm. There is not a single nerve that controls the hand, nor can the hand be divorced from other portions of the anatomy. Therefore the cause of the numbness must be psychological.

In this early paper, Freud postulated that hysteria was a reaction to traumatic events in childhood, which have been repressed: "Hysterical symptoms can be resolved if, starting from them, we are able to find the path back to the memory of a traumatic experience. If the memory which we have uncovered does not answer our expectations, it may be that we ought to pursue the same path a little further; perhaps behind the first traumatic scene there may be concealed the memory of a second, which satisfies our requirements better." What did he mean by that? Obviously Freud had an object in mind, a childhood event that was not only powerful enough to supply what he called the "traumatic force" that would give rise to hysterical symptoms in later life, but also sufficiently universal to account for the syndrome in each of his patients—the psychological virus, in other words, that would generate this neurotic disease.

Freud saw memory as a chain of associations; each symptom was attached to a particular chain, which would then call up another chain. For example, the symptom of hysterical vomiting may be associated with a memory of eating a rotten apple, and that memory itself may be linked to an earlier scene in which the patient discovered a putrid animal corpse while gathering windfalls in an orchard; that scene calls up another chain of memories, connected to another symptom, such as a headache. The task of the analyst is to retrace the pathways of memory through this converging chain of associations until arriving at what seems to be the traumatic source. Eventually, said Freud, "we come to the field of sexuality and to a small number of experiences which occur for the most part at the same period of life—namely, at puberty." At this point, however, there is a new disappointment for the analyst, because many of these experiences are "astonishingly trivial." He gave examples of one of his women patients whose neurosis seemed to be based on the experience of a boy who stroked her hand and, on a different occasion pressed his knee against her dress; for another patient, the traumatic event was an obscene riddle that had brought on an anxiety attack. Were they really such delicate flowers that they wilted under such tepid advances?

No, Freud reasoned; there must be yet another cause, further back in the chain of memories. "If we have the perseverance to press on with analysis into early childhood, as far back as a human memory is capable of reaching, we invariably bring the patient to reproduce experiences which, on account both of their peculiar features and of their relations to the symptoms of his later illness, must be regarded as the etiology of his neurosis for which we have been looking." To the dismay of his eminent colleagues in Vienna that day, Freud proposed that "at the bottom of every case of hysteria there are *one or more occurrences of premature sexual experience* [Freud's emphasis]."

Anticipating the objections that would arise from the suggestion that childhood sexual abuse was the "source of the Nile" in neuropathology, as he then believed, Freud defended himself by saying that doubts about the genuineness of these memories can be erased because of the anguish on the part of the patients as they remember scenes of seduction in childhood and their own resistance to believing in them once they have been produced. "While they are recalling these infantile experiences to consciousness, they suffer under the most violent sensations, of which they are ashamed and which they try to conceal; and, even after they have gone through them once more in such a convincing manner, they still attempt to withhold belief from them, by emphasizing the fact that, unlike what happens in the case of other forgotten material, they have no feeling of remembering the scenes." To Freud, the patients' distrust of their own memories was conclusive proof that they had not made them up. He was struck by the similarity in details that his patients reported. Either there was a conspiracy among the patients, or else they were suffering from nearly identical traumas. As for the obvious argument that the doctor himself had forced these memories onto his patients, through suggestion, that also seemed unlikely to Freud: "I have never yet succeeded in forcing on a patient a scene I was expecting to find."

There were, of course, many people who clearly recalled childhood sexual experiences who did not suffer from hysteria; as Freud pointed out, however, it was not the *memories* but the *repression* of them that caused hysterical behavior. The memories haven't disappeared; they've been shoved into the unconscious, where they work their poisonous influence until dragged into the light of awareness.

Freud spoke movingly of the reality of child abuse, which was rarely discussed in his time:

> All the singular conditions under which the ill-matched pair conduct their love-relations—on the one hand the adult, who cannot escape his share in the mutual dependence necessarily entailed by a sexual relationship, and yet is armed with complete authority and the right to punish, and can exchange the one role for the other to the uninhibited satisfaction of his moods, and on the other hand the child, who in his helplessness is at the mercy of this arbitrary will, who is prematurely aroused to every kind of sensibility and exposed to every sort of disappointment, and whose performance of the sexual activities assigned to him is often interrupted by his imperfect control of his natural needs—all these grotesque and yet tragic incongruities reveal themselves as stamped upon the later development of the individual and of his neurosis, in countless permanent effects which deserve to be traced in the greatest detail.

These passionate words were coldly received by Freud's colleagues, who believed that the stories of hysterics were lies or fantasies. To the formidable Richard von Krafft-Ebing, who was presiding over this conference, young Freud's remarks were "a scientific fairy tale." Moreover, there was the unstated implication that the abusers Freud was indicting in his daring seduction theory were respectable family men—such as the psychiatrists and neurologists gathered in Vienna that day. Indeed, Freud's theory was categorical. He had come to the conclusion privately that "in all cases, the *father*, not excluding my own, had to be accused of being perverse."

Freud suffered humiliating rejection and damage to his professional reputation. He would later be accused of rejecting his seduction theory out of a craven need to please his colleagues, who were almost exclusively male. There were other sources for his misgivings, however. In October of 1896, only a few months after Freud's disastrous presentation in Vienna, his own father died. During the grieving period that followed, Freud recognized that it was absurd to classify this lighthearted sage as a child molester, even though his own siblings showed traces of hysteria. His beloved theory was at war with his sense of reality. In order to account for the common diagnosis of hysteria, child abuse would have to be practically universal, since only a portion of the cases would give rise to neurotic illness. "Such widespread perversion against children is scarcely probable," he realized.

Adding to his qualms was the fact that some of his patients reported events that he took to be fantasies rather than memories. One of his patients reported that the devil himself had stuck pins in her fingers and placed a piece of candy on each drop of blood. "What would you say," Freud wrote to his friend Wilhelm Fliess, "if I told you that my brand-new theory of the early etiology of hysteria was already well known and had been published a hundred times over, though several centuries ago?" He was referring to the European witch trials. Freud was no believer in witches, and yet he wondered, "Why did the devil who took possession of the poor things invariably abuse them sexually and in a loathsome manner? Why are their confessions under torture so like the communications made by my patients in psychological treatment?" He had come to the same juncture that the profession he created would confront again a century later.

The abandonment of the seduction theory left Freud in a period of helplessness. In 1925, when he wrote his brief autobiography, a penitent but defensive tone is still apparent. "I must mention an error into which I fell for a while and which might well have had fatal consequences for the whole of my work," he wrote.

> Under the pressure of the technical procedure* which I used at the time, the majority of my patients reproduced from their childhood scenes in which they were sexually seduced by some grown-up person. With female patients the part of seducer was almost always assigned to their father. I believed these stories, and consequently supposed that I had discovered the roots of the subsequent neurosis in these experiences of sexual seduction in childhood. My confidence was strengthened by a few cases in which relations of this kind with a father, uncle, or elder brother had continued up to an age at which memory was to be trusted. If the reader feels inclined to shake his head at my credulity, I cannot altogether blame him. . . . When, however, I was at last obliged to recognize that these scenes of seduction had never taken place, and that they were only fantasies which my patients had made up or which I myself had perhaps forced upon them, I was for some time completely at a loss. . . . When I had pulled myself together, I was able to draw the right conclusions from my discovery: namely, that the neurotic symptoms were not related directly to actual events but to fantasies embodying wishes, and that as far as the neurosis was concerned psychical reality was of more importance than material reality. I do not believe even now that I forced the seduction-fantasies upon my patients, that I "suggested" them. I had in fact stumbled for the first time upon the *Oedipus complex*, which was later to assume such an overwhelming importance, but which I did not recognize as yet in its disguise of fantasy. Moreover,

---

*Freud may have been referring to his early enthusiasm for hypnosis.

seduction during childhood retained a certain share, though a humbler one, in the etiology of neuroses. But the seducers turned out as a rule to have been older children. . . .

When the mistake had been cleared up, the path to the study of the sexual life of children lay open.

This momentous shift in Freud's perceptions was the turning point in his thinking and in the history of the psychoanalytic movement. It is important to note in his statement above that he never repudiated the reality of child abuse and its—admittedly, more modest—role in psychopathology. In his new understanding, Freud realized that his patients' fantasies were masking their own childhood sexual longings, and that what they were repressing were not actual seductions but their wishes for the same.

Freud compared the function of repression to that of a watchman who stands guard between the large entrance hall of the unconscious mind and the small drawing room in which consciousness resides. The watchman is a censor, examining mental impulses to determine whether they will be allowed to enter further. "If they have already pushed their way forward to the threshold and have been turned back by the watchman, then they are inadmissible to consciousness; we speak of them as *repressed*," Freud wrote. Such an impulse, for instance, might be the desire of a young girl for her father. The watchman would certainly frown on that; and although the image would be pushed back into the entrance hall, that doesn't mean that it is banished forever. Years, even decades, later, the forbidden desire might return, but this time in a clever and frightening disguise. In its exile from consciousness, the forbidden desire has become an unconscious fixation, enlarging itself on fantasies. "It ramifies like a fungus, so to speak, in the dark and takes on extreme forms of expression," Freud wrote in 1915, "which when translated and revealed to the neurotic are bound not merely to seem alien to him but to terrify him by the way in which they reflect an extraordinary and dangerous strength of instinct." In this way, Freud accounted for the bizarre nature of the fantasies his hysterical patients produced. The shameful sexual desire of a young girl for her father is reexperienced as her father's desire for her; her fantasy of sexual union is recast as a remembered assault.

An unfortunate consequence of Freud's rejection of his seduction theory was that society took a more skeptical stance toward all reports of child abuse, not merely those that had been achieved through recovered memories. That state of affairs began to change in the 1970s, as feminist writers began to speak up about the issues of rape and incest. The question of recovered memories did not arise; indeed, it was the persistence of memory, and not its repression, that was seen as the hallmark of childhood trauma.

Several forces produced the vector that we may call the recovered-memory phenomenon. Among them was the publication in 1980 of *Michelle Remembers*, which not only awakened popular interest in satanic-cult activity but also established the notion of massive repression, such that an entire secret life could be hidden away in the unconscious, waiting to be coaxed into consciousness by a caring, believing therapist. No longer ruled by psychiatry, the counseling profession itself was undergoing an informal deregulation. Psychologists and social workers were at least trained to practice, but increasingly counselors of varying ability and experience were simply being certified, or—as in Washington State—registered for a small fee, with no credentials required. Undersheriff Neil McClanahan, who has a bachelor's degree in human behavior from Evergreen State College, is a registered counselor; Pastor John Bratun is not registered, nor does he need to be unless he charges for his services. Bratun never even took a course in psychology in college; he was trained to be an art instructor, which is what he did before taking up counseling. The lack of credentials is not at all unusual. In New York, for instance, anyone can call himself a psychotherapist. This trend has left the profession prey to fads and malpractice.

At the same time, the field of psychotherapy was under attack within its own ranks. In 1984 two books appeared that challenged Freud's abandonment of the seduction theory: Alice Miller's *Thou Shalt Not Be Aware: Society's Betrayal of the Child* (which had been published in German three years earlier) and Jeffrey Moussaieff Masson's *The Assault on Truth: Freud's Suppression of the Seduction Theory*. These books struck a deep chord, coming at a time when child abuse suddenly seemed to be far more prevalent than society had ever been willing to recognize. A number of counselors began to wonder whether Freud had been right the first time; perhaps trauma—specifically, childhood sexual assault—really was at the root of most neurotic behavior, as Freud originally had claimed. (This revisionist theory quickly became so entrenched with some practitioners that they began calling themselves "traumatists" rather than therapists.) Using the same techniques that Freud himself renounced, particularly hypnosis, therapists and other counselors began uncovering memories of abuse which had apparently been repressed for most of the patient's life. In some cases, the patients reported abuse that had continued well into their teen or adult years, without being consciously acknowledged. Many of these patients were diagnosed as suffering from multiple-personality disorder.

Soon the discoveries in the counseling offices spilled out into the families and the communities, as patients were encouraged to confront their abusers, notify the police, or bring suit. "You cannot wait until you are doubt-free to disclose to your family," admonished Renee Fredrickson in her 1992 book, *Repressed Memories: A Journey of Recovery from Sexual Abuse.* "Avoid being tentative about your repressed memories. Do not just tell them; express them as truth. If months or years down the road, you find you are mistaken about details, you can always apologize and set the record straight."

Whether truthful or mistaken, recovered memories have had the effect of breaking apart thousands of families. A 1991 civil suit in Orange County, California, is characteristic of hundreds of cases that have flooded the legal system. Two adult daughters and a granddaughter accused their elderly mother/grandmother of gross, ritualistic crimes over a period of twenty-five years. The daughters contended that they had been tortured, sexually abused, and forced to kill babies in caves and church basements in Southern California. The women said that they had repressed the abuse until just a few years before, when the older daughter entered therapy after the breakup of her third marriage. In therapy she learned that she was a multiple personality, and she began remembering satanic-ritual abuse. Soon she brought her sister and her daughter (who was eleven when the trial began) into treatment with the same therapist, and they began having similar memories. Eventually all three were diagnosed as multiple personalities. They sought half a million dollars in damages. The defendant, who was a wealthy woman, contended that none of this abuse had ever happened. She believed that her older daughter was after her money, while her younger daughter and granddaughter were simply trying to please her older daughter. The jury decided that the defendant had neglected her daughters but had not intentionally harmed them. No damages were awarded. These claims have become sufficiently routine that some attorneys have standardized forms for their clients, in which the accusations of rape, torture, sodomy, and ritual abuse are already specified.

In 1992, in reaction to the rise of charges and lawsuits, a number of accused parents formed the False Memory Syndrome Foundation, in Philadelphia. By June of 1993, more than four thousand families had come forward (including the parents of Roseanne Arnold). The foundation discovered that these people had much in common. Most of their marriages— about 80 percent—were still intact, and usually only the husband had been accused, although wives had also been accused in nearly a third of the cases. The couples were also financially successful, with a median annual income of more than sixty thousand dollars. The majority had college educations. Most of them reported having frequently eaten meals together as a family and having gone on family vacations. More than half reported being active or very active in religion. About 17 percent of the accusations involved satanic-ritual abuse.

The accusers were adult children, 90 percent of them daughters. Most of the accusers had read *The Courage to Heal*. In 11 percent of the cases, siblings echoed the allegations, although 75 percent of the time the siblings did not believe the charges. Most strikingly, the accuser was a single child in only 2 percent of the families; larger families were predominant, with 3.62 children being the mean. Eleven percent of the families contained 5 children—the size of the Ingram household.

In almost every case, the allegations arose in therapy. It is difficult to know what part therapy may have played in the Ingram case. Julie was briefly in therapy before she made her outcry in her letter to her teacher. Ericka told the defense attorneys, "I'm going to a counselor and she's helping me to remember," but she would not elaborate or disclose the counselor's name. She also told Karla Franko, the speaker at the Heart to Heart camp, that she had gotten counseling, and she sought Franko's counseling over the phone.

Many people who feel themselves to be falsely accused believe that their children were coaxed or bullied into bringing charges by therapists or counselors who used their authority to persuade vulnerable clients that the complex problems they experience in adult life can be attributed to a single, simple cause: childhood abuse. Like their children, some of these aggrieved parents have taken their complaints to the courtroom by filing lawsuits against their children's therapists. There have also been cases brought by former clients who have recanted their stories of remembered abuse and charged their therapists with a form of mind control. Judges and juries all over the country are struggling with the concept of repression and the reality of recovered memories.

"In Salem, the conviction depended on how judges thought witches behaved," notes Paul McHugh, who is director of the Department of Psychiatry and Behavioral Sciences at Johns Hopkins University. "In our day, the conviction depends on how some therapists think a child's memory for trauma works." McHugh contends that "most severe traumas are not blocked out by children but are remembered all too well." He points to the memories of children from concentration camps and, more recently, to the children of Chowchilla, California, who were kidnapped in their school bus and buried in sand for many hours. They remembered their traumatic experience in excruciating, haunting detail. These children required psychiatric assistance "not to bring out forgotten material that was repressed, but to help them move away from a constant ruminative preoccupation with the experience," McHugh says.

McHugh finds a parallel between the recovered-memory phenomenon and an episode involving hysterics in nineteenth-century France. The distinguished neurologist and psychiatrist Jean-Martin Charcot was Freud's teacher at the Salpêtrière hospital in Paris. At one time, the hospital reorganized its patients and happened to place the hysterics in the same ward with epileptics. The hysterical patients began to display odd attacks that were similar to epileptic seizures, but different enough that Charcot believed he had discovered a new disorder, which he named "hystero-epilepsy." With his usual exactitude, he began to study this new condition. "Strangely, the patients became more and more disturbed, had more spells, and progressively more intriguing kinds of fits," McHugh relates. Audiences of doctors and the Parisian intelligentsia gathered to view this enthralling phenomenon. Finally, one of Charcot's students suggested that the great doctor had induced this behavior out of his own authority and enlarged it through his interest. Unless the doctor changed his approach to the patients, the student suggested, they would not improve.

As it developed, the student was correct. Two new methods of treatment were employed. First, the hysterics were isolated from the epileptics; and second, they were given a counter-suggestion, which offered the patients a different view than the one they currently held—that their condition was fascinating to Charcot. Instead of focusing on their condition, the staff began to turn to the question of the hysterics' life condition and the circumstances that had brought them into care into the first place. "This was the beginning of psychotherapy," writes McHugh in a paper titled "Historical Perspectives on Recovered Memories":

> How does this set of events relate to repressed memories?
> Charcot showed that just as there was epilepsy, it was also
> possible to create a pseudo-epilepsy. If one had a pseudo-
> epilepsy and focused on its counterfeit manifestations, they
> would worsen. If the patient remained amongst groups with
> both epilepsy and pseudo-epilepsy, she would not improve.
> The patient does improve when diagnostically distinguished
> from the actual epileptics and a common-sense management
> then devised.
>
> In the contemporary era patients who were sexually
> abused and those with pseudo-memories of sex abuse are of-
> ten placed together by therapists in "incest survival" groups.
> The patients with the pseudo-memories tend to develop pro-
> gressively more complicated and even quite implausible mem-
> ories of their abusive childhood. Particular ideas seem quite

contagious and spread throughout the group—such as satanic-cult explanations for parental excesses and vile abuse including cannibalism. The patients often do not get better. Years of therapy continue to keep many of these repressed-memory patients angry, misinformed. The lesson from Paris is that it is crucial in practice to differentiate the incest-injured from those with false memories.

In 1987, Judith Lewis Herman and Emily Schatzow of the Women's Mental Health Collective in Somerville, Massachusetts, published a study of fifty-three female participants in a therapy group for incest survivors, such as McHugh describes. The paper was titled "Recovery and Verification of Memories of Childhood Sexual Trauma," and it is often cited by those who believe that abuse that has been remembered through recovered-memory therapy is just as real as abuse that has never been forgotten. The object of the study was to determine the link between traumatic childhood memories and symptoms in later life, and "to lay to rest, if possible, the concern that such recollections might be based on fantasy." Finally, the authors wished to explore the therapeutic effect of recovering and validating memories of early trauma.

All of the patients either reported having been sexually abused by a relative or else strongly suspected that was the case but could not remember. The sexual experiences the women described ranged from indecent exposure and propositions, which involved no actual physical contact, to vaginal or anal rape. Seventy-five percent named their fathers or stepfathers as the abusers. "In Freud's time, these women would undoubtedly have been diagnosed as suffering from hysteria," the authors stated. "They would readily have recognized their own afflictions in the anxiety attacks, the bodily disgust, the 'mental sensitiveness' and hyperactivity, the crying spells, the suicide attempts, and the 'outbursts of despair' that Freud described in his hysterical patients almost a century ago." In modern-day terminology, the women had received a variety of diagnoses, the most common being dysthymic disorder, which is a tendency to be despondent. Their backgrounds strongly resembled the family profiles described by the False Memory Syndrome Foundation survey.

Just over a quarter of the women reported severe memory deficits, which meant that they recalled little of their childhoods but were recovering or trying to recover memories of abuse. These patients stood out from the others. "Often they described almost complete amnesia for childhood experiences but reported recurrent images associated with extreme anxiety. Attempts at sexual intimacy often triggered flashback images of the abuser and panic states. These women were preoccupied with obsessive doubt over whether their victimization had been fantasized or real. Some had previously sought treatment with hypnosis or sodium amytal." When their memories erupted, they were often of a violent, sadistic, and grotesquely perverse character.

The authors claim that three-fourths of the women were able to obtain confirmation of their abuse from another source. They did not specify whether the fourth who were not able to do so was the same fourth with severe memory deficits—a significant omission, given their bold conclusion. The confirmations came from the perpetrator himself or other family members or from physical evidence, such as diaries or photographs. "The presumption that most patients' reports of childhood sexual abuse can be ascribed to fantasy no longer appears tenable," the authors asserted. "No positive evidence was adduced that would indicate that any of the patients' reports of sexual abuse were fantasized. In light of these findings, it would seem warranted to return to the insights offered by Freud's original statement on the etiology of hysteria, and to resume a line of investigation that the mental health professions prematurely abandoned 90 years ago. . . .

"Massive repression appeared to be the main defensive resource available to patients who were abused early in childhood and/or who suffered violent abuse."*

Following up on the Herman-Schatzow study, John Briere, of the Department of Psychiatry at the University of Southern California School of Medicine, and Jon Conte, of the School of Social Work at the University of Washington, surveyed 420 females and 30 males who described themselves as having been sexually abused. They had been recruited by their therapists to respond to the study. "During the period of time between when the first forced sexual experience happened and your eighteenth birthday, was there ever a time when you could not remember the forced sexual experience?" the questioners asked. Nearly 60 percent responded yes. That figure is now being used as a benchmark for measuring the size of the population of people who were abused but repressed that memory, versus the number of those who were abused and never forgot.

---

*A more recent study, by Linda Meyer Williams at the Family Research Laboratory of the University of New Hampshire, located one hundred women who had reported abuse in 1973, 1974, or 1975 at a major northeastern hospital. The abuse ranged from fondling to intercourse, and the age of the females at the time they reported the abuse ranged from "infancy" to age twelve. In 1990 and 1991 the women were asked about childhood sexual experiences in order to elicit the memory of the reported abuse. Thirty-eight percent either forgot the abuse or chose not to report it. However, Williams does not say what percentage of them were infants when the offenses occurred. Those who were younger than four at the time could not be expected to remember much, if anything; nor is it likely that very young children would have been the primary reporters of abuse—presumably they had been taken to the hospital by a parent or caretaker who did the actual reporting.

However, there was no attempt to verify the abuse; the fact that the respondents remembered it was taken as sufficient evidence that it occurred. "It is likely that some significant proportion of psychotherapy clients who deny a history of childhood sexual victimization are, nevertheless, suffering from sexual abuse trauma," the authors concluded. They proposed that clinicians continue to entertain the hypothesis that their clients have been abused, even when there are no memories.

Briere and Conte also found, along with Herman and Schatzow, that the abuse recalled by those who claimed to have been amnesiac was far more violent than the abuse that had never been forgotten. But wouldn't more violent experiences also be more memorable? The theory that many have used to explain this paradox is that violence increases the level of repression; that subjects "dissociate" during the experience—that is, they mentally go away in order to protect themselves, then bury the pain in another part of their psyche, even in another personality. But if that is so, why don't children who experience other extreme forms of cruelty, such as life in a concentration camp, repress those memories or turn into multiple personalities? In one study, not a single child aged five to ten who had witnessed a parental murder had forgotten it. Why is it specifically sexual memories that are so often forgotten?

People often do forget details of traumatic events, especially when they are physically injured. Prosecutor Gary Tabor was in a traffic accident in college, but he can't remember a thing about it, except what people have told him. Sheriff Gary Edwards fell out of a tree he was pruning and lost the memory of the experience for ten years, until he was persuaded to take a bungee jump for a charitable event. Just before he jumped, the whole awful memory returned. In both cases, however, they knew something terrible had happened to them. Traumatic amnesia often accompanies combat or savage rapes, but the people who have suffered those experiences know what they've been through. It's the details that escape them.

Despite the common acceptance of the concept of repression, some clinical researchers, such as Loftus, make the point that repression has never been demonstrated experimentally. David S. Holmes of the University of Kansas has reviewed sixty years of attempts at proving the existence of repression. Early tests concentrated on subjects' ability to recall pleasant versus unpleasant memories. Unpleasant memories were less available, and this was taken as evidence of repression; but the same data also demonstrated that the more intense the memory, the more likely it was to be remembered, whether it was pleasant or unpleasant. Holmes himself conducted a study demonstrating that emotional intensity attached to unpleasant experiences declined over time at a greater rate than was the case with pleasant ones, thereby making unpleasant memories less memorable. Learning experiments were conducted in stressful versus nonstressful environments; when subjects were less able to remember the materials that they studied under stress, that, too, was taken as evidence of repression. However, those tests are better understood in terms of the difficulty of learning under stress. Other experiments presented insoluble problems to various personality types, with the hypothesis that certain individuals would be more likely to repress their failures. "The only consistent finding in this line of research was that subjects with a high need for achievement recalled more incompletions under high stress than low stress," Holmes reported. "They persisted in working on or thinking about their failures rather than repressing them. Not only do these findings fail to provide support for the concept of repression, but they are the opposite to what would be predicted on the basis of repression." Holmes concluded that it might be time to abandon the theory of repression. Of course, without the concept of repression, the edifice of psychoanalysis collapses.

Even if repression does function in the way that therapists who work with recovered memory suppose, is it possible to repress repeated, long-term abuses, some of which began in infancy and lasted well into adult years? This certainly goes far beyond what Freud had in mind. Richard Ofshe terms this new, aggrandized version "robust repression." The awkwardness of explaining this mechanism is evident in the answers that members of the Ingram family gave to investigators and defense attorneys. After Ingram had described a mass rape of his family by Rabie and Risch, Schoening asked, "They leave; then what—you as a family do what?"

"As I recall, I lock up the house and, uh, I don't recall any conversation," Ingram said. "It's kind of like, once the situation's over, we go into a different memory. . . . We're back to normal, if that's a way to put it."

Again, explaining how he would forget, as he drove home, that he had taken part in a satanic ritual, Ingram theorized, "At some point you block the memory and your conscious memory takes over. It's like I couldn't function up here on a day-to-day basis knowing what I had done."

Frequently, the victims remember being told not to remember. Sandy explained how she forgot having been raped on the kitchen floor by Rabie in August of 1988 this way: "Then he said . . . that I wouldn't remember anything and for me to finish washing the dishes." Ericka related that after a satanic ritual "my father would carry me back to my room and he would always say, 'You will not remember. You will not remember. This is a dream.' "

These theories were supported all along by the police officers and mental-health professionals who had been brought in to counsel the Ingrams and who often reassured the victims and the investigators alike that such wholesale, instant repression is completely normal.

"Tell me why it is that you wouldn't leave," Sax Rodgers

asked Sandy after she described newly recalled incidents of abuse.

"Well, what they've explained to me is that because of what happened to me, that I repressed everything as a defense or a survival mechanism, and that's why it's hard for me to remember. That it's all there and that I will remember it all, but it's . . ." She trailed off hopelessly. Her psychiatrist had provided her with this explanation.

One can see the handiwork of five different psychologists and counselors who talked to Ingram during six months of interrogations. "Two guys just anally rape you against your will, you say," Rodgers observed, referring to one of Ingram's accusations against Rabie and Risch. "You have been a police officer since 1972. . . . Why didn't you go report them?"

"I have also been a victim since I was five years old, and I learned very early that the easiest way to handle this was to hide it in unconscious memory, and then you don't have to deal with it," Ingram replied.

"The more severe the incident the deeper the repression and the more difficult it is to disclose," argues Undersheriff McClanahan. Like several of the other officers in this investigation, McClanahan sees himself as a psychological authority. He has written several papers on the Ingram case and has counseled with Olympia's survivor groups. Many members of these groups claim to have been ritually abused and have received diagnoses of multiple-personality disorder. McClanahan has also lectured on satanic-ritual abuse in survivor workshops. "Just to hear the words 'I believe you' can make all the difference in the world to a ritual-abuse survivor and oftentimes begins the process of trust, hope, and healing," McClanahan says. Those are words he has often spoken to Julie and Ericka Ingram.

These two hypotheses form the intellectual framework of the Ingram investigation: first, that the depth of the repression is a function of the intensity of the trauma; and, second, that victims must be believed. Once a victim's account is believed, however, the evidence must be stretched to fit it. Often, it's a big stretch. McClanahan accounts for the absence of scars on the Ingram daughters by saying that it is not uncommon for survivors to believe there are scars, because they've been conditioned to believe things that aren't true. He also explains why the sisters couldn't be given lie detector tests: "Our survivors are very traumatized. To question their credibility would cause them to be retraumatized. They're so fragile." In response to the fact that teams of officers and an anthropologist from the local college dug up the Ingram property looking for the burial ground of murdered babies and turned up only a single elk-bone fragment, McClanahan says that the ground was so acidic that the bones disintegrated. Months of the most extensive investigation in the county's history produced no physical evidence that any crimes or rituals ever took place, but Joe Vukich explains this by saying, "We shouldn't have found any. These guys were police officers. We expected to find a lot or nothing. We did find a couple pieces of bone. Obviously, something had happened."

In a paper that Elizabeth Loftus presented to the American Psychological Association in 1992, she asked, "Is it fair to compare the current growth of cases of repressed memory of child abuse to the witch crazes of several centuries ago?" Posing that question has caused her to become an object of scorn to many victims' advocates and to some other researchers who believe that her research is part of a social backlash against abused women and children. Loftus wrote about the "great fear" of witches that caused the witch-hunts to occur:

> There are some parallels but the differences are just as striking. In terms of similarities, some of the stories today are actually similar to stories of earlier times (e.g., witches flying

into bedrooms). In terms of differences, take a look at the accused and the accusers. In the most infamous witch-hunt in North America, 300 years ago in Salem, Massachusetts, three-fourths of the accused were women. Today, they are predominately (but not all) men. Witches in New England were mostly poor women over 40 who were misfits. . . . Today, the accused are often men of power and success. The witch accusations of past times were more often leveled by men, but today the accusations are predominately leveled by women. Today's phenomenon is more than anything a movement of the weak against the strong. There is today a "great fear" that grips our society, and that is fear of child abuse.

13

In February 1989, Jim Rabie and
Ray Risch waived their right to a speedy trial in exchange
for limited freedom: they were fitted with electronic brace-
lets and confined to their homes. It was just as well that they
couldn't go out in public, for the satanic-ritual abuse allegations had surfaced in the pretrial hearings, and the county
was in shock.

Richard Ofshe sent a report to the prosecutor outlining his
concerns about the truthfulness of the alleged victims' stories.
He pointed to the many inconsistencies in Ericka's accounts
and her inability to recall anything about the ordinary life of
the cult beyond the fact that "they chant." After his first interview with Ericka, she began to claim traumatic amnesia in
order to explain the new information she was providing. No
one had been able to confirm her stories. When Ofshe had
asked Ericka why she hadn't moved out of her house sooner,
if her life was so awful, she suggested that she didn't want to
take a cut in her standard of living. "If she is capable of lying
about numerous infant and adult murders and the other heinous acts of the group, one must seriously consider the possibility that all of her accusations are fabrications," Ofshe
wrote. As for Julie, Ofshe believed that many of her accusa-

tions were false as well. "The timing with which she reveals information about the group is strangely similar to the timing with which her sister reveals information," he noted. "Even with her sister in the lead, Julie Ingram did little more than concur with her sister's report that a group existed." Ofshe discounted Paul's confessions because of the apparent ease with which he was persuaded to fantasize events and confess to imagined crimes, as he did in Ofshe's "little experiment." Sandy's statements were the result of a process of influence rather than real recollections based on memories of events, Ofshe wrote. "It is my opinion that Mrs. Ingram is not aware that she is inventing the scenes she came upon during the sessions with Reverend Bratun. I believe that she does not realize that the images are the result of her compliance to the demands of the situation. If she is permitted to continue to retell these stories over and over again her confidence in their validity will increase." Ofshe assured Tabor that there was no known technology available to Ingram, Rabie, and Risch that would induce Sandy's amnesia. "The implications of my opinions should be clear to anyone who reads this report," Ofshe concluded. "They are clear to me. I fear that my conscience would trouble me greatly were I not to communicate these conclusions to you in the most forceful and direct manner available. If I am correct in my judgment about the general truthfulness of Ericka and Julie Ingram and the extreme degree of suggestibility of Paul and Sandy Ingram there is a substantial danger that innocent people will be made to undergo a trial and a danger that they might be convicted."

When Tabor refused to turn the report over to the defense as exculpatory evidence—on the ground that, in his opinion, it was not real evidence—Ofshe complained to the presiding judge of the court. The judge agreed to make the report available to the defense attorneys. The report landed a shattering blow to the prosecution's already shaky case.

When Rabie and Risch were offered deals that would slash their jail time if they confessed, neither man would agree. In addition, other people who had been named by the daughters as members of the cult maintained their innocence, and there was no evidence to dispute their word. Beyond that, the months and months of work around the clock had taken an immense personal toll on the detectives. One marriage had ended. Tom Lynch had been a pal and fishing buddy of Sax Rodgers's, but their friendship broke apart over this case. Brian Schoening had begun dreaming about Ericka's abortion. He saw her lying on a table in a satanic ritual as her baby was being chopped up. At the end of the dream, the baby's little severed arm was forced into Ericka's vagina. Joe Vukich noticed that other officers were shying away from him in the hallway; he could only imagine how zombielike he must look to them. The fact that the investigation was consistently thwarted by a total lack of evidence added to the explosive pressures. The defense attorneys worried that Vukich, especially, was lurching out of control. During one court hearing, they stationed a private detective in a chair directly behind him because they were concerned that he might draw his gun and shoot the defendants.

What set this tinderbox ablaze was a discovery made thousands of miles away, in the Mexican border town of Matamoros, in April 1989. Police uncovered a ritual slaughterhouse on a ranch operated by a gang of drug smugglers. Thirteen mutilated corpses were exhumed, including that of twenty-one-year-old University of Texas student Mark Kilroy, who had been kidnapped as he walked across the international bridge toward Brownsville, Texas, a month before. The cult blended elements of witchcraft and Afro-Caribbean religions, but the main influence seems to have been a 1987 John Schlesinger film about devil worship called *The Believers*. The Matamoros cult lent an air of reality to the satanic hysteria that had taken root in the media. Agents for Geraldo Rivera and Oprah Winfrey were quickly on the scene.

"The discovery sent a shock wave through this part of Mexico and Texas and throughout the rest of the world," Rivera said on his show a couple of weeks later. "But, unbelievably bizarre as the Brownsville incident is, it is nothing viewers of this program haven't heard before." Rivera had on his show a former FBI agent named Ted Gunderson, who identified himself as a satanic-cult investigator. "I'd like to tell you right now, the next burial ground that we will learn about will be in Mason County, Washington," Gunderson announced, naming the county next door to Thurston County. "We've located a number of burial grounds in Mason County, and they can't possibly go out and dig them all up, because there's too many of them," he added.

Gunderson's announcement rocked the state of Washington. Soon he arrived and led a search team of private aircraft and television-news helicopters through the river valleys in the Olympic National Forest. Heat-seeking devices scanned the terrain, searching for the warmth of decomposing bodies. One of the helicopters landed on property belonging to Undersheriff McClanahan's parents. The searchers informed them that there was a satanic burial ground close by.

Although Thurston County authorities looked upon this frenzied hunt for bodies with official dismay, the truth is that they felt somewhat relieved, for the county had exhausted its own budget on the Ingram case and on the additional expense of conducting nighttime aircraft patrols that were intended to spot the bonfires of satanic cults. (Several fraternity beer busts had been raided.) Governor Booth Gardner now approved a $50,000 grant to continue the investigation, and the sheriff's office went to the state legislature seeking $750,000 for bullet-proof vests, night-viewing scopes, and electronic surveillance equipment. (That request was denied.) The sheriff's office also petitioned the county commissioners for $180,000. McClanahan showed the commissioners a short video about satanic-ritual abuse, in which a number of therapists spoke of the need for greater public support of its victims. "We are now hearing these reports from literally hundreds of therapists in every part of the United States that have amazing parallels," Dr. D. Corydon Hammond, a mild-faced professor at the University of Utah School of Medicine, said on the video. "What we are talking about here goes beyond child abuse or beyond the brainwashing of Patty Hearst or Korean War veterans. We're talking about people in some cases who . . . were raised in satanic cults from the time they were born—often cults that have come over from Europe, that have roots in the S.S. and death-camp squads, in some cases." The full extrapolation of Hammond's theory, not included on the video, goes on to postulate that the mind-control techniques used in such cults were developed by satanic Nazi scientists, who were captured by the CIA after the war and brought to the United States. The main figure was a Hasidic Jew, Dr. Green (an alias for Greenbaum), who saved himself from the gas chambers by assisting his Nazi captors and instructing them in the secrets of the cabala. Thus a note of anti-Semitism, which is almost always present in demonology, was sounded.* "The observa-

---

*According to Hammond, multiple personalities have been deliberately created in satanic ceremonies. "People say what's the purpose of it? My best guess is that the purpose of it is that they want an army of Manchurian Candidates, tens of thousands of mental robots who will do prostitution, tions of experienced therapists leave little doubt that children in our society are at risk of being ritually abused," the narrator of the video concluded. "An appropriate response on the part of professionals requires that we be willing to suspend disbelief and begin to watch for the telltale indicators of this most severe and destructive form of child abuse." The commissioners granted the request, at a time when schoolteachers were unable to get a scheduled pay raise because of budget restrictions. Eventually, the Ingram investigation would cost three-quarters of a million dollars.

For weeks, Schoening and Vukich had pressured Ingram to come up with names of cult members to match the additional names that Julie had produced for Ofshe. Ingram had been praying and visualizing with Pastor Bratun, and when he was alone he fasted and spent much of his time speaking in tongues. On April 13, he began four days of disclosures, which produced ten names of past and present employees of the Thurston

do child pornography, smuggle drugs, engage in international arms smuggling, do snuff films—all sorts of very lucrative things—and do their bidding, and eventually, the megalomaniacs at the top believe, create a satanic order that will rule the world." The logic of SRA hysteria permits no other conclusion. Hammond, incidentally, was instrumental in persuading the governor of Utah to create a ritual-abuse task force. He reports that, largely as a result of this effort, 90 percent of the citizens of the state believe that SRA is real, and that there are two full-time ritual-abuse investigators working through the attorney general's office. According to the September 13, 1993, Salt Lake *Tribune*, the investigators spent $250,000 and found nothing to prosecute.

As for the mysterious Dr. Green, Sherrill A. Mulhern, an anthropologist at the University of Paris who has studied the SRA phenomenon, traces him to the 1989 Lisa Steinberg case in New York City. A Dr. Michael Green was supposedly a member of a cult that Joel Steinberg was in. See also Joyce Johnson, *What Lisa Knew: The Truths and Lies of the Steinberg Case* (G. P. Putnam's Sons, 1990).

County Sheriff's Office. He also named members of the canine unit—the actual dogs, not their handlers—and described a scene in which the animals raped Sandy.

That was too much, even for investigators who had been willing to believe everything so far. A parade of outraged employees of the sheriff's office took lie detector tests. All passed except one, and no one paid any attention to the man who failed. The common wisdom in the department now was that Paul Ingram had controlled the investigation from the beginning. This latest series of disclosures was his masterstroke, the thinking went; he had been protecting the cult all along, and by discrediting himself in this fashion he would ensure that his testimony was completely worthless. Even so, the demoralized detectives had to reconsider their case against Rabie and Risch. The possibility that the two were innocent apparently never arose in the discussion. The question was simply: Is there any way left to prosecute them—any evidence at all? As the case was falling apart, Ericka and Julie finally consented to allow Loreli Thompson to examine them for scars, the idea being that perhaps she could see something the doctor in Seattle could not. Thompson found nothing. Earlier, Ericka had told of being cut with a knife on her torso and had said she had a three-inch scar; but when she exposed her stomach and pointed to the area, Thompson couldn't see anything. Paula Davis thought she could see a slight line, but Thompson stretched the skin to make sure, and she still couldn't make it out. A family doctor finally said she had discovered a tiny, L-shaped scar, but no one else could discern it.

"I'm writing this to you to maybe help fill in the blank in your investigation," Julie stated in a letter to Tabor on April 26. She maintained that she really did have a scar on her left arm, from a time when her father had nailed her to the floor. She told of other scars from ceremonial incisions. Then she described a scene in which she had been tortured by her father,

Rabie, and Risch with a pair of pliers. Paul had visualized such a scene months before, and on several previous occasions Julie had denied that it had occurred. She also wrote: "One time, I was about 11, my mom open my private area w/them and put a piece of a died baby inside me. I did remove it after she left it was an arm." Apparently, Julie was now remembering Brian Schoening's dream.

"On May 1, 1989, the trials of Jim Rabie, Ray Risch and Paul Ingram are scheduled to begin," wrote McClanahan in an effort to buoy his depressed investigators. "This office has done a remarkable job in uncovering the first ritualistic abuse investigation that has been confirmed by an adult offender involved directly with the offenses in the nation's history. . . . Clearly we are on the cutting edge of knowledge being gained from ritual abuse." At the bottom of the letter, he appended the names of four therapists who were available to counsel the officers.

McClanahan had taken the trouble to put together a chart titled "The Formal Investigation of Ritual Abuse," which might be a model for similar investigations around the world. He was trained in "link analysis," and the chart attempted to place all the elements of the case into a display of associations. The centerpiece was a square, which McClanahan labeled "Ritual Abuse." Inside this box were four rectangles, titled "History," "Control," "Abuse," and "Organization," as well as two ovals, "Criminal" and "Non-Criminal." These were linked by tangents, forming a kind of web; and from each of these, other lines branched out to other rectangles and ovals outside the central square. From the "Abuse" rectangle, for instance, there were lines leading to "Physical," "Emotional," "Sexual," "Spiritual," and "Psychological" ovals. Each of those ovals, in turn, became a hub for new spokes radiating from it. From the "Psychological" oval, for instance, there were spokes labeled "Killing Babies," "Sacrifices," "Eating Urine/Feces," "Sex with Animals," "Self Pleasure," "Who Will Believe," "Tricked Humans/Animals Buried— Later Moved," "It's Victim's Fault Others Die," "Killing/ Eating Pets." A spoke from "Psychological" made a connection to yet another oval, "Concealment," which had its own sunburst of spokes, and each of them had subspokes: the "Victims Conditioning" spoke, for instance, branched into "Others Will Die If You Remember," "You Will Die If You Remember," and "Satan Can Read Your Mind." McClanahan was proud of his chart, which he hung prominently on his wall. It seemed to capture the multiplying complexity of the Ingram case and arrange it all into a single, comprehensible, if awe-inspiring, graphic display. The detectives, however, were mortified. "It looks like a schizophrenic's brain exploded on him," one of them remarked sourly.

Actually, the Ingram case was no longer a ritual-abuse investigation. All charges of satanic abuse had faded away as prosecutors worked to salvage something. Ingram spared them any further embarrassment by deciding to plead guilty to six counts of third-degree rape. On Bratun's advice, he had not read Ofshe's report, because it might confuse him. Both Ericka and Julie had written him, however, saying that he owed them a confession. Sandy, who had initiated divorce proceedings, also urged him to plead guilty. The judge delayed the sentencing when it was learned that Julie had been sent a threatening letter. "Hows my very special little girl?" the letter read. "Do you realize how much trouble you caused our family? You've really blow this one and to tell you the true you've broke us up forever you'll never be a part of our family again. You've hurt you mom so bad you've destroy her she wants to die . . . you do realize that there are many people that would like to see you dead and a few that are hunting for you." It was signed, "Your ex Father, Paul." As soon as Detective Thompson saw the letter, she recognized the handwriting: Julie had written it to herself. Undersheriff McClanahan explained the forgery as behavior typical of ritual-abuse victims, who have been conditioned to exaggerate. "She just wanted us to believe her," he said.

On May 3, 1989, two days after Ingram pleaded guilty, the prosecutor dropped the charges against Rabie and Risch. They had been in custody a hundred and fifty-eight days.

14

In May 1989, Richard Ofshe had a telephone conversation with Paul Ingram in which he urged him to try to withdraw his guilty plea before the sentencing. Ingram said that although he had been having doubts himself about the validity of some of his memories, he was still hopeful that he would be able to fill in the blanks with new memories that would explain the many contradictions in his own stories and those of his wife and children.

"I'll tell you something, Paul—you are never going to get them," Ofshe said. "There is no way that you are going to be able to remember anything that is going to reconcile all the lies that have been told about this in the last few months."

"Assuming that you are right, you know I am still not willing to make the girls get up on the stand if there is a chance that I am going to emotionally damage them for the rest of their lives," Ingram replied. He said both the prosecutor and his own attorney had told them this might happen. Besides, he still believed that he was repressing material that could explain everything. "Let's even look at the guys that go through, like, Vietnam," he added. "They hide a lot of those memories."

"Maybe somebody can blank out one event that was just life-threatening to them, terrifying, disgusting beyond belief," Ofshe conceded. "Nobody can blank out as many events as you think you blanked out—it has never happened," Ofshe went on. "Paul, everything that you have told me this evening adds up to one thing. There exists a process that you have learned to use that allows you to invent images that are consistent with what you think should be happening."

Ingram was unmoved.

Two months later, however, in his prison cell, he reconsidered. He had been keeping a log in which he divided his memories into three categories: "Definitely Happened," "Not So Definitely Happened," and "Not Sure." At the time of his plea, most of his memories had been lodged in the first category, but afterward they began an insidious migration into the other two. On the morning of July 19, 1989, the anxiety that had been building within him reached a crisis. While he was praying, he later related, he heard a murmur, "Let go of the rope." A deep feeling of peace settled over him. His mind began to clear. Suddenly, he could see that all the visualizations of rituals and abuse had been fantasies, not actual memories. He no longer believed that he was a satanist or a child abuser, or even the victim of child abuse himself. The experience approximated for him a religious conversion. He wrote in his Bible, "PRI DIED TO SELF 7-19-89."

Ingram got a new lawyer, who filed a motion to withdraw his guilty plea on the grounds that he had been coerced in the course of being interrogated and had given incriminating testimony while in a trancelike state. Unfortunately, it was too late to stop the train that Ingram boarded when he pleaded guilty. All the lawyer could do was to petition for leniency at the sentencing hearing, which took place in April of 1990.

"I'm Ericka Ingram. I was the daughter of Paul Ingram," Ericka stated in a surprise appearance at the hearing. Ericka wore a simple, pale dress, and she looked wan and stricken. She asked the judge to impose the greatest possible sentence.

Otherwise, "I believe he will either kill me or Julie," she warned. "He destroyed me and Julie's life and our entire family, and he doesn't care. He is obviously a very dangerous man." As she spoke, Schoening and Vukich sat in the back of the court and wept openly.

When Ericka finished, the judge asked Paul Ingram if he had anything to say.

Ingram rose and said in a clear voice, "I stand before you, I stand before God. I have never sexually abused my daughters. I am not guilty of these crimes." The judge showed no interest in this change of heart. Ordinarily, under the worst circumstances, Ingram would serve thirty-three to forty-three months for each count, running concurrently, which meant that he would be in prison for no more than three and a half years. The standards in the state of Washington are such that most first-time sex offenders receive a six-month sentence if they agree to urdergo treatment—a sentence Ingram had already served. The judge agreed with the prosecutor, however, that this was not an ordinary circumstance. Moreover, because Ingram was now saying that the events didn't happen, the judge believed that treatment would not be helpful. He sentenced Ingram to twenty years in prison, with the possibility of parole after twelve years.*

When the county prosecutor's office dropped the charges against Rabie and Risch, Ericka asked an attorney named Thomas Olmstead to file a suit against Thurston County for negligence in failing to supervise Ingram and Rabie.† Ericka

---

*Ingram's motion to withdraw his guilty plea was rejected by the appellate court in January of 1992, and by the Washington State Supreme Court in September of that same year. At this writing, the case is in federal court, but Ingram's chances there would appear to be slim, since the courts have shown little interest in granting an appeal to anyone who has pleaded guilty.
†The suit was still pending as this was written, in September 1993.

has asserted that some thirty satanists controlled the county and conspired to derail the case. Undersheriff McClanahan and Detective Schoening are among those Ericka has named as satanists. "How high does this go?" asks Olmstead, who is a fundamentalist Christian and a former FBI agent. "The governor? Who knows?"

Sandy Ingram, now divorced from Paul, has changed her name and lives in another town with Mark. Both Chad and Paul Ross have married and moved away. Ericka is living in California. Julie remains in the Olympia area, but she now uses a different name. The Ingram family, such as it was, has been destroyed. In the end, what had once held them together, their memories, is what blew them apart.

Jim Rabie and Ray Risch still live in Olympia, although they are widely believed to be guilty men who got away with heinous crimes. Risch works in the same automobile repair shop where he worked before, but he is rarely given any supervisory tasks. "There isn't a day that goes by that it doesn't get brought up," he says. "The cloud is still there. It's not a good memory." His wife reports that his mind is still scattered, and that it has been hard to keep up payments on their mobile home.

After abandoning his lobbying consultancy, Rabie worked for several months for a friend who owns a carpet shop, until customer complaints about his presence began to hurt business. Now he has a job with a vehicle-transport company. His legal bills, along with Risch's—which Rabie helped to pay—have exceeded ninety thousand dollars. Both men sued the county for false arrest and malicious prosecution, but their suit was dismissed by the United States District Court.* At this reporter's request, Rabie agreed to take another lie detector

---

*It was before the Ninth Circuit Court of Appeals at this writing.

test, which covered the same material as the one he had failed earlier. This time, he passed it.

As for the investigators, most of them have not altered their views. Undersheriff McClanahan, despite being denounced himself as a satanist by Ericka, remains unswayed. "Satanic abuse is real," he contends. "This case proves it."

Indeed, with Ingram's conviction, the case has become a primary exhibit in the SRA controversy. On December 2, 1991, many of the principals met in a television studio in New York. "Today, this woman will come face to face with the man that she says sexually tortured her in satanic rituals for seventeen years. A show you don't want to miss," said Sally Jessy Raphaël to her television audience. The camera focused on Ericka Ingram, wearing a cobalt-blue sweater and sitting meekly in a chair beside Raphaël. Arguably, it was shows like this one that created the Ingram fantasy in the first place.

"They were people in the community, like policemen," Ericka said as she described the cult. "There were some judges, doctors, lawyers. Different people in the community that had high political standings."

"What happened at the rituals?" Raphaël asked, her voice full of prodding compassion. "I know it must be pretty awful, but what happened?"

"First they would start with just, like, chanting," Ericka said. "Sometimes they would kill a baby."

"A baby?" Raphaël echoed. "Where would they get babies?"

"Sometimes people in the cult would have them just for this."

"Did this happen to you?" Raphaël asked. "You remember being on a table and people having sex with you?"

Ericka nodded.

"Wow. What else?"

"Sometimes they would drink blood," Ericka said. The members of the audience looked at her gravely and occasionally shook their heads in dismay. "One time, when I was sixteen, they gave me an abortion. I was five months pregnant. And the baby was still alive when they took it out. And they put it on top of me and then they cut it up. And then, when it was—when it was dead, then people in the group ate parts of it." A gasp arose from the thrilled audience. Later Ericka asserted, "I spent most of my life in the hospital. And that is true. And, I mean, doctors were just, like, looking at my body, just going—*ugh*!"

Raphaël introduced Jim Rabie, who was there trying to reclaim some of his reputation in the only forum available. "He says, even though he is innocent, his life, and that of his family, has been permanently damaged," Raphaël said.

"It destroyed a business that I had," Rabie explained, his voice cracking. "It has caused my family untold heartache."

But the audience wasn't interested in Rabie's problems. "Ericka, I feel so sorry for you," one woman in the audience said. "I have no idea why she would ever bring up this guy if he was not guilty."

Richard Ofshe was also on the show, matched against Bob Larson, a radio evangelist who has built his ministry by spreading satanic hysteria. "What is this whole thing about satanism, Dr. Ofshe?" Raphaël asked.

"Right now, there is an epidemic of these kinds of allegations in the country," Ofshe said. "They are totally unproven."

"There's an epidemic of satanism in the country, not allegations," Larson interjected.

"Why would you say there is this epidemic, as a sociologist?" Raphaël asked.

"In part because it's a way of reasserting the coherence and authority of fundamentalist perspectives in society," Ofshe said.

"All right, let's talk to Bob," said Raphaël, turning to the evangelist, who has thinning reddish-blond hair and a beard. "Bob, you've got a man here saying that in no case—and there have been one hundred court cases, I believe, maybe even more, involving satanic rituals in our country—in no case has there ever been any evidence, hard-core evidence, nor has anyone, except Ericka's father, ever said that they've done that. In other words, there's never been a confession."

"He's only technically correct," Larson said.

"Technically correct," Raphaël repeated flatly. When Larson cited the enormous number of people in therapy who have complained of satanic abuse, Raphaël asked again, "Why, if there are all these people under care, why isn't there one shred of evidence?"

"The difficulty is that the evidentiary basis of the justice system is not commensurate with what you deal with in a therapeutic process," Larson said. "When are we going to start believing people who come forward like this, instead of putting them through some type of legal litmus test?" One supposes that the "legal litmus test" he was referring to was the need for Ericka to provide credible testimony in order to convict Rabie of the crimes she accuses him of. Larson's voice rose in indignation. "These are people who suffered the most incredible abuse!" he cried. "My God! This woman has been defecated on, urinated on—"

"By him!" Ericka cried, pointing at the hapless Rabie.

"She's experienced bestiality and group sex by this man!" Larson said as he laid a pastoral hand on Ericka's knee. "When are we going to start believing the victims?"

"Believe us!" Ericka cried.

Love in the Time of Algorithms

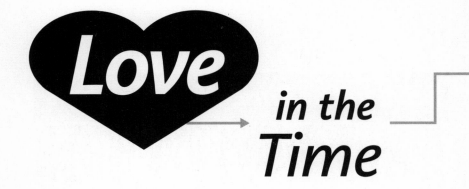

Love *in the* Time

of

Algorithms

+

WHAT TECHNOLOGY DOES
TO MEETING AND MATING

=

DAN SLATER

CURRENT

CURRENT
Published by the Penguin Group
Penguin Group (USA) Inc., 375 Hudson Street, New York, New York 10014, U.S.A. • Penguin Group (Canada), 90 Eglinton Avenue East, Suite 700, Toronto, Ontario, Canada M4P 2Y3 (a division of Pearson Penguin Canada Inc.) • Penguin Books Ltd, 80 Strand, London WC2R 0RL, England • Penguin Ireland, 25 St. Stephen's Green, Dublin 2, Ireland (a division of Penguin Books Ltd) • Penguin Group (Australia), 707 Collins Street, Melbourne, Victoria 3008 Australia (a division of Pearson Australia Group Pty Ltd) • Penguin Books India Pvt Ltd, 11 Community Centre, Panchsheel Park, New Delhi – 110 017, India • Penguin Group (NZ), 67 Apollo Drive, Rosedale, Auckland 0632, New Zealand (a division of Pearson New Zealand Ltd) • Penguin Books (South Africa), Rosebank Office Park, 181 Jan Smuts Avenue, Parktown North 2193, South Africa • Penguin China, B7 Jiaming Center, 27 East Third Ring Road North, Chaoyang District, Beijing 100020, China

Penguin Books Ltd, Registered Offices:
80 Strand, London WC2R 0RL, England

First published in 2013 by Current,
a member of Penguin Group (USA) Inc.

10   9   8   7   6   5   4   3   2   1

Portions of this book first appeared in *GQ* magazine.

Author's Note
This book attempts to be a factual inside account of the development of an industry, and a chronicle of how that industry has affected the lives of the people whose stories I've told. The casual nature of online interaction, however, required taking liberties with some of the secondary material quoted—namely, the conversations, profiles, and messages pulled from online-dating sites and the Phantasy Tour forum. Occasionally, I relocated or transposed a sentence or paragraph, adjoined remarks written by the same person at different times, removed words or phrases from quotes without inserting marks of ellipsis, and cleaned up spelling and grammar. None of these changes are intended to alter meaning or make the material more interesting, but rather to privilege clarity and narrative flow over fidelity to the precise original. Also, the names of most online-dating users have been changed to protect their privacy.

LIBRARY OF CONGRESS CATALOGING IN PUBLICATION DATA
Slater, Dan.
Love in the time of algorithms : what technology does to meeting and mating / Dan Slater.
p. cm.
Includes bibliographical references and index.
ISBN 978-1-59184-531-7
1. Online dating. 2. Courtship. 3. Dating (Social customs)—Technological innovations.
4. Marriage brokerage—Technological innovations. I. Title.
HQ801.82.S58 2013
306.730285—dc23   2012036921

Printed in the United States of America
Set in Diverda Serif Com with Aroma No. 2 LT Pro
Designed by Daniel Lagin

For G & G

The Internet did not develop in order to facilitate relationships, any more than newspapers were invented to publish personal ads. Like the panda's thumb, evolution, whether natural or technological, takes unexpected directions.

—Monica Whitty and Adrian Carr, *Cyberspace Romance*

CONTENTS

Love in the Time of Algorithms

INTRODUCTION

Liquidity in the Market

THE iDATE AWARDS

t's January 2011, and Sam Yagan and Markus Frind are trying to chat casually by the pool behind Miami's National Hotel. Their reflections shimmer in the water as a humid evening breeze shakes the palm fronds. The two men, both in their early thirties, are dressed identically in blue button-downs, navy blue blazers, and khakis. But these similarities belie their true relationship. They are stiff competitors, and the presence of the other unnerves them both. Yagan and Frind shift on their feet, beers in hand, waiting for the other to speak.

"Why didn't they ask you to give the talk on free dating?" asks Yagan.

"Because," says Frind, "I hate public speaking."

This is true: Despite running what's believed to be the largest online-dating site in the world, Frind is loath to appear on television or radio. When he does, he speaks of "programming languages" and rattles off statistics. In a 2009 appearance on a Toronto-based talk show, Frind said the average online dater "needs about 3.8 dates for a relationship."

Yagan, meanwhile, has been a media fixture since college. Cable, newspapers, magazines, tech-news sites, investors, Silicon Valley—they all love Yagan and he loves them right back. His question to Frind barely conceals his excitement that his rival was not asked to speak.

"Then why not get one of your illustrious team members to do it?" responds Yagan, his quip divided evenly between mockery and jealousy over Frind's entourage of beautiful female executives, all of whom are mingling a few feet away. Some tension is released as Frind and Yagan gaze appreciatively.

Yagan is a slender man, about five feet eight inches tall, with a narrow chin, an aquiline nose, thick eyebrows, a broad forehead, and cropped hair that's gone prematurely gray. With friends Yagan is intensely congenial but turns quickly to disgusted and derisive when a subject or viewpoint arises that conflicts with his agenda.

Frind is taller, paler, more reserved. He tends to press his chin in while casting his bespectacled eyes down, as if expecting an insult or a punch to the face. His look, wrote *The Globe and Mail*, is that of a "true coder," his style reminiscent of men "twice his 33 years, boomers whose only exertion is to toddle to the first tee." Frind uses his fame to surround himself with attractive women, including his new wife, Annie, a charming and radiant blonde.

They've come to Miami to attend the iDate Awards dinner, the featured event of the online-dating industry's annual conference in South Beach. Yagan, a cofounder of OkCupid, and Frind, the sole founder of Plenty of Fish, are celebrities in this place where relationships are the business, a very lucrative business that has reached $2 billion in North America, with billions more being made abroad, as millions of customers join, and return to, dating sites every day. From New York, Los Angeles, Quebec, Vancouver, Sydney, Moscow, Kiev, London, and Rio de Janeiro, the one hundred dating executives who turned up at the conference are here to show their faces and shore up their interests in an industry that has arrived at a crossroads, saturated with players and facing an uncertain future. The online-dating industry may service thirty million of America's ninety million single adults, but momentum is slowing. Following a period of explosive growth between 1998 and 2005, the Facebook-led rise of social networks began stealing market share. Meanwhile, popular matchmaking sites like eHarmony and Chemistry face attacks from academics who say the science behind their algorithms is bunk.

For three days, the dating execs have been cutting advertising deals, buying and selling dating sites, and arguing over the future of the industry. Now they're ordering drinks, posing on a red carpet, and waiting for the awards dinner to begin.

Yagan, the son of Syrian immigrants and a graduate of Harvard and Stanford Business School, is CEO of OkCupid, a dating site known for its community of urban-creative types. Frind, a Canadian who comes from German-farmer stock, attended a vocational school before starting Plenty of Fish. Frind's site is thought to attract a certain kind of customer, one who feels at home among grammar-free profiles comprised largely of text-speak and emoticons—a sizable population, as it turns out: Frind owns 20 percent of the world's online-dating traffic.

Yagan says Plenty of Fish, because of its unmanageable size, is infested with "romance scammers," people who create fake dating profiles to wring money from the desperate. Frind dismisses Yagan's OkCupid as a "niche site" with a limited following among "the writer-slash-hippie-slash-whatever crowd." Frind says Plenty of Fish grows an OkCupid a day. All sallies are partially correct: Plenty of Fish is much larger than OkCupid, and therefore more vulnerable to infiltration by scammers.

But as antagonistic as they fancy themselves, Frind and Yagan are aligned when it comes to one key element of the business: They both believe online dating should be free. Yagan's anger over not being asked to give the conference talk about the state of free online dating is palpable. He campaigned to give the talk. When the conference organizers refused him, citing the need to let others in the industry speak, he nearly boycotted the conference, agreeing to make the trip from New York only after the organizers hinted that OkCupid would receive several honors at tonight's ceremony.

That Frind and Yagan are two of the savviest entrepreneurs in an industry that markets human relationships is, to put it mildly, totally bizarre. Both are married. Neither has dated online. Yagan often jokes that he and his OkCupid partners know nothing about dating. They are business-minded, unemotional math guys. Dating, relationships, and

love, on the other hand, are irreducible products riddled with variables

Or are they?

My phone buzzes with a text: "Just walked in. You here?"

When I asked the conference organizers about the possibility of
bringing an online date to the awards dinner, I expected some pushback.
The one-hundred-dollar-per-head event was sold out, after all, and I was
lucky to get a last-minute press pass. But instead of resistance, my request met with universal encouragement. I was in Miami for three days
and had lined up a date through Match.com. This, I suppose, was precisely the kind of dating adventure their business models encouraged.

I walk through the hotel's foyer and find my date standing patiently
beneath the chandelier. I don't know much about RedPepper—her
online-dating nom de plume—other than a few dating vitals: thirty
years old; a Jew of Dutch descent; Michigan-raised; the director of marketing for a global ice cream brand. Two weeks before my trip to Miami,
she'd written to me via Match's messaging system:

> So, you're probably thinking: Why is this girl from Florida e-mailing
> me on Match? Well, I was sitting here alone in South Africa on a
> business trip in the middle of the night and talking to my best friend
> in Brooklyn. She said why don't you switch your search parameters to
> Brooklyn and see who shows up. You showed up first, we match on
> all the green bubbles, and you made me laugh. Anyway, you should
> write me back. What have you got to lose?

There was something serendipitous about getting this message so
close to my trip. South Africa, Florida, New York: What were the chances?
Yet after nine months of online dating from my home base of Brooklyn,
the situation didn't *seem* that unusual. I'd become conditioned to the
message-in-a-bottle randomness of it all, having received queries from
London, Hanoi, San Francisco, and even the Upper East Side.

RedPepper is tall and slender, with large blue eyes, a cheery disposition, and long frizzy hair that is almost platinum. We greet in one of those slapstick ballets of mistimed lunges and errant cheek kisses. The awkwardness contains itself, and we make for the pool. "I'm always up for an adventure," says RedPepper. "But I did wonder why you didn't respond to my second message asking what brings you to Florida." Indeed, I had needed some time to figure out how to ask an online date to an online-dating conference.

While RedPepper and I wait for the awards dinner to start, we sip our drinks beneath the palm fronds that wrap around the pool. Nearby is Markus Frind's entourage, led by Kate Bilenki, Plenty of Fish's chief operating officer. Doe-eyed and porcelain browed, Bilenki gets hit on by pretty much every heterosexual male at iDate. Particularly relentless is a team of British dating executives, one of whom boasted that he was flying Bilenki to England in the spring to take her to "the polo." When he said this I wondered if he was referring to a business meeting or a cross-continental date of some kind. But this was the point. Nowhere else in corporate life do work and play merge so shamelessly as they do among these dating mavens.

Whereas prior to RedPepper's arrival I was an interloping reporter with too many questions and uncertain motives, I am now part of a couple, one half of which is inarguably attractive. As such, we begin drawing dating execs to our area beneath the palm fronds. A Chinese American man introduces himself as Jason Du, the founder of MillionaireMatch, whose members include "professional athletes, beauty queens, fitness models, and Hollywood celebrities." The actor Charlie Sheen, he says, was an early customer. Du also runs PositiveSingles, a dating site for people with sexually transmitted diseases. "Because of privacy concerns, it's very tricky for people with STDs to date," he explains. "So on the site we have a button labeled Quick Exit for those times when your pesky boss walks by."

A post-forty-five-ish blonde drifts over. She's Julie Ferman of Cupid's Coach, an offline matchmaker. Ferman flashes a toothy smile and looks like a cross between Julia Louis-Dreyfuss and Glenn Close. "It's very hard to find good guys for my great women," she laments. "These are women who live in great million-dollar homes, have great careers, and just need that great special someone, that great relationship with that great stable guy."

"Like what's an example?" asks RedPepper.

Ferman purses her lips, happy to be asked, and relates a recent conflict: "I matched up a client in L.A. with a great guy. But then the client went out of town. When the client returned, the guy was not calling her. So the client called me, and I told her she had two options. Either she could wait it out, or she could take the situation into her own hands and call *him*."

When RedPepper realizes this is the sum of the facts, she becomes slightly hostile, asking Ferman whether it's "problematic" that a forty-year-old woman is paying thousands of dollars for advice that "seems kind of basic." Ferman turns to me and says she loves to take care of her friends in the media, and that she recently arranged a very successful date for Dr. Phil. This name drop piques the interest of Jason Du, who appears to be envisioning Dr. Phil as MillionaireMatch's next celebrity dater.

After Du and Ferman leave, RedPepper says, matter-of-factly, "Me and my friends, we're well-educated and successful and all that. But I guess we focused on other things after college. Career stuff. Now it's hard to find anyone. Some are already resigned to waiting for a divorcee to pop up. Or just marrying guys they're not very excited about."

The gist of what RedPepper describes happens to be highly relevant for the online-dating industry. The ascension of women at work and their rising financial status, the lagging prospects of men, the ebb of the marriage rate, and the ever-rising marriage age—these are societal trends that have dovetailed with, and been a boon to, online dating in recent years. "My friends think I'm crazy for being on Match," she says. "They tell me I don't need it. But quote unquote need isn't really the point, is it? It's about taking control."

On and off, for the last nine months, I, like RedPepper, had been taking control. Three events accounted for my foray into online dating: I turned thirty-one, got out of a long-term relationship, and then lost my job. I was single at a point in life where all my friends were married or settled down, and I suddenly had a lot of free time on my hands.

Then, a few months into my online-dating adventure, a fourth thing happened. A package, sent from my father, arrived, containing a stack of old letters and postcards dated 1966 and addressed to him at Harvard University, where he'd gone as an undergraduate. The correspondence had been written by my mother, a student at Mount Holyoke College, during the early months of their courtship. My parents had separated in the eighties, when I was three. I'd always just assumed they met at a dance, or were introduced by a friend, but I'd never bothered to ask.

Among the materials was an annotated cartoon booklet given to my father on his twenty-second birthday. On the first page, adjacent to a drawing of a girl and her dog, my mother had written, in her neat tight scrawl: "Thank you, you old mathematically-minded-can't-mind-your-own-business-mass-production-post-card-instigating-work-of-art-in-stainless-steel computer. Thank you."

What computer could she possibly have been thanking, and why?

Flipping through the rest of the pile I came upon a questionnaire entitled "CONTACT Personality Preference Inventory."

"Oh yeah. You didn't know?" my father said, when I called to ask him what CONTACT was. "Your mother and I met through a computer dating service. These days they're all over the Internet. I think they're mostly for desperate people though."

There were a few flops in my online-dating experience. But most of the people I met were, like RedPepper, the kinds of people I might've pursued had we run into each other "IRL," in real life. The main difference was that I no longer had to rely on real life. From the convenience and privacy of my laptop (or cell phone), I could browse through hundreds or thousands of people I would likely never meet otherwise. In the past I'd had to rely on my social circle—family, friends at school and work, friends of friends—or the occasional chance encounter in the subway or on the street. But even at my most outgoing, opportunities to make a connection were limited; potential partners, rare.

For virtually all of human history the search for a mate has been predicated on scarcity: One met only so many people in his or her life-time. They optimized their options within a circumscribed pool, chose someone, settled down, and, in the best of cases, found something they called happiness. Even when women's lib came along, and the legal and cultural restraints surrounding divorce began to ease in the 1960s and 1970s, making it easier to leave failed relationships, many chose to stick with the devil they knew because of scarcity, believing it was better to be in a so-so relationship than no relationship at all.

Today, however, companies in the online-dating arms race are building ever more efficient, "frictionless" systems for bringing together people who are likely to like each other. By posing hundreds or thou-sands of questions and quizzes—or asking nothing at all—these sites offer endless choice, combining to form a vast mate-seeking arena I came to think of as the "date-o-sphere," not a physical construct but not an entirely virtual one either, a special category of social media that yokes together enormous online communities for the purpose of offline relationships. So in 2010, when I discovered that thirty million single adults in the United States—about one-third of all American singles—had an online-dating profile, and that I couldn't sit through a dinner party without meeting at least one couple, if not several, who'd met on-line, I became hooked by a simple question: What does all this connec-tive technology mean for the future of relationships?

This isn't a book about me, or my parents. It's about how online dating—as both a revolutionary medium and a quirky, virginal industry—is remaking the landscape of modern relationships. It's about a man in Oregon whose plans to settle down took a detour when he discovered how easy it was to meet new women online. It's about a young woman in New York whose compulsion to broadcast her online-dating adven-tures in social media seemed to foil her offline relationships, and about another online dater in San Francisco whose Facebook monitoring had become the enemy of her new relationships. It's about an asthmatic in Atlanta who realized, thanks to a cutting-edge algorithm, that he could be happy with a smoker; and about a cancer survivor in southern California whose isolation inspired her to start a niche dating site for people, like herself, who can no longer have sex. Authenticity, deception, commitment, intimacy, paranoia, sex, and trust—technology is changing all these aspects of relationships. Those changes are what this book is about.

It's also about how, over the last half century, a bunch of geeks reengineered romance and serendipity, redefined our values around meeting and mating, and fought through a heavy societal stigma in the process. Beginning with the early computers of the 1950s and 1960s, the video cameras of the 1970s, the bulletin board systems of the 1980s, the Internet of the 1990s, and the smartphones of the last decade, every new format of electronically intermediated introductions has faced a stigma of some kind.

Only recently has the discredit that's dogged traditional online-dating sites like Match.com begun to dissolve, only to pop up elsewhere in the date-o-sphere. Today, more risqué incarnations—from sites that facilitate marital affairs to those that connect Western men with women in the developing world—are hoping to travel a similar path toward wide acceptance. The profits made by these companies tell a fascinating (and, for some, disturbing) story of shifting sexual mores, as easy access to hitherto unimagined liaisons slowly erodes the taboos that surround them. This, too, is the subject that *Love in the Time of Algorithms* explores: how these new means of connection are threatening the old paradigm of adult life.

My journey took me to the headquarters of dating sites around the country, where I saw dating executives struggle with how to balance their business interests with the interests of their users; into the private lives of dozens of online daters across America; and then abroad, to England, France, Russia, and Colombia, where Latin women, many of whom don't own a computer, use online dating to meet men from North America.

I also went back in time, to understand how technology has influenced our relationships throughout history. As it turns out, this is not the first time that technology has upended the old ways. In the past these changes have been fueled by the personal ad, the bicycle, the car, the movie theater, and contraception. Today it's the Internet. In all cases the narrative is similar: One generation considers its social norms around meeting and mating to be inviolable, only to see them disregarded by the next.

When the awards dinner begins, the emcee, playing to the supposed proclivities of his audience, tells a series of jokes featuring his mother and sister in outlandish sexual scenarios. RedPepper and I laugh. Nothing will come of our date. She's great. But the chemistry isn't quite right. Sparks would really need to fly to pursue a long-distance relationship with someone in Miami.

For the moment, however, we're still on a date, and seated next to Sam Yagan, who's treating the event as a kind of companion-media to his smartphone, which he thumbs furiously while at the same time telling us how much he dislikes his rivals. A special hatred is reserved for Match, the oldest and largest online-dating site in the paid category. Yagan claims Match has built a business around bamboozling its customers. But his contempt masks the truth about his own business: OkCupid, in spite of its loyal following, hasn't performed very well in terms of revenue. Without the enormous traffic of Plenty of Fish, it's hard to be profitable as a free site, depending wholly on advertising to make money. With around 1.5 million paying subscribers, and many million more free users to fill out its database (more on that later), Match makes nearly $350 million a year in revenue. OkCupid makes less than $5 million.

For the last year, Yagan has been quietly courting potential buyers, including AOL, MSN, Google, Yahoo, Viacom, and the Hearst Corporation. Viacom's MTV and Hearst's magazines are all about relationships and sex. AOL owns the domain name Love.com but doesn't use it. A dating site, he's tried to convince these companies, would fit perfectly in their empires. But no luck. "The idea is interesting enough for them to talk to me for thirty minutes," says Yagan. "But the conversations end the same: 'no thanks.'" The only major acquirers of online-dating sites are other online-dating sites, namely Match, the company Yagan and his partners have made a sport out of slamming publicly.

He's called up to accept OkCupid's first award of the night, for Best

Up and Coming Dating Site. "Seven years in business and we're still 'up and coming,'" he mumbles on his way to the podium, where he graciously accepts the award.

Next up is offline matchmaker Julie Ferman, who wins for Best Matchmaker. Ferman remarks that the award—a long, arcing glass statuette—looks like a giant dildo, which it sort of does, and then proceeds to frog hop off the stage while pretending to ram the award into her rear end.

During a lull, I ask Yagan a version of the same question I'd posed to other dating execs: "If dating through the Internet becomes more and more popular, and sites become more efficient, what do you think will happen to commitment when people discover how much easier it's become to find new relationships?"

"That's really a point about market liquidity," Yagan replies, "which I like."

His answer is technical but not surprising. Even though Yagan and his Harvard pals created one of the industry's top dating sites, he distances himself from the notion that they're relationship gurus. Yagan married his high school sweetheart. His OkCupid cofounders are also married. "We're a bunch of math guys," he told the *Boston Globe* in 2007. "We don't know anything about dating."

OkCupid wins four awards, including Best Dating Site—the iDate equivalent of a Best Picture Oscar. At the podium, Yagan thanks the conference organizers and bows to his industry colleagues. "What I like most about this business," he tells the crowd, "is that all of us here are committed to helping people find love."

CHAPTER ONE

Your Pleasure Is Our Business

THE BIRTH OF THE ORIGINAL SOCIAL NETWORK

It is clearly the most unusual entry on the resume of Judge Douglas H. Ginsburg, President Reagan's nominee for the Supreme Court.

According to a spokesman, Judge Ginsburg left college for more than a year in the mid-1960s and founded a nationwide computer-dating service known as Operation Match.

— **"Nominee Left College to be Matchmaker,"**
New York Times, **October 30, 1987**

B efore he achieved notoriety for his crazy handlebar mustache and film criticism on the *Today* show, Gene Shalit was a journeyman culture reporter for *Look* magazine. A general-interest publication and a runner-up to *Life*, *Look* was trying to stay on top of the computing revolution when, in 1965, it spotted a good story coming out of Boston. Some industrious Harvard students were putting computers to novel use. *Look*'s editors dispatched Shalit, then twenty-nine years old, to investigate.

It was still several decades before Facebook and the phrase "social media" would come into vogue, but the earliest pioneers were still aware of the computer's social implications. In 1959, two Stanford engineering students who were known to throw epic parties, complete with home-brewed beer and nurses from the veterans' hospital in Menlo Park, designed a class project around using the IBM 650 to match up the people in their readymade mating pool: forty-nine men and forty-nine women. Jim Harvey and Phil Fialer called their project Happy Families Planning Services and wrote a questionnaire asking about age, height, weight, religion, hobbies, and personality traits. They programmed the IBM to measure differences in their respondents' answers. But the pool was small, making for some odd couples. Although the project received an A, and even produced one marriage, it never moved beyond the classroom.

In the early sixties, some colleges used computers to optimize the meeting potential at dances. In 1963, Ed Lewis, a psychology professor at Iowa State University, served as "personality consultant" in an initiative to match up one thousand students. Answers to a lengthy questionnaire were transferred onto punch cards and fed through an IBM. Short on females, the university had to bus in nursing students from Des Moines. The value, said Lewis, was simply pairing people up; the question of why they'd been matched was a good icebreaker. There was also scientific value. Iowa State professors squeezed in some research, and the results surprised them: Men tended to fall in love more quickly and less deliberately than women; men also reported feeling more romantic attraction and were more optimistic about the prospect of marriage. One or two happy couples emerged. *Time* published a story. *Life* planned a big spread for its November issue but had to scrap it to cover the JFK assassination.

Back then, computers occupied entire rooms and were prohibitively expensive, and therefore were owned mostly by universities and corporations. Harvard had owned computers since 1944. Weighing in at ten thousand pounds, the steel frame of the Harvard Mark I was fifty-one feet long and eight feet high. The machine used five hundred miles of wire with three million connections: 3,500 multipole relays with 35,000 contacts; 2,225 counters; 1,464 tenpole switches; and tiers of 72 adding machines. The Mark I's dizzying complexity tended to obscure its function. It could perform long computations automatically. Basically, it was a giant calculator.

Even while more companies, such as Xerox, entered the computing market, the potential of computers remained a matter of speculation in the sixties, making them a subject of sci-fi fantasy. In the fall of sixty-five, when *Look* sent Gene Shalit to Harvard, the film director Stanley Kubrick was starting work on what would become his most enduring film, *2001: A Space Odyssey.* The story starred a sentient computer named HAL 9000 and even featured a tabletlike device. As for the Internet, it was still in seed form. In sixty-three, a Defense Department employee named J. C. R. Licklider had sent a memo to the nation's top computer scientists ("Members and Affiliates of the Intergalactic Computer Network") in which he suggested it might be "interesting and important . . . to develop a capability for integrated network operation."

But how interesting or important was it? How different might this integrated network be from telephones or wireless transmissions?

Of course it was quite different. By merging these old technologies with a new search-and-discovery tool, the Internet would endow users with a degree of control and decision-making power unprecedented in the history of the communication and information industry. It was this idea of control that interested Gene Shalit. At the pre-Internet Harvard of sixty-five, the computer's human-augmenting effects were finally being revealed to the masses. Two rival companies, both student-run, were making money hand-over-fist by using what Shalit called the "Great God Computer" to help college students find dates.

The concept had taken root at Harvard earlier that year, when a junior math major named Jeff Tarr decided he was fed up with coming home alone from the same mixers with Radcliffe, the women's college across the way. Despite Tarr's towering stature in the math department, he was, at five feet seven inches, less than a heartthrob. Tarr's eureka moment, like that of so many innovators before and after him, reflected the desperation of a guy who couldn't get a date. That he could also make a fortune by expanding the mating pool from Wheaton to Wellesley, from Pembroke to Mount Holyoke, was an afterthought. His primary goal was meeting girls.

Tarr raised $1,250 in start-up capital, and recruited classmate

Vaughan Morrill. Tarr wrote a matching questionnaire that asked students to answer seventy-five questions about themselves and another seventy-five about their "ideal date," and passed it around. Feedback was good. Then the plan hit a snag: Tarr knew nothing about computers. He was just a math guy; computer science did not yet exist as a major. So he paid a friend one hundred dollars to program an IBM 1401 to match up the responses to the questionnaire. Tarr and Morrill distributed the questionnaire to Boston-area colleges. Students filled it out and returned it with a three-dollar subscription fee. Tarr then paid "punch-card ladies" to transfer the answers from each questionnaire onto Hollerith punch cards—similar to voting cards—which were then run through the 1401, which was a little smaller than a library bookcase and could be rented from an IBM susdidiary across town in Roxbury. Within days the student would receive a sprocket-fed computer printout with the names, phone numbers, addresses, colleges, and graduation years of six people. Tarr and Morrill gave their parent company a scientific-sounding name: Compatibility Research Inc. They called the dating service Operation Match.*

In March, just weeks before the official launch, a science editor and future Pulitzer Prize winner at the *Boston Globe* received a tip from his alma mater. Timothy Leland ('60) rushed over to Tarr's corporate headquarters—dorm room G-35, Winthrop House—where he was greeted by a sign on the door: YOUR BUSINESS IS OUR PLEASURE. YOUR PLEASURE IS OUR BUSINESS. Half naked and shaving when Leland barged in, Tarr improvised. Operation Match, he jested, had done a study on which kinds of women prefer which kinds of aftershaves.

"And?" Leland asked.

Tarr explained that Old Spice attracts the All-American ladies, while Royall Lime gets the preppy types. Fascinated, Leland jotted this down and put it in the *Globe* article, the first in-depth piece ever produced on the computer-dating industry, which ran under the front-page headline, "2 Harvard Men Replacing Cupid With Computer." The breathless Leland wrote that Tarr was "masterminding the cleverest business enter-

---

* No relation to today's Match.com.

prise since J.D. Rockefeller invested in oil." The computer, Leland explained, would "analyze all the personality profiles and match the couples up scientifically in less time than it takes to blow a kiss."

"A computer," Tarr told Leland, "can find the right date for a person in a split second, when it might take him or her three years to do it alone." Leland wanted to know if Tarr planned to run his own questionnaire through the computer. "Darn right I do," said Tarr. "Two or three times at least. That's the beauty of being a company president."

The idea, to use modern parlance, went viral. Tarr had tapped into a vein of loneliness and frustration at single-sex schools in the Northeast, and beyond. Operation Match hit colleges across the country.

"This is the greatest excuse for calling up a strange girl that I've ever heard," wrote a computer dater from Williams in a letter to the company.

"No dogs please!" wrote another from Dartmouth.

"The girl you sent me didn't have much upstairs," wrote a third, from Northwestern, "but what a staircase!"

A female computer dater from Connecticut College suspected "that boys don't level" on their questionnaires. "I was honest with mine," she told Shalit, "but I wonder if some guys fill out theirs to see if they can get a first-nighter."

By the fall of sixty-five, six months after the launch, some ninety thousand Operation Match questionnaires had been received, amounting to $270,000 in gross profits, about $1.8 million in today's dollars. Not bad for a scholarship student from small-town Maine. Tarr would need a bigger staff. He pulled in another classmate, a chemistry major named David Crump. Then, walking through Cambridge one day, Tarr struck up a conversation with a dropout from Cornell University named Douglas Ginsburg. A pot-smoking free spirit looking for a cause, Ginsburg was not yet on his way to becoming a Harvard Law School professor and Supreme Court nominee. "A computer-dating service?" laughed Ginsburg, whose friends called him Fug. He signed on right away.

Profits aside, Gene Shalit wanted to know the same thing as the rest of the world: Did it work? Did the computer really make good matches? Was Operation Match a gift from the Great God or mere technogimmickry? "I approve of it as a way to meet people," said an Operation Match subscriber from Yale, "although I have no faith in the questionnaire's ability to match compatible people. The machine has no way of telling whether or not the girl has pizzazz!" By pizzazz, the student referred to that mysterious aspect of romantic connection, chemistry. How could such an elusive quality be quantified and commercialized?

Tarr made no claims. "We're not trying to take the love out of love," he told Shalit, "we're just trying to make it more efficient. We supply everything but the spark." It was an honest response, one rarely heard from today's online-dating companies, which like to differentiate their brands based on scientifically groundbreaking algorithms.

Operation Match might get ten thousand questionnaires returned from any given geographical area. Tarr and his partners would then do a series of "sorts"—sorting the questionnaires, for instance, according to age, then height, then religion, etc. After five or six sorts, the pools would become too small to further differentiate. The vast majority of the 150 questions never came into play. Computer dating was about *more* dates, not better dates.

Harvard being Harvard—a place where students have historically evaded traditional career paths by creating their own jobs—it didn't take long before Operation Match met its first competitor. In the summer of sixty-five, an MIT graduate named David Dewan was preparing to enter Harvard Business School. Having followed the success of Operation Match as it was chronicled in the pages of the *Harvard Crimson*, Dewan thought he could steal some market share.

Over the summer he drafted his own dating questionnaire and taught himself how to write matching code for the Honeywell 200, a car-sized contraption that, at around three o'clock in the morning, could be rented for thirty dollars an hour from a small Boston-based mutual fund company called Fidelity.

Unlike Tarr, whose main interest in computer dating was as a means of self-help, Dewan came to the business with a seriousness that Harvard people associate with their more buttoned-up geek rivals at MIT. Dewan played the part: A rich kid who wore Brooks Brothers and drove a Jaguar, he borrowed ten thousand dollars from his grandfather to start his own computer-dating service. He called the service Eros and its parent company Contact Inc.

Shalit called Dewan "a brilliant math and engineering student" and "a frugal man" who "runs deep in the black." With no full-time employees, Dewan operated Contact out of his grandparents' home near Cambridge. In one distribution of questionnaires, he drew eleven thousand responses at $4 each, or $44,000 in gross profits, about $250,000 in today's dollars.

Dewan entered the fledgling market with guns blazing, telling the *Crimson* that Operation Match's questionnaire was "less sophisticated, appealing to the big, Mid-west universities." In truth, very little distinguished Contact from Operation Match. Operation Match sold its questionnaires for three dollars while Contact charged four dollars. The questions reflected the politics and preoccupations of the era. Both offered three options for race: Caucasian, Oriental, or Negro. Contact's questionnaire was more straight-laced, seeking daters' opinions on whether civil rights laws should be strengthened, whether censorship of students is justifiable, and, prophetically, whether the computer is invading too many aspects of personal life. Dewan asked daters to correlate qualities in themselves with the qualities they desired in a date, such as sociability (friendly versus reserved), conformity (conventional versus eccentric), role in the group (center of attention versus spectator), and sexual history (limited versus experienced).

Operation Match took a more playful approach with its questionnaire. Question 69 posed this dilemma:

> Your roommate gets you a blind date for a big dance. Good looking, your roommate says. When you meet your date, you are sure it's your roommate who is blind—your date is friendly, but embarrassingly unattractive. You:
>
> 1) suggest going to a movie instead.
> 2) monopolize your roommate's date, leaving your roommate only one noble alternative . . .

3) dance with your date, smiling weakly, but end the evening as early
as possible.
4) act very friendly the whole time and run the risk of getting
trapped into a second date.

"If there's some chick I'm dying to go out with," Tarr told Shalit, "I can drop her a note in my capacity as president of Operation Match and say, 'Dear Joan, You have been selected by a highly personal process called Random Sampling to be interviewed extensively by myself . . .'"

Tarr may have been a jokester, but he wasn't going to stand by while Dewan cornered the industry that he had pioneered. In retaliation for Dewan's trash-talking to the *Crimson*, Operation Match alerted authorities that Dewan intended to paper Harvard Yard with questionnaires for Contact. Things got ugly, fast. On September 29, 1965, campus police collared Dewan for the dubious crime of "distributing questionnaires without a permit." The next day the *Crimson* splashed the news across its front page: "University Police Eject Man from Winthrop House."

"Funny," an Operation Match employee later recalled. "The last I heard you didn't need a permit to distribute questionnaires in a dorm. I think our guys were messing with Dewan."

Dewan's enthusiasm was unmarred. "The way I envision things, in 50 years computers may well have reduced our work week to zero hours," he told the *Sarasota Journal*. "We'll date through computers, mate through computers, select our home with the help of computers, and plan our recreation with computers. It will be a fantastic time and my company and I hope to be a large part of it."

Going back to the Newtonians, Dewan's exuberance echoed earlier eras of intellectuals and scientists who believed man's innovations would liberate him from pain and drudgery. Today we can laugh about the zero-hour workweek Dewan predicted. What an idealization to think the machine would supplant the workaholic in us rather than accentuate him! But even while Dewan turned out to be a visionary (everything else he predicted came true, after all), his first taste of utopia was bittersweet.

"Back then I was going out with a girl from Wellesley," he recalled four decades later. "I gave her a free questionnaire, because she helped me distribute in the dorms there. When we ran it through the computer, she and I matched. That was exciting! But I forgot that she also received five other matches, including a guy from Amherst, whom she later dumped me for."

Somewhere in there lurked a lesson about the relationship between technology and the people who use it. Did the machines remain ours to control? Or did they control us?

Meanwhile, on campus, a political science major named Gerry coasted through his last months in Cambridge, pondering his own relationship future. Gerry kept himself busy with bartending jobs, membership in the Hasty Pudding Club, and a term paper about the psychology of speech impediments. Gerry stuttered. He'd come to Harvard via boarding school, where he was mocked savagely for the way he spoke. Despite good looks and charisma, he was, by his own admission, a late bloomer when it came to girls. He tended to seek out self-esteem and identity through friendships with professors.

So when David Dewan swung by Adams House with questionnaires for Contact, Gerry carefully answered all one hundred questions. Accuracy of self-assessment varied. Gerry ranked himself as assertive and said he was looking for someone who was more submissive. He said he was uninhibited and wanted someone more restrained. He preferred security, as opposed to risk taking, and was looking for the same. He was sexually experienced and wanted his date to be similarly experienced. He thought of himself as particularly perceptive, considered himself highly self-confident, and said he appreciated "the aesthetic experience." When asked about verbal fluency, the inveterate reader marked himself inarticulate. He returned the Contact questionnaire with the four-dollar subscription fee.

On Halloween, Gerry received a computer printout in the mail: "Dear Gerry," it began, "My name is Eros. I'm the Contact computer. In the last minute I have introduced you to 4,122 people. Here is your first group of computer matched dates." The list included six Boston-area coeds: Mimi of Wheaton; Ellen of Simmons; Pamela of Wellesley; Romana of Pembroke; Hinda of Boston University; and finally—just for good measure, it seemed, given the distance—Nancy, a nineteen-year-old English major at Mount Holyoke, an all-women's school located ninety miles west of Boston.

Gerry went out with Pamela and Hinda because they were nearby. Both dates were unimpressive.

He set his Contact sheet aside and returned to his studies. In December, as final exams approached, he received a one-line postcard from the sixth girl on his Contact sheet. "Dear Gerry," she wrote, "Do you exist?"

Intrigued, Gerry poured himself two fingers of Prunier, a hard-to-get cognac he enjoyed, and sat down to compose a response.

Dear Nancy:

First let me say that I think it was ingenious of you to write postcards to the negligent boys on your Contact list. I confess that because Mt. Holyoke is so far away, I probably would not have pursued your name. However, your postcard really impressed me. Either you are a very inventive, outgoing girl, or the social life in South Hadley is horrible. Whichever it is, I will look forward to meeting you.

Ten days later, a reply:

Dear Sir Gerald:

How are you so sure you weren't the only guy privileged with receiving a post card? As a matter of fact, you're right. I sent them to everyone, except for 3 names that had already "come to life." "Flop" is a good word for two of them. The other was successful enough, but nothing special. "Contact" seems to have been pretty much a failure for everyone—except for one girl in my dorm who is now pinned, thanks to Eros.

After weeks of correspondence, Gerry drove to Mount Holyoke for a Saturday date. Nancy wrote to him the day after: "I did have a very nice day—and want you to know that I appreciate very much your having driven ¾ of the way across the state and back again! Thanks for showing me around my home town area. Hope you didn't find it all unbearably bucolic."

If he did, the correspondence didn't say. But he enjoyed himself enough to return the invitation, responding that when Nancy visited him in Cambridge, she should be prepared to do "some horseback riding very early on Sunday morning." Pulling out all the stops, he added: "I usually follow that up with bagels and lox in some Jewish restaurant."

Sure, people debated whether Operation Match and Contact worked, whether the chance of meeting someone you liked "via the punch cards" was any better than trolling at a mixer. On campus there was little embarrassment or shame. Odd, given that thirty years later online dating would encounter a strong stigma; to "date online" suggested an inability to meet people in real life. But in the sixties, when Jeff Tarr and David Dewan brought the first incarnations of computer dating to college kids, stigma didn't surround the medium as it later would.

For one thing, a celebrated singles culture was emerging outside Harvard's walls. In urban areas across the country, the energetic young were spending disposable income in "singles bars." Maxwell's Plum, on Manhattan's Upper East Side, was one of the first bars that "respectable" single women could visit alone. (Dorrian's Red Hand, more familiar to today's UES singles, opened in 1960.)* City papers announced upcoming singles events. The *New York Review of Books*, known for its highbrow readers, began its famous personals column in 1965. Developers con-

---

* Project TACT—an acronym for Technical Automated Compatibility Testing—was New York City's first computer dating service. TACT's founders, a young accountant and a programmer from IBM, got their inspiration from Tarr, figuring that the Upper East Side would be a good testing ground: "The demolition of the Third Avenue Elevated subway line set off a building boom and a white-collar influx, most notably of young educated women who suddenly found themselves free of family, opprobrium, and, thanks to birth control, the problem of sexual consequence," Nick Paumgarten later wrote in *The New Yorker*. "Within a year, more than five thousand subscribers had signed on."

structed youth-oriented apartment complexes. Guidebooks helped the unattached navigate the scene.

In some ways this world of urban nightlife and go-go courtship resembled the post–World War I era, when young people took to cars and movie theaters and other commercial amusements. The Roaring Twenties and the Freewheeling Sixties shared an enthusiasm over new technology. Again, though, a taboo greeted one but not the other. The youth of the 1920s "had elicited pity, scorn or fear from the middle class who sought to control their behavior and made them the object of reformation efforts," wrote John D'Emilio and Estelle Freedman in *Intimate Matters: A History of Sexuality in America*. By contrast, in the 1960s "young adults of the middle-class were glamorized; they embodied the unspoken fantasies of a consumer society extended to the sphere of sex."

Rebelling against their parents' suburban sprawl and soulless conformity, youth of the sixties saw staying single as an exciting adventure for those up to the challenge. The new singles culture, said one commentator, was regarded as a "privileged, spotlighted, envied group."

As for computer dating, it's possible that whatever stigma existed at the time was outweighed by the medium's novelty, a coolness factor that comes with being in the know about new gadgetry, particularly for a generation that was reveling in the first film adaptations of Ian Fleming's James Bond series, featuring colorfully blinking walls and programmable computer boards, as well as a dashing Sean Connery carousing his way through a world of killer fountain pens and sports cars with ejector seats, not to mention an endless stream of beautiful women.

"I wanted people to see Operation Match as a novelty," Jeff Tarr remembered, "something neat. I advertised it as a social experiment."

Certainly it was a social experiment. But finding dates via the punch cards was a much different proposition than today's online dating. The pool to which computer dating provided access had known limits: college students in your area. So what if a guy from Harvard was driving ninety miles to date a girl from Mount Holyoke? How much different might she really be from the Radcliffe chick across the Yard? Yes, computer dating brought a new efficiency to the college mating scene. But it merely extended the connections within an already cloistered world. It was not too surprising, then, when early correspondence between the budding lovers revealed that Gerry knew Nancy's brothers from summer camp.

Their relationship progressed into the summer of 1966, with vigorous correspondence between Europe, where Gerry was taking a graduation trip, and the Rocky Mountains, where Nancy spent the summer vacationing with her family. She wrote of her "cumberless rovings" in the woods and of her thoughts on books she was reading, such as *Love Without Fear*, a 1947 marriage guide by Dr. Eustace Chesser, billed as "one of England's most reputable marriage counselors" and "the foremost authority on sex technique."

From Goose Prairie, Washington, Nancy reported on a special guest: "William Douglas, the Supreme Court Justice, came for dinner last night with his new wife—#4, age 23. I'd always expected a Supreme Court Justice to be a very imposing person, but he's not. He's just an ordinary, nervous individual—especially when I spoke to him. He knows people are thinking about his marrying a girl 1/3 his age."

Despite her precocious acuity, the twenty-year-old Nancy did not know that her dinner guest was, in both his private and public lives, a crusader for the liberalization of relationship politics in America, not unlike Nancy was, albeit unwittingly, when she decided to write to the negligent boys on her Contact list. In June of sixty-five, two months after Jeff Tarr opened for business, the Supreme Court handed down one of its most progressive decisions. In *Griswold v. Connecticut*, the sixty-six-year-old Justice Douglas reasoned that even though "privacy" is mentioned nowhere in the Bill of Rights, a "right to privacy" could be divined in the "penumbras" and "emanations" of other constitutional protections. The holding in *Griswold*, which struck down Connecticut's ban on contraception, established a right to marital privacy. While state laws against sodomy and abortion remained on the books, the Court's decision in *Griswold* sent a strong message to state legislatures: Mating decisions are sacrosanct. Two years later, in *Loving v. Virginia*, a unanimous Court struck down Virginia's antimiscegenation statute, the Racial Integrity Act of 1924, ending race-based legal restrictions on marriage. In 1972 the Court expanded *Griswold*'s holding to unmarried couples; that case, *Eisenstadt v. Baird*, established a more fundamental right to control reproduction and laid groundwork for the Court's landmark abortion decision in *Roe v. Wade* the following year.

For a culture whose courtship practices were undergoing rapid liberalization, these Supreme Court rulings can be seen as a response to, an accommodation of, or just the obvious result of recent developments in American mating. In the 1950s, the crude competition of dating's early years—when men showed off their assets and expressed their interest in terms of resource expenditure, while women worked hard to cultivate an aura of popularity—was giving way to the postwar generation's desire for security in an uncertain world. This desire for security transformed dating into the custom of "going steady." Many young people, by going steady, did not expect to marry but to act as if they were already married: The boy gave the girl some visible token (class ring, letter sweater, etc.); he had to call her a certain number of times per week and take her on a certain number of dates; and exclusivity was assumed. Under the new going-steady complex, a "beleaguered system of sexual control based on the resolve of young girls to say no, at least to the final step of actual intercourse, was further breaking down," writes Beth Bailey in *From Front Porch to Back Seat: Courtship in Twentieth-Century America*.

The old dating system versus the new going-steady complex: both located power in the control of the scarce resource—access to sex. "Through at least the first two-thirds of the twentieth century," writes Bailey, "Americans thought of courtship as a system governed by laws of scarcity and abundance, and acted in accordance with that perception." Regardless of which courting system reigned at a given time, *scarcity* would always be the natural social control reinforcing the system du jour. Scarcity would always be the irrefragable regulatory device that—along with religion and moral dogma—would keep the youth in line with certain expectations, forestalling the doomsday scenario of a society run amok in the pursuit of unchecked desire.

But wait. Suppose some Harvard math whiz came along with an idea to harness technology in a way that was so big, so fresh, that it could change the game entirely? Not by solving some riddle of scarcity, but by smashing the whole concept of scarcity to pieces, eradicating its relevancy altogether. Why settle for the smug and entitled Cliffies, asked the height-challenged Jeff Tarr, when I can meet every girl at every school?

Like the *Griswold* case, the revolutionary technology that brought Nancy and Gerry together was a portent, if not a precursor, to what would become the sexual revolution of the late 1960s and 1970s. And yet, in the narrative of that sexual revolution, from the Pill to *Playboy* magazine to the North American Swingers Club to the countercultural battle cry of "free love," computer dating never became a character. This is probably because the technology faded out before it could spread past college campuses. There was no Internet to optimize matching or let users search for themselves, discreetly.

When Gene Shalit left Harvard to write his article, Tarr planned to install hundreds of "special typewriters" around campus, all linked to "a centralized mother computer." A boy typing in his requirements would receive in seconds the name of a compatible girl who was free that night. The project never panned out, but the computer dating pioneered by Tarr and Dewan was still a major first step in applying a new tool and a new way of thinking to the mating dance, what Justice William Brennan termed the "great and mysterious motive force in human life."

As for Nancy and Gerry, they would marry in 1967. Medical careers would take them from Boston to Syracuse to Denver to Minneapolis, where, in 1977, they would become your correspondent's parents, just as their marriage was careering toward divorce.

The story of how my parents met seems quaint when one compares those clunky old IBMs to the complex algorithms, flashy Web sites, and smart-phone applications employed by dating services today. But it shows that the subject of how technology affects relationships is hardly new.

In the 1920s, Judge Ben Lindsey sat on Denver's Juvenile and Family Court, where he witnessed, firsthand, the chaos of the technologically driven sexual revolution. Judge Lindsey held heart-to-heart meetings with the youngsters who came through his court, during which he gathered stats on teen pregnancy and how teenagers were mating. He condemned adults for their silence in the face of youthful questioning.

Judge Lindsey came to believe that certain modern conveniences had changed mating practices so quickly that Jazz Age youth were left in a kind of cultural lurch: The rules and values they'd been raised with no longer applied. While Lindsey knew that young people had been rebellious in plenty of earlier eras, he argued that Jazz Age youth were different. The youth of past generations didn't have the same economic independence. "Now," he wrote, "it has it. Machinery has made that possible." The "agencies of modern life" to which Lindsey referred in his 1925 book, *The Revolt of Modern Youth*, were ubiquitous:

> Those that immediately present themselves are the automobile (and soon the aeroplane with the kids spooning in the clouds), the telephone, the motion picture, the radio, the jazz dance, jazz music, jazz booze, jazz journalism, "crime wave," the permanent wave, the permanent passing of the chaperone, the parking of the corset, the feminine invasion of the barber shop, growing and changing standards of living, rising wages . . . electrical appliances that make women something more than drudges in their homes. . . . The list, you see, includes among other things physical comforts and speeding-up devices of all kinds; and the effect of it all is enormously stimulating.

The social upheaval that Lindsey described began in the early twentieth century, around the time of World War I, when courtship shifted from the privacy of the home to the public sphere of dance halls, movie theaters, and automobiles, giving young people more control over their dating lives and access to a wider social circle. Sound familiar?

Before dating there had been "calling," a system taken from the English upper class, in which a gentleman would visit a woman at her home in the presence of her family. Tea, cakes, doilies, a meddling aunt perched on the couch's arm—these things made a proper setting for the negotiation of love. Calling, by controlling access to a scarce resource, placed control over mating and sexual limits in the hands of women and their families. The idea was that women, through their special virtue, helped men reconcile morality (a devotion to family) with instinct (the sexual urge), while the change a man brought to her life was more tangible, a material rather than spiritual alteration.

The rise of "dating" coincided with the advent of the automobile and the rise of cinema. Unlike the carriage that preceded it, the motorcar had speed, which meant *exploration! adventure! excitement!* Henry Ford and his ilk believed they were marketing something to bring the family together. The car may have achieved that. But it also released youth from the tyranny of parental oversight. Forget tea parties and hay rides. Now every date was a bedroom on wheels. In 1919 the country had seven million registered cars; ten years later that number would have more than tripled. Some cars had front seats that folded back to blend with the backseats. For those who couldn't afford a car with a backseat (the Model T sold for $290, $3,300 in today's money), there was always the back row. Though many in the upper class continued to regard movies— "flickers"—as morally repugnant, working-class society, less restrained by rigid sexual mores, found privacy and romance in the darkness of the cinema. "Oh, oh, that picture show spoon," went a popular jingle, "that's what put kissing on the boon." Marathon sessions of "necking," "heavy petting," and close dancing known as "button shining" replaced the buttoned-up courtship of old. These technologies marginalized old controls by providing islands of privacy to lovers who were suddenly flung out into the public realm, free at last to remake the rules.

But more freedom meant greater uncertainty in courtship, and thus more confusion. When a man came to visit a woman in her family's home, the agenda was clear: an interview couched in a chaperoned social call. But . . . a *date*? What was that about? A date was supposed to end in . . . *something*, yes. But what exactly was the date itself? And more important, what did it imply? Radcliffe College's *Red Book*, which furnished girls with the school's rules of conduct, printed a list of approved restaurants in which they could dine with a young man. Some were acceptable only before 7:30 P.M.; others posed a threat to reputation. The etiquette expert Emily Post wondered why, even though "she may not lunch with him in a restaurant, she is sometimes (not always) allowed to go to a moving picture matinee with him! Why sitting in the dark in a moving picture theater is allowed, and the restaurant is tabu is very mysterious." Miss Manners threw up her arms.

"With the old order of things," wrote Frederick Lewis Allen, a historian of the 1920s, "had gone a set of values which had given richness and meaning to life, and substitute values were not easily found."

For most of the nineteenth century, couples tended to encourage openness with each other, as seen in the letters that flew back and forth prior to the age of the telephone and other innovations, such as the bicycle, that provided connection and proximity. In place of premarital petting, the sharing of confidences defined intimacy. In 1926, *Harper's* magazine reported that, until 1913, "the rule for young couples was conversation in pairs about serious things. There weren't many cars, most movies were not approved of. . . . Couples would spend hours discussing each other." While close dancing and the picture show spoon meant more "contact," emotional openness suffered.

With the birth of broadcast radio and mass advertising in the 1920s, conformity became the new value. "A growing emphasis on personality and physical attractiveness made self-exposure a risky proposition," writes courtship historian Ellen Rothman. To catch a mate you needed to know the right fads, have the right *line*.

Never had standards for behavior undergone such radical change in such a short period of time. The youth that came of age in the 1920s, writes Rothman, "were separated from their parents by as wide a gulf" as had ever separated two American generations. "By 1930, the terrain through which young Americans passed en route to marriage would be almost unrecognizable to their parents." The new code was accompanied by a disillusionment that no amount of fast driving could outrun. Values are primal in their hardwiring. It's difficult to substitute one for another without causing distress. Now, thanks to the widespread acceptance of contraception and a more liberal attitude toward premarital sex, young people faced a new reality: Sex could be divorced from child-bearing. So what was marriage for? Did good sex make for good marriage?

People may have reveled in the new freedom, but that didn't mean they were happy. The trending divorce rate of today began in this postwar decade: In 1910 there were 8.8 divorces for every 100 marriages; by 1928, the rate had doubled—to almost one divorce in every six marriages.

What distinguished the post–World War I generation, wrote journalist Walter Lippmann, was not its rebellion but rather its disillusionment with its rebellion. That "they should distrust the new freedom no less than the old certainties" was "something of a novelty," Lippmann wrote in his 1929 bestseller, *A Preface to Morals.* The wild success of Lippmann's book, which tried to lay the foundation for a new system of belief, suggested that people were tired of tobogganing into mental chaos. "The inexperienced," Lippmann wrote, "must be offered some kind of hypothesis when they are confronted with the necessity of making choices: they cannot be so utterly open-minded that they stand inert until something collides with them."

Lippmann would die in 1974, two decades before the Internet went mainstream. As the pace of technology quickened, his words would gain in resonance for generations to come.

ALEXIS, PART I

It's Hard Meeting Men in the City

IT WAS THE SUMMER OF 2005, DURING COLLEGE, WHEN ALEXIS FELL hard for a guy. They had great, memorable dates for several weeks. Then it came out that he had a serious girlfriend who was out of town. "At this point," she remembered, "I was in too deep and stupidly forgave him. He swore to me that he would come clean to her. He did. But she flew home the next day, and he left me for her anyway. Good times."

After college in Colorado, Alexis moved to New York City to attend Parsons, the prestigious fashion and design institute. She'd loved the laid-back vibe of mountain life. But, like her hometown of Chicago, it was too clean, too banal. As an artist, she much preferred the grime and grit of her new Lower East Side neighborhood, where she became addicted to falafel, the Mister Softee ice cream truck, and deli sandwiches with fried eggs and cream cheese. She hummed Lou Reed's "Rock n' Roll," pretending she was the Jenny he sang about, who one fine morning put on a New York station and couldn't believe what she heard at all.

With wit, freckles, a fun sense of humor, and a body toned by frequent yoga, Alexis was confident in her appearance and only a little self-conscious about her jowly cheeks. Men were attracted to her, she knew. She just needed to learn how to avoid the bad ones. But sometimes Alexis got lonely. So she spent time on social-networking sites, where any decent-looking woman could get the attention of at least a dozen guys. "The attention," she said, "revives me."

"I'm twenty-four," she would remind herself when feeling down, "and I'm awesome."

Shortly after moving to New York Alexis began dating Chad, a law student she met at a party. Her father is an attorney. So Chad felt right. He lived across the river in Brooklyn Heights and had a big trust fund. She'd always dreamed of living in a nice house in Kentucky, where she has relatives, and she could see it happening with this guy. They both loved the jam band Phish—an important glue in their relationship—and even though he still had an ex-girlfriend in the picture, when Alexis forced him to choose between them, he chose Alexis.

There was some weirdness, though. He became angry when Alexis wore revealing clothes, such as a tank top with low-cut armholes that showed her bra. "My professors live around here," he would scold her. "Keep that outfit in the Lower East Side!"

"What does he expect?" she thought. "I'm a fashion student."

They also did a lot of drugs, a habit she'd hoped to leave behind in college, when she'd struggled through a relationship with a recovering heroin addict. For her twenty-fourth birthday, Chad took Alexis to a sex shop in Soho called Kiki de Montparnasse, and told her to pick out anything she wanted from among the haute couture whips, leather pony harnesses, and headbands with horse ears. Intimidated, Alexis chose a tamer offering, the Mia vibrator by Lelo, a lipstick-sized travel companion that recharges in any USB port. Then they checked into a fancy hotel, where, on a table, he traced their names, "Chad + Alexis," through a pile of cocaine.

Eventually Chad's insecurity and fawning turned her off, and she left him, feeling a little bad about having been so attracted to his money in the first place. Soon after she began seeing a forty-year-old man she met on a social-networking site for music. He lived just a few blocks away and helped her get an internship at a music label. He was urbane and mature, and this turned her on despite his inconsistent nature. She would wait anxiously in her apartment for his text messages before realizing that, to him, she was nothing more than a plaything. She knew she needed to set boundaries but found it difficult.

"It's hard to meet people in the city," Alexis said. "It seems to be one disaster after the next. They're fine hanging out, talking all the time, and of course fucking. But the second they smell you actually caring about them, they bounce. The ones who are crazy about me, I'm not into. The ones I'd do anything for don't care."

Alexis always thought of online dating as a place for desperate people—until a friend of hers had success on Match.com. For months the friend enjoyed a couple of dinners out a week, with a bunch of different men, and then got engaged to a nice guy. Maybe, Alexis thought, she should give it a shot.

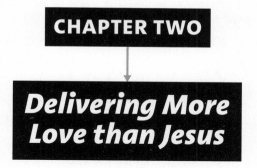

CHAPTER TWO

Delivering More Love than Jesus

HOW ONLINE DATING BECAME MODERN

We are the most important search engine on the Web, not Google. The search for companionship is more important than the search for song lyrics.

—Sam Yagan, chief executive officer, OkCupid

As a youngster in Skokie, Illinois, during the late 1970s, Gary Kremen's future did not seem bright. Half geek, half hoodlum, he recalls getting into the "usual juvenile stuff"—busting windows, breaking into schools, and computer hacking. With his parents' blessing, the police picked Kremen up one day and showed him the inside of a jail cell.

Short, heavyset, and socially awkward, Kremen was accustomed to losing many of life's contests. Making money, he knew, was the one metric on which he might be able to compete, but not if he was locked up.

Although Kremen's high school grades were less than stellar, he managed to talk his way into Northwestern University in an interview by touting his entrepreneurial zeal and technological skills. In 1981, he began a double major in business and electrical engineering. At graduation he turned down several offers from corporate recruiters in favor of a job with a government aerospace contractor, where he was introduced to ARPANET—the Advanced Research Projects Agency Network—the U.S. Defense Department's online network, which eventually became the Internet.

Kremen went on to pick up an MBA from Stanford, and then became one of the Internet's first entrepreneurs. His roommate worked for Sun Microsystems and had a high-speed Internet connection. At night they would download Unix software for free, repackage it, and then sell it. Kremen led the company, Los Altos Technology, until investors replaced him with a new CEO in 1993.

Weeks later, he was taking a shower when the idea struck him: What if I put classified ads online?

Kremen took a $2,500 advance on his credit card and acquired several domain names from the government: Jobs.com, Housing.com, Autos .com, Sex.com, and a fifth domain name that was less literal than the others, Match.com. Match, according to Kremen's vision, would be the personals "vertical" in a larger entity called Electric Classifieds.

"I thought it would be really interesting to use the Internet for relationships, and to do it right," he told *Wired* magazine at the time. The tone of the *Wired* story gives a sense of how Kremen's plan was received: "Cyberlove and chat room couplings are as much a part of online lore as hacker fiends and wild viruses. So, connecting and tracking these millions of plugged-in lonely hearts is a prime business opportunity." Even at a tech magazine, online dating was fodder for derision. But Kremen didn't care. He bought a $750,000 server on credit from Sun Microsystems and, with $1.7 million in venture capital financing, unveiled Match in 1995.

The idea, like Jeff Tarr's idea for Operation Match, was not completely original. Both Tarr and Kremen were second-comers who did it better and with more propitious timing.

Over in France, in the 1980s, Marc Simoncini, who would eventually run Meetic.com, Europe's largest online-dating site, got his start in the computer matching business by hosting services, known as *messageries roses*, or pink chat rooms. These were essentially dating chat rooms, made possible by the Minitel, a text-only computer that hooked into the phone and connected 90 percent of French homes.

The Minitel chat rooms had a precursor in the United States: bulletin board systems, or BBSs, which comprised the online world before the online world went mainstream. The BBS revolution began during Chicago's Great Blizzard of 1978, when Ward Christensen was shut in by the snow. Bored, Christensen, a computer hobbyist and former IBM employee, decided to invent a way to digitize his computer club's message board, a pushpin board on which members posted three-by-five-inch cards with things like "Need ride to next meeting," "Let's get together for a group-purchase of memory chips," "Anyone else have a KIM-1?"

Christensen's creation became the world's first bulletin board system. Early BBSs would be used by clubs and communities to stay in touch and share information. Users needed a computer—such as an IBM XT, an Apple II, a Commodore 64, or Radio Shack's TRS 100—plus a software package; a modem; and a phone line. You accessed a BBS by dialing into the phone number allocated to it. Each BBS was run by a person known as the system operator, or sysop, who was usually the creator of the BBS. It was his phone number that users dialed into.

Nearly everything on BBSs was presented in text, called ASCII, or rendered in low-resolution images called ANSI art. Some BBSs experimented with high-resolution formats, such as remote imaging protocol. Unlike the Web pages of today, BBSs operated as individual systems: They did not converge or connect; information contained on one BBS was not shared with another. The original 110- and 300-baud modems made the first BBSs painfully slow. With the introduction of 1200-baud modems, speed improved dramatically, and so did the popularity of BBSs. The BBS universe would grow to more than sixty thousand boards during the eighties. Geeks could finally unite online. It was their moment. The movie *Weird Science*, a 1985 sci-fi comedy written and directed by John Hughes, portrayed two young geeks who, inspired by the story of Frankenstein, used a computer to create the woman of their dreams by turning on a modem and feeding magazine photographs into a scanner, literally dialing her up.

These movie geeks were close contemporaries of Jon Boede and Scott Smith, two young computer whizzes in Texas. In 1984, Boede and Smith launched the Matchmaker Electronic Pen-Pal Network, known simply as Matchmaker, the first online social network geared toward romance. "We had some awful press coverage," Boede told Andrea Orr for her book about the early years of online dating. "The editors would always turn the story into something like, 'Computer Nerds Need Love Too.' But it was clear to us that we were on to something." In eighty-five, Boede met his girlfriend online.

The Matchmaker network grew into a nationwide chain of fourteen local BBSs spread throughout Texas, California, Florida, Arizona, New York, Illinois, and Virginia. But Boede remained national network administrator, or master sysop. "We call him God," said twenty-seven-year-old Bobby Dominguez. "He's the guy who created it all." Dominguez ran Matchmaker's local BBS for Tampa, Florida. Nonmembers could browse free of charge for three and a half hours. After that, he charged fifty dollars for one hundred hours. Users chose "platonic" or "romantic" mode. A woman whose data showed she was only interested in pen pals would not be introduced to men seeking romance.

In 1992, as BBSs were waning, the *Tampa Bay Times* covered Dominguez's Matchmaker franchise. The paper foreshadowed the imminent demise of BBSs when it noted, at the end of the article, that "Matchmaker also offers a link to the Internet, a worldwide system." Users could soon log in through Matchmaker.com. In a couple of years, when the Internet— along with its most popular application, the World Wide Web—went mainstream, the world of BBSs would try to keep up by becoming more visually appealing. But they could do nothing to offset the appeal of the Web, and eventually faded out.

BBS inventor Ward Christensen saw the usurpation as a good thing. BBS users, he would later say, had been "more elitist, more computer people." Even though early Internet communities seemed to lack the vibrant social energy that had characterized the best BBSs, the Internet meant greater utility, efficiency, and access. Not just for geeks but for everyone.

For online dating, however, the battle was just beginning.

Once computer dating left Harvard in the late 1960s and began to be marketed to the general public, the notion that only the desperate or the criminal would turn to such a scandalous and seemingly scattershot method finally caught up with it. It was one thing for college kids to find each other through a computer-matching system. Quite another for the population at large.

In the early seventies, James Schur, a former advertising executive in Boston, ran a computer-dating company called Phase II. Schur was scheduled to appear on Johnny Carson's *Tonight Show*. But the invitation was rescinded at the eleventh hour when NBC executives became concerned that advertisers would flee.

Even the era's literature reflected societal suspicion. In 1971, an upstart author named Don DeLillo referenced computer dating in his debut novel, *Americana*. The book's opening scene contains a hostile exchange between the protagonist, a philandering television executive named David Bell, and a young woman named Pru.

"Quincy tells me you've got a new boyfriend," David says to Pru. "Quincy tells me you met him through a computer dating system."

Pru replies: "That lying bastard."*

Dating services had a reputation for drawing losers, Phase II's Schur conceded. He also pointed out that there are "losers everywhere."

That's not to say the fledgling industry wasn't producing happy couples. Data-Mate, a service that cropped up at MIT in 1968, brought together Lawrence Krakauer, a grad student in engineering, with Margret Berman. Forty-five years later, they're still married. "Despite the detailed questionnaire," Krakauer said, "Margret always thought we were matched because we were both short, educated, and Jewish. But, hey, it worked."

Others were less pleased. *Dear Dating Computer*, a book published

---

* I wrote to DeLillo to ask him where, in the late sixties, he'd heard of computer dating. The author replied, somewhat mystified: "I can only speculate that I heard about such a service from someone I knew. Certainly I had no firsthand experience in the matter, and until I saw your letter I would never have guessed that computer dating had somehow sneaked into the novel." There's a decent chance that DeLillo, who in 1964 left his advertising job at Ogilvy & Mather to become a writer, heard of such a service through reports or gossip concerning TACT, New York City's first computer-dating service.

in 1968, compiled letters sent to computer-dating services around the country. The book divided the letters into two sections: The Requirements ("I have studied your questionnaire and frankly I would be most compatible with someone who hates his parents as much as I do") and The Results ("The date was bow-legged, wore glasses, had a faint mustache, and talked with a lisp. I didn't have to pay $6 to find her. If I wanted that kind of a girl I could have gone out with one of my sister's friends").

Given the stigma and the lack of an Internet to spread the word, computer dating remained a small industry. A few video-dating services, like Teledate and Introvision, tried and failed in the early seventies. Finally, one had success. In 1976, Jeffrey Ullman, a handsome young techie and former sixties radical, had been working in broadcasting ever since graduating from the University of California–Berkeley with a journalism degree. Back home in Los Angeles one night, twenty-six and newly married to the first of what would be several wives, Ullman began complaining that he couldn't find a job because it was too hard to meet people in LA. Then he remembered a party he'd videotaped, years earlier, with a camera he got for graduation, a Sony AVC 3400 Porta Pak. When he'd played the tape for a friend who hadn't been at the party, the friend spotted a woman he wanted to meet. Ullman arranged it, and they dated for a year.

The Sony Porta Pak technology, invented in 1967, was archaic. But in the midseventies, several Japanese electronics companies had started backing the new VHS format to compete with Sony's Betamax. Bingo.

Ullman founded Great Expectations, naming his company after the novel by Charles Dickens. The idea was to take old-school matchmaking methods and mix them with modern technology. Members would go to a Great Expectations office, where they would read through three-ring binders of printed profiles. If they liked a profile, they could check out the person's videotape. Ullman would then place personal phone calls to his members with news of a "mutual consent."

It wasn't a bad idea, but there were some problems. For one thing, the tricky logistics—users had to visit a physical place—made it onerous and inefficient. While some people were open to selecting dates based on videos, far fewer were keen on being filmed themselves. The often mannered performances posed difficulties for editors. "I'm a twenty-five-year subscriber to both *Playboy* and the *New Yorker* magazine," emphasized one video dater in a popular montage viewable on YouTube. "Hi Mom," chirped another.

It was just, well, really awkward.

MADtv, the sketch-comedy series that began competing with *Saturday Night Live* in the nineties, ran a regular skit called "Lowered Expectations." In one, a young Shaquille O'Neal dressed in drag posed as "Denise Rodman," the fictional sister of eccentric basketball great Dennis Rodman. In another episode, the company representative of Lowered Expectations pitched the business like this:

> Are you desirably impaired? Do you find yourself serving punch at parties? Would you describe yourself as shy? Old-fashioned? Not on anyone's A-list? Is your ideal date someone in their early twenties with a perfect body and a sparkling personality? Well, unless you win the lottery, you're never going to land that dreamboat. But that doesn't mean you can't find . . . *somebody*. And that's why Lowered Expectations may be for you.

Ullman loved the mockery. It meant his business was becoming relevant. It also helped shape his marketing. Losers, Ullman would argue, are those singles who complain bitterly about the people they're meeting yet do nothing about it. But when Santa Monica Bank advertised that it handles "more zeros than a dating service," Ullman was livid. He organized a demonstration on the bank's doorstep. "Since Santa Monica Bank believes that single people are zeros," he said, "we're asking all people, single and married, to reduce their bank accounts to zero." He handed out bumper stickers that said "I'M NO ZERO." The ploy won him mention in the *Wall Street Journal*. And later, when TV talk-show host Montel Williams asked Ullman if he was preying on lonely people, Ullman shot back: "Yes. Just like restaurants prey on the hungry and doctors prey on the sick and talk-show hosts prey on the people who are too bored to read a book."

Video dating grew in the 1980s and early 1990s, and facilitated many marriages. It also brought in big bucks for Ullman and his partners. At its peak, Great Expectations had forty-nine franchises and grossed $65 million per year, bolstered by a huge direct-mailing campaign. Ullman drove a Cadillac and collected African art. He hired and fired his mother, twice. In the press he derided his sister, who also worked at Great Expectations, for being overweight and a lesbian. "Sometimes he seems to be incredibly proud of being an asshole," his sister told the *Los Angeles Times*. "Jeffrey would call it tough love. It just gets to a point where you say, 'Do I want to be loved that way?'"

In 1995, as Gary Kremen was launching Match, Great Expectations was sold to a financial-services firm for $88 million. But despite Ullman's business success, video dating never won wide acceptance or overcame its stigma. It would remain a punch line. The matchmaking industry was anxious to see whether its next iteration would break through, go mainstream. "The only people online in the nineties were socially awkward geeks," says OkCupid's Sam Yagan. "So, by definition, they were the bulk of the people doing online dating."

Was that the reason for the stigma? What did membership in a dating service imply that was so bad? For the answer, we must flash back three hundred years, to the beginning of media itself.

In 1690 in Britain, not long after the newspaper was invented, mate seekers began using the "personal advertisement" to find husbands, wives, and "unspecified arrangements"—code for someone seeking a homosexual partner. "Being single past the age of 21 was considered almost shameful in that era," writes H. G. Cocks in *Classified: The Secret History of the Personal Column*, "and the ads were often a last resort for the men who advertised and the women who read them. If a match resulted, it is unlikely that you boasted the fact to your friends."

Even though matchmaking had been around for centuries, this new form of mate finding—more a searching system than a matching system—garnered harsh criticism. Part of this stigma stemmed from a major ideological shift in how Western culture viewed marriage.

Prior to the eighteenth century marriage was still an arrangement for building a home and a family. And for as long as these arranged marriages existed there had been arrangers: the priest in medieval Catholic society; the rabbi, *yenta*, or *shadchan* in Judaism; the *nokado* in Japan; the *portador* in Mexico; the *kalyn* in Russia. Women were kept inside in Plato's ancient Greece while Athenian men, guys with names like Draco and Heron and Lysander, postponed marriage as long as possible, preferring a public to a domestic life. When the time finally came, female matchmakers, instructed either by the bride's father or husband-to-be, would conduct negotiations. The first known dating agency was run by parish priests in sixteenth-century England, when vicars assembled lists of candidates and paired them based on supposed compatibility.

As spiritual advisers and authority figures, matchmakers were trusted to form wise pairings based on practical considerations such as wealth, politics, and property. The transactions they facilitated could be just as commercially and religiously driven as the relationships sought out on today's more no-nonsense dating sites, such as WealthyMen.com, for men who make at least eighty-five thousand dollars a year and "want to meet interesting and beautiful women," and Jdate.com, which "ensures that Jewish traditions are sustained for generations to come."

It was not until the middle of the eighteenth century, shortly after the personal ad came along, that certain intellectual trends—namely, Romanticism—put a new emphasis on self-expression. The Romantics, according to the *Encyclopedia of Human Relationships*, cast courtship as nothing less than "an individual heroic quest for life meaning, personal identity, and a kind of terrestrial salvation." In a trend that continued from the 1700s to the 1970s, "marriage became redefined from a practical social arrangement . . . to the formal public recognition of a private romantic love."

Classifieds made a comeback in America in the 1960s and 1970s, encouraged by the era's inclination toward individualism and social exhibitionism. "Everybody was letting it all hang out in other ways," said Raymond Shapiro, a business manager for the *New York Review of Books*, "so suddenly it was okay to display oneself in print. It was very important to be 'self-aware.' So you'd get ads like: 'Astrologer, 27, psychology student, desires to establish non-superficial friendship with sensitive, choicelessly aware persons who are non-self-oriented, deep, and wish to unearth real, personness relationships.'"

People got picky. This created some inconsistencies: While the romantic ethos and its emphasis on pickiness reignited the demand for marriage intermediaries, it also made the idea of getting help ideologically unattractive. Romantic love, after all, was "a supernatural force existing outside of conventional social institutions." The use of a commercial intermediary risked profaning "love's sacred essence and was the admission of personal failure." Westerners adopted a view of how two people should meet that went hand in hand with romantic love: Since our relationships are a product of fate, one should leave the problem of finding a soul mate to the universe. This is serendipity: finding good things without seeking them out.

It's been a classic critique of online dating that too little happens online that's not planned out. In 2011, *The New Yorker* observed that the "Internet subverts Kismet," while *GQ* announced, "Technology has trumped serendipity." Technology expands our choices. But it also requires instructions, narrowing inputs: no kids; over five feet eight inches; makes upward of one hundred thousand dollars a year; etc. With all our Googling activities, we no longer "happen upon." Instead, we heat seek via search engine, stuck inside what one author coined the "filter bubble." The thing that was thought to be one of online dating's biggest virtues—the ability to control and direct one's relationship life—was also bothersome.

At the moment, much of society still clings to the idea that two people are "made for each other" even while it conflicts with what we know to be the less romantic reality: Had those two people never met, each would have, most likely, found someone just as unique. And still, we can't resist a good "meet cute"—a Hollywood term describing the most important consideration for the writer of romances: How will the couple *meet*? Regardless of how *uncute* the real-world meeting may actually be—*he bought me a drink at happy hour; she shared her notes in criminal law*—it's a story nonetheless, something that can be told and embellished over time, and one that is unique to each couple. The stigma that attached to meeting through an intermediary reinforced how hardwired this idea had become.

So when Gary Kremen came along with Match.com, it remained to be seen whether, given the utility of the Internet, people could be enticed to see serendipity in a new light.

In the early 1990s, Trish McDermott, a recent college graduate, helped market an offline matchmaking service in San Francisco. The service, called the Patricia Moore Group, charged singles anywhere from five thousand to fifty thousand dollars to find "high-end, needle-in-a-haystack matches." One male client demanded to meet only women involved in the arts. Another narrowed it to the ballet.

The job taught McDermott that no amount of career success guarantees someone will find love; wealthy people have the same fundamental problems as everyone else when it comes to relationships. The matchmaking business taught her something else as well: Singles, rich and poor, would pay good money in the pursuit of companionship.

Toward the end of 1994, shortly after Netscape launched its Web browser, McDermott read an article in the *San Francisco Chronicle* about someone out of Stanford Business School who was doing something with the Internet related to dating. When McDermott met him, Gary Kremen oscillated between awkwardness and confidence. After launching Match, he came to his first television interview wearing a tie-dyed shirt and declared that his Web site would "bring more love to the planet than anything since Jesus Christ."

To lure in people who were already using newspaper personals, Kremen experimented with membership fees at or below the cost of the print competition. In early 1996, after building the membership up to sixty thousand users, he turned on pricing, starting at $9.95 per month.

"Today, a dating site that has sixty thousand people would feel like a pretty light community," says McDermott, whom Kremen hired to handle Match's marketing. "But at the time, to be able to find twenty-five people who matched your basic criteria and lived in your area—that was awesome. Some argued that we'd never make money, since everyone thought everything on the Internet was supposed to be free. But coming from my old job, where I saw people pay fifty thousand dollars to find someone, I knew that dating was a unique service."

In the days of newspaper and magazine personals, mate searchers were advised to place their ads in the publications they read, suggesting that mutual allegiance to a print product might be a proxy for compatibility. In this way, personals provided a measure of search capability but not the matching service that online dating offered. With Kremen's simple idea of putting the personals online, search and match had finally been merged, and the introductions business took a giant step in the direction of user control.

It was this control that separated online dating, and the Internet in general, from all other media that came before. The Internet, writes communications historian Tim Wu in *The Master Switch: The Rise and Fall of Information Empires*, "defies every expectation one has developed from experience of other media industries, which are all predicated on control of the customer, whereas the Internet abdicates control to the individual; that is its special allure, its power to be endlessly surprising."

In the mid-1990s, the online community was still quite small. About 5 percent of Americans had Internet access, and the majority of people online were men. So Kremen got every woman he knew to post a profile on his site. Even though he was in a relationship, he signed up for Match and asked his girlfriend to do so as well. When membership reached critical mass, Kremen discovered that his success, like that of David Dewan thirty years earlier, would come at his own expense: Kremen's girlfriend met someone else through Match and left him. Oh well. At least he knew the site worked.

The problem, however, was that the site's most satisfied customers were unlikely to spread the word. Meeting your mate online was like getting a nose job—you'd just as soon not tell anyone about it. "In those first few years at Match," McDermott says, "people who met their partner or spouse on the site would lie about it. At one wedding, I watched a couple who met on Match stand up before their friends, relatives, and church community and lie about how they met. They felt it would cast a shadow over their marriage." When successful Match users called the company with requests to have hard copies of their profiles mailed to them for posterity, they'd often request that the profiles be sent in blank envelopes, without the Match emblem, so the mailman wouldn't see. "Here people were, meeting the love of their life and feeling like they'd done something wrong!"

But the stigma they felt was real. Lois Smith Brady, the journalist who began writing the Vows column for the *New York Times* in the early nineties, remembers hearing about a couple who met online. She was reluctant to cover the wedding: "It seemed so risky and dangerous. What if other people followed?" The stigma was also felt by Match's financial backers. Kremen's venture capitalists never fully embraced the online-dating industry, even as success stories abounded: more than two hundred marriages reported; a dozen babies; and countless dates. As membership grew by as much as 10 percent a week, Kremen clashed with the board over issues like whether to include gays on the site. The board removed Kremen but failed to find a CEO replacement, and decided to wash their hands of online dating. In 1997, Match was sold to a consumer-services company for $7 million, of which Kremen walked away with a small fraction—and no girlfriend.

"It's really a bummer," he told the *San Francisco Chronicle* at the time. "I've helped a lot of people, but it just hasn't helped me."

Copycats followed. Jdate, the site for Jewish singles, and Lavalife, based in Canada, entered the market. Nerve Personals, the personals portion of an online magazine for "literate smut," was a hit with the kinds of intellectual, edgy urbanites found on OkCupid today. Gradually, the industry gained ground. Matchmaker.com, born in the BBS era, built a loyal following, with about four million registered daters. In 2000, it sold to Lycos for $44.5 million.

Customer patronage and societal acceptance were different things, however, and the lingering stigma meant that the online-dating industry was largely ignored during the Internet boom of the late nineties—with one exception.

Having dropped out of UCLA after one semester, Barry Diller found himself working in the mailroom of the William Morris Agency during the 1960s. Following an improbable rise through the ranks of ABC's television unit, he became the head of Paramount Pictures at age thirty-one, created the Fox Broadcasting Company in the eighties, and built up USA Network in the nineties. In 1999, Diller bought Match for $50 million. The dating site would become the crown jewel in Diller's Internet empire, IAC (InterActiveCorp), joining the travel Web sites Expedia.com and Hotels.com, the search engine Ask.com, the borrowing site LendingTree.com, and the news site TheDailyBeast.com.

While Diller enjoyed the bragging rights that came with being a leading aggregator of Internet brands, he had no specific interest in online dating. What drew Diller to Match, and to the Web in general, was a vision he had about the future of media convergence, what he called "interactivity at scale." The vision for IAC had come to him many years earlier, in the early nineties, while standing on the selling floor of QVC, the home teleshopping network in which he owned a $25 million stake. Born in 1942, Diller was accustomed to thinking of media in its distinct forms: There was print, broadcast, and film, and they didn't mix. But QVC's business combined telephones, televisions, and computers. Diller saw them all work together in a kind of primitive convergence. When phone calls came in from home shoppers, he watched their orders register on a computer screen, with the digital bars rising and receding in waves. He thought, "This is going to change things."

Diller probably didn't realize the full extent of what convergence would mean for dating. But his thinking put him ahead of his time. The matching of computer dating, the searching of personal ads, the virtual reality of video, and eventually, the pinpointing capability of GPS—they could all one day converge on one screen. Over the next decade, his IAC would come to own more than two dozen dating sites, including Europe's Meetic and OkCupid, the industry darling.

"I wish I could say it was all planned," says Greg Blatt, the young lawyer who helped take Martha Stewart's company public before de-camping to Diller's Web empire, where he became CEO of Match and then of IAC. "But back in those days the company was simply buying up a bunch of Internet businesses. Dating just happened to be something that worked out, so we stuck with it."

Back in the sixties, when the average marriage age was twenty-three for men and twenty for women, students turned to computer dating be-cause they were sick of coming home empty-handed from college mix-ers. But during the first decade of the new millennium, with the average marriage age creeping toward thirty (twenty-eight for men; twenty-six for women), singles faced a new set of efficiency problems. Bars fell out of favor after the postcollege years. The primacy of work left less and less time for mate searching. Women's biological clocks were already ticking away by the time they got serious about settling down. And as people remained single for longer, they grew to be more discerning dat-ers, pickier about what they wanted and what they'd settle for.

"I prefer younger guys," said Miriam, a thirty-three-year-old speech pathologist from Maryland who joined the secular community after living as an orthodox Jew for twenty-five years. "Because I date online I can go with whoever I want." An easily accessible, rationalized marketplace of relationships: This was the big, game-changing difference between online dating and the other forms of relationship intermediation that came be-fore. The online-dating industry sold choice and control at a time when choice and control were exactly what many people wanted and needed.

By 2011, the eighteen-to-twenty-nine demographic accounted for 44 percent of the online-dating market; people aged thirty to forty-nine comprised 35 percent.

"I believe it all came down to *You've Got Mail*," says Trish McDer-mott, referring to Nora Ephron's 1998 hit romantic comedy about a cou-ple of book lovers played by Meg Ryan and Tom Hanks. The movie wasn't about an online-dating site, but the two met in an AOL chat room. "A lightbulb went off for single people. Suddenly it was seen as possible to meet someone who's smart and interesting online."

Surely many societal trends overwhelmed the online-dating stigma. Major pop-culture events like *You've Got Mail* may have helped. But most industry execs interviewed for this book believe it came down to one thing: access. This theory is also supported by findings from social science. Researchers say that attitudes toward online dating become more positive as social milieus provide less access to partners. Over time people lack the social capital to afford a stigma.

Up the age ladder, baby boomers divorced in droves: In 2010, nearly 33 percent of people between forty-six and sixty-four were divorced, separated, or had never been married, compared with just 13 percent in 1970. Being single later in life no longer carried the stigma it once did—and neither did online dating. For Match, eHarmony, and Plenty of Fish, three of the largest dating sites in North America, the fifty-and-over crowd became one of their most reliable demographics, accounting for 21 percent of the market, a valuable 21 percent because these were the people who were (a) likely to have money and (b) unlikely to believe that everything online should be free. Match launched a new site, OurTime .com, for singles fifty and up. The press release cited corporate research that singles over fifty are "considerably happier than their younger counterparts." With the pressures of child rearing and career lifted, the over-fifties "experience less stress about their personal lives." They also have fewer options.

Throughout the first decade of the 2000s, the stigma gradually reversed itself. Match employees got invited to weddings, where they were asked to give toasts. Happy couples, proud to have met online, put Match-branded matchbooks on the wedding tables as gifts. Groomsmen wore Match baseball hats. One bride even designed her wedding cake to look like the Match homepage. "Now," McDermott recalls, "it was as if people wanted to say, 'I'm tech-savvy. I was there at the beginning of the online-dating movement!'"

After fifteen years the online-dating industry reached a tipping point. The U.S. industry had become saturated, with over fourteen hundred dating sites making $2 billion per year. The top ten players—led by Match and Plenty of Fish—owned 60 percent of the U.S. market's approximately thirty million customers. A widely parroted 2010 finding estimated that one in five committed relationships originated online. The ratio was expected to climb dramatically in the coming decade.

Dan Winchester runs a free dating site in the United Kingdom. Like many of his colleagues, Winchester is an online-dating evangelist. Given this amazing tool, he wonders, why would anyone leave the most important decision of their life to chance? He predicts that the prospects of access and control will, in time, turn every adult into an online dater; and that the vast selection of online dating—expanding one's pool by hundreds or thousands of people—will mean a future of smarter mate selection and better relationships.

"When I meet someone," says Winchester, "I always ask where they met their boyfriend or girlfriend, or wife or husband. If they say, 'In a bar,' which they often do, I ask, 'How did you know what his interests were, or whether he had that same problem that you had with your last six relationships? How do you know you're not just making the same mistake over and over?'"

Just how much *do* daters control when they go looking online?

ALEXIS, PART II

Go Ask Phantasy Tour

AS AN ART STUDENT, ALEXIS SHOWCASED HER WORK ON A PER-
sonal Web site. As an intern at a music label, she marketed content online. As an aspiring set designer for film and television, she networked
for jobs on social-media sites like Facebook and Twitter. As a music enthusiast, she posted regularly, sometimes obsessively, on a fan forum
devoted to her favorite jam band, Phish.

The forum, called Phantasy Tour, is less about music per se than
bringing Phish fans together in a place where they can sound off on relationships and sex, posing questions and seeking advice. Whatever
Phantasy Tour may have been intended for originally, it functions as a
place for young adults of a similar cultural bent to crowd-source feedback on common coming-of-age conundrums in their personal lives.

Unlike, say, the vast connectedness of Facebook, the PT community
is limited, specific, and isolated. Because Phantasy Tour members,
known as PTers, or "bears," post under anonymous screen names, their
conversations tend to be characterized by heavy disclosure, blunt honesty, braggadocio, and lots of off-color humor. It works like this: A PTer
poses a conversation topic, or thread: "Can you be friends with an ex?"
"Tell me about your worst breakup!" "Sex on the first date?" Conversations then unfold over hours, days, or months, reading like raw, often

R-rated streams-of-Millennial-generation-consciousness. Typical fodder ranges from the normative—whether, after a first date, one owes the other an official "I don't want to see you again"—to the prescriptive: "Don't date girls who won't admit to mastying [masturbating]. They will never let you hit it from behind, touch your balls, give frequent Bjs, have sex with the lights on, or SIIHB [stick it in her butt]." The Web site operator caps conversations at seventeen pages, a limit that is often reached.

In the winter of 2010, Alexis initiated a thread entitled "Match.com." As the so-called original poster, or OP, she asked: "So, who's done it? Weird experiences? Horror stories? I'm just curious if it's essentially a bunch of dudes looking to date/fuck multiple girls as sport."

Comments flowed: a mixture of encouragement ("If you can trudge through that initial awkwardness, it might be a fit"); caution ("It's the electronic version of the bargain bin at Filene's"); and leavening perspective ("I find it truly comical that people in this thread are poo pooing online dating. We're all message-board dorks! Online is where it's at!").

"Okay," Alexis wrote after several hundred comments had been posted. "I will just enjoy some random dinners, see what happens, and let you all know, of course. Side note: facepalm [head in hands]."

CHAPTER THREE

The New Serendipity

HOW A BUNCH OF GEEKS REENGINEERED ROMANCE

It's all about hooking people up and being as fast and efficient as possible.

—Markus Frind, founder of Plenty of Fish

A couple of years before Carrie and her husband moved from Salt Lake City to New York, when their son was new and their marriage was still healthy, they filled out OkCupid profiles and answered some questions on the site. It was just for fun, to see if they were good for each other, and, according to the algorithm, they were: a 96 percent match.

The OkCupid site had a soft blue background with writing in blue and pink. "I liked the whole tone," Carrie recalls. "Nerdy and coy. There was this strong sexual edge to the questions they asked, but they were nice about it, like friends asking you incredibly intimate things but without judgment. It was all in the name of efficiency."

Carrie, thirty-four, was born in England and raised in Iowa. She met her husband during college at the University of Illinois, while getting a degree in industrial engineering. She loves her son and enjoys talking about him. She thinks of herself as a highly rational person. She calls herself an "atheist and borderline antitheist," and says religion is "a force for evil in the world."

So after the move to New York, when Carrie's husband announced he was unhappy and wanted to split up, these two criteria—antireligion, prochildren—were foremost in her thinking about a new partner. "I haven't dated since college," she says, "when all you do is get drunk and see what happens."

When I meet her, Carrie is seated among children's toys in the living room of a one-bedroom apartment in downtown Manhattan. Her ex moved out recently. At the moment she's trying, without success, to remove iced-tea stains from an expensive wool carpet. "I knew OkCupid from their blog, which is about patterns and trends in data," she says. "As someone who knows statistics, I like their matching process, the way they do it with questions and a weighting system rather than just have you define yourself by ticking off a bunch of boxes."

Doing things better based on data—that's what Carrie's job at a credit card company is about. A devotee of corporate America, she believes human greed is too strong to regulate, and that transparency is the only antidote to Wall Street corruption. Her friends call her the Plutocrat.

Carrie tried Match but didn't like it. "On Match the guys can sort profiles by what body shape they want," she explains, "which pisses me off." If Carrie were a petite woman, her red mop of hair would look devilish, almost too cute. But size gives her aspect a certain seriousness. "I wouldn't qualify as 'curvy,'" she says, "not like Kim Kardashian. I'm definitely bigger than that. But I'm not quite 'big and beautiful' either. So out of the five options on Match I picked 'full figured.' But I'm pretty sure that most of the guys on there, even if they're chubby, check off 'skinny' or 'average' as their requirements for women. Give me a break! We all prefer to go out with someone insanely sexy. But be realistic about it! *You* get to stay skinny after kids, but I don't. In any case, I don't think Match picks up on the fact that I'm passing over all these guys because of their weight requirements. But OkCupid can because it allows me to rate the importance of guys' answers to their weight questions."

Carrie logs onto OkCupid. The homepage greets her: "The Internet rejoices in your return!" says a message from the OkCupid staff. There's nothing written in her profile, but the site still has her basic stats from when she and her ex tested their compatibility.

Ethnicity: White. Height: 5' 4". Body Type: Full figured. Diet: Mostly anything. Smokes: No. Drinks: Socially. Drugs: Never. Sign: Capricorn, but it doesn't matter. Religion: Atheism, and very serious about it. Education: Graduated from masters program. Job: Executive/Management. Income: $150,000–$250,000.

Carrie adds her age, zip code, and a screen name: VociferousInNYC.

Immediately she receives a message from Chris Coyne, an OkCupid cofounder, who writes: "If you want the best people to contact you, you should share interesting facts about yourself on your profile page. . . . Around the site you'll encounter match questions. When you see them, you can answer them in three parts. First, you'll give your own answer. Second, your ideal match's answer. And finally, you'll tell us how important (if at all) that question is to you. In this way OkCupid lets you—and only you—control how matches are sorted. The more you answer, the better your matches."

Users can answer thousands of questions, or none at all. Carrie goes to the lifestyle and dating tabs, where she answers questions about the topics that are most important to her: Are you Christian? "No," she replies. "I much prefer Aesop's fables." Should evolution and creationism be taught side-by-side in schools? "No, and it's very important that my partner agrees." If you made a bright orange bowel movement that had glowing purple polka dots, would you tell your partner about it? "Yes." How much can intelligence turn you on? "A lot!" Do you believe that men must be the heads of their households? "No." Do you have a child? "Yes, and it's very important that my partner be okay with that." Is your ideal match well-off financially? "I don't think I want to be a sugar mama," she writes, "but I'm not too picky." Do you think boys should be circumcised? "No! Keep your knife away from my son's penis!" Do you Google someone before a first date? "Yes. Knowledge is power!"

Carrie then answers questions in the sex category, marking many of them "irrelevant" in terms of how important they are to her relationships:

Orgasms are clearly the most important part of sex. "I agree." Do you prefer to achieve orgasm by intercourse, oral sex, masturbation, or pure force of will? "Masturbation." Would you date someone just for the sex? "Not very likely but maybe." Do you usually feel the need to shower or bathe after having sex? "No." Have you ever tasted your own sexual fluids? "Yes." Is there such a thing as having had too many sexual partners? "No." Under the right circumstances would you allow your partner to lick your anus? "Yes." Would you find shaving your partner's pubic hair exciting? "No. (I wouldn't like brushing his teeth either. It should be done beforehand.)" Would you consider inviting someone to bed with you for clearly stated nonsexual purposes on a first date? "Yes. (I did. It was nice!)" Have you ever had sex in a place where there was a high risk of getting caught? "No." If your partner asks you to have sex in a sex-shop booth with others watching, would you? "Yes." Would you rather be tied up during sex, do the tying, or avoid bondage altogether? "Be tied up." Would you play out a rape fantasy with a partner who asked you to? "No." Would you do a striptease for your mate? "Yes." Have you ever had sex with a person within the first hour of meeting them? "No." Can you remember the names of everyone you've ever had sex with? "Yes." Would you ever consider cutting a partner in sexual play who asked for it? "No." Do you have a hidden stash of pornography? "Yes." Would you be okay with your significant other thinking about someone else while having sex with you? "Maybe. It would depend who they're thinking about." Do you own sex toys? "Yes. Who doesn't these days?"

The next step is photos. Carrie uploads five pictures: two of her in a black evening dress, sitting down; another of her typing on her Black-Berry; a fourth "strategic photo" of her holding her son; and a fifth of her doing yoga. She presses a button labeled "My Best Face." The site tells her which photos are most attractive, so she can order them accordingly. She decides to remove the yoga picture, because it shows too much cleavage. In the about section she writes a few paragraphs. She says she is "warm and fun" but has a "cynical side." She's "enthusiastic" and has "been trying to do more things out and about in the city," like "biking, seeing plays and taking yoga classes." She says she has a son who lives with her part-time.

Days go by: Carrie receives no messages from eligible candidates, nor does she get many responses to the messages she sends. After browsing profiles she realizes that her own is, well, pretty boring. It doesn't sound much different from the profiles of those guys who say "I like to work hard and play hard." She takes another stab, beginning with a joke from her sister:

> An atom walks into a bar and says, "I've lost an electron." Bartender says, "Are you sure?" Atom says, "I'm positive."
>
> I grew up in Iowa but have been in NYC for 9 years. I like to think that I'm nice like a classic Midwesterner but can keep up with life in New York. My undergraduate degree is in engineering but I turned to the dark side, business, soon after I graduated. I have a 5-year-old son who lives with me part-time (read: my biological clock has gone off once and is now on snooze). I love raising him in the city and he inspires me to broaden my horizons.
>
> I have a weak spot for people who are intelligent and a little geeky but with a touch of sophistication. Perhaps someone who has seen a few Woody Allen movies but won't judge me when I sing along to Adele. Someone who is generally optimistic but can get annoyed by politicians or people who block the doors on the subway.

Under "The most private thing I'm willing to admit," Carries writes: "I had a C-section, didn't breastfeed (read: everything is still as it was!), and dropped my son on his head when he was 6 months old."

Messages begin rolling in. The atom joke proves to be a good conversation starter. About half of her suitors reference it or come with a joke of their own. Carrie goes on ten dates in the next two months. The main criteria she uses are kids, atheism, and education—the guy needs at least a college degree.

Many of the dates go well. But "the kid thing" seems to get in the way. "Many men without kids seem to like kids and say they want kids of their own," Carrie says. "But the fact is, if you don't have kids, then you only think kids are entertaining for a while. Eventually you want to move on to other conversations, about going out at night and skiing in the Alps and things that parents don't have the time for. I'm like, yeah, I did that stuff—eight years ago."

When Carrie's son becomes a sticking point on yet another date with an otherwise promising twenty-nine-year-old guy with a graduate degree and a good job, Carrie comes home, opens her laptop, and does an "advanced search" on OkCupid using just two criteria: He must have kids and he must be an atheist. "My money is taken care of," Carrie says. "I don't need money. I need the rest of it." She leaves the education, job, and income fields blank.

While Barry Diller was buying Match and other Web sites in the nineties, the math geeks of Generation X—those born in the late 1970s who had dial-up connections in high school—were also trying to capitalize on the Internet. Back at Harvard, a math geek from Maine named Chris Coyne saw eBay.com, the auction site, go public and sell for insane multiples. He began brainstorming ideas for his own Web site.

Coyne is a waifish six feet five inches with spiky blond hair and steely eyes. He looks like a male model conflated with a basketball prospect—not your typical geek. In the spring of 1998, as Coyne approached the end of his junior year at Harvard, he heard about the Last Chance Dance. Seniors listed up to fifteen secret crushes and were then told which of the fifteen liked them back. Coyne wondered why someone hadn't put this on the Web. Seemed like it would spread really fast.

He asked a friend to build a Web site called Pimpin' Cupid. They listed some people who they thought were hot. Then those people would get an e-mail asking them to list the people *they* thought were hot. There were no profiles, no photos, no searching. The site just matched people who said they liked each other. It quickly spread around Harvard and other universities for a few weeks and then crashed, but it was the start of something.

Coyne's math buddies from Kirkland House, Max Krohn and Sam Yagan, shared Coyne's ambition—however ambiguous it was—and joined him.

The goal wasn't to build a dating site; certainly the idea of online classifieds never occurred to them. "There was an Internet boom happening," Coyne recalls. "People our age who were building things online didn't necessarily think of their creations as specific businesses. We talked about making sites that would 'grab eyeballs.' I thought of a Web site as a portal into something engaging or entertaining or interesting that would keep users coming back." Coyne, Yagan, Krohn, and a fourth geek—a double math and English major named Christian Rudder—kept testing ideas. The next project to catch fire was a humor blog called TheSpark, much of which was written by Rudder.

"When spring rolled around," recalls Yagan, "I was in Chris's dorm room with a bunch of guys, saying, 'You know, being funny every day is going to be really hard. We need to make something that will have lasting value.'"

Krohn suggested putting their own version of *CliffsNotes* online; he recommended hiring students to write their own study guides for Shakespeare and other subjects.

Two years after they launched SparkNotes, *CliffsNotes*, publisher of the iconic yellow and black study guides founded in 1958 by Nebraskan Cliff Hillegass, had had its monopoly disrupted. In 2001, SparkNotes was bought by iTurf, and then shortly thereafter Barnes & Noble bought SparkNotes from iTurf for $3.5 million. By then the site had published over six hundred free online study guides on topics such as literature, history, economics, math, and chemistry. Barnes & Noble turned SparkNotes into one of the leading education brands in the world.

After selling SparkNotes, the guys disbanded for a year. At the end of 2002, Coyne was stumbling drunk around Manhattan's East Village when he called Yagan with an idea.

"We should make a site that has a big blind-date button on it!" he said. "You just push the button and you get a blind date. We'll send people to bars to meet each other. The site will be free. The bars will subsidize us."

"Okay," replied Yagan. "Call me back when you're sober."

Coyne's idea, which would eventually launch, fail, and launch again, was called CrazyBlindDate.

"But OkCupid was the launchpad," says Max Krohn, who graduated summa cum laude from Harvard with a degree in computer science, and now also has a PhD in computer science from MIT. "We thought from the beginning we could only launch CBD once we had a sufficiently successful dating site."

Shortly before the acquisition of SparkNotes the team had been working on a dating site called SparkMatch. SparkMatch offered a personality test, called the Purity Test, that was based on the Myers-Briggs Type Indicator. It classified people on four dimensions: independent/dependent; good/evil; love/sex; taker/provider. This resulted in sixteen personality types, each of which Rudder, who had a knack for funny writing, named: a man who qualified as a Furry Dildo (dependent, evil, sex, provider) might do well with the female character Battleaxe (dependent, evil, love, taker) but should avoid the Mermaid (independent, good, love, provider).

"Chris and Christian always believed that consumer Web products should have a personality, an attitude, that they should be fun to use," says Yagan. "If you look at the SparkNotes and OkC brands, they really share an irreverence and a (sometimes not-so) subtle sense of humor."

SparkNotes had become a success by 1) being better than its incumbent competitor and 2) being free. SparkNotes relied on advertising rather than subscriptions to make money. What other industries could Coyne & Co. disrupt with this two-point business plan? It needed to be an industry in which the user gives something in return for the free service—something that would appeal to the advertisers the site would need to court in order to make money. Online dating, with all its potential for massive data collection, could be a good one. But they would need to ask their users to do more than just push a button.

In 2004, the reorganized company launched under a new name, OkCupid, and was now prepared to tackle online dating full time. Krohn wrote the OK Web Server (OKWS), Coyne worked on the matching system, and Rudder cultivated a voice.

Early on the site featured a version of the Purity Test. A man might learn that he's a Billy Goat, a Backrubber, a Vapor Trail, a Poolboy, or the Last Man on Earth. The Hornivore ("roaming, sexual, subhuman") might want to consider the female type Genghis Khunt ("master of man, bringer of pain") and avoid the Sonnet ("romantic, hopeful, composed"). To figure out what you were you had to answer questions about yourself, some of which were written and submitted by users. Over time, the questions multiplied.

At OkCupid's headquarters—a no-frills loft office in Midtown Manhattan—Coyne explains how his matching system works today. "The objective," he says, "is to figure out what you want. To accomplish that we play a giant question-and-answer session with everyone on the site at once."

The prototypical user, let's call him John Dater, is not required to answer any questions. But OkCupid is premised on the idea that the more questions John D. answers, the better the site works for him. Questions range from the abstract (Would you prefer that good things happened, or interesting things?) to the specific (How often do you feel the need to get really drunk?); from penal policy (Which of the following is the more appropriate penalty for rape: death, castration, prison, or community service?) to trust (Would you be okay with your significant other spending a lot of time with his/her ex?); from the forward looking (Does finding a long-term partner give you license to "let yourself go"?) to the practical (Ideally, how often would you have sex?) to the downright intimate (How do you feel about kissing your partner after he/she goes down on you?).

For each question, John provides three answers: 1) his own answer, 2) the answer(s) he's willing to accept from a match, and 3) the level of importance he attaches to the question: irrelevant, a little important, somewhat important, very important, or mandatory.

When John clicks on a new profile he's shown a "match percentage" that accounts for all the questions that he and the potential match have *both* answered. If they've both answered the same one thousand questions, for instance, then OkCupid's algorithm generates a match percentage based on six thousand answers: the product of one thousand questions times three answers per question times two daters. Beyond that, John is welcome to go "behind the numbers," so to speak, to see how his potential mate has answered any given question, provided she's chosen to make her answer public.

The innovation of OkCupid—and what distinguishes it from other "matching" sites, such as eHarmony—lies in its pliability. Coyne believes he can give members the power to sort through matches online the same way they would offline, assuming a world of perfect information. "Suppose," he explains, "that your buddy tells you he has a girl he wants to set you up with. No matter how much you trust him, you're not going to say yes without asking questions first. In your mind, you have a filtering process that's built in, which is different from another guy's filtering process. eHarmony would say they know everyone's filtering process. We say we don't. But we can give you the tools to express your filter. We can show you how everyone stacks up against your filter, and how you stack up against theirs. Then you're on your own."

Offline, when you're on your own, you're not relying on such detailed data. The most obvious difference between meeting someone in real life and meeting someone online is, of course, what you see first. Instead of assessing and greeting a physical person, you assess and greet an avatar, some combination of text, photographs, and match percentages flashing in the corner of the screen. Biological attraction gets replaced with something far less sexy, "computer-mediated communication," or CMC.

In broad strokes, the science of human attraction is something we all grasp, intuitively, even if we've never thought much about it. In a 1991 study, for example, researchers observed 109 "attraction tactics" in a singles bar, including sucking seductively on a straw, offering to buy someone a drink, puffing out one's chest, and staring. Women say the most effective tactics for attracting them are displaying good manners and acting sympathetic. Men, meanwhile, favor signals that are more easily quantified: accentuated curves; a strut in her step; a sexualized appearance that might include tight clothes, short skirts, and low-cut tops that slip off the shoulder. On a seven-point scale, men placed a woman's act of rubbing her chest or pelvis against him at 6.07, the second most effective tactic. Only an explicit agreement to have sex beats the chest/pelvis rub.

Women experience strong physical reactions too, though they tend to place more importance on scent. Pheromones—from the Greek words *pherein* (to carry) and *hormon* (to stimulate)—are secreted by apocrine glands in the skin, mouth, feet, and vagina. In *The Evolution of Desire*, David Buss defines pheromones as "chemical messengers secreted by one person's body that produce physiological and behavioral changes in another person." Women are attracted to men with symmetrical faces. We think of symmetry as a visual quality, not an olfactory one. Scientists report, however, that symmetry has its own natural perfume: Women have evolved an ability to *smell* it. In one famous study, T-shirts worn by symmetrical men smelled more pleasant to ovulating women than the dirty T-shirts of less symmetrical men.

Ovulation sends its own signals: Her voice becomes sexier; her skin color becomes lighter and vascularized—she glows. During the fourteen days approaching ovulation, called the follicular phase, she emits more copulins—vaginal fatty acids—than she does during the luteal phase, the next fourteen days. In another dirty T-shirt contest, men found odors emitted during the follicular phase to smell more pleasant than odors emitted during the luteal phase.

When computers began talking to each other in the 1970s and 1980s, scientists believed that because nonverbal cues—the hair flip, the straw, the copulin—were filtered out of the process, CMC felt too unreal to facilitate social bonding. In the 1990s this perspective was debunked: Given an unlimited time frame to correspond, as well as "richer" online media—photographs, more text, interactive questions—studies found that even without a physical presence, people will use whatever communication tools they have at their disposal to connect. A mood becomes an emoticon. A fast e-mail response communicates warmth.

That people can bond online doesn't come as a huge surprise. People have been meeting through personal ads and bonding through letters for centuries. What's different about online dating is not necessarily that you're selecting mates through a digital representation of a person but rather that you're doing it through an interactive medium, entering loads of detailed information into a Web site that runs that information against the information of others. Of course you can't smell the person you're looking at—until later—but meanwhile, the computer is crunching more information than you could ever gather in a glance across the bar, or a chest/pelvis rub.

The online-dating industry has experimented with different ways of imitating real-world attraction online, making self-presentation more authentic and communication more effective. How best to let someone express who they are and what they want? How to let them search? What kinds of information should be prioritized? At the moment the industry is heading in the direction of greater user control, with different ideas about how to achieve that. The goal, however, is always the same: Within any given pool, matching up potential mates should be as efficient as possible, getting you what you say you want, or what the site observes that you seem to actually want.

"You can ask people surface stuff or more psychologically penetrating questions," says Gavin Potter, a retired business consultant with a degree in psychology. "But either way, in the past it's always depended on the person filling out a questionnaire. I'm not interested in that."

Potter made his name in 2007, when Netflix ran a competition offering a million dollars to whomever could create a movie-recommender algorithm 10 percent better than its own. Math geeks and scientists teamed up to compete for the prize. Early on, Potter emerged as the dark horse. He worked alone in his London home, using an old computer to run math formulas on data sets. Rather than going with the purely mathematical approach favored by other contestants, Potter based his Netflix algorithm on human psychology. What does this mean? It gets abstract. But basically Potter designed an algorithm that takes account of, and corrects, psychic concepts like "ratings inertia," whereby a Netflix user who has recently given a lot of above-average ratings to movies is likely to continue to do so, out of habit. Potter's approach has been compared

with the field of behavioral economics, which incorporates into traditional economics those features of human life that are lost when you
think of a person as a rational machine, or as a list of numbers representing cinematic taste, or taste in people.

Potter lost the Netflix competition. But it would lead him to a new
line of business. Through a company called IntroAnalytics, he now sells
a matching algorithm that prioritizes implicit preferences over explicit.
"Why would I trust a woman to tell me whether or not she likes facial
hair when I can simply monitor her browsing behavior and get a definitive answer?" Potter explains. "Even assuming people are good judges of
what they want, which they aren't, there are so many options. I help
people discover what they want and then recommend people who will
want them in return." By letting users design their own filter, Potter does
something similar to OkCupid. The difference is that they design the filter without answering questions. He calls the approach "revealed preferences," and a version of it is being used increasingly at dating sites,
including Match.

"In any mating pool, you have a supply and a demand," says Amarnath Thombre, the chief of algorithms at Match. "It's a numbers game.
Our job is to match people up within the pool we have, keeping in mind
that people are not great at describing themselves or what they want."

Match's headquarters in Dallas is located on the top two floors of an
office building in Highland Park, one of the wealthiest suburban neigh-
borhoods in the world. When Thombre arrives each day he passes fresh
orchids and a wall of digital clocks announcing the time in London,
Tokyo, Beijing, Madrid, Munich, Paris, and Stockholm. A coffee table dis-
plays clay pots of wheatgrass and paperback copies of *The Cheat Sheet:
A Clue-by-Clue Guide to Finding Out If He's Unfaithful*, *The Breakup Bible:
The Smart Woman's Guide to Healing From a Breakup or Divorce*, and *Love
for No Reason: 7 Steps to Creating a Life of Unconditional Love*. The lobby,
with its velvet-covered chaise longue and Boho-chic couches, feels as
though someone dimmed the lights on the furniture section at Anthro-
pologie. Affixed to the wall is a porcelain sculpture entitled "Penrose
Tilting." The piece, according to its description, consists of repeating kite

and dart shapes that "connect to create patterns but will never form the same area of pattern twice—no matter how large the piece gets."

Lining the elegant staircase that Thombre climbs to get to his office are three flat-screen TVs looping real Match.com first dates and real Match.com success stories. A sign at the top of the stairs reminds employees of their mandate: POSITION MATCH AS A PLACE WHERE REAL PEOPLE MEET AND FALL IN LOVE; DISPEL CUSTOMER CONCERNS, GIVE THEM A REASON TO BELIEVE US; SHARE OTHER CUSTOMER SUCCESSES PROMINENTLY AND OFTEN.

Conference rooms are labeled "Chapel of Love," "Dirty Dancing," and "Casanova Executive Office."

With a degree from the Indian Institute of Technology in Bombay, and an advanced degree in chemical engineering from the University of Arizona, Thombre's qualifications as head of analytics—the algorithm guy—go unquestioned. He, along with the head of product, a serene and precise Indian woman named Sharmistha Dubey, were recruited to Match by the current CEO, Mandy Ginsberg, a spunky, dimpled Jewish woman in her early forties who looks like she could still be captain of the high school soccer team. Ginsberg, Dubey, and Thombre all came to Match from i2 Technologies, a supply-chain management company where they found ways to move products around the country with ever greater efficiency.

Before Thombre arrived at Match, in 2008, the site's searching and matching functions reflected an earlier state of the art. "Originally," explains Thombre, "it was very simple. The site created a bunch of dimensions on which you could define yourself and what you want in someone else. The technology was a basic evolution from personal ads: Your dimensions or parameters would be matched up against those of others, and when you looked at another's profile you'd get a visual representation"—the matching green bubbles that RedPepper referred to—"of how your specifications lined up with theirs. This was the original Match. Over the first decade of online dating, systems grew, in the sense that they added more users and more parameters, but the basic technology stayed the same."

Thombre continues: "Eventually we realized that not all parameters are equal. You may say you like people with red hair and a college degree. But education is a much more important parameter. So if she has a college degree but no red hair, that doesn't mean it's only a 50 percent match. Education should count for more. Things like age, height, political preferences, smoking versus nonsmoking, wants kids versus doesn't want kids—these are the really defining parameters. So it's possible for people to match on only seven of fifteen parameters and still be a 90 percent match."

The algorithms got smarter at defining what mattered and what didn't, but they were still based on what people said they wanted.

That began to change in 2008, shortly after Thombre arrived. "I wanted to understand why, when the algorithm says two people are a 100 percent match, it can still lead to a bad match," says Thombre. "When we dug further into the data, we began to see how frequently people break their own rules. When you watch their browsing habits—their actual behavior on the site—you see them go way outside of what they say they want. We realized that people were creating a much more holistic idea of what a person really is. The mind makes a very complex judgment that can't really be defined, beforehand. This is when the whole idea of dissonance came into focus."

Dissonance, a popular concept in social psychology, is the difference between what you say you want and what you'll actually go for. Think of it in terms of movies. Just because you can tell Netflix why you like a movie, and perhaps even describe features of movies you tend to like, doesn't mean you can describe all the characteristics a movie must have in order for you to like it. The hard-core horror guy can still be pleasantly surprised by a well-done romantic comedy. The right plot twist, joke, or character flaw can pull him in, appeal to an unrecognized side of himself.

After an early divorce, CEO Ginsberg tried out Jdate. But being a single mother made dating hard. She was surprised, eventually, to find herself married to an engineer she met offline, at i2 Technologies. "If I had laid out criteria for what I was looking for, it would not have been a guy from south India," she says. "People are complex. You're constantly making trade-offs about who's too tall, too short, too smart, and too dumb. People come in and tell us a bit about what they're looking for. But what you say and what you do can be different." A woman might tell Match she wants a nice Catholic guy between thirty and forty who's never been married, Ginsberg says, by way of example. But after weeks on Match she might get an e-mail from a guy who has kids, and accept that.

When he signed up for Match, Tom, twenty-eight, a nice Catholic guy who'd recently moved to Atlanta and didn't know anyone, was in search of a nice girl. A world traveler, Tom had once been engaged to a Chinese woman he met while working in Hong Kong. Socially reserved and buttoned-up, he is an accountant who enjoys movies, Garth Brooks, and sleeping in. He lives for Italian food, hates salad, and struggles with asthma. Smokers were out, no exceptions.

On paper, Kelly, twenty-three, was horrible for Tom: an extrovert who tends to gravitate to "dramatic, indie-type guitar players" and can't sit still for long periods. Kelly loves salad, hates Italian, and pops out of bed in the morning. She had no experience with long-term relationships, nor had she traveled outside the country. And the ultimate deal breaker: She smoked. Intellectual incongruities aside, Tom should've been physically revolted.

But Kelly showed up in Tom's "Daily 5"—the five matches that Match sends its users each day—for other reasons: The matching algorithm determined that neither Kelly nor Tom had married, and they both wanted to meet someone who'd never been married; both have college degrees; both are social drinkers; and both want children (Kelly: "definitely"; Tom: "someday"). The behavioral algorithm took account of Tom's likelihood of getting in touch—he had sent winks to some smokers, despite his no-smoking rule—as well as Kelly's probability of responding.

Lastly, Thombre's "triangulation" algorithm considered the messaging habits of other men who tended to like the same women that Tom liked: Of the women Tom had winked at, other men who also liked those women had contacted Kelly as well. "The triangulation algorithm helps determine someone's type," explains Thombre. "It says, 'The men who like the same women that you like also tend to like this other woman over here.'"

From Tom's perspective, Kelly's profile showed a fit blonde with green eyes and a big smile. One photo showed her strolling along the beach in a turquoise summer dress. In another she looked away from the camera, model-like, as the wind blew back her hair. In a third photo, taken at a party, she sat atop a guy's shoulders while pumping her fist.

Kelly had been on Match for six months, the average "lifetime" of a Match user. Tom, a newbie, had been on for two weeks and had not yet subscribed. He was still a free user, meaning he could send winks but not messages until he paid. He sent her a wink. She replied with a message. He subscribed in order to correspond. Tom suggested a date at the Georgia Aquarium and Kelly agreed.

"I saw her on the site," recalls Tom, "and said to myself, 'Okay, she looks *really* attractive. Is that how she actually looks?'"

Yes, it was. "I guess it was my looks that attracted him on Match," Kelly says, "though I doubt that's maintained his interest for over a year."

At first Kelly wasn't crazy about Tom. "It took a while," she says, "because he was nice, and I wasn't used to nice guys. It didn't start out intimate. I was just open to seeing where it would go. The whole thing about being on Match in the first place was that I felt more open to trying new things and not being tied so much to some image of who I should be with."

Tom learned how to play the guitar. She was impressed. "He told me, 'I don't want to be your friend. I want to be more than that. I'll treat you better than anybody will ever treat you.' I've been told a lot of things by a lot of guys," Kelly says, "but I believed him because he's so honest and upfront."

"She said on her profile that she smoked occasionally," Tom says. "When I found out that she actually smokes *daily*, I was like, holy shit! I would usually never go out with anyone who smokes. But at that point I liked her so much—her high energy level, how she treats me, that she's always smiling—that the smoking didn't mean anything. The biggest difference from past relationships is that she's really low maintenance. I don't have to spend much money on her, and if I do, she tells me I don't need to and suggests free things. She's a lot more into spending time than spending money. I was used to a girlfriend being a big investment."

Now they're living together in a new city, Las Vegas, where Tom works as an accountant for casinos, and Kelly is looking for work. Is it a great match? Time will tell. Tom was alone, now he's with a beautiful woman. Kelly had never been with a nice guy, now she is. Both say they've found the love of their life. Neither, when filling out their Match profiles, imagined the other as an ideal partner.

Back in Manhattan, Carrie also found someone she'd never imagined, but with the help of a different algorithm.

"It was like he'd been pulled out of the pile especially for me," she recalls. "His username was AteoBoricua, and the first line of his profile said something like, 'My main focus is trying to raise my children right.' And I was like, yes!"

She sent a message:

> AteoBoricua—Puerto Rican atheist. I'm probably the last person in the US who doesn't speak Spanish so I have to admit I googled that!
>
> I have to head to bed but I wanted to drop you a note so I don't lose track of a nice person among all the "hey sexy lady" messages (groan).
>
> Hope to hear back from you!
>
> - Carrie

He responded saying he'd just returned from the Poconos, where he'd been on vacation with his kids. But for Carrie the thing that nailed it was their mutual response to OkCupid's question about whether women should keep their legs shaved: Both said shaving was "preferred but not required."

"Any guy who can tolerate that I don't wax my legs in the winter," she says, "is good for me."

AteoBoricua doesn't have a college degree, which had been one of Carrie's main criteria. As a computer technician he makes a fraction of what she makes in her management job. She comes from an upper-middle-class family. He was raised by high school dropouts. "It creates some interesting gender-role issues," she says, "because he's used to being the provider." AteoBoricua wanted to pick up the check on their first date, but Carrie insisted on splitting it. "That first night turned out to be a great test case for how things are now," she says. "He was gracious, and I was bold, and it worked."

Socioeconomic status is thought to be a fundamental aspect of compatibility, but between them there are enough similarities and good things to override its importance. They're both divorced, and they both live for their children. He's three years older—thirty-seven to her thirty-four—and is attracted to how opinionated she is. "We both work for big companies," she says, "so there's that. I think I was rude the first time we discussed moving jobs offshore, but I'm better at this now. At work I have direct reports and he doesn't, which was awkward at first. But he's really good at his job, and takes it seriously, and that's what matters. It would be an issue if he didn't think our work lives were important. Maybe he hasn't read as many books as I have, but we've got plenty to talk about."

On their first date he told her about moving back to Puerto Rico as a kid and not speaking Spanish. She told him about working in Asia. Even though their backgrounds are different, their politics align on some key issues. "We bonded over the fact that we both support universal health care," she says. "He influenced my views on minimum wage, and I think I influenced his."

They share a love of pubs and good barbecue. Most important, Carrie's son met AteoBoricua on a Fourth of July weekend, and they hit it off.

"We still bump into each other when we go to pay the check," Carrie says, "but he always takes my hand when I step down a curb in high heels, and that kind of thoughtfulness is what's really important to me. Our differences are less of an issue because we aren't twenty-two-year-olds looking to weave our entire lives together and define ourselves by our relationship. I don't care how he decorates his apartment, because I have my own. He doesn't care how often I do the dishes, because he doesn't have to see them every day. It's fantastic!"

"If you're geeky and you get excited about everything and have a clear idea of what you want, then OkCupid's algorithm is going to work better for you," says Match's Thombre. "If you want to put in less effort but still learn what might work for you, then I think Match is better. OkCupid goes deeply into hundreds of questions. We're focused more on behavior."

Match, OkCupid, and eHarmony represent different parts of an industry spectrum between "search" and "match." Match, despite its name, is more of a searching site. Even though it asks some questions, the filters are minimal. On the other end of the spectrum is eHarmony, a matchmaking site with a fixed filter. In the middle somewhere is OkCupid, a matching site that lets users design their own filters.

But despite their differences, they all combine written profiles, photos, and some kind of matching algorithm based on responses to questions. These sites—along with the many that resemble them—represent Phase I of the online-dating industry's evolution.

Phase II occurred between 2007 and 2011, when the rise of smartphones allowed online dating to go mobile. In 2003, a service called Proxidating used Bluetooth technology to alert users when a person with a matching profile was within fifty feet. Match also introduced a mobile version that year. But these apps were ahead of their time. It wasn't until the 2007 introduction of Apple's Web-friendly iPhone that people could easily access a new world of mobile-ready sites on-the-fly.

For online-dating entrepreneurs, this was a no-brainer. Three of the biggest complaints about the medium in its traditional form, say dating execs, are the problems of distance (becoming attached to someone online only to find out they live too far away); "funnel time," the days or weeks that lapse between the initial online introduction and the first in-person meeting (known in the industry as "asynchronicity"); and a lack of transparency, the idea that, online, a man can't see how "surrounded" a woman is by other men, which results in inefficiencies because women get overloaded with messages while guys get ignored.

"When I walk down the street," said Google CEO Eric Schmidt, "I want my smartphone to be doing searches constantly." Schmidt's utopia can be described as search-without-search, a world in which your phone knows to search for what you want before you do and can help you find the people and things you don't yet know but might like to get to know, right around you.

In Europe, Latin America, and, more recently, the United States, a "social-discovery" app called Badoo facilitates meeting on-the-fly, based on little more than a photograph, an age, and an interest or two. Badoo was invented in 2006 by a young Russian, Andrey Andreev, while he was living in Spain, a country where people tend to be more gregarious in public places.

"It's no coincidence that Badoo was built in Spain," says Badoo's chief of marketing, Jessica Powell. "When I was living in New York, you'd go out with your friends but you wouldn't talk to the people next to you. When you're out in a place like Rio or Madrid, it's just much easier to start conversations. There's more natural social lubrication in those cultures." Meeting people is the basis of evolution, says Powell. And unlike with dating, with meeting there's no pressure, no unnecessary work up to something that may not go anywhere. On Badoo, dating becomes a less distinct activity, one integrated with the rest of life's activities. By 2012, it claimed 35 million active users, with another 120 million registered.

"If we were a normal dating site," explains Powell, "we'd have a matching algorithm and long user profiles that don't tell you anything. We view interests as just an icebreaker. The most successful conversations don't start with 'Hi' or 'I like your profile.' They start when you say something that's interesting to the other person. After all, when a woman sees a guy on the street, there's no voice on her shoulder saying, 'He's thirty-six, works on behalf of animal rights, and likes the same cereal you do.' No, she sees a person who looks good. She experiences something, and sends a signal."

Generation Y, the people born in the eighties and nineties, have grown up on things being very visual, says Lloyd Price, another marketing executive at Badoo. "There's not a lot of text, not a lot of substance. It's about appearance. And everything's very quick. 'Show me your photo, tell me how old you are, then let's connect.' Badoo just makes the world work faster. Do you want to meet people in your neighborhood? Do you want to do this quickly and in a noncommittal way? The key reason for Badoo's success is that Badoo reflects society. It's all about you."

Badoo and its competitors, such as Skout, another popular meeting app, are part of a growing universe of smartphone apps specializing in social discovery with a dating bent. "Any site that can be used for flirting will be," says Paul Davison, who founded Highlight, another location-based dating app. "But this is much bigger than that. You'll be able to walk into a room, look around you, and know everyone's name and everything about them. It can make profound, new things happen." The field of social-discovery apps includes others with names like Intro, Qrious, Mingle, Sonar, Kismet, and Glancee, which was bought by Facebook in 2012.

Traditional online-dating sites are hoping to keep up. "We are thinking more about ourselves as simply a dating site rather than an online dating site," said Sam Yagan in 2012. "We want the focus to be getting people to meet in person, actually going on dates." Earlier that year, at iDate Miami (where Yagan was finally allowed to speak), he told a conference room: "Now we're seeing a lot of sites that are starting off as dating sites, and then trying to do things to move into social, like taking the pink hearts off the homepage. Because think about the offline world: In a bar, you don't announce you're there to meet women. So sites like Zimride"—a social-discovery site geared toward carpooling—"are finding that you don't have to be explicitly for dating in order to generate datinglike behavior."

Just as important as the change in technology—going from Web site to mobile—is the subtle shift in branding. Savvy entrepreneurs hope to beat the lingering taboo and draw in more users by offering social discovery (a sunny-sounding product that only a philistine or hermit would reject) rather than online dating (an icky redoubt of the desperate). In 2012, Sean Parker, the former Facebook president, teamed up with his old Napster cofounder, Shawn Fanning, to build Airtime, a social-discovery site in video format that works in conjunction with Facebook. Airtime, Parker told CNN, "allows me to use my interests, and all the other information I've built up about myself on Facebook, to match with people who I haven't met, people I might like to get to know." The word "dating" appeared nowhere in the company's press materials nor in the media's massive coverage of Airtime's launch.

Could any heavily trafficked Web site be a potential dating site? What about other sites that operate on matching algorithms? In 2012, Spotify, a music-streaming app similar to Pandora, integrated with a dating site for music lovers called Tastebuds.fm. Tastebuds scans your most frequently played music on Spotify, shows you people nearby who have similar tastes, lets you browse their playlists, listen to their music, and send them messages.

Dating through Badoo or Tastebuds versus dating through OkCupid or Match changes how we meet people, as well as how we think about what we want. But whether online or off, we ultimately select mates based on a small handful of key attributes: age, looks, income, education, ethnicity, children, and marital history. Men and women weigh these attributes differently. But any pool, small or large, online or off, tends to sort itself out automatically, as if by magic.

A 2010 study coauthored by Duke University's Dan Ariely, a leading scholar of online-dating behavior, found that the "natural equilibrium mechanism" by which people pair off in any online-dating pool generates "sorting patterns that are qualitatively similar to those observed offline." The study found, in other words, that dating online is different from dating offline largely—and perhaps only—because it turbocharges that equilibrium mechanism, creating what Ariely calls "an efficient, frictionless market environment."

Had it not been for Match, Tom may never have wound up with a smoker. But given the opportunity to browse and meet hundreds of women offline, he may have. This, then, is the new serendipity. Yes, Tom and Kelly were both on Match and therefore both looking for a partner. But technology helped them stumble on something good that they might never have discovered on their own.

"The question for us," says Match's Thombre, "is always the same: Who's the best person we have to show you today?"

Relationship success, on the other hand, is another issue. It's one thing to put a pretty, low-maintenance smoker in front of Tom and watch him bite, or serve Carrie up the child-friendly divorcee she requested. Whether they're "made for each other" is a much tougher question. Still, many dating sites claim they can predict compatibility, and, in some cases, they may be telling the truth.

ALEXIS, PART III

↓

What's the Etiquette Here?

DESPITE HER PROMISE TO SHARE HER ONLINE-DATING ADVENTURES with a large community of people she's never met, Alexis is serious about finding a boyfriend. In her Match profile, she writes:

> I'm a passionate person with a big personality, I suppose not for the faint of heart. Always trying to live healthier, learn more, read more, see more, do more.
>
> My Kentucky-raised mother says I am "very loving and loyal but not one of those nice girls." Thanks mom. She's referring to my sarcasm and my at-times inappropriate sense of humor, but I get more from my Southern upbringing than she thinks. I mean, I keep my nails perfect and wear lots of dresses. I was raised in ballet to be graceful. When I drink it's always Kentucky bourbon on the rocks. I have a charming, diplomatic demeanor and love entertaining. I'm very traditional in the sense that I love cooking for friends and loves . . . but I must warn you I can be a control freak about it, and unless you have verified skills you can best help me by sitting on the couch and enjoying your beer.
>
> Looking for a guy who takes pride in being good to his friends and family. Who's looking for something serious. Who dances at

shows, who can take a joke and tell a story. Who is happy having a quiet night in sometimes, but can play hard as well. Who is good to his body and challenges himself. Who perhaps likes Phish and The Grateful Dead but does not live in a van down by the river.

Immediately, in the first few days, Alexis is inundated with messages from people she calls "icky folk." For laughs, she posts one on Phantasy Tour: "Love, Do you want to go clubbing? Me and my friend are going this Friday. It's not the best place to get to know someone but the music is bitching. Bring friends if you want. I'll pay for you but not your friends."

"Tell me," she asks Phantasy Tour, "do you actually send the 'not interested' automated thing? Or should I just ignore people? What's the etiquette here?"

"There is nothing more infuriating," replies a PTer, "than spending several hours carefully crafting a letter to someone with whom you think you'd have a connection only to be ignored. I make it a point to politely thank writers for their interest, but say I'm not sure it's a match. I feel better treating people the way I'd like to be treated, even when it's awkward to do so."

"My suggestion, from the girls I know, is to be pro-active," writes another. "Don't just wait for guys to message you, or you'll be inundated with creep-shows. Search for people with common interests, and say what's up to them."

Alexis agrees there's no reason that the offline tradition of men initiating a relationship should apply online. The point, after all, is control. So she takes matters into her own hands, searching the Match database for exactly what she wants—a college-educated professional in his early thirties who doesn't post annoying pictures and has written a funny, sex-free profile. Must love music.

"I prefer older guys," she tells Phantasy Tour. "My peers can be annoying. Plus I like to see how a guy shakes out as a man. I don't need some jobless wook [a hippie without ambition] I have to pay for. I don't have an income listed for my match," she writes, "but I work really hard and don't want to be the one pulling the weight, and they need to be able to support my potential babies. I come from a long line of lawyers, so they get a plus one." Her comments set off a Phantasy Tour debate over modern gender roles.

"Holy shit," writes a PTer, "what a trixie [prostitute]."

"Let me point out that men and women live in two entirely different universes," writes another PTer. "What you ladies have to do is consent. That is all. What men have to do is . . . everything. We have to charm you, prove our worth, be indifferent, be cool, have an attractive career, be talented and sexy, buy you stuff, go in for the kiss, fuck you (but not cum too soon!)."

But Alexis believes men of her Millennial generation suffer from a kind of schizophrenia: On one hand, they decry feminism and women who think they can have it all, children and a career; on the other, they resent traditional women who expect men to be breadwinners. Men her age, it seems, want stay-at-home Stepford wives but also think it's a crime for them to have expectations. "A woman giving up a career to raise your babies and wash your balls with a warm wet rag deserves a payoff of security without resentment," she writes.

Some male PTers defend themselves, but Alexis continues: "Fantasy football, video games, shaving hairs left all over the sink, treating women like trash, reading Tucker Max books and *Maxim* magazine (aka men's *Cosmo*)—you all have your own annoying issues. ESPN is just as gossipy as E!. And women who dress slutty or act ditzy do it because they're taught it's what you want. Maybe if you reinforced that you actually want a woman of character, instead of idolizing *Playboy* sluts, you could change the culture."

CHAPTER FOUR

It Knows My Anal Preferences?

AMAZING REVELATIONS FROM
THE SCIENCE OF DATING

No one knows what chemistry is at work when two people fall in love, least of all a computer. The claim that some scientific match has been made is obviously misleading.

—Dr. Igor Aleksander, British scientist, 1973

I n his 2010 novel, *Super Sad True Love Story*, satirist Gary Shteyngart imagines a future of perfect information transparency. Every character carries an "äppärät," an iPhone-like device that can access every piece of information imaginable, including, for instance, the financial and property holdings of a prospective date's father.

In an early scene, the novel's bumbling hero, Lenny Abramov, meets his friends at a Staten Island nightclub called Cervix. Inside the club, Lenny's friend Vishnu tells him to take out his äppärät and set the "Community Parameters" at "Immediate Space 360," then to look at a woman he likes—any woman—and press the äppärät to his heart.

Lenny narrates:

The girl across the bar laughed immediately without even turning my way. A bunch of figures appeared on my screen: "FUCKABILITY 780/800, PERSONALITY 800/800, ANAL/ORAL/ VAGINAL PREFERENCE 1/3/2 . . ."

"But I don't even know her personality," I said. "And how does it know my anal preferences?"

"The personality score depends on how 'extro' she is," Vishnu explained. "Check it out. This girl done got three-thousand-plus Images, eight hundred streams, and a long multimedia thing on how her father abused her. Your äppärät runs that against the stuff you've downloaded about yourself and then it comes up with a score. Like, you've dated a lot of abused girls, so it knows you're into that shit."

As I write this, just two years after the novel was published, Shteyngart's hi-tech fantasy world isn't really much of a fantasy. Much of the dating technology he describes in *Super Sad True Love Story* already exists in some form. As for the transparency Shteyngart imagines, it's easier to speculate about what information about us will be accessible online in the future than to guess what *won't* be. Facebook founder Mark Zuckerberg predicts, not without self-interest, that over the next decade a thousand times more information about each individual could flow through Facebook. "People are going to have to have a device with them at all times that's [automatically] sharing," he told David Kirkpatrick for *The Facebook Effect: The Inside Story of the Company That Is Connecting the World.*

Four decades after Jeff Tarr had the idea to install hundreds of special typewriters around Harvard so that a boy could type his requirements and immediately receive the name of a girl who was free that night, location-based dating services—GPS applications that show you every eligible dater within, say, five hundred feet of your Immediate Space 360—are becoming all the rage. Grindr, the premiere mobile-dating application for gay men, was so successful that it released a heterosexual version, Blendr. HowAboutWe.com, the popular dating site based on first-date ideas ("How about we grab brunch and tackle the Sunday crossword puzzle?"), has a location-based app. eHarmony released a "location conscious" app called Jazzed. Match has Crowded Room. OkCupid has Locals. Now many dating sites, or social-discovery platforms, launch primarily, or even solely, as mobile applications.

"OkCupid Locals merges a Twitter-like broadcast feature, Foursquare's location database, and insights on OkCupid's 8-million person membership to give you nearby connection opportunities," wrote Sam Yagan in an e-mail to users notifying them about the launch of Locals.

Notice how Yagan chooses his words carefully. He doesn't use terms like "personality profiling" or "compatibility." Instead, he says that OkCupid generates "insights" on its users, the implication being that the system can glean a little more about you than you can and then use that knowledge to provide you not with soul mates or matches but with "connection opportunities."

What's the difference?

Even in the early days of Jeff Tarr's computer dating, people assumed, or hoped, that the fact of technology-as-mediator would mean not just *more* dates but *better* dates. The Great God Computer must know something we don't, the thinking went. It just *must*. Even while academics doubted that something as complex as compatibility between two people who've never met could be predicted, the notion that it could became a wonderful marketing tool, and red meat for the media. "Every journalist just assumed we were making better matches," Tarr recalls of the Operation Match era, "and we were happy to perpetuate that thinking."

From the company's perspective, claiming a superior "scientific matching system" or "personality profiling test" could distinguish you from the field. The truth, Tarr and Dewan knew, was something else. "Any date was a good date," Tarr recalls. "The idea that we were matching based on compatibility was purely a marketing thing. It was always more art than science."

Dewan agrees: "There was a lot of randomness to it. 'Do you like pizza?' 'Me too!' 'What kind of movies do you like?' 'Romantic comedies?' 'Me too!' Then you go meet her, and most of the time you put your head in your hands because she was so ugly—and she was thinking the same about you. Everyone lied about their looks. We found that 96 percent of women and 92 percent of men said they were above average in terms of looks. On the other hand, the matching worked when it came down to the basics. The big hang-up was appearance. But we were dealing with computers that had twelve kilobytes of memory. We couldn't do pictures."*

Digitally intermediated introductions have evolved quite a bit from the days of Contact and Operation Match. Back then, two companies battled for domination over a market that extended to thousands of students in the United States. Today thousands of sites are going after *tens of millions* of mate searchers around the world. It's not enough for these companies to say, as Dewan did, that their questionnaire is more sophisticated. The pitch must be more elaborate, more official sounding. The computer must know something we don't.

The first five years of the online-dating industry evolved in two stages. First there were sites like Match and its progeny, which were basically searchable personal ads. Whether on a general site like Match or a site that targeted a specific niche, such as Jdate, you answered some questions about yourself and about your ideal partner, and then the search was left to you. This changed in 2000, when Neil Clark Warren introduced a new online-dating model—or marketing gimmick, depending on one's point of view.

Born in 1934, Warren was by far the oldest of the online-dating pioneers—three decades older than Gary Kremen. Warren's interest in compatibility developed early, during his childhood in rural Iowa. His parents' marriage may've lasted seventy years, but Warren's childhood was spent with two people who never talked. "They had a nice marriage," he said, "but they were not a very well-matched couple. . . . My

---

* On a modern computer, five kilobytes of memory are allocated just to display the cursor on the screen.

dad was just so stinking bright, and my mom was so sweet, but she was two standard deviations below him in intelligence." Warren's father, who owned a Chevrolet dealership, a John Deere outfit, and a grocery store, wanted to talk about things like "Why do you think the Jews and Arabs are continuing to fight over the earth?" while his mother, Warren said, "didn't know there was a Middle East."

When Warren's father ran for office in Polk County, his mother voted for another candidate, because she thought politics was a dirty business. Warren remembers being bored to death growing up.

After receiving an undergraduate degree from Pepperdine University, a Christian liberal arts college in California, Warren got a master's in divinity from Princeton Theological Seminary and a PhD in psychology from the University of Chicago. For fifteen years, between 1967 and 1982, he served as a professor and then as dean of Fuller Theological Seminary's Graduate School of Psychology while maintaining a private practice as a psychologist.

Warren considered his own longtime marriage to his wife, Marilyn, to be a lucky success. Many of their friends suffered "the excruciating pain of divorce," Warren said, while he and Marilyn wound up having broad-based compatibility without knowing it. Warren refused to let his three daughters rely on luck alone, however, because it would be, he said, like sending them out to skate on thin ice. Warren focused his practice on marriage compatibility, counseling couples, and performing "divorce autopsies" on failed marriages. In 1975, he published a pamphlet entitled "Selecting a Marriage Partner," and then went on to write ten books, including *Learning to Live With the Love of Your Life*, *Loving the Life You Live: 3 Secrets to Feeling Good—Deep Down in Your Soul*, and *Date . . . or Soul Mate? How to Know If Someone Is Worth Pursuing in Two Dates or Less*. Warren curated an image of grandfatherly affability: square glasses, elegant sport coats, and a well-manicured white coiffure that matched his teeth. There was something distinctly welcoming about his pillowy lips. His soft blue eyes beamed trust and understanding.

In 1993, Warren published *Finding the Love of Your Life*, a "primer on all the qualities that two people should consider before committing to marriage." Two years later, he and his son-in-law, a former real estate developer named Greg Forgatch, started Neil Clark Warren & Associates. The company, which offered seminars and teaching tools based on the book, quickly moved online. "We came to the conclusion that single people in America do not want more education about relationships," Warren said. "They're sick of that. They want somebody."

In early 2000, Warren and Forgatch redesigned the site as a matchmaking service called eHarmony. The goal, however, wouldn't be creating great first dates. It would be creating great marriages. "Not every marriage made at eHarmony is going to last," Forgatch said. "But the purpose of being here is to lower the divorce rate. That's Neil's vision—literally to change the world."

Warren's matchmaking process on eHarmony began with the user filling out a 436-question personality profiling test. The user then received a list of other users on the site with whom he or she was most compatible. In order to correspond with others, they were required to subscribe. There followed a "Guided Communication" process through which the site regulated interaction.

Rather than a big searchable database of singles based on the idea of newspaper personals, eHarmony was about science, algorithms, and a secret sauce. The system determined matches and predicted compatibility based on "29 Dimensions of Compatibility." These dimensions were divided into "Core Traits" ("defining aspects of who you are that remain largely unchanged") and "Vital Attributes" ("based on learning and experience and are more likely to change based on life events and decisions you make as an adult"). The "scientific precision at the core of eHarmony's matching methodology" was, according to corporate literature, "proven to predict the success of long-term relationships." Warren's system focused on similarity—rather than difference—and was based on research he conducted with five thousand married couples.

Further elaboration was vague. But some hard-and-fast rules did apply. The system would not match women with men who were shorter than them. Nor would it match people who were already married—a group that, eHarmony claimed, accounted for nearly one third of the million users it rejected. A thirty-year-old woman would be matched with men between twenty-seven and forty, while a thirty-year-old man would be matched with women between twenty-three and thirty-three. People who had been married four or more times were rejected, as were gays and lesbians, as were people whose responses to the questionnaire failed eHarmony's "dysthymia scale," indicating depression.

eHarmony's paternalism felt reassuring, both to those who entered the date-o-sphere with trepidation and to those who felt like they needed help with their search. A huge TV marketing campaign fueled eHarmony's growth. Within three years it had more than two million registered users. The site claimed to have a 20 percent "conversion rate" of free users to paying subscribers. That was four times the industry average.

Success, however, became a problem. Much of eHarmony's initial popularity was due to Warren's relationship with James Dobson, founder of Focus on the Family, the nonprofit evangelical organization aimed at "nurturing and defending the God-ordained institution of the family and promoting biblical truths worldwide." It had been through Dobson's radio show that eHarmony attracted users. Around 2005, Warren realized that for eHarmony—a for-profit enterprise—worldwide influence would require a more secular vision.

"I think there is something very incredible about Jesus," Warren said. "I don't back away from that. At the same time . . . the public we want to serve is the world."

Warren bought back the rights to three of his books that Focus on the Family had published. He said the public recognizes Focus on the Family as occupying "a very precise" political and spiritual position and to have its name on the top of his books would be a killer for the company. eHarmony grew to be less exclusive, accepting gays and lesbians after a lawsuit forced its hand. Not long after its break from Focus on the Family, the site claimed to have fourteen million registered users from more than two hundred countries.

The story of eHarmony showed that the market for "scientific matching" was strong. Naturally, competitors arrived and quickly tried to differentiate themselves. Duane Dahl, the CEO of PerfectMatch.com, which was founded in 2003, referred derogatorily to eHarmony's approach as "marriage in a box." Dahl said his members are looking for a genuine person "who can respect them for who they are, what they are about, before getting married."

Really, though, there were more similarities than differences. Just as Warren mugged for eHarmony, the copycats would also put professionals on the homepage, people with official titles who claimed to have cracked the code of human compatibility: Relationship Scientist; Sexual Anthropologist. These sponsors tend to hold doctoral degrees and write self-help books. In labs, they reproduce the conditions of relationships, study interactions, and generate conclusions. People of type A are compatible with people of type B. Here's why they worked. Here's why they failed. Here, read this new book.

Dr. Pepper Schwartz, coauthor of *Love Test* and author of *Getaway Guide to the Great Sex Weekend*, *Everything You Know About Love and Sex Is Wrong*, and much, much more, is one such promoter. Dr. Schwartz is a professor of sociology at the University of Washington in Seattle, and in her spare time she poses for PerfectMatch, with whom she helped develop The Duet® Total Compatibility System. A pocket-sized woman with a calming smile, Schwartz says the system is based on the Myers-Briggs Type Indicator, a questionnaire designed to measure how people perceive the world and make decisions. You can read about The Duet® Total Compatibility System in her book, *Finding Your Perfect Match: 8 Keys to Finding Lasting Love Through True Compatibility*.

GenePartner.com took scientific matching to the cellular level. For $249 users receive a kit with which to swab the inside of their mouth Then they send the swab back to the company and receive a Gene Partner ID. For an extra fee they can hunt for their genetic soul mate on the site.

The media eats it up, often parroting the claims of scientific matching sites as hard news. When ABC's *Good Morning America* covered GenePartner, it introduced the segment in awed tones, reporting: "Now, hard science is making it easier to find true love. A new matchmaking system uses DNA to help you find your dream date, and it's redefining what it means to be compatible. . . . Making that first match has always been an inexact science, kissing a few frogs, unavoidable. Until now. With the use of DNA technology, the science of dating has become a whole lot less inexact."

The academic community called bullshit. In 2012, a team of five psychology professors, led by Eli Finkel at Northwestern University, published a withering rebuttal to what sites like eHarmony, PerfectMatch, and GenePartner claimed to do. It is "virtually impossible," the authors argued, "to succeed at the task many matching sites have set for themselves"—specifically, "their promise to identify potential mates who are uniquely compatible with their users."

Finkel and his coauthors laid out their argument in a paper published in *Psychological Science in the Public Interest.* According to the paper, the most dubious claim made by scientific matchmaking sites is that the likelihood of any two people having a successful relationship is knowable *in advance* of their meeting. It is one thing to look at a couple that's already together and predict the likelihood of their success. Indeed, it's been practiced for nearly thirty years by John Gottman, a psychologist at the University of Washington who was made famous in *Blink: The Power of Thinking Without Thinking,* Malcolm Gladwell's 2005 book. By measuring certain emotions and reactions that a couple might express during a conversation—for instance, contempt, defensiveness, stonewalling—Gottman can predict, with 95 percent accuracy, whether a couple will still be married in fifteen years. Other research teams have reported similarly high levels of accuracy in predicting marital outcomes for couples who are already together.

This line of research has been taken as encouragement for matching sites that claim to predict compatibility between strangers. But Team Finkel argues that the success of Gottman's technique means nothing for matching sites. Why? Because the Gottman marriage prediction studies don't actually predict anything. They merely: 1) assess a couple on many variables; 2) follow the couple to see if they divorce; and then 3) use a computer to identify the combination of variables that best accounts for the outcome. This is not *pre*diction. It is *post*diction. The Gottman studies can identify things like "contempt" as a relationship killer, a strong determinant of a certain outcome. But that is all. In a way, Gottman's ability is the same one that Warren, as a marriage therapist, claimed to bring to eHarmony. He had diagnosed problems in *existing* couples. Did that mean he could predict compatibility between strangers?

No, Team Finkel says, because prior to meeting the most important elements of relationship success are unknown and, therefore, excluded from the matching process. Granted, there are some concrete factors, such as geography and socioeconomic status, which are important to relationship success, and they can be measured easily in a questionnaire and plugged into an algorithm. These concrete factors are meaningful. Whether someone dates online or off, he or she tends to look for people who live nearby and share a background. But these factors don't narrow the pool much. Meanwhile, far more relevant factors are unknowable in advance, such as the way a couple will experience and handle stress, particularly stress arising from things outside the couple's control—unemployment, career unhappiness, infertility, and illness.

Team Finkel then takes aim at the matching models themselves. Sites that claim to offer scientific matching generally adopt one of two perspectives: the "relationship aptitude perspective" or the "compatibility perspective." The relationship aptitude perspective is more simplistic; it functions on the premise that some people are more likely to succeed at relationships than others. You can spot these people by asking about certain traits, preferences, and aspects of their personal history, such as whether they had positive relationships with childhood caregivers. As the term "aptitude" suggests, this perspective considers relationship ability to be a sort of talent, a quality that, though it can be nurtured and improved over time, remains relatively stable. Team Finkel concedes that the effects of these personality differences on relationships are well supported by research but argues that they leave "most of the variance in adult romantic relationships unexplained."

The compatibility perspective, on the other hand, assumes not that some people are bound to fail in relationships and others succeed, but rather that there is someone for everyone. The most frequently cited basis for compatibility is similarity—as eHarmony believes. But similarity, Team Finkel says, is difficult to measure: The perception of similarity between two people can have as much to do with relationship satisfaction as with actual similarity. Second, there's no clear consensus on what kinds of similarity matter. Again, concrete things like religion, wealth, and education have been associated with relationship happiness. But scientific matching sites aren't claiming to match on these concrete variables. They focus, rather, on psychological variables such as personality, the idea being that two people will succeed romantically if they interact with and view the world in similar ways. In any case, Team Finkel argues, similarity, whether actual or perceived, accounts for only a tiny variance in overall relationship satisfaction. Besides, matching on negative personality traits, such as neuroticism, is unlikely to yield relationship bliss.

At eHarmony, Gian Gonzaga, the relationship scientist who took over for Neil Clark Warren, sees it differently: "A very anxious person," Gonzaga says, "will be better off with someone who has experienced anxiety, even in just one area of their lives, because that person will be empathetic."

On Valentine's Day 2012, WBEZ, a Chicago affiliate of National Public Radio, invited two locals, Eli Finkel and Sam Yagan, to debate the issue of just how much dating sites can deliver on their matching claims. OkCupid, to be clear, does not pitch itself as a scientific matching site. But it does collect as much information from its users as any dating site and feeds that information through an algorithm to generate match suggestions.

"It *is* the case," began Finkel, "that people in same-race marriages are less likely to divorce than people in interracial marriages. But it's not like these matching algorithm sites are saying, 'Hey, you're white. I can introduce you to someone who's also white.' No, they're claiming that they match you to someone who's similar to you based on psychological dimensions, like personality or values. And the evidence [from eighty years of relationship scholarship] is just very weak that that actually predicts long-term relationship well-being."

Yagan didn't address Finkel's point directly. Instead, he argued that OkCupid can narrow down large pools of people and suggest the ones you're likely to like: "But Eli . . . wouldn't [your critique] apply equally to Google? Online dating is a search for a person. Google is a search for anything. When you type something into Google, it takes all the billions of pages on the Web and says, 'Here are the ten that we think are the best *options* for you.'"

Yet the position of Team Finkel, if taken to its logical extreme—that predictive matching on psychological variables is a false promise— would deny Yagan's claim. If anything, their NPR debate highlights a fundamental incompatibility between a social psychologist and a math guy, a professor and a salesman.

In fact, Team Finkel's argument came as no surprise to the dating industry. For a decade the people at Match had disbelieved scientific matching. "When eHarmony took so much market share in the early 2000s, we hired the best science people," recalls Brian Bowman, who at the time was Match's vice president of product strategy. "It was clear that there was absolutely no validity to personality profiling. But eHarmony was doing a huge marketing push. The good white-haired doctor was the big presence on TV. So we had to offer what he was offering."

Match considered buying eHarmony. Instead, it spun off a competing site called Chemistry.com in 2006 and paid anthropologist Helen Fisher (*Why Him? Why Her?: Finding Real Love by Understanding Your Personality Type*) to put her face on the homepage. Dr. Fisher developed a matching system built around four personality types: Explorer (adventurous, creative, energetic); Builder (calm, cautious, conventional); Director (dominant, analytical, decisive); and Negotiator (empathetic, idealistic, emotionally expressive). Fisher's questionnaire asks Chemistry's daters about the length of their index finger compared to the length of their ring finger. The differential, she claims, is associated with the level of testosterone, which in turn corresponds to one of the four personality types, which in turn determines who you are scientifically compatible with.

Chemistry ran competing TV ads that differentiated it from—and bashed—eHarmony. "I mean, I *am* a good person, right?" asks an actress in one of the Chemistry spots, just as a giant red "Rejected by eHarmony" graphic slams onto the screen, followed by a note that eHarmony has denied more than a million mate seekers. eHarmony tried to punch back. Lanny Davis, eHarmony's crisis management lawyer who served as special counsel to Bill Clinton during the Monica Lewinsky affair, asked NBC and *People* magazine to stop running the Chemistry ads. But to no avail. Chemistry soon ranked among the top twenty dating sites in the United States, not far behind eHarmony.

The online matchmaking space was heating up. Between 2007 and 2010, personality-profiling sites—which were defined as those sites that require users to fill out lengthy questionnaires—grew steadily, coming to account for a quarter of the market. Plenty of Fish spun off its own matchmaking site, eVow.com, which advertised "an innovative compatibility matching system" for long-term relationships. "No more browsing online dating profiles wondering if that person is actually serious about finding someone! In fact, we reject more than 10% of people who we know aren't serious."

To Brian Bowman's mind, the concept of scientific matching is no different than any other dating niche. "As a marketing hook," he says, "it works great. Because consumers are eager to latch onto this idea that you hit a button and your soul mate pops up. That's why the industry is obsessed with relationship success metrics."

Bowman calls this obsession pedantic. "What you have to remember about the dating industry—and this is one reason why even top dating sites rarely sell for more than $100 million—is that the products are largely undifferentiated. In any undifferentiated market, you're left to fight a branding battle with the guy who's spending the most to go on TV. In the dating business, that's meant that the message to the customer must be: 'We're asking you to invest in something that has unique value, i.e., high marriage rates.' Meanwhile, everyone knows that all personality profiling is bullshit. Statistically, you can't put people into categories and say, 'Here's a formula.' If dating sites were being fully honest, they'd stick to one success metric: 'Did you have a good first date?'"

The great algorithm debate is unlikely to be resolved. The academics who do not work for dating sites will continue to be skeptical. Sites will continue to guard their secret matching formulas while producing studies that support whatever conclusions benefit their bottom line. At the moment, the consensus for how far technology can go in predicting compatibility seems to fall somewhere between Finkel, on the one hand, and Bowman and Yagan on the other: *We can show you the people you are mostly likely to connect with on a first date. After that, we make no guarantees.* But the story doesn't end there.

The industry's obsession with predicting compatibility overlooks one of the more intriguing implications of the Internet's rising dominance as a matchmaker. On personality profiling sites, and even on sites that don't ask any questions, online daters provide an incredible amount of information. Not only when they fill out a questionnaire, but every time they post a photo, send a message (or ignore a message), leave a site (or return to one). What are sites doing with all this data? Does it exclusively benefit their business, or does the Internet's novel ability to monitor and document the many details of social interaction help us arrive at a better understanding of what we really want, how to go about getting it, and what those people we like want from us?

Let's take Shteyngart's scene in the Cervix nightclub a step further. Curious about the brunette, Lenny approaches her at the bar. Thanks to his äppärät, he knows they align on certain metrics. But he's still nervous. What does he say? Hmmm. Well, he sees she's Asian and drinking a beer. Do these facts mean anything for how he should comport himself? Has he learned anything useful from past encounters that he could apply to this one? Will he learn anything useful from this encounter that he can apply to the next?

Suppose there was a robot following Lenny around, cataloging his every move, her reaction to his every move, and providing a feedback loop of information advising him on how to enhance his likelihood of success, cluing him in to the mistakes other guys were making and setting him straight on the disconnect between what he says he wants and what he actually seems to want, with every interaction saved, broken down, and analyzed? Lenny is closing in now. He hears the brunette talking to her friends about a horror movie. Lenny likes horror films too! He can see that she has a curvy figure, is eating a salad, and has a crooked tooth. What does it all mean?

The study of how we behave on online-dating sites is a kind of sister science to the studies of mating and sex that began around the turn of the twentieth century. It was then that two pioneering sex surveys—one by Katherine B. Davis, the other by Dr. Clelia Mosher—penetrated the shame surrounding America's hush-hush sexual culture. They reported, among other things, high rates of contraceptive use, high sex drives, and regular masturbation among married women. A majority of the women polled confessed to believing that pleasure was a legitimate purpose of conjugal relations. More studies followed. At midcentury, Alfred Kinsey's investigation of male and female sexual behavior represented the first prominent coupling of science and sex. *Look* magazine predicted that Kinsey's studies could "have a tremendous effect on the future social history of mankind. For they are presenting facts. They are revealing not what *should* be, but what *is*. For the first time data on human sex behavior is entirely separated from questions of philosophy, moral values, and social customs."

The dispassionate format of science became its own kind of religion. In 1966, William Masters and Virginia Johnson, the other pioneers of sex research, published *Human Sexual Response*, their write-up of a ten-year study of sexual physiology. Among other conclusions, they reported: 1) as female climax is reached, the clitoris, counterintuitively, becomes too sensitive for direct contact and therefore retracts shortly prior to the moment of truth, becoming a potential source of confusion for her partner; and 2) the head of the penis, or glans, becomes oversensitive after ejaculation, and therefore a woman should not resent a man for pulling out before she's done.

Kinsey, Masters, and Johnson believed there were social values to be obtained by the spread of such knowledge—about sexual physiology, sure, but also about what your neighbor thought about sex, or how your neighbor was doing it better, or differently, or the same. Fast-forward four decades: The math geeks and data wonks behind online dating own gobs of raw data, the quantity and quality of which would turn Kinsey, Masters, and Johnson green with envy. "We can't even say what the learning curve looks like," says Markus Frind, referring to the amount of data Plenty of Fish accumulates. "Because every day we climb the slope of new information and learning, and every day it gets steeper." The date-o-sphere begged for a Masters and Johnson.

In 1999, Christian Rudder was a senior English major at Harvard when he decided to add a math concentration. In addition to becoming an indie film actor* and rock-band guitarist, Rudder became a partner in OkCupid. In 2009, when OkCupid became popular, Rudder began playing around in the site's data trove as if it were his own personal sandbox. He started writing a corporate blog called OkTrends. Its mission: No truth, no matter how ugly, would be spared. In an early post about racism in dating, Rudder wrote:

> Welcome back, dorks. We've processed the messaging habits of over a million people and are about to basically prove that, despite what you might've heard from the Obama campaign and organic cereal commercials, racism is alive and well. It would be awesome if the other major online-dating players would go out on a limb and release their own race data, too. I can't imagine they will: multi–million dollar enterprises rarely like to admit that the people paying them those millions act like turds. But being poor gives us a certain freedom to alienate our users. So there.

Alienating users became integral to Rudder's aesthetic: "The basic currency of the Internet is human ignorance," he wrote, "and, frankly, our database holds a strong cash position!" While his style incorporated elements of shock and humor, Rudder set himself a rather serious

---

* Rudder appeared in Andrew Bujalski's *Funny Ha Ha*, for which Rudder's band, Bishop Allen, supplied music. The movie, which was named to a 2005 Top 10 list by *New York Times* film critic A. O. Scott, is said to have invented the "mumblecore" genre.

course: to present empirical proof that many perceptions and assumptions about modern mating were out of sync with reality. Like his progenitors, Rudder wanted to get down to what was really real. Able to monitor and catalog the behavior of millions of people who didn't know (or, because of the anonymity accorded by the site, didn't care) that they were being watched, Rudder embarked on a social scientist's dream, becoming something of an industry oracle. Here's a smattering of lessons he taught the online-dating community:

> Even though white men get the most responses to their messages, they write back 20 percent less often than other men; they do tend to reply often to Middle Eastern women. Black women reply to messages at the greatest rate, yet get by far the fewest replies to their messages, including those sent to other blacks.

> White women—even though they have above average compatibility with almost every group—prefer white men, to the exclusion of everyone else. Asian and Hispanic women prefer white men even more exclusively.

> Jewish and agnostic men, on the whole, get along with people much better than Hindu and Muslim men, and Jewish men match Muslim women better than Muslim men match Muslim women, *not* meaning that Muslim men are bad people, just that they're harder to please.

> When categorized by religion and gender, Jewish women are the most likely to claim they've never masturbated.

> The ideal length of a first message is two hundred characters, and you should never use text-speak, except for those phrases that denote humor, keeping in mind that "haha" beats the slightly evil-sounding "hehe."

> You should compliment anything *except* looks. Guys should be self-effacing but women should not.

> Vegetarian women are twice as likely as nonveggies to enjoy giving oral sex (for those intrigued: VeggieDate.com).

A woman's desirability, measured in messages received, peaks at age twenty-one. At age forty-eight, men are nearly twice as sought after as women.

Women are harsher judges of physical beauty than are men.

As men get older they're more likely to develop a yen for rough sex, whereas the rate of women who like it rough, which was never very high in the first place, descends with age.

As women get older they are more reluctant to emphasize their bodies in profile photos, opting instead to show themselves in nonsexual contexts, such as being outdoors, despite the fact that striking sexual poses is a very good strategy for achieving increased message volume. Photos showing the woman doing something interesting, however, such as playing the guitar or scuba diving or walking through a desert, are more likely to lead to actual conversations, Rudder points out, rather than just "Hey, nice rack," which is unlikely to get a reply.

Women prefer photos in which men are looking away from the camera (hypothesis: less intimidating), and men prefer the opposite (they want a woman's full attention). Profile photos should be taken with a Panasonic, a low *f* number, and no flash.

iPhone users report having more sex than BlackBerry and Android users.

If you're a twentysomething guy with a nice body, you should take off your shirt, but if you're over thirty, you should not.*

---

* As one twenty-seven-year-old OkCupid-ite put it: "You should message me if you enjoy shirts, and wearing them in photos." Older male online daters I spoke to agreed that candid shirtless shots are more successful than posed shirtless shots, implying some kind of link between shirtlessness and maturity: As men age they are expected to do useful things, or at least active things, rather than just pose naked with pectorals and six-pack flexed—a strategy that remains successful for younger guys. However, if older men happen to be photographed shirtless while doing useful/active things, then the resulting image may be an asset in mate acquisition. Whereas women should just be naked all the time.

The average thirty-year-old man spends as much time messaging eighteen- and nineteen-year-olds as he does messaging women his own age.

Men who chase teenagers sacrifice more than just their souls because:

➡ 75 percent of thirty-nine-year-old women rank sex as one of their favorite activities versus only 25 percent of eighteen-year-old women;

➡ 81 percent of thirty-year-old women enjoy giving oral sex versus only 63 percent of nineteen-year-old women;

➡ 40 percent of thirty-five-year-old women would be interested in a threesome with another woman versus 29 percent of twenty-four-year-old women; and

➡ (as if more evidence is needed) younger men tend to want to be dominated in bed, and it just so happens that older women are interested in doing precisely that.

White men like Tom Clancy and *Ghostbusters* while white women prefer Jodi Picoult and *When Harry Met Sally*. The top preferences of white women—bonfires, boating, horseback riding, thunderstorms—demonstrate what Rudder calls "a rural self-mythology," while the preferences of white men amount to the "frat house" stereotype. It's unclear whether one begot the other.

Among gay people, 2 percent have 23 percent of the total reported gay sex, despite the image of gay people and promiscuity. But other stereotypes of gay men hold entirely true. To wit, their top preferences: *The Devil Wears Prada*, Britney Spears, *Mean Girls*, and Kelly Clarkson. Online daters are, on average, two inches shorter and 20 percent poorer than their profiles claim.

Based on their browsing history, 80 percent of users who claim to be bisexual are in fact interested in only one gender.

One in every seven straight men and two in every seven straight women would like their partner to put a strap-on dildo inside them.

The more men, as a group, disagree about a woman's looks, the more they end up liking her, and having some men think she's ugly actually works in her favor. To simplify: If *some* men think a woman is ugly, then other men (who don't think she's ugly) are *more* likely to message her. Whereas if *some* men think she's cute, then other men (who think she's more than cute) become *less* interested. "Suppose you're a man who's really into someone," Rudder writes, attempting to unpack this better-to-be-ugly-to-some-guys-than-to-be-cute-to-some-guys paradox. "If you suspect other men are *uninterested*, it means less competition. You might start thinking: maybe she's lonely; maybe she's just waiting to find a guy who appreciates her; at least I won't get lost in the crowd. Maybe these small thoughts, plus the fact that you really think she's hot, prod you to action. You send her the perfectly crafted opening message: 'sup.'"

By contrast, says Rudder, someone who's "conventionally cute, but not totally hot" might appear to be more in demand than she actually is: the curse of cute. This is mathematical evidence that minimizing your flaws is the *opposite* of what you should do: "If you're a little chubby, play it up. If you have a big nose, play it up. If you have a weird snaggletooth, play it up: Statistically, the guys who don't like it can only *help you*, and the ones who *do like it* will be all the more excited."

Women who do not like to exercise report twice the orgasm problems of women who do.

When it comes to self-confidence, curvy women pass skinny women at age twenty-nine, and curvy women consistently have the highest sex drive among body-type groups that include skinny, thin, average, full-figured, a little extra, and overweight.

Tall people have more sex.

Black men like soul food more than anything else, and black women like soul food even more than that. Latino men like merengue and *bachata* more than anything else, and Latino women like merengue and *bachata* even more than that.

Asian men and Asian women tend to describe themselves, above all, as "simple."

To determine whether you and your date have potential, see if you align on three questions: 1) Do you like horror movies? 2) Have you ever traveled around another country alone? 3) Wouldn't it be fun to chuck it all and go live on a boat? One third of the couples that meet via OkCupid agree on all three questions, which, Rudder calculates, is 3.7 times the rate of simple coincidence.

Cutting to the chase: If you want to know whether your date will have sex with you on the first date, you should ask whether he or she likes the taste of beer. Because of all OkCupid's casual questions—the questions users answer that are not specifically about sex—whether someone likes the taste of beer is the single best predictor of whether he or she has sex on the first date, suggesting there is something empirically true in the image of beer drinkers as practical, unfussy, free of pretension.*

---

* On this issue of first-date sex—who's likely to go for it, who's not—more data exists. A free dating site in the UK, FreeDating.co.uk, correlated certain physical and non-physical attributes with a willingness to knock mops on night one. As it turns out, women who are overweight and/or over five feet nine inches—obese and/or tall—are prime candidates for first-date sex. (Whether a man is overweight has no effect on first-date sex. Although men with athletic builds are most likely to be open to it.) Bizarrely, an interest in cars predicts a *decreased* likelihood of first-date sex in men, while in women the reverse is true. Meanwhile, women under twenty-five are most open to first-date sex, and their willingness *decreases* with age. Whereas the opposite is true for men: A man in his thirties is more open to first-date sex than a man in his early twenties. As for education, a man's propensity for first-date sex increases with his education level, whereas the opposite is true for women. Reducing these principles to their core meaning, Free Dating advises: "The youngest, largest, most drunken woman is about as open to first-date sex as an average sixty-year-old guy."

———

OkTrends underscored a crucial feature of online interaction: It leaves a trace. "Vast digital trails of social interaction," writes Jon Kleinberg, a data scientist at Cornell University, "allow us to begin investigating questions that have been the subject of theoretical inquiry and small-scale analysis for a century or more—a reflection of the broader principle that science moves forward whenever we can take something that was once invisible and make it visible."

Technology and time separated Rudder's work from that of his predecessors. Whereas Rudder used a computer to run mathematical processes on data sets, Masters and Johnson relied on somewhat cruder instruments; e.g., a thrusting mechanical penis-camera that could have sex with a woman and *film it from the inside*. Whereas Kinsey led a team of men on fact-finding missions, zigzagging the country in planes, trains, and automobiles, rounding up interview subjects in restaurants, libraries, and bars, Rudder sat in a Manhattan office, shoeless and sipping tea while the data rolled across his screen.

The mainstream print media jumped all over Rudder's dispatches. In 2010, the OkTrends blog served as fodder for at least half a dozen *New York Times* articles and blog posts. "The PR that was generated from the blog was transformational for our brand," says Yagan, who appeared on CNN and elsewhere to discuss some of the OkTrends findings. "We were able to take dating into the workplace. Because we can tell where people are reading it. Whether it was an investment bank or a consulting firm, people would read this stuff at work and share it around with colleagues."

Social scientists descended like vultures, purchasing OkCupid's raw data for five-figure amounts in order to study topics such as how political opinions factor into choosing social partners. In 2012, the rights to Rudder's forthcoming book about how the profusion of data is changing our understanding of everything from humor to history fetched a seven-figure advance.

Rudder's findings attracted attention because he was not interviewing online daters or chronicling his own experiences or bringing his own biases to bear. He was aggressively analyzing data on how OkCupid's membership used the site, which, like a bar, is an enormous laboratory of human behavior.

There are differences, of course, between a bar and a dating site. In a bar the interactions and behavior are *un*structured. Nothing is documented and little is remembered. On a dating site the preferences and histories and tendencies become highly structured, saved, and analyzed. A dating site owns what online marketers call the "structured version of your preferences." The next step for dating technology, then, is to capture real-world behavior by gathering data on how daters actually date, IRL. At OkCupid, Yagan continues to believe in the power of data to improve relationships, or at least first dates.

"When people talk about the impact of mobile dating," he says, "everyone focuses on real-time meeting—this idea that my pocket will vibrate every time a hot girl walks by. That's important. But it's not transformative. The thing that's underdiscussed in mobile is the ability it will give us to understand how people are actually behaving in the real world. Historically, the only way we could measure success on OkCupid was by asking, 'Did an online conversation occur between these two people?'" (OkCupid defines "conversation" as a message, a response, and a reply to the response; they call it a three-way.) "But with mobile," Yagan continues, "we're going to be able to verify who actually went on a date. That alone is huge, but then we can also ask, 'How'd the date go?' Whether Foursquare or Facebook, people are feeding their phone information constantly. So this won't require any huge shift in consumer behavior. Being able to put that data back into our matching algorithm will just make it that much richer."

Even Eli Finkel, the industry scold, agrees that data on real-world behavior could mean major advancements in what we know about attraction and compatibility. "I think it's possible that really smart people working with loads of data could increase the chances of predicting initial attraction, and perhaps by a significant amount," Finkel says. "I hedge only because this ability has never been proven. But the promises get a lot more plausible once you stop talking about soul mates and start talking about increasing the likelihood of hitting it off on a first date. That, to me, is entirely reasonable."

ALEXIS, PART IV

↓

It's Good to Say You Want a Real Relationship

THANKS TO ALEXIS, HER FELLOW PTers FLOCKED TO ONLINE-dating sites—Match, eHarmony, Plenty of Fish, OkCupid.

"This is the power of PT!" one rejoices.

"I hope my height and lack of funds appeal to women who like short broke men," writes another.

"I Googled 'best first message,'" reports another. "Found one that someone had put max effort into, and then mailed it to the 6 hottest girls on Plenty of Fish. No responses. But I was contacted by a chick that looks like Snookie and has a kid. LOL."

Another online-dating initiate shares the introductory message he's sending to women on Match: "Hey, I know of this great little Italian place. Their salad and breadsticks are to die for. It's called the Olive Garden. You may have seen their commercials on the cable TV. I would love to take you there some time. If things go well, maybe I can hide your engagement ring in the breadsticks. Hope to hear from you soon!"

"Sarcasm," advises a female PTer, "is hard to read online. I wouldn't respond to that in a million years. Just saying."

"I don't like that OkCupid tells you exactly who is viewing your profile and WHEN," writes another. "On Facebook the whole point is that you can view people's profiles without them knowing, which is essential for stalking people. I don't want a chick to know I was checking her out at 10pm on a Saturday (loser) or 3:30 am on a Tuesday (crackhead)."

"If y'all like creepin' online," writes another, "I have a way to find girls' Facebook pages. Often they'll use the same picture for their dating profile as they use for their profiles on LinkedIn or Facebook. So just drag and drop their photo into the search bar on Google Image. It can be helpful. I have three mutual friends with a girl I'm going on a date with from OkCupid."

"I can't believe how many women say they're bi on OkCupid."

"I hate when they write on their profile that they find online dating bizarre. Do they really expect me to be impressed that they're above this shit, when their method of telling me was their fucking online-dating profile?"

"These are girls that are obviously tired of getting stuffed by dudes they met at bars, or just got out of a shitty relationship with a dude like that," offers another. "Spin this to your advantage. Also, have a reason to be on there, i.e. work doesn't give you time and shit like that. Being a pussy who can't talk to girls is pretty easy to spot."

"I think that when a chick gets a message, she immediately starts to look for things not to like about the guy's profile. And if I'm being honest, I do the same thing. Online dating is making us far too judgmental and dismissive of each other."

For the benefit of the guys, Alexis posts her own advice manual on online dating:

→ Have your primary pic be one where you can actually see you. You can keep the Halloween pic in your secondary album to show some personality, but as the default pic, I would probably assume you were immature and annoying at first glance.

→ It's good to say you truly want a real relationship. Don't talk, infer, or gesture about sex on your profile.

→ Take the time to write a short, lighthearted paragraph about what kind of girl is ideal for you. The checklist approach comes off a little douchey. This is a harder thing to accomplish, but if in your "about

me" paragraph you can show who you are without explicitly saying you are funny, smart, caring, whatever, then that is better than
just listing qualities. Everyone says the exact same shit. They like
to party but stay in sometimes. They live to travel. How fascinating.
Instead, tell an anecdote that exhibits who you are and the way
you interact with people.

→ Lastly, put some pictures up of you with family, pets, guy friends.
Having 5 pictures of you with hot girls does not impress hot girls. It
makes it seem like you are insecure and needing to show off all
your bitches.

On Match, she comes across a thirty-three-year-old lawyer who seems
to fit the bill. His main photo is a picture of him smiling at a party and looking off screen. Other photos show him being active outside—in a kayak, on
a road trip. In his profile he pokes fun at the online-dating process:

I don't require much from a lady, except that she be perfect in
every respect. I want a bookish girl who can throw down when it's
time to party. I want Type-A competitiveness sometimes, a devil-
may-care attitude others. I want blue eyes. But I also want green
eyes. I require a woman who can effortlessly manage the sched-
ules of three teenagers, rake in a six-figure salary, and be attentive
to my every need—while also taking responsibility for maintaining passion in the relationship . . .

"Your profile," she writes to him, "WINS."

His name is Ben, and in his response he mentions that he's seen
Phish in concert, a big plus for Alexis. She responds. He asks her out for
a drink.

Back on Phantasy Tour, Alexis posts an update: "I've been e-mailing
this guy. He is hilarious and eloquent. I have my first online-date on Friday! I think this is the preliminary meeting when they see if you have all
your fingers and toes and didn't post pictures of yourself 30 pounds ago.
Right?"

"Is Poundtown a possible post-date destination?" asks a PTer.

"No Poundtown till the 5th date," she replies. "I plan to put off sleeping with any of these online dudes for as long as possible." She's trying not to have high hopes, she writes, because for all she knows this Ben may be "banging biddies all over town." In past relationships she's been too open to sex too early, and it never goes well.

Alexis's first love, she tells Phantasy Tour, "began with a first date bone. But we were young, 18. Now that I'm a bit older I can't just bone everyone I'm attracted to who wants me. My numbers would be sky high and every new relationship would have high emotional stakes. I just feel like it's wise to have discussed what you're looking for in a relationship before you bone. Once you do, there are usually feelings at stake, most likely for the girl. So if the dude doesn't want a relationship it burns, eventually. And it drags on longer than it should because the dude stays in it just for sex. It's a good sign if sex is tempting on the first date. But I'd rather know their intentions and their character before sex. Personality can shine on a first date, but character takes time to reveal. If you both just want to fuck, go for it. If you want real feelings, it's always better to wait."

CHAPTER FIVE

Better Relationships but More Divorce

WHAT TECHNOLOGY MEANS FOR COMMITMENT

Fast Company: If you were standing in front of a group of business school students who were trying to decide what industry to go into, what would you tell them about online dating?

Greg Blatt: First . . . you can ask them how many people in their own lives they know who are single who complain that they're not meeting the right people, and yet they're not using online dating. That creates a huge market opportunity. . . . Second, this is going to sound a little cheesy: If you go into retail, and you successfully sell someone a coat, you've sold someone a coat. But you really change people's lives with Match.com and other services.

—interview with *Fast Company* magazine

B ack home in Oregon, after college on the East Coast and a few years bouncing around, Jacob was surprised at how difficult it was to meet women. He was used to small, ready-made social scenes. In Portland most of his friends were dating people they met in college, pursuing careers, and discussing marriage. When Jacob wasn't coaching youth football and basketball, he liked to watch sports on TV. He also took an academic interest in the city's microbrew scene, frequented concerts, and enjoyed the occasional poker game. Past girl-friends found Jacob's pursuits tiresome. He'd been called lazy, aimless, and irresponsible with money.

Following a long period of singleness, Jacob met a slightly older woman—thirty to his twenty-six—who seemed independent and low maintenance. She moved in, but soon demanded more than just brunch on Saturdays. "I've never been able to make a girl feel like she was the most important thing in my life," he says. "It's always 'I wish I was as important as the basketball game or the concert.'" An only child, Jacob tended to make plans by negotiation: She would watch the game with him, he would go hiking with her. He was passive in their arguments, hoping to avoid confrontation. Whatever their relationship amounted to, he told himself, it was better than being single in Portland again.

After five years, she left.

In 2009, at thirty-one, Jacob felt he had no idea how to make a rela-tionship work. Was compatibility something you learned? Would per-manence simply happen, or would he have to choose it? Just meeting people seemed hard enough. It was around this time that he signed up for two dating sites: Match, because he'd seen the ads; and Plenty of Fish, because word of the site had spread down to Portland from its Vancou-ver headquarters.

"It was fairly incredible," he remembers. "I'm an average-looking guy. I wasn't used to picking and choosing that way. All of a sudden I was going out with one or two very pretty, ambitious women a week. At first I just thought it was some kind of weird lucky streak."

After six weeks Jacob met a twenty-two-year-old secretary named Rachel through Match. Her youth and looks reinvigorated Jacob's out-look. His friends were jealous. Was this the one? They dated for a few months and then she moved in.

Markus Frind did not go to Stanford or Harvard or MIT. To say that his roots are small-town doesn't quite describe the obscurity of his upbring-ing. He was raised in Hudson's Hope, British Columbia. Closer to the

Yukon Territory than to the United States, Hudson's Hope, a logging town of one thousand people, is near the start of the Alaskan Highway. Frind's parents, German farmers, emigrated there after his fourth birthday. They bought a twelve-hundred-acre plot, where they lived in a trailer without electricity, phones, or running water. It was lonely and desolate. The boy played a lot of chess, struggled to learn English, and didn't have many friends.

At eighteen, Frind drove fourteen hours south to Vancouver and enrolled in a technical school. In 1999, just as the tech bubble was preparing to burst, he graduated with a two-year degree in computer programming.

"Every six months I got a new job," he said a decade later. "It'd start with thirty people, and then five months later there'd be five. It was brutal."

But Frind was learning how to simplify complex code and make computers run faster. By early 2003—as Sam Yagan and Chris Coyne were getting their Harvard buddies back together on the opposite coast—the technology economy in Vancouver continued to struggle. Facing the possibility of another layoff, Frind devoted a couple of weeks to learning about Microsoft's new tool for building Web sites, ASP.net. He decided he would teach himself by building the hardest kind of site he could think of, an elaborate network of user-designed avatars that gawked at, winked at, and spoke to one another.

The idea came to Frind when he looked at Lavalife, Canada's then-largest dating site. "I thought it was ridiculous," he said. "It was this rinky-dink little site charging money for something anyone could make. I was like, I can beat these guys."

The task, however, was not to build a better dating site than Lavalife or Match. The challenge, rather, would be how to make a free site profitable, relying exclusively on advertising instead of subscriptions to make money. For users, the value proposition would be great. The challenge would be finding them. On a per-user basis, paid sites could afford to spend one hundred times more on their advertising budget. Match, with its thirty dollars to forty dollars per month subscription, could spend at least that much, if not several times more, to acquire a single user. A free site could spend maybe forty cents.

Back East, Yagan and Coyne set out to make OkCupid not only free but *better* than the competition. Frind set his sights lower: simple functionality. The key would be dispensing with all frills. No customer service, no employees, no user feedback taken into account. With its drab light-blue background, it looked as though it had been built by a retiree selling used auto parts out of an attic, circa 1995. The site's hallmark was its distorted profile photos, squished or elongated, that required users to click through in order to get a sense of what a user actually looks like. This resulted in more page views and, consequently, more advertising revenue.

In the summer of 2003, Google introduced AdSense, a tool that allowed small businesses to automatically sell advertising space on their sites. By the end of the year Frind was making more than thirty-three hundred dollars a month, largely by selling ad space to paid dating sites that hoped to persuade Frind's free users to trade up. By mistake or design, Frind had built a place for paid sites to spend those enormous marketing budgets. If he could serve as a gateway for the rest of the industry, he wouldn't need Madison Avenue or a huge sales force to make a go of free dating. When the tech community doubted Frind's claims that he was making ten thousand dollars a day through Google AdSense in 2006, he posted a picture of a check from Google for nearly a million Canadian dollars, representing two months' worth of revenue and implying that his site was making nearly $5 million a year.

"The thing that amazes me is that I'm becoming some sort of icon in Canada," Frind wrote on his corporate blog. "There are no counterparts to Bill Gates, Facebook founder, Myspace founders, Amazon, etc. I assume the conversations go something like this. He makes how much??? That is the ugliest site ever."

As Plenty of Fish membership hit the roof, becoming the most heavily trafficked dating site in the world, Frind found it necessary to keep the site free not only of scammers—people trying to con his legitimate users out of money—but also of those whose searching and messaging behavior indicated they were in pursuit of sex, even if their profile stated otherwise. The women who date him on the premise that he's looking for a relationship come away with, as Frind put it, a bad experience. A bad experience for a Plenty of Fish user is bad news for business. He needed to organize people according to *intent*.

"It's easy to spot them," says Frind, when asked how something as cerebral as intent can be monitored. "Suppose a guy says he's looking for a long-term relationship but then messages people in the Intimate Encounter section, or uses sexual language in his profile or his messages. The program will pick up on that and stop showing him women who are interested in a relationship. I don't care what the user says he wants. Most guys, regardless of what they're really looking for, will say they're looking for a long-term relationship. Why? Because they think they need to say that in order to meet women online—and they may be right. But I know whether he's telling the truth. I can see everything he does."

In ordering his site, Frind can make money at the same time by bombarding sex searchers with ads for Fling and Adult Friend Finder, which function like steam valves for Plenty of Fish. These sites are part of the adult date-o-sphere, which also includes Online Booty Call and XXX-Cupid, where daters often forego headshots in favor of genitalia close-ups, selecting mates based on vasculature and labial presentation, cutting through deception at least on these dimensions.

By 2011, Plenty of Fish was drawing 2.8 billion page-views and a little over six million unique visitors per month. With so many people providing so much personal information, all kinds of advertisers, from book publishers to tobacco-addiction remedies, loved the opportunity for targeted marketing. For just a few dollars you could have one thousand lonely smokers see your ad for nicotine chewing gum or the latest self-help book.

Frind wrote on his blog:

> I figured I should go back to the basics and see what dating is all about. . . . This weekend I'm taking my girlfriend and 4 of her really hot girlfriends for a week-long trip to Mexico in a 5-star all-inclusive

resort in Cancun. I'm going to sit on my big plush bed under a ca-
bana with a steady stream of drinks supplied to one hand by my
girls, while holding my laptop with the other hand. Being that it is
spring break, I can watch how people behave—people in Mexico
are similar to those who go online and date because they all behave like no one is watching, and nothing matters. . . .

In between the time it takes you to read this and my next drink
arrives I'll have made your weekly salary. Now that is either going
to make you angry, or it's going to inspire you to go create something. The choice is yours.

"I feel like I underwent a fairly radical change thanks to online dating,"
Jacob says. "I went from being someone who thought of finding someone
as this monumental challenge to being much more relaxed and confident about it. Rachel was young and beautiful, and I'd found her after
signing up on a couple dating sites and dating just a few people."

We all know what a dreadful relationship looks like, how it unfolds
from day to embattled day in tremors, each party's misery redounding
to and justifying the other's. Hell-bent on the correctness of your
choice—or merely resigned—you adapt to a life in which obscene stores
of energy are frittered away in the effort it takes to live with someone
you secretly hold in contempt, or just don't really enjoy that much. Why?
Because it would take even more energy to start over, and no one wants
to run the risk of being alone. It could be years until another suitable
mate comes along. Whatever it is, it's better than being single in Portland
again.

It's what the behavioral scientists call "learned helplessness" and
what everyone else calls "settling"—relegating yourself to your current
situation on the assumption or belief that no escape route exists, that
you have no control. Evolution drives this. It's thought that the "brain
pain" of lost love—the extreme anxiety one feels at the prospect of relationship failure—evolved as a physical alarm to alert us to the dangers
of social isolation, not unlike the alarm system that keeps our hands
away from hot stoves and makes us look both ways at an intersection.

The relative difficulty of moving on heightens the intensity of this alarm system; it can skewer our standards for happiness and keep us in sub-prime relationships.

There were good things about Jacob's relationship with Rachel. She didn't mind his sports addiction and enjoyed going to concerts with him. But there were issues too. She was from a blue-collar military background. He came from doctors. She placed a high value on things he didn't think much about: a solid credit score; a forty-hour workweek. But Jacob was thirty-four now. He felt pressure. His parents were getting anxious to see him paired up. While a younger girlfriend bought him some time, biologically speaking, it also alienated him from his friends, who could understand the physical attraction but couldn't really relate.

In the past Jacob had always been the kind of guy who didn't break up well. His relationships tended to drag on. His desire to be with some-one, to not have to go looking again, had always trumped whatever doubts he'd had about the people he'd been with. But now, after having met Rachel so easily online, he felt differently. He felt like he could as-sess the situation and acknowledge their problems with a clearer mind. He felt no need to pretend to be sure of something he wasn't sure of.

"I'm about 95 percent certain," he says, "that if I'd met Rachel offline, and if I'd never done online dating, I would've married her. At that point in my life I would've overlooked everything else and done whatever it took to make things work. Did online dating change my perception of permanence? No doubt. When I sensed the breakup coming, I was okay with it. It didn't seem like there was going to be much of a mourning period, where you stare at your wall thinking you're destined to be alone and all that. I was eager to see what else was out there."

The day Rachel informed Jacob she was moving out, he logged on to Match. His old profile was still up. A few messages had even come in from people who couldn't tell he was no longer active on the site.* The site had improved in the two years he'd been away. It was sleeker, faster,

---

* When you stop paying for Match, the company leaves your profile up. Many Match users I interviewed reported having to call customer service to have it taken down.

more efficient. The population of online daters in Portland seemed to have tripled. He never imagined there were so many single people. Now he could see them all.

We live in an age of customization. Homes, cars, vacations, college degrees, even children—they can all be specialized and designed to suit every need, fad, desire, and whim. Love and relationships have also become customizable things, defined in a boardroom, built to fit, and pushed out by sites like eHarmony and Chemistry, or offered up by Ok-Cupid and Match as one choice among many, as a box that can be checked along with other boxes, such as long-term dating, short-term dating, new friends, casual sex, activity partners, long-distance pen pals, have children, (definitely) want children (someday), not sure about children, do not want children but it's okay if my partner already has children, etc.

Or consider the Gaggle, a theory of relationship customization that looks a lot like segmentation, an industrial term for gaining efficiencies by dividing up and isolating the means of production. The Gaggle is a multimedia franchise—a Web site, a book, a movie—invented by two women in their twenties named Jessica Massa and Rebecca Wiegand. A term they coined to describe the romantic arrangement adopted by their peers in the face of "hook-up culture," the Gaggle lays out the new relation-scape of a postdating society: Instead of dating individual men consecutively, just long enough to be disappointed by one before seeking out the next, the Gaggle philosophy encourages young women to maintain relationships with a gaggle of men, each of whom fulfills a specific role: the Accessory; the Boyfriend Prospect; the Ex-Boyfriend Who's Still Around; the Hot Sex Prospect; the Career Booster; the Unavailable Guy; the Ego Booster. It's important for women to understand how they fit into each man's gaggle. If he's her Career Booster, for example, then she might be his Work Wife. Perhaps she sees him as the Hot Sex Prospect, and he sees her as the Last Resort. ("He is not seeing you as the cool girl that you are.") Of course it's bad if her Boyfriend Prospect considers her to be his Short-Term Investment. ("He is asking you to hang out, but not in supermeaningful settings" or "He starts pulling the slow fade. . . . And then you become a bitter, paranoid woman.")

On their Web site, "WTF is Up With My Love Life?!" Massa and Wiegand explain:

> Looking at the guys in your Gaggle, you might be explicitly romantically involved with some of them. But many of them are just "friends"—co-workers, teammates, bandmates, neighbors, etc.—who play different roles in your life and allow you to explore your romantic desires and needs, in a time when traditional dating relationships can't be expected. We've found a way to get all the perks of dating, without actually having to sit around and wait to be asked out to dinner . . . to figure out who you are, what you want, and where you're going to be hanging out on Saturday night. It's about living an awesome life and having guys be a part of it.

Even assuming young women feel that traditional dating relationships can't be expected, many may still seek out long-term monogamy. But that's not really the point. The Gaggle is less a solution-oriented scheme than it is a theory of how to perceive the world around you. Recall what Walter Lippmann wrote in 1929, after technological innovation helped foment the twentieth century's first sexual revolution, unmooring the young from an earlier value system: "The inexperienced must be offered some kind of hypothesis when they are confronted with the necessity of making choices: they cannot be so utterly open-minded that they stand inert until something collides with them."

Once again, aspects of modern life—remoteness, access to all manner of relationships through social networks and online-dating sites—have elevated efficiency and convenience but also deepened the confusion when it comes to romance, especially for the first generation of people to have been born and raised in the postprivacy (and perhaps postdating) era of the Internet. Massa and Wiegand, by expanding choice and offering a broader view, are trying to impose a working structure on modern norms. The Gaggle, with its go-girl undertone, is about options. Don't settle. Don't sit at home waiting. Instead, adapt. This is their hypothesis.

Relationship advice-givers have been trying to define America's new relation-scape since the 1960s, when the old marital ethos founded on a good job and a neat home entered decline, buffeted by a wave of anti-institutionalism. Abraham Maslow's Human Potential Movement mocked the idea that human growth culminated with a singular peak accomplishment, marriage. Life was fuller than that. It was an adventure marked by an ascending sequence of growth experiences, including, but not confined to, the loss of a job, divorce, and even, eventually, dying as a growth experience. Maslow's fervent individualism was, in a sense, the inexorable capstone of a movement that had begun two hundred years earlier, when romanticism put a new emphasis on self-expression and turned courtship into that heroic quest for life meaning, personal identity, and terrestrial salvation.

Dr. Albert Ellis, a Maslow contemporary, tried to chart this new world of permissiveness in a string of books, including *The Case for Sexual Liberty* and (with Edward Sagarin) *Nymphomania: A Study of the Over-Sexed Woman*. In his writing, Dr. Ellis came across as a sex-crazed quack, though an assiduous and practical one. "Without experience and practice at heterosexual relations," he wrote in *Sex and the Single Man* (a response to Helen Gurley Brown's *Sex and the Single Girl*), "there is a very low probability that you will succeed with them." In a chapter devoted to picking up women, Ellis concluded: "*How* to meet suitable girlfriends is a more difficult question. . . . The general answer in this regard is clear: stop defining yourself as a no-goodnik whenever you fail, and keep trying, trying, trying."

What's different about today's revolution, of course, is its covertness. We can't see young people frolicking for the first time in movie theaters and steaming up car windows. We can't turn on the evening news and see baby boomers dancing naked in the mud at Woodstock. Instead, for information we turn to opinionistas like Massa and Wiegand, data-wonks like Christian Rudder, and bloggers like Chiara Atik and Scott Alden.

Alden and Atik are the male-female blogging duo at How About We, the dating site based on first-date ideas. Alden was fed up with the overly simplistic distinction between "casual" and "serious" relationships. There are actually ten varieties of casual-but-emotional-sex, he says, including intense orgasm sex ("And there you are. Feeling more vulnerable than you intended to."); rough sex ("It doesn't matter if you met that night and never intend to see each other again—if you're beating the heck out of each other, it's not casual."); I hate you sex ("Being pissed at someone doesn't mean you don't feel anything for them, especially if you're expressing it sexually."); accidental pregnancy sex ("Maybe you *thought* it was casual, but if the stick turns pink, it's definitely not casual anymore."); anal sex ("Unless you're one of those people who just finds butt sex super easy to pull off [and bless you if you are], you're going to need to deal with lube, possibly toys and a lot of trust to make it work. Again, you *can* have anal sex with someone you don't know very well, but it's never 'whatevs.'").

There are degrees of disinterestedness. And any variety of deceptively noncasual sex could be a stepping-stone toward (or away from) any one of nine "pre-exclusive relationships," or PXRs, of which Alden compiles a litany, including OGBC (ongoing booty call: "You've probably never seen your OGBC before midnight"); FWB (friends with benefits: "The most infamous of all PXRs. . . . we keep acting like we're emotionally invincible until we ruin a perfectly good friendship"); SEO (seeing each other: "You're not necessarily exclusive, but you're interested in the *possibility*"); XWSEX (ex with sex: "There were probably a lot of reasons that you and your ex called it quits. But maybe the sex wasn't one of them"); PMX (pretty much exclusive: "The PMX period is a time when you're basically obligated to take advantage of any and all uncomplicated sex that comes your way—because it won't last long"); and, perhaps the most perplexing of all PXRs, the SF (significant frother: "You're not dating them. You're not sleeping with them. But whoever you are dating or sleeping with will probably get inexplicably jealous of them. Your SF is your 'When-the-hell-are-you-two-just-going-to-get-married?!' friend").

There's a biological basis for our obsession with choice: The experience of choice—confronting, say, forty-five versions of peanut butter at

Whole Foods or a dozen styles of tattered cuffs at The Gap—elevates activity in brain regions associated with motivation and reward. The perception that one has options instills feelings of autonomy, which in turn contributes to psychological and physical health.

At the same time, however, the notion that too many options makes us miserable is a well-documented phenomenon in late-capitalist America. Acquisitions of things that used to be viewed as utilitarian and standardized, such as cars or blue jeans, can now cause a gnawing distress, a suspicion that you chose nonoptimally. As early as 1970—thirty-five years before Barry Schwartz published *The Paradox of Choice*—Philip Slater (no relation) wrote *The Pursuit of Loneliness*, in which he argued that "the major problem for Americans is that of choice: Americans are forced into making more choices per day, with fewer 'givens,' more ambiguous criteria, less environmental stability, and less social structural support, than any people in history."

In online dating, choice influences mate seekers in at least two ways. First, there's the choice one confronts at the selection phase. Second, there's the mere existence of online dating as an easy, discreet mate-finding channel *after* selection has occurred. At selection, researchers have seen that as choice sets grow larger, mate seekers are liable to become "cognitively overwhelmed." They deal with the choice overload by adopting lazy comparison strategies and examining fewer cues. After selection, researchers say three ingredients determine the strength of relationship commitment: 1) satisfaction level (one's subjective evaluation of the relationship); 2) investment size (such as time and effort, shared experiences and emotions, and the importance that the relationship holds for one's identity); and 3) quality of alternatives.

Both satisfaction level and quality of alternatives could be directly affected by a larger mating pool. No studies in the romantic realm have looked at how choice affects satisfaction.* But when it comes to quality

---

* Research elsewhere has found that people are less satisfied when choosing from a larger group: Those who selected their chocolate from an array of six think it tastes better than those who select the same chocolate from an array of thirty.

of alternatives, evidence shows that the perception of appealing alternatives to a current romantic partner is a strong predictor of low commitment to that partner and eventual breakup. The opposite situation—the perception of *diminished* choice—supports the same conclusion: People exhibit stronger positive illusions about a partner when they believe that access to alternative partners is scarce.

"You can say three things," says Northwestern's Eli Finkel, of Team Finkel fame. "First, the best marriages are probably unaffected. Happy couples won't be hanging out on dating sites. Second, people who are in marriages that are either bad or average might be at increased risk of divorce because of increased access to new partners. Third, it's unknown whether that's good or bad for society. On one hand, it's good if fewer people feel like they're stuck in relationships. On the other, evidence is pretty solid that having a stable romantic partner means all kinds of health and wellness benefits."

If online dating can blunt the emotional pain of separation, if adults can afford to be increasingly demanding about what they want from a relationship, including when and how they want it, the effect of online dating seems positive. The bar for what we consider a good relationship will be raised. But what if it's also the case that the prospect of finding an ever more compatible mate with the click of a mouse means a future of relationship instability, a paradox of choice that keeps us chasing the illusive bunny around the dating track? Does it matter that the latter—serial online daters returning to the date-o-sphere—is what the industry is hoping for?

Despite their competing business interests, a majority of the dating execs interviewed for this book agreed with what research appears to suggest: The rise of online dating will mean an overall decrease in commitment.

"The future," says Dan Winchester, "will see better relationships but more divorce. The older you get as a man, the more experienced you get. You know what to do with women, how to treat them and talk to them. I often wonder whether matching you up with great people is getting so efficient, and the process so enjoyable, that marriage will become obsolete."*

"Historically," says Greg Blatt, CEO of Match's parent company, "relationships have been billed as 'hard' because, historically, commitment has been the goal. You could say online dating is simply changing people's ideas about whether commitment itself is a life value." A forty-something bachelor in Manhattan, Blatt underscores the role that mate scarcity plays in people's relationship decisions, including his own: "Look, if I lived in Iowa I'd be married with four children by now. That's just how it is."

Another online-dating exec hypothesized an inverse correlation between commitment and the efficiency of technology. "I think divorce rates will increase as life in general becomes more real-time," said Nic Formai, the head of social-media marketing at Badoo. "Think about the evolution of other kinds of content on the Web. Stock quotes, news. The goal has always been to make it faster. The same thing will happen with meeting. It's exhilarating to connect with new people, not to mention beneficial for reasons having nothing to do with romance. You network for a job. You find a flatmate. Over time you'll expect that constant flow. People always said that the need for stability would keep commitment alive. But that thinking was based on a world in which you didn't meet that many people."

"Societal values always lose out," says Noel Biderman, the founder of Ashley Madison, which bills itself as "the world's leading married dating service for discreet encounters," i.e., cheating. "Premarital sex used to be taboo," explains Biderman. "So women would become miserable in marriages, because they wouldn't know any better. But today more peo-

---

* U.S. Census data from 2010 showed that 39 percent of all Americans believe marriage is becoming obsolete. Yet 47 percent of the unmarried adults who believe marriage is becoming obsolete say they would like to marry someday. This suggests that a huge chunk of the population, despite disbelieving in marriage, has not discovered a satisfactory alternative. At the moment, the marriage void is being filled partly by an increase in cohabitation, indicating that a wish for some kind of stability remains a driving force in the absence of legal commitment.

ple have had failed relationships, recovered, moved on, and found happiness. They realize that that happiness, in many ways, depends on having had the failures. As we become more secure and confident in our ability to find someone else, usually someone better, monogamy and the old thinking about commitment will be challenged very harshly."

Even at eHarmony, where marriage and commitment are billed as the only acceptable goals of dating, Dr. Gian Gonzaga, the relationship psychologist who replaced Dr. Warren, acknowledges that technology is at odds with commitment. "You could say online dating allows people to get into relationships, learn things, and ultimately make a better selection," says Gonzaga, who wrote *eHarmony Guide to Dating the Second Time Around: Finding Love That Lasts.* "But you could also easily see a world in which online dating leads to people leaving relationships the moment they're not working, an overall weakening of commitment."

In 2011, Mark Brooks, a consultant to the online-dating industry, published the results of an industrywide survey entitled, "How Has Internet Dating Changed Society?" From the survey responses of thirty-nine executives, here are some conclusions:

- → "Internet dating has made people more disposable."
- → "Internet dating may be partly responsible for a rise in divorce rates."
- → "Low quality, unhappy, and unsatisfying marriages are being destroyed as people drift to Internet dating sites."
- → "The market is hugely more efficient. People expect to—and this will increasingly be the case over time—access people anywhere based on complex search requests. Such a feeling of access affects our pursuit of love. Increasingly, the whole world (versus the city we live in) feels like the market for our partners. Our pickiness will probably increase."
- → "Above all, Internet dating has helped people of all ages realize that there's no need to settle for a mediocre relationship."

Alex Mehr, a cofounder of the dating site Zoosk, is the only executive interviewed for this book who disagrees with the prevailing view. "Online dating does nothing more than remove a barrier to meeting," says Mehr. "Online dating doesn't change my taste, or how I behave on a first date, or whether I'm going to be a good partner. It only changes the process of discovery. As for whether you're the type of person who wants to commit to a long-term monogamous relationship or the type of person who wants to play the field, online dating has nothing to do with that. That's a personality thing."*

Single again, Jacob cut his hair close and started working on his paunch. "Ever since college I've been a little loose in the cage," he says. "But I'm doing this DVD program called P90X, Tony Horton's extreme home fitness. It didn't seem to be working at first, but now women are telling me how athletic I look. It's amazing how much of a difference that stuff can make, even if just for confidence."

Back online, Jacob is meeting all kinds of women. Some like going to basketball games and concerts with him. Others enjoy bar hopping. Jacob's favorite football team is the Green Bay Packers, and he has success using Packers fandom as search criteria on OkCupid, the latest site he's trying out.

Many of these relationships become physical very early, sometimes before the date happens. Prior to a first date with a zookeeper from OkCupid, she sends him a text message: "Do you want to just meet at my place?"

Jacob is seeing a paralegal and a lawyer who work at the same law firm; a naturopath; a pharmacist; and a chef. Three of them he slept with

---

* Fidelity might be a genetically programmed trait. "As far as researchers know," writes Louann Brizendine in *The Female Brain*, "human males represent behaviors on a spectrum from totally polygamist to totally monogamous." Brizendine, a neuropsychiatrist, speculates that there's a link between the length of a man's vasopressin gene and his likelihood of being unfaithful—the longer the vasopressin gene, the less likely he is to stray. "So the current joke among women scientists is that we should care more about the length of the vasopressin gene in our mates than about the length of anything else."

on the first or second date. The others are headed toward intimacy. The chef says she has hips like handlebars and encourages him to grab them. The naturopath wants to wait until she gets waxed, but emphasizes how much she enjoys threesomes. He likes the pharmacist most. She's a girl-friend prospect. The problem is that she wants to take things slow. This worries Jacob. If need be, he knows he'll just get it somewhere else. There's always a pepperoni pizza in the trunk, is how Jacob thinks of it. A publicist who enters the picture via Plenty of Fish requests to be choked during sex.

"Some of these women are sort of losers," Jacob says, "but they supplement my life while I pursue the long-term prospects." In addition to the pharmacist, Jacob envisions long-term potential with a fellow fly-fishing enthusiast after they exchange twenty-two messages on OkCupid. But shortly after the first date the relationship morphs into a sex-only situation.

On Match one day, he comes across a twenty-five-year-old. "Curiously obsessed," she writes in her profile, "with random things like cleaning out my iTunes, always having a pen on me, and pointing out inefficiencies. I have an amazing life but am frustrated with the lack of assertive men in this town."

"I've been hearing this a lot lately," he writes to her, "and I have to agree with you. I think it's a ton of factors, starting with Portland's laid-back lifestyle. There are also a lot of niche interests here to take up our time. I'm sure there's more to it."

She responds, seeming interested, but he doesn't ask her out. She strikes him as too demanding.

One night the paralegal tells Jacob a workplace anecdote that references the lawyer whom Jacob is also seeing. The paralegal then confides in him: Her prior relationships haven't gone well, she says. But he gives her hope. All she needs in a relationship is honesty, she says, and Jacob thinks, "Oh my God." He wants to be a nice guy, he says, but Jacob knows that sooner or later he's going to start coming across as a serious asshole. While out with one woman he has to silence text messages coming in from others. He must start paring down "the clubhouse."

He tries calling the naturopath. She doesn't answer, so he sends a text message: "Hey, I wanted to talk to you about what's been on my mind. I started online dating thinking that I just wanted to see what was out there and not jump into something with one person again too soon. In other words, I want to date other people right now and not be exclusive. I am uncomfortable that we haven't spoken about this yet and wanted to tell you because it's the honest thing to do."

"You are making a huge mistake," she replies. "I will be your biggest regret in life. Lose my number."

Women seeking commitment have evolved strategies to detect deception and guard against it. They might withhold sex in order to assess his intentions and/or whether there's competition or prior commitments. Theoretically, her withholding sends him a message: I'm not that kind of girl. Theoretically, his willingness to wait sends a message back: I'm interested in more than sex.

But the pace of technology is upending these rules and assumptions. Relationships that begin online, Jacob finds, move quickly. He chalks this up to a few things. First, familiarity is established during the messaging process, which also often involves a phone call. By the time they meet face-to-face there's already a level of intimacy, which often feels particularly strong because they connected online, without physical chemistry. Second, if she's on a dating site there's a good chance she's eager to connect. But for Jacob, the most crucial difference between the date-o-sphere and offline meeting is the sense of urgency. Occasionally, he has an acquaintance in common with the women he meets. But by and large they come from different social pools. "It's not like we're just going to run into each other again," he says. "So you can't afford to be too casual. It's either, 'Let's explore this' or 'See you later.'"

Social scientists say that all sexual strategies carry costs, whether risk to reputation (promiscuity) or foreclosed alternatives (commitment). As online dating becomes increasingly pervasive, the old adaptive problems of a short-term mating strategy will give way to a new set of problems. Jacob, for instance, notices he's seeing his friends less often. Their wives get tired of befriending his latest girlfriend only to see her go. Also, he finds himself unable to dismiss certain women even when he's seeing someone, or several people, he likes better. Research shows that people will often overinvest to keep an inferior option open, even when doing so means underinvesting in the superior option. Some say a desire for flexibility drives this tendency. Others chalk it up to an aversion to loss, that we're not pursuing the pleasure of utility but rather avoiding the pain of disutility.

Historically, men pursuing a short-term strategy have faced at least three constraints: 1) the problem of partner number, or variety; 2) the problem of identifying which women are "sexually accessible"; and 3) the problem of minimizing commitment and investment. Whether by accident or design, online-dating technology innovated around all three of these constraints, known in social-psychology literature as "adaptive problems."

Any new medium originates, often, as a solution to a problem—*I need to communicate in real time with people who live in other places; I can't find a date*—and in solving the problem it creates a new irritant: *I can talk to everyone all the time; I can go on a date every night.* Communication mediums, argued media guru Marshall McLuhan, change us by changing our perception of the world, of reality, of what is possible.

Jacob has mixed feelings about his altered perception. "Each relationship is its own little education," he says, "you learn more about what works and what doesn't, what you really need and what you can go without. That feels like a useful process. I'm not jumping into something with the wrong person, or committing to something too early, as I've done in the past." But he does wonder: When does it end? At what point does learning become an excuse for not doing what it takes to make something last? "Maybe I have the confidence now to go after the person I really want," he says. "But I'm worried that I'm making it so I can't fall in love."

Over time Jacob feels less excitement over each new date. "Is that about getting older," he wonders, "or about dating online?" How much of the enchantment associated with the experience of romantic love had to do with scarcity? *This person is exclusively for me.* How will romantic love hold up in a marketplace of abundance? *This person could be exclusively for me, but so could the other two people I'm meeting this week.*

Using OkCupid's new Locals app, Jacob can broadcast his location and desired activity and then meet people on the fly. Out alone for a beer one night, he responds to the broadcast of a woman who's at the bar across the street, looking for a karaoke partner. He joins her. They spend the evening together, and never speak again. When Jacob wants to be taken off the grid, he hits a button on his iPhone. When he wants back in, he hits another button. The choice between dating and not dating: It's hardly a choice at all.

ALEXIS, PART V

↓

Sometimes Things Do Work Out

HER FIRST DATE WITH BEN, OVER A DRINK, GOES WELL. THEY MEET the next day for dinner and music.

Alexis likes the way he looks, likes that he's affectionate and laid-back but takes control when appropriate. That she met Ben online and doesn't know much about him makes her nervous. But she Googles him obsessively, finding out everything she can, and he seems legit. "I am pretty much smitten," she writes on Phantasy Tour. "I want to wait on the sexy time front though because I really am looking for an actual boy-friend and don't want him to think I'm a sloot [slut]." Then she asks: "Is it really kosher though to go home with someone and not get it on? I would hope there would at least be some cab make out sessions or something in the meantime. . . . The no sex sleepover seems a bit cruel."

"I don't mind no sex sleepovers if I like the girl," replies a male PTer. "It's a great way to get quality time in."

"I think it's rather presumptuous to think you're going to sleep with someone the first time you sleep over," writes another. "So I wouldn't expect the declaration. If that bothers someone, they're clearly not quality."

Meanwhile, the chatter turns to other relationship issues. "I came home from work and I could tell she was pissed about something," writes a PTer. "Then she said she found a tissue and wanted me to say, honestly, if it was from me jerking off. I just said, 'Yeah,' and laughed. But I guess she figured since we live together now that I don't need to do that anymore? I got through my teenage years without getting busted. Now it's finally happened and I'm 26 years old."

"She should be telling you to jerk off on to her," Alexis offers. "Get a new girlfriend."

"Having a solo session is not a big deal," someone else replies. "Just because you're living together doesn't mean you have to share every moment of your lives. People need their space and private thoughts."

"If I was the OP," writes another, "I would David Blaine her and keep on walking."

"'David Blaine her'?"

"A David Blaine is when you're fucking somebody from the back, and, goddamn, you let your friend slide in without her knowing, and then you run around and bang on the window and wave at her ass. That's called a David Blaine."

A week later Alexis updates the PT community on Ben: "Date #3 tonight," she writes. "If your prophecies are correct, and I wind up in the East River, know that I have always loved you Internet." But Alexis is enamored with online dating: "The people you meet might live a mile away from you, but you'd never run into them IRL," she writes. "Plus, the online profile screens for red flags. If you're serious about meeting someone with long term potential, there's no need to waste time on 3 dates only to find out homeboy still lives with his mom and failed out of junior college. It's still exciting and scary and new to get to know someone you meet online, and a bit magical as it starts to work out."

"Oh gimme a break," writes a PTer. "You know what's going to happen? This guy, who is probably pretty good looking if you're going to bang him a week after meeting—this dude is going to walk man. Twenty-to-one he walks after 5 bangs. I know like 35 dudes in NYC who just mack it up on Match. Most have 2 restaurants they take the girls to. One that's darker if they're ugly and one that's a little brighter."

Others agree that Alexis should proceed with caution.

"I will tread lightly," she writes. "But it's kind of depressing that everyone's response to this is just some warning about how he is probably ill-intentioned and has no real interest in being any good to me. Blah. Thanks for the concern PT. But sometimes things do work out, mmmkay?"

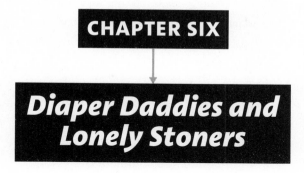

CHAPTER SIX

Diaper Daddies and Lonely Stoners

NICHE DATING AND THE ULTRAREFINED SEARCH

aura Brashier's diagnosis amounted to a mixed blessing: Stage IV cervical cancer was rare in a woman of thirty-seven, but her youth opened a greater range of treatment options, a full menu of chemotherapy along with extensive radiation ranging from below her breasts to the top of her legs. In the surgery to scrape metastasized cancer cells from her groin, thirty-three lymph nodes were removed, leaving her with a permanently swelled right leg that would need a stocking. During radiation, the omentum, a sheet of tissue that covers the organs around the stomach, melted. The doctors had to cut it away and tack it back on. The colon was irreparably damaged, maiming her digestive system. At the cancer site, radiation turned her vagina to scar tissue; it nearly closed completely. The doctors advised her to keep having sex.

"A cancer liability with a scarred vagina," Brashier recalls. "No one was going to sign up for that."

Brashier, an attractive California blonde who works as a hairdresser in Orange County, was given a dilating device to help keep her vaginal canal open. They told her to use it for ten minutes per day. But scar tissue doesn't expand like normal tissue. The burning pain was unbearable.

She bore the ordeal patiently, with little remonstration, and then the difficult part began. Three months after the diagnosis, she was cancer-free. She was also postmenopausal, having lost her ovaries before her thirty-eighth birthday. She figured she was just going to live alone. She felt reclusive and quiet, especially these days, with so much of everything revolving around sex and discussion of sex. It didn't matter whom Brashier met, or how she met them. The likelihood of hitting it off on a first date was nil. There was something about her that she couldn't talk about. "We live in our brains anyway," she says. "So you're trying to date and just talk about life and substance, and meanwhile you have this heavy thing on your mind. Do you tell them, straight up, that you can't have intercourse? Or do you wait?"

Brashier began dating someone she met at a party who lived an hour away. She liked him. There was chemistry. But then he lost his job and said he couldn't afford to court her anymore. "It was for the best," she thought. At least she wouldn't have to tell him the secret.

During the 1980s, personal ads enjoyed a resurgence in the United States. Americans could advertise in a number of publications geared toward their needs. In New York City, at least fifteen publications carried personals, including *Chocolate Singles*, a bimonthly magazine for blacks, and the *Mensa Bulletin*, for the high-IQ set. Elderly singles met through *Sweet 'n' Sexy Seniors*.

The modern mail-order bride industry originated in these pre-Internet personal ads. American men unhappy with the women's lib movement at home could shop for submissive Asian wives in a catalog published by Cherry Blossoms, one of the oldest mail-order bride agencies, founded in 1974 by John Broussard. A Harvard graduate and former hippie, Broussard had been importing Oriental bowls and vases when he decided to diversify his business to include Philippine women. By 1986, one hundred mail-order bride agencies had blossomed in North America. The Philippines exported twenty thousand mail-order brides per year. At the time, Alfredo Perdon, the director of the Philippine government's Commission on Filipinos Overseas, told Reuters that his country had "become a real shopping market for the foreigner in search of a wife." In 1992, after the fall of the Soviet Union, one hundred more agencies would surface to meet the new demand for Russian and Ukrainian brides.

Gay people mingle in gay bars. Bikers congregate in biker bars. Significant minorities—religions, political interest groups, sports fans—often enjoy some real-life venue in which to mix and date. But what about the thousands of other disparate, marginal, or downright deviant interests that lack nonvirtual meeting places? And what about people like Laura Brashier, who face "thin markets" for partners?

The nichification of personal ads coincided with the rise of cable television, another niche media product. Many later blamed cable, as they would blame the Internet, for dividing Americans and degrading their tastes with "down-market" content. Highbrow or low, there was no question that these innovations changed the way people lived. "There is a difference," writes Tim Wu in *The Master Switch*, "between a nation in which on any given night conservatives are watching Fox News, sports fans are tuned to ESPN, and teenagers are glued to MTV, as compared to the America of television's yesteryear, where the nuclear family would watch *I Love Lucy* and the *CBS Evening News* together, whether they would have preferred to or not." By targeting one demographic, other demographics were, as a matter of course, turned away or excluded. "The alienation was, in a way, the message, and the product," writes Wu, invoking the aphoristic language of an earlier media theorist, Marshall McLuhan, who famously said, "The medium is the message."

After Barry Diller's IAC bought Match in 1999, it moved the dating company from California to Texas. Trish McDermott, in charge of marketing, was one of the only original execs to stay on. Shortly after the move, she recalls, the option to list yourself as bisexual suddenly disappeared from the site. McDermott, a lesbian, was annoyed by this. So she brought it up in a meeting. Management explained that since Match was building a brand about monogamy, about finding your special someone, it couldn't allow bisexuals, because if you were bisexual, you'd always be looking for something else. If you were a bisexual man who found a great woman, you'd still always be looking for a man. "Huh?" McDermott protested. "I'm pretty sure bisexual people still have monogamous relationships."

McDermott won that round. Bisexuality was restored as an option. But it was the beginning of what she calls Match's identity crisis. Internally, the company wanted to be everything to everyone. Tim Sullivan, Match's CEO at the time, called it the bookend theory: The Match brand must speak to all the "books" on the shelf, everything from "just messing around" to "serious about marriage," from fat to skinny, black to white, religious to non, gay to straight. The bookend theory meant excluding no one in particular. It also meant speaking to no one in particular. In 2001, McDermott was instructed not to use the word "single" in press releases. Match's research showed that "single" had a negative connotation; it was a temporary status that people wanted to shed. Later she was told not to use "marriage." Match didn't want to discourage those who weren't looking to get hitched.

When Dr. Warren's eHarmony, the marriage-minded site, began accumulating a big membership in the early 2000s, Match considered buying it. But Match's leadership was concerned that the eHarmony brand defined "appropriate" too narrowly.

But to many at Match, it was bad business to remain general, to try to be CBS in an MTV world. By catering to more niches you removed a big barrier to meeting for the people who were interested in the niches. Because Match refused to be specific, it opened the door for others to be specific. Match had more Jews than JDate, but JDate marketed to them and Match refused to.

Frank Mastronuzzi, a young gay man, wanted to change this. As Match's head of business development, it was his job to strike up partnerships with other Web sites in order to drive traffic to Match. He urged the company to spin off separate dating sites—for gays and lesbians, for Asians, African Americans, Latinos, and Christians. He urged Match to purchase People Media, one of the industry's first niche dating companies. Leadership wasn't interested. Instead, the company continued to pursue partnerships with general media sites, like AOL, MSN, and Village Voice Media. Eventually Mastronuzzi did an advertising deal with Black Entertainment Television. BET put a banner ad for Match on its Web site, showing a black couple laughing. When BET's customers clicked on the ad, however, they were taken to Match's homepage, where they got bombarded with white people.

"Match," Mastronuzzi recalls, "just wasn't relevant for tons of communities. Take gays. We have our own unique concerns. Are you a top or a bottom? What's your HIV status? A general dating site can't get at that stuff."

During the first decade of online dating—between roughly 1995 and 2005—many in the industry thought the best site was the site with the most people on it. You'll recall that in the early days of Match, Gary Kremen envisioned an electronic version of a personals column, a giant, undifferentiated arena of mate seekers. But as the date-o-sphere grew and choice expanded, efficiency problems arose: Women got deluged with messages from guys they weren't interested in; men got ignored. The best site, went the new thinking, was not the one with the most people on it but the one with the most people on it for *you*. Through the questions asked in the sign-up process and the content posted on its site, a niche site like JDate could make itself feel culturally relevant to Jews (JDateTV, JMag, Jblog) in a way that Match's one-size-fits-all approach could not.

When Greg Blatt took over as CEO of Match in 2009, he saw niche dating as a sensible branding play and decided to buy People Media for $85 million. "People's decisions about what they do are a lot more random than they think," Blatt says. "Someone joins a dating site because they happen to see the advertising for that site, which frankly is the reason people do most of what they do. If it works for them, helps them get whatever they're looking for, they use it again. Most of our users are return customers." The People Media empire includes about thirty communities, such as Black People Meet, Senior People Meet, Single Parent Meet, Little People Meet, and BB People Meet ("Meet big and beautiful singles today!").

By 2011, niche dating sites had taken nearly a third of the market, or roughly ten to fifteen million online daters in North America. But across the pond, a young innovator had beaten Match to the punch.

In 2002, after moving back in with his parents, Ross Williams, a twenty-four-year-old Brit, started a company that designed Web sites. At night he dabbled in online dating. In the UK then there were two big dating sites, Match and Dating Direct. In Europe there was another online-dating company called Dating Central that allowed affiliates to build their own dating sites, which then tapped into Dating Central's main user database. Williams tried building his own site within Dating Central, but it didn't work very well, because traffic was hard to come by. But the idea of partnering with affiliates, he thought, was solid.

Building traffic on a new dating site can cost millions. Williams couldn't afford to buy and market new sites like Match could. And even if he could, how would a Brit know what kind of dating site would work in a far-flung place like, say, South Africa? Or how best to market that site to South Africans? Even more tricky would be developing sites that accommodated niche interests with which Williams was unfamiliar. Tattoo enthusiasts, swingers, fetishists—the list was mind-boggling.

So he borrowed a marketing concept that had worked in other industries: white labeling. A white-label business model is often used for mass-produced, undifferentiated products, such as electronics or food. The white-label product—say, cornflakes—is made by one entity and marketed by another, or by several others. A second entity brands the cardboard box, a third entity brands the store in which the box of cornflakes is sold.

After building up a small membership base through a generic dating site called Singles365, Williams began partnering with affiliates who wanted to operate their own niche sites that would then tap into Williams's mother database. To create an optimal dating site for South Africa, Williams would partner with a South African and let that person design and market the site locally. This would also solve the traffic problem: The local affiliates—the "storefronts"—funneled business to the "manufacturer," and vice versa. The affiliate gets a cut of money for each subscriber he pulls into the network through his white-label site. Williams called his company White Label Dating, and its parent company Global Personals.

Rather than market to users with the promise of raw size, he would claim to offer endless choice on the assumption that someone joins a dating site because they happen to see advertising for that site. Someone who wants to date a redhead can visit a virtual redhead bar, such as Date Ginger: "If you have the good taste to know that red is best, if you want to linger with a ginger, if you like pale and interesting, fiery personalities and partners that look fabulous in green. . . ." While another person who wants to be collared during sex can visit a virtual bar full of people who enjoy doing just that, at CollarMe.

But niche dating wasn't just about creating culturally relevant dating communities for specific interests. It was also about branding interests and fetishes that might not be socially acceptable to acknowledge publicly, creating judgment-free zones where the like-minded can mingle freely and furtively through a friendly flashing portal that screams: *See how many people are just like you?*

See, for example, goth dating;* pet-lovers dating;† sites for military widows;‡ nerd dating;§ plus-size dating;¶ a large subset of dating sites for rich guys and the women who love them; sites for prisoners;** a site for

---

* GothDating, GothicMatch, GothScene. (GS member Sara says: "Music rapes my life. Some of my favorite bands are The Birthday Massacre, Cradle of Filth, and Psyclon Nine. I'm a really sweet person. I have a one-eyed black cat, a ferret, and a pretty cool snake.")

† DateMyPet ("Date Me. Date My Pet.")

‡ MilitaryCupid, USMilitarySingles, MilitaryDatingOnline.

§ NerdPassions, SweetonGeeks, Gk2Gk.

¶ LargeFriends, LargeandLovely, Fat Singles, FatDatingService. FDS explains: "You'll find big fat women, proper fat chicks, college fat girls, fat black singles, fat white babes, the working class fat guy, cute fat females, old fat lovers, beautiful fat strippers, reserved fat Christians, fat Indian men, fat moms, bi fat people, hot fat Japanese singles, or even the ever popular skinny fat man. . . . Tired of hanging out at the night clubs for fat people with no results? Let us be your fat cupid."

** Meet-An-Inmate, ConjugalHarmony, WomenBehindBars. WBB advertises thusly:

Are you tired of wondering if she's cheating on you? Do you love to leave the toilet seat up? Want to enjoy freedom on the weekend and watch a little football with your buddies, rather than work on your "honey do" list? Well, now you don't have to worry about any of that with the latest craze in adult dating, dating and marrying inmates for conjugal visits. With a conjugal marriage, you will finally have a wife with the perfect amount of freedoms and rights, and more importantly, you will finally start enjoying your own.

people who look alike;* a site for Star Trek fans;† sites for cowboys;‡ a site for sea captains;§ sites for the fitness obsessed.¶ Some of these sites appear to have rather vibrant communities, and some of them appear to be fake.

The following, however, are all real: cougars (and their cubs) have Urbancougar, CougarLife, Date A Cougar, Cougarfling, and Toyboy; while the more traditional variety of age-incongruent relationship—sugar babies and sugar daddies—can be sought out on Seeking Arrangement, where sugar babies, who list compensation demands ("open—negotiable," "$3,000 to $5,000 per month"), emphasize that they are "easy" and "drama-free." The CEO of SeekingArrangement, Brandon Wade, also owns What'sYourPrice, where rich men bid on dates with beautiful women; and MissTravel, which pairs "generous travelers who hate to travel alone with attractive travelers who would love the opportunity to travel the world for free." Wade, a Chinese American with two degrees from MIT, says his sites are not about prostitution but are simply being "honest" and more efficient, by treating the dating game as it really is—an exchange of female beauty for male resources.

Honesty, particularly when it comes to expectations about lifestyle, is crucial to the success of any relationship. For the marijuana enthusiast in search of a mate who won't see red flags in his bloodshot eyes, there's LonelyStoner. Those obsessed with their iPhones, but who also want to find love, can scroll for mates at Cupidtino ("find other Machearts around

---

* FindYourFaceMate: A dating site for the "facially compatible." (See, e.g., a study of this phenomenon, by Liliana Alvarez and Klaus Jaffe, published in 2004 in Volume Two of *Evolutionary Psychology*, and titled, "Narcissism guides mate selection: Humans mate assortatively, as revealed by facial resemblance, following an algorithm of 'self seeking like.'")

† TrekPassions: "Feel like you are always wearing a red shirt in your relationships? In Pon Farr?"

‡ CowboyCowgirl, SinglesCorral, HorseandCountryLovers, FarmersOnly. One FarmersOnly member testifies: "The city folks that dominated these online dating sites couldn't relate to my lifestyle. They wanted to meet at 9:00 p.m. for a cup of coffee when I would typically be preparing for the next day, which started at 5:00 a.m. Caffeine at that hour was the last thing I needed!"

§ SeaCaptainDate. "In the unforgiving ocean of love, let us be your lighthouse."

¶ FitnessSingles: "Where relationships workout!"

you"). Lest one overlook the bonding power of shared virginity, abstinence, too, is a niche. Those choosing to retain their V-card until marriage have We Waited: "Before you ever get into any relationship at all, you need to be right with God." In the niche dating world there are all kinds of ways to be right with God. Liberal Christian swingers have libchrist: "Hell fire and save the matches, fuck a duck and see what hatches." Beautiful people date through BeautifulPeople, which expels users who transgress into ugliness, becoming, say, too fat after the holidays. Not even those with sexually transmitted diseases need remain lonely with niche dating, what with PositiveSingles, STDFriends, and Herpes Online, to name but a few of the sites that have, as one dating executive put it to me, "niched out everything from crabs to cottage-cheese discharge, a veritable Sunday buffet." Speaking of eccentric tastes, vampire enthusiasts can sink their teeth into dating profiles at Vampire Passions where, in addition to selecting among blood types, the garlic-averse daters must choose between "sanguine vampirism" and "psychic vampirism." If your thing is minimalism, Diapermates ("No scat videos please!") boasts of more than eleven thousand diaper-loving members, among them, WetBabyGirl, a twenty-nine-year-old who poses with a pink pacifier, a bib, and, of course, a diaper, and in her profile explains that she's looking for "a strong daddy" to take her to the movies. World Singles specializes in nationality niches, with sites like ArabLounge, IranianPersonals, RomaniaKiss, and VietVibe. A white-label dating company called Dating Factory has over three hundred sites for people with disabilities. Toy collectors once dated through PlasticSouls, but it folded for lack of subscribers—too niche-y.

Again, some of these sites are spoofs, but many niche sites are very real; and even if a niche site doesn't have a sufficiently large community, the member can always be fed into a larger database, such as Ross Williams's Singles365 or Markus Frind's Plenty of Fish, and introduced to people whose behavior indicates they're a good match.

The suburb of Windsor lies twenty miles west of London, south of the Thames River. Home to Windsor Castle, a royal residence, along with some of the most expensive real estate in the United Kingdom, Windsor doesn't seem like a hotbed of mate seekers. But just off Windsor's cute cobblestone strip, Global Personals, one of the largest online-dating companies in the world, does business from a comparatively bland office building.

Inside, an open-desk plan is divided among departments with names like Global Development, Business Intelligence, User Experience, Retention, and Fraud Moderation. Nearly one hundred employees chug coffee and fluorescent-colored energy drinks as they shift between an in-house deli, a miniature golf course, and a pool table. When they need a break, they relax in beanbag chairs and play video games. A sign by the door says: YOUR BRAND. YOUR SITE. OUR PLATFORM.

"Ultimately online dating is about understanding yourself," says Ross Williams. He's seated in a zebra-striped beanbag chair between the pool table and the flat-screen TV. "What online dating does, in my opinion, is allow me to experience more encounters and relationships. You can condense what would be years or decades of learning into months."

Going small and local, Williams effectively went large. In 2011, White Label Dating had more than six thousand affiliate sites across seven countries, from England to New Zealand, and was making $70 million a year in revenue. Some in the industry call Williams the Ray Kroc of dating, after the founder of McDonald's. There's also a more modern analogy. By creating a platform on top of which others build their own sites, Williams did for online dating what Mark Zuckerberg is attempting to do for the entire Internet by opening his Facebook platform to outside developers to build their own applications within the site. The affiliates of White Label Dating, some of whom make tens of thousands of dollars per month in revenue, operate niche sites such as the infamous Ugly Bug Ball ("If you are one of the millions of people that don't always like what they see in the mirror, then this is the place for you!"), and GILF Dating, a site that features thousands of British grandmothers in various states of froufrou and frippery.

"We've got a platform for people to create whatever they want," says Williams. "Life's too short. They should enjoy themselves."

Williams racks the balls for a game of pool. He's tall and lumbering, with a ready smile and jolly red cheeks devoid of judgment. Shortly after Williams started the main site, Singles365, he met a woman through it, fell hard for her, and proceeded to block messages from other guys until he'd solidified the bond. They dated for four years, then broke up. But he says that's just life, nothing to do with the site. (Williams's business partner, Steve Pammenter, met his wife through Singles365.) At the moment Williams is in a long-distance relationship with a woman from Arizona, whom he met offline. "I'm not totally sure about it," he says, cracking the balls apart. "I'm a homebody and she loves to go out all the time." A month from this interview she'll move to England to be with him, the relationship will fall apart immediately, and she'll return to the States.

"You don't learn much in life when things go perfectly right," says Williams, pragmatism unifying his sensitive side with the renegade businessman. "You need to experience some bad things. Hopefully we'll see a reduction in divorces, because people will be making smarter choices. Online dating is fantastic for building the confidence you need to date the person you want, and also for realizing that we're all in the same boat. We're all a bit nervous. We're all a bit shy. Some are better actors than others."

Many White Label sites seem very much on the fringe. But in a way, niche dating, whether it be GILF or LonelyStoner, is no different than general dating sites. Just as your Google searches become increasingly tailored to your interests and opinions, and your Pandora account tries to predict your music taste, relationship search engines also put you in a box. Niche dating simply markets, individually, the thousands of options out there. As the Internet grows vaster, technology is allowing us, and in some cases forcing us, to be more specific. This means John Dater can find people who are like him, and quite easily. It also means that, out of necessity, he will exclude those with qualities he may not realize he needs or enjoys. Opposites like Kelly and Tom are more likely to run into each other on Match, perhaps, than on CollarMe or Date My Pet. On the other hand, Atheist Passions or SingleParentMeet might have been good options for Carrie and AteoBoriqua.

But niche dating will likely have the largest impact on the lives of people who, for reasons beyond their control, lack choice. "If your dating pool is limited," says Trish McDermott, "online dating in its 'miniform' has been amazing in reducing some of that limitation."

Growing up gay in a suburb of New York City during the 1990s, Joel Simkhai faced a limitation. At the dawn of the Internet he would meet other gay teenagers through Compuserve's gay channel, an early version of a niche chat room, striking up long-distance relationships with people in places like Minnesota, Boston, and Washington, D.C. It was thrilling to make these connections, but also impractical. Simkhai's father would yell at him about the long-distance phone bills. There had to be a better way.

Not only does the gay community amount to a small fraction of the heterosexual community, but it can be hard to tell who's what. "I walk into a place, I don't necessarily know who's gay," says Frank Mastronuzzi, the former Match business developer. "This is why gays have always been on the cutting edge of technology. It's so much harder for them to connect. If their family casts them out, then it's also crucially important for them to connect."

Simkhai thought he had a pretty good "gaydar" until he realized, in his midtwenties, that both of his brothers were also gay. "With problems," he says, "come solutions."

He wanted to make it very easy to meet the gay people right around him, to see if there's chemistry, and move on if there's not. In 2009, Simkhai released a smartphone application through Apple's new app store. He gave his app a bold name: Grindr. On their smartphones, Grindr members are shown the profiles of other members within several hundred feet. Grindr has a reputation for facilitating sex on the fly, but Simkhai rejects the notion. "Here's the deal: The name 'Grindr' was chosen because it embodied the idea of 'grinding' people together in the same way that a coffee grinder grinds coffee beans," Simkhai explains at conferences and on the Grindr Web site. "The name is also a combination of the words 'Guy' and 'Finder.'"

Whatever the original intent, the app took off, and Simkhai became something of a rock star in the gay community. By 2012, Grindr had more than 3.5 million users in 192 countries, including in many with cultures that are intolerant of gays, such as Sri Lanka, Djibouti, Haiti, Iraq, and Iran. The UK is Grindr's biggest market, with 1 in every 60 male Londoners using the app. Assuming a 10 percent rate of homosexuality, that's 1 in 6 gay men. At the 2012 summer games, when the first Olympians arrived in London, Grindr melted down from overuse.

After her recovery from cancer, Laura Brashier spent the better part of a decade inside her head, wondering what she was meant to do with this hand she'd been dealt. She told no one of her condition, instead throwing her energy into her garden in Orange County, where she would relax in the evenings with food and wine. One day, in her late forties, Brashier was at a restaurant when a friend asked her why she wasn't dating. For the first time she told someone: "I can't have sex."

"When I finally heard myself say it out loud," she recalls, "I could imagine others in similar situations." She researched the reasons why intercourse might not be possible: diabetes, high blood pressure, cancer, the list went on. "It turns out that there are all kinds of reasons why people either don't want to have sex or can't have sex, yet still seek intimacy," she says. "I suspected that the group of people out there, if I could find them, was large enough to warrant a dating site."

In 2011, Brashier introduced 2Date4Love, "a dating site that enables people who cannot engage in sexual intercourse to meet and experience love, companionship and intimacy at its deepest level." Members began signing up, slowly at first, then faster.

"We all want to portray that we're perfect," Brashier says. "With clothes and makeup we can hide a lot. But when you have to admit this, you have to admit you're not perfect anymore. My goal is to make this a subject that people no longer have to hide from."

Thank-you letters rolled in from people whom the site had coaxed out of isolation. "I am smart, fun and very social," wrote Renee, an ovarian cancer survivor whose treatments hindered sexual functioning. "However, until now, I've shied away from dating. When men approached me, I would immediately act uninterested even if I was. I anticipated rejection and found it easier to dismiss them. I also got defensive when topics related to sexuality and relationships arose, which made me feel like I was in my own little bubble, separate from the rest of the world."

"Unlike a traditional dating site, I'm focused on what I call 'digital lip-stick,'" says Noel Biderman. "I realized early on that my role in this was twofold—create the connection, and help you not get caught. That's what the perfect affair is."

A law school graduate who became a sports agent, Biderman used to work out of Chicago and Italy, helping move basketball players around to keep their careers alive. "My fantasy was to be Jerry McGuire," he recalls, referring to the sports agent played by Tom Cruise in the eponymously named 1996 movie. "Instead I became the Jerry McGuire of Lebanon."

In 2001, after leaving sports agenting to join some friends in a real estate concern, Biderman (pronounced BEE-der-man) began thinking about online businesses. The first Internet bubble had just burst, meaning it might be a good time to invest. A Toronto native, Biderman recalls reading an article by a female journalist in Canada. The piece, he remembers, was about how, even though the bubble had burst, the Internet had made an irreversible impact on our lives. Napster changed how we thought about music. Online pornography meant no longer wearing disguises out to the video store. Online dating was changing the way we meet people. Anecdotally, the writer estimated that a third of the men on dating sites were married.

"I was in an entrepreneurial mind-set at the time," Biderman recalls. "That statistic jumped off the page. I looked at dating sites. They were all subscription businesses that promised better relationships. I thought, 'Hmm, who's more motivated than a married man to put down a credit card to get what he's missing in his marriage?' These people should have their own site." Biderman ran the idea by his friends. The response from men was the same—laughter, either nervous or excited. The response from women was more interesting. They were silent at first. "There would be this moment," he remembers, "when they sort of peered into

DIAPER DADDIES AND LONELY STONERS 145

my soul, as if maybe I was testing them, as if I'd found them out. I always suspected that a lot of guys cheated. But I would've never guessed that half my female friends had had affairs."

If you're on a niche dating site, you may lie about your height, weight, and income, but at least you're not lying about the one attribute that makes you eligible for the niche. If you post a profile on DateGinger, you're either a redhead or you want to date one. If you go on Grindr, you're gay. If you're on SalaamLove, you're presumably Muslim. What happens when the relevant qualification is relationship status itself?

In 2003, Biderman started Ashley Madison, naming the company after the two most popular names for baby girls. Ten years later, the site claims thirteen million members in seventeen countries. With slogans like "Monogamy is Monotony" and "Life is Short. Have an Affair," Biderman's advertising is often turned down, particularly for primetime television slots like the Super Bowl. So he compensates by going on TV talk shows, where he's often booed.

On these shows Biderman has become skilled at defending the societal contribution of his business: Affairs will happen with or without online dating to facilitate them, he argues. Would divorce cease if divorce attorneys couldn't advertise? Do limits on alcohol stop drinking? Workplace affairs, he says, jeopardize jobs and livelihoods. By creating a space for discreet affairs, you limit fallout and keep families together. The children—Ashley and Madison—are the ultimate beneficiaries.

After talk-show appearances, the traffic on Ashley Madison spikes.

Biderman sees himself as a crusader on behalf of the online-dating industry's taboo-busting efforts. "I'm happy to be a one-man wrecking crew making the industry better for everyone else," he says. But he's also careful to distinguish Ashley Madison from traditional dating sites. "eHarmony has a terrific trick up their sleeve. If you're patient enough to fill out hundreds of questions, then you might get along with someone who's also patient enough to do that. These sites want you to think that dating is about getting married. Yet a small percentage of people out there are seeking only permanence. Most of the rest of society is willing to date for lots of reasons besides dating-into-relationships-into-permanence."

Ashley Madison's success spawned copycats in North America and abroad. Gleeden, founded by two French brothers, got its start by serving a culture of infidelity in France. A Scandinavian cheating site called Victoria Milan prompted a record number of complaints to Sweden's advertising authorities after introducing a billboard campaign that read: "Are you married? Liven up your life—have an affair."

Since the mainstream advertising world treats Biderman's cheating empire as toxic, he does what a lot of online-dating businesses do. He puts out reports showing how popular Ashley Madison is. So while Match and eHarmony distribute studies showing that more marriages are originating from online dating, and that online-dating sites result in better marriages, Ashley Madison sends out press releases claiming, for instance, that Hispanics are "the fastest growing community when it comes to infidelity," and that, according to its own data, "Hispanic members have affairs at the youngest age: Average age of 27 for women and 34 for men (compared to 33 for women and 40 for men in the general U.S. population)." Another press release, quickly parroted by the media, announced that Washington, D.C., was Ashley Madison's biggest market. "Powerful men and women, particularly those in politics, tend to take multiple 'risks' on their way to the top," explained Biderman. "Taking a risk within their personal life, since they feel they are made of Teflon, is a natural extension. Simply put, the more successful you are, the more prone to cheating you are."

People scoff at Biderman for promoting a pastime still generally regarded as immoral by most of the population. But his efforts don't seem as outlandish when you think of the ways our views on relationships—from premarital sex, to divorce, to gay marriage—have progressed over the years. "As an entrepreneur, part of my responsibility to society is to help it evolve, the way an artist does," Biderman says.

This theme—helping society evolve past old traditions, whether marital fidelity (Biderman) or privacy (Zuckerberg)—runs through the world of social media. The message is: Conventions should be revised to conform with the behavior enabled by technology, which has been tooled to accommodate all possible behavior.

For at least a century, America has been "preparing to meet the challenges of a more permissive society" trumpeting some new "emerging culture of chaotic indulgence," celebrating and ruing another "conquering of taboo." Declaiming a sexual revolution is practically a generational rite of passage: From the perverse poetics of Catullus (80 B.C.) to the sixteenth-century Rabelaisians to the seventeenth-century libertines, the men and women of every generation have thought they reinvented fornication. For all we know, granny fantasies and diaper fetishes date to Catullus's *polymetra*, or at least to the invention of diapers.

And still, today *is* different. Even if there is nothing new under the covers, the mode of *finding* it has been revolutionized by the Internet, by the radical connection that is unique to *this* era. Perhaps a diaper fetishist is a diaper fetishist is a . . . and so on, all the way back, and what has been will be again. But a diaper fetishist living in a world with immediate access to similarly pampered people is a new baby. The player still suits up one leg at a time, but the game has changed.

It doesn't matter who you are or what you do. You can be a closet swinger, an out-of-closet deviant, or a U.S. congressman. You can be them all. Between Twitter and Facebook and Phantasy Tour, as well as the thousands of sites and smartphone applications designed explicitly for dating, there is bound to be someone in the cloud of faces who's interested in whatever it is that you've got. These portals not only present the whole human grid of desire and stimulation but make that grid real and attainable, nonvirtual, bounded by only the limitations of curiosity and imagination.

Although Biderman catches a lot of flak for branding infidelity, he is not alone among online-dating execs in his belief that monogamous marriage is at odds with the reality afforded by technology. With a courtside seat to the behavior of enormous mating populations, those who run dating sites see infidelity firsthand. "At the moment," says Dan Winchester, founder of Free Dating in the UK, "there's a glaring inconsistency between the old convention—in which people are still very much geared toward maintaining traditional relationships—and the way people are actually using the Web today to get together. Some of the most well-trafficked sites are those for affairs, swinging, or so-called deviant behavior of one kind or another. These are not tiny ecosystems, mind you. Sooner or later we reach a point where people say: 'What is actually wrong with this behavior? Why are we not openly engaging in it?' This is the real story of our industry."

When *The New Yorker*'s Adam Gopnik reviewed a bunch of books about life online in 2011, he argued that the Internet's first two decades sparked "a revolution less in morals, which have remained mostly static, than in means: you could already say 'fuck' on HBO back in the eighties; the change has been our ability to tweet or IM or text it." The Internet is certainly a revolution in means, but those new means are not properly identified as IM or text, which are merely updates of the letter and the telephone. What's revolutionary about the Internet is the way it combines communication with ever-enhanced search-and-discovery capability.

On HBO in the eighties you could hear people say "fuck," and you could see people have sex. What you could not do then, which you most definitely can do now, is crawl through the screen, meet anyone, go anywhere, even abroad, and forge relationships on whatever grounds the free market permits. The kind of online connecting that leads to offline relationships is an Internet breed apart. The measure of power that it abdicates to the user is unprecedented, far from theoretical, and it's changing the way people approach their relationship lives, giving rise to a new normal.

CHAPTER SEVEN

Like Everyone, I'm Looking for My True Love

MARRIAGE AND MIRAGE IN THE INTERNATIONAL DATE-O-SPHERE

I like women from countries that have sustained political turmoil. Western culture seems to forge women that are valueless and inane. OK. Not only women!

—OkCupid profile of WikiLeaks founder Julian Assange

The online-dating honchos in Europe and America are trying to free the date-o-sphere from its stigmatized roots. They want to expose the old encased world of online dating to the great wide open of social discovery, lose the pink hearts on the homepage, skirt the taboo, and make their product universal by conditioning the world that meeting new people online is amazing.

Neal Bryant, a British dating exec based in Moscow, is waging a branding battle that is similar and different. The site he represents, AnastasiaDate, specializes in connecting Western men with women in Russia, Ukraine, China, Africa, Latin America, and beyond.

The stigma here is mighty, well, stigmatizing. Always has been. Even in the Old West of nineteenth-century America, when pioneers would strike out for the Territories, and then, once settled, advertise for wives in newspapers back east, it was assumed that the mail-order bride industry relegated prostitutes, old maids, and hopeless spinsters to the nation's grubby backcountry. As an Anastasia rep, it's Bryant's job to make over the mail-order bride industry, to convince the buying public that there's nothing weird about this, nothing untoward. It's just another way of meeting people.

It's early fall in Russia, 2011. This afternoon Bryant spoke at iDate Moscow, an international online-dating conference organized by the same people who handle Miami. The conference was sponsored in part by Mamba.ru, a dating site for Russians seeking Russians. "Mamba," states the corporate poster, "creates happy couples and families, makes people feel better, feel needed and important. Mamba is not just a business but, in a way, it's a business that helps children to be born." This local online-dating market is not substantially different from what goes on back home. I've come to Moscow, rather, to investigate this cross-border format in which the Russians specialize, to see whether it could really one day go mainstream, assuming it hasn't already.

The business is certainly cash-positive. In 2012, *The Daily*, an iPad publication owned by Rupert Murdoch, reported that the international marriage brokering business had reached $2 billion, making it equal in size to the entire online-dating industry in the United States. Although numbers are hard to substantiate, Anastasia appears to be grossing something on the order of $1 million per day, perhaps substantially more. Its main competitor, A Foreign Affair, is owned by Americans and based in Arizona. Both companies are doing everything they can to get the word out. Times have changed, they say: You can find love at your local church, at work, in a pub, and now you can find it in the foreign country of your choice. This is the way of the world now.

"We don't say mail-order brides!" Bryant told his audience of online-dating colleagues. "People say Anastasia is about mail-order brides, but you can't order a bride by mail or the Internet. If you could, Amazon would be doing it!" The joke played well. He continued: "Many people ask what our clients see in Russian girls. From our research and understanding, we think the art of attracting a male is more developed in Eastern European culture. In Russia, it's frowned upon for ladies not to look after themselves. They walk more, eat less junk food. There's no gender-role confusion."

In the evening, the conference-goers—comprised of online-dating execs from the United States and Europe—convene at a cavernous underground restaurant across town, where they dine on vodka, beef, boiled potatoes, and smoked fish. Bryant sits down at my table with a bottle of Russian Standard. "Drinking," he says, "this is a serious problem here in Russia. Escaping the fate of an abusive, alcoholic husband is one good reason the Russian and Ukrainian women have for shopping their wares overseas."

Bryant's ironic smirk hardly bears the courage of conviction: He pours a shot of vodka, then another. A female dating exec from London joins us. "If you don't call it mail-order brides," she asks Bryant, "what do you call it?"

"We call it 'premium international online dating,'" he says.

But the question, coming from a Western woman, seems to rattle Bryant, almost shame him in some way. "Oh my God," he says, leaning hard on the Russian Standard. "I can't believe what I do for a living."

Following the 1991 collapse of the Soviet Union, the market for mail-order brides began to heat up. Many bridal agencies in the United States that had dealt mostly with women from the Philippines switched their focus to Russia and Eastern Europe. The business was mediated almost entirely by catalogs. New York–based Scanna International, a pioneer in the Russian mail-order-bride industry, set up an office in Vladivostok as early as 1989. Scanna published a five-dollar catalog every two weeks, with profiles of two hundred new women. The catalogs, which often featured poorly printed photos, didn't put much of a gloss on the industry, or help convince would-be customers that the women were real. Media reports about mail-order brides helped spread the word, but without a more efficient way to connect the market would remain limited. Throughout the nineties, and even into the early 2000s, the Internet didn't figure much in Russian life. Even in 2007, when Ericka Johnson wrote *Dreaming of a Mail-Order Husband*, only one of the hopeful mail-order brides she interviewed in Moscow had ever "surfed the Net."

Still, women found a way to connect. In 2003, when Anastasia started its Web site, many Russian women flocked to their local "bridal agencies" to have their photos taken and uploaded into profiles to be seen on the other side of the world. These local agencies, which are now said to exist in most Russian and Ukrainian cities, are essentially Anastasia's subcontractors, or white-label partners, feeding women into the main database. This model would prove handy as the mail-order-bride business spread across Eastern Europe, Asia, and Latin America, from 2003 to the present. Anastasia now partners with over one thousand bridal agencies around the globe.

In 2011, *Bloomberg Businessweek* reported that "venturing abroad for love has taken on a more acceptable mien," as international matchmakers comprise "a growing segment of the U.S. online dating industry." It's the poor economy in the United States—rather than the desperation of disadvantaged women abroad—that's responsible for the flourishing growth in recent years of premium international online dating, the magazine said: Struggling financially and losing out in the gender wars, American men were doing the rational thing by looking abroad for a low-maintenance alternative to that entitled and difficult American woman to whom he no longer measured up. Those who run Anastasia and A Foreign Affair don't disagree with this view. But they chalk up their success to a rising awareness among men that, yes, you can meet young, beautiful, *real* women from foreign places and actually pursue a relationship with them.

At the restaurant, Bryant and the female dating executive are joined by a fortyish man from Los Angeles named Tai Lopez. Like Brandon Wade, Lopez operates dating sites that target the sugar-daddy/sugar-baby niche. Bryant and Lopez don't see themselves as being in the same business. Yet they both match older men with younger woman, based either explicitly (Lopez) or implicitly (Bryant) on a financial imbalance. In the States, this is stigmatized as sugar daddies and sugar babies. When the connection is cross-border, it's mail-order brides, or premium international online dating.

"I was going to bring my Ferrari to Moscow," Lopez says. "After racing it across the States."

"Why would you do that?" Bryant asks.

"The women here are such gold diggers," Lopez says. "It's not like Sweden. If you go to Sweden, the women don't care what you have, because everyone in Sweden has the same amount."

Vodka is drunk. Lopez then asks Bryant: "Are the girls on your site real? Aren't you just selling them to a bunch of weirdos?"

This is the perception. Some high-profile murders of women who came to the United States via so-called international marriage brokers prompted President Bush to sign the International Marriage Broker Regulation Act of 2005, or IMBRA, which mandates background checks for men. Before flying abroad to meet a woman through one of Anastasia's Web sites, the client is required to fill out a form answering questions about restraining orders, domestic violence, arrests for prostitution, rape, kidnapping, stalking. and incest. as well as marital status, past marriages, and biological and adopted children. Clients must list all the states they've resided in, so the appropriate sex-offender registries can be checked. According to Bryant, Anastasia's staff in Moscow spends the majority of its time satisfying IMBRA regulations. Those in the United States who advocate on behalf of trafficked women say it's not enough.

"We're going to let the journalist decide," Bryant says. He and I had previously discussed the possibility of my tagging along on an Anastasia romance tour. "We've got a tour running down to Colombia in November. We'll send him along."

Like normal online dating, the international date-o-sphere is another venue for matching people who are looking for the same thing, optimizing market efficiency just as eBay does with goods bought and sold. But unlike local online dating—Match in the United States or Mamba in Russia—the technology in its cross-border format is as much about expanding one's options as it is about exploiting a gap in options. This gap is often financial, but not always. When Western men use the Internet to meet women in China, for example, the Chinese women who sign up for the service often come from well-off families. These women don't want to meet an American for his money, necessarily. Rather, they're looking abroad because they *can*. Female infanticide, part and parcel of China's one-child policy, resulted in a gender imbalance that left women in a competitively favorable position. Of course, this won't be the situation in Colombia, one of South America's poorest countries.

Welcome to Medellin, City of Eternal Spring. Seventeen of Anastasia's male clients have descended on Colombia's second-largest city for a weeklong romance tour. In the cultural primer provided by the company, the romance tourists have been warned not to be offended if they're called "gringo."

For the past several months, if not several years, these men have been members of Amo Latina (Find Your Princess), the Latin sister site of Anastasia, where they pay to correspond with women in Brazil, Colombia, Costa Rica, Panama, Peru, and Uruguay. Amo Latina is one of three Web sites owned by Anastasia. The other two are Asian Beauties, which markets relationships with women from Chongqing, China, as well as from select outposts around Southeast Asia; and Africa Beauties, the company's newest site. There are no monthly membership fees on these sites. Instead, male clients buy credits, which they dissipate in the sending and receiving of e-mail messages and instant chats. Bulk purchases bring the cost down: one thousand credits cost $399 ($.40 each), while twenty credits cost $15.99 ($.80 each).

The service is "premium" in part because all communication requires a human translator. One e-mail or chat correspondence—a message sent, a message returned—can cost the client between one and two dollars. Anastasia claims to exchange 2.5 million letters per day through all of its sites combined. The sites offer male clients other methods of mobile courting too, such as the delivery of flowers and chocolates. "When a lady you've corresponded with has a birthday upcoming," the Amo Latina Web site promises, "you will receive a birthday notification to remind you about the significant date."

As for the romance tours, they're billed as a very special experience for clients who see the value proposition: $1,595 gets you one week at the Dann Carlton Hotel, located in El Poblado ("the Beverly Hills of Medellin"); two "socials," at which women outnumber men 20 to 1; access to a support staff of Russian ladies, who function as dating concierges, suggesting restaurants and arranging in-country transportation should a client wish to swing through, say, Bogotá, to meet more women on his way home; and a crew of able translators for hire. For fifteen dollars an hour, a translator can accompany the client on dates. If he has a phone number written in the little black book that is provided for the purpose, the translator can even make the date. While the translator's presence jacks up the dinner tab, she becomes an indispensable third wheel, not only translating languages but arbitrating emotions, a kind of relationship mediator brought to the table to help hammer out terms.*

Poolside at the Dann Carlton, the gringos eat a buffet breakfast while discussing their motivations for turning to premium international online dating.

"American women took me to the cleaners," says Andy, a fifty-two-year-old window-installer from Florida. "They'll basically say, 'I'm going to fuck you up the ass and take 150 percent of everything you ever dreamed about.'"

In his Amo Latina profile, Andy calls himself a "Texas-raised gentleman" looking for his "Latin Princess." He enjoys dinner on his boat under the stars and bubble baths by candlelight. He warns all those seeking "rich sugar daddies" to stay away. Andy came to Colombia to find love, to be appreciated for who he is, not for what he can provide. He feels that his first two marriages were brought down by gold digging, not by his alcoholism; Andy says he's stopped drinking. His third marriage, which ended recently, was to a young Brazilian he met in a Miami bar. She offered him ten thousand dollars in exchange for a sham marriage and a green card. He turned down the money, said he'd marry her only for love, and two years after the wedding she disappeared.

"American women won't say, 'I want a relationship,'" agrees Bart, a fifty-four-year-old air-conditioner salesman from Alabama. "They'll say,

---

* The romance tours to Russia and Ukraine typically cover two cities and three socials. They cost twice as much as the Latin America tours.

'Fuck you, I want to see how much money you got first'—at least to a certain extent."

Bart is also coming off a difficult divorce. Despite giving his wife of thirty years "horses in the barn, vacation cruises, and cars," she became addicted to crack and left him for her dealer. But Bart is eager to accept responsibility for the failed marriage. Through a regimen of competitive ballroom dancing, hunting trips, and attendance at relationship semi- nars, such as those run by guru David Deida, author of *The Way of the Superior Man*, Bart's been striving to improve himself for the next woman. "You must be passionate enough to understand we have a very short window to make a connection," says Bart's Amo Latina profile, "and do whatever you must to make that connection unbreakable."

The opacity of Bart's actual intentions speaks to a basic divide among the group. While decorum requires all of the men to express hope of a re- lationship, only about half of the seventeen romance tourists (sixteen Americans, one Canadian) are in Medellin to find a wife, I am told by Charles, a former bodybuilder who became an Anastasia rep after going on a romance tour. The rest, he says, are here for "a week of fun."

A third romance tourist, a fifty-six-year-old doctor from California named Richard, says, "Women in the States are confused. They don't know if they want to be the man or the woman. I sure as hell don't want to be the woman."

"Burn the bra and everything else," Bart says. "Gloria Steinem started all that stuff."

"It'd be nice to find a girl who thinks gym clothes are for the gym," Richard says. "That's why I'm down here."

Bart, Andy, Richard, and several other men on the trip say they came to Amo Latina after failing to find happiness on mainstream dating sites like Match and eHarmony. They came on the romance tour because it's easier and more efficient than planning a trip on your own.

After breakfast, the gringos convene in a hotel conference room for the introductory session. "These tours serve as huge public relations tools," they are told. "We don't really make any money on the tour. It brings you here to meet women, but also to understand that these women are for real, so that you can return home and hopefully spread a good word about us, dispel any naysayers who think the women on our site are just pictures. Remember: If you can think of it, if you can imagine it happening, we can help you make it happen."

Historically, the media has written off the mail-order bride industry as a business that services the West's most undesirable men— ignoramuses, racists, misogynists, repeat offenders. In press accounts, the red-faced lecher with a walrus mustache is a standard of the genre. A few of Amo Latina's clients fit that bill. But what's unique about the foreign niche's stigma is the perception that only older men use it. If the stereotype was ever true, it's no longer. According to sources who work for the local bridal agencies in Medellin, the women in foreign countries who sign up for these sites are getting younger and younger, and so are the men. On this trip there is Derrick, a soft-spoken twenty-seven-year-old Hispanic American from Houston. Derrick came on the trip because his job at a petroleum company keeps him long at the office and he wants to settle down with a Latin woman. Eddie, a thirty-two-year-old Hispanic American chef from Brooklyn, also speaks Spanish, also works long hours, and is determined to marry a Latin woman. Eddie worked two jobs to support his ex-fiancée in New York, until she cheated on him with his best friend. The group contains three additional members under thirty-five. Almost half the group is under forty.*

The men, showered and dressed, gather in the lobby of the Dann Carlton. Brody, a thirty-year-old nurse from Michigan, wears jeans and an untucked black button-down. A tour veteran, this is Brody's third trip to Medellin. "It's a little overwhelming at first," he explains, referring to the unusual ratio at the socials. "But then you get used to it, and all the

---

* This comes as a shock to Norma Ramos, the executive director of the New York–based Coalition Against Trafficking in Women. The paradigm of the older troglodytic male preying on the underprivileged foreigner makes a more compelling argument in favor of her agency's work against trafficking and exploitation. When told that male clients are getting younger, Ramos said it "just demonstrates the increasing commodification of women, based on intense poverty and dramatic inequality."

attention makes you cocky. You go back to the States and not even the girl behind the McDonald's counter smiles at you."

Almost goofy with optimism, Brody is not a particularly good-looking guy, though he's not unattractive. His last American girlfriend, whom he met on eHarmony and planned to propose to, was unfaithful. Now, according to his Amo Latina profile, he's looking for a woman who is "worth the white dress," one who knows that "matrimony is not a game but a glorified dimension if we obey our heavenly father." His colleagues at work rib him about these trips, suggesting that he comes to Colombia to sleep with prostitutes. Like Bart, Brody's mission is a matter of some urgency: His previous tours have earned him a reputation as a player among Medellin's bridal agencies.

"I can't find a woman at home," he says. "Yet thanks to the Internet I can develop a reputation as a player in a foreign city where I don't speak the language."

A trim man with a perma-smile slaps Brody on the back and says, "Ready to go, buddy?" This is Tony, a poster child for Amo Latina. "I'm already with a girl down here," he explains. "But I'll be doing the same thing as you tonight, walking around and talking to them."

Tony is a forty-nine-year-old emergency-room doctor from Oregon. Last week he proposed to a thirty-seven-year-old woman he met on an earlier Amo Latina tour. They're commencing paperwork for a K-1 visa, known as a fiancée visa, which allows a woman to live in the United States for ninety days. (During that time she must either marry an American or leave the country.) Once married, she can apply for a green card. Whenever the paperwork for the fiancée visa gets processed, she can return to the States with Tony. In the meantime he rents a condo in Medellin and flies back and forth. "I'm addicted to these tours, man," he says. "You'll see tonight at the social. You can't put it in words. You go in there, and it's like you're punch drunk. You feel like a rock star. See, I don't work for the company, but I help promote the company. And for these girls to come back to the Amo Latina socials, they've got to be able to say, 'Hey, I came here and I met some guys, and it was okay.'"

Tony will repeat these lines many times over the next few days. Billing himself as a perennial promoter seems to help Tony maintain a risky illusion—that he can send his fiancée shopping, or tell her to wait at home and study English, while, in the name of keeping Amo Latina in business, he trawls for women at the socials.

The gringos are now in a tour bus heading to their first social of the week, at a nightclub called Mango's, where, according to the *Lonely Planet* travel guide, Medellin's "rich and beautiful come to show off."

"This city has a history, sometimes a rough history," the gringos were told during the introductory session. Medellin was home to the late drug kingpin Pablo Escobar. Much of the city doesn't feel safe. Vendors return change in counterfeit bills. Taxis stray from course. Nicer areas are guarded with guns. "You have a safe in your room—use it. Only take as much cash as you need. Don't flash your cash, don't bring your bling, don't go anywhere without a buddy. It's more fun to double-date or even triple. It's also a courtesy to the ladies, because many don't speak English, so they'll feel more comfortable with another girl at the table."

Bart, the air-conditioner salesman from Alabama, is giving a counterhistory of the Confederate War. "Redneck," he says, "is as insulting to whites as nigger is to niggers. I tell you, there should be no quotas or affirmative action, because on the sports field the most powerful wins, the best wins. Why should it be turned around in life? It's like they want to eradicate any form of a moral code."

Andy, the window guy from Florida, is more focused. Though divorced three times, Andy's spent most of his adult life as a married person. The prospect of mingling with dozens of women makes him more nervous than excited. He carries a digital pocket translator. Compounding Andy's angst is an experience he had a couple days before the rest of the crew showed up. He came down to Medellin early to meet a woman he'd been communicating with through the Amo Latina Web site.

"The only downfall was that she's twenty," he explains. "But man, did we click. I tried to shoot her down right away when she invited me to chat online. 'What are your parents going to think? What are your friends going to think?' I tried to give her something to really think about. I even said, 'If we're together in the States we wouldn't have a lot of friends, because they wouldn't agree with our arrangement.' A thirty-two-year age gap. People look down on that shit. I even mentioned that she's seven years younger than my youngest daughter. But she said, 'I don't want to talk about age.' Then she started talking about things she liked. She liked everything I like: swimming, the beach. And man, she don't look twenty. And she conducts herself like a lady, not like a kid. When we went out, she had a sore throat. I said she should go home and sleep. But she said, 'No. I want to spend time with you.' So we went to dinner and to the mall to shop. She wanted pictures of everything. A picture of the translator. A picture of her and the translator. A picture of me in front of the fountain. Of me in front of the Christmas tree. She wanted all these pictures for memories. So I thought, 'Man, that's pretty good.'" With the pocket translator, Andy told her she should call him when she got done with work the next night. But she never called. He sent her a letter through the site. He knows she opened it yesterday. "Maybe with being sick she couldn't respond," he speculates. "But it went so good. I don't know what happened."

Dave, an Amo Latina client liaison, asks Andy what the company can do to help.

"Maybe you can get me her phone number," Andy says, "so I can text her, and if she doesn't text back, then at least I can move on."

"Okay," Dave says, "we'll take care of you, buddy." Dave is a former Amo Latina client who met his girlfriend on an earlier tour. Now he owns a vacation house on the beach in Cartagena. Dave says he made it "to the top of the tree" in the nightclub business back in London, where he "banged pretty much everything." Dave's girlfriend runs one of the local bridal agencies. She's responsible for the rumor going around that Brody is a player.

Tony intervenes. "Trust me," he tells Andy. "After tonight you won't even remember her."

Andy's misfire with the twenty-year-old is a reminder that, just like other online-dating portals, the reality of international online dating is complicated: For every Western man looking not for a wife but for quick sex abroad, there is a woman looking not for a relationship but for a free night out in her hometown, shopping for shoes at the mall, and eating at restaurants that she and her family could never afford. As for explicit scamming, it's well-known among Web site users that the staffs of local bridal agencies will often pose as the women in the profiles, responding to incoming messages in order to keep the rubles rolling in. Nearly every man on the tour has a story of chatting up a beautiful woman online and then offering to fly down, only to be told, suddenly, that she'll be out of town or busy working during those dates. Two of the romance tourists on this trip came specifically because they'd been corresponding with women they wanted to meet. In both cases, the men explained, with more pride than disappointment, the women were away doing a modeling tour and couldn't meet up.

According to Neal Bryant, about 80 percent of male clients are so-called keyboard Romeos, lonely guys looking to make pen pals and nothing more. Therefore, much of the scamming goes undetected by Anastasia's users—no harm, no foul.

But Arturo, a Mexican American truck driver from Fresno, has found the Amo Latina Web site frustrating for this reason. That's why he came on tour. "I no want no woman with kids," he says. "In States, the young girls with no kids—they think I'm too old. But if I date older, then she already have kids. That mean father come to my house to get kids on Saturday. I don't like that." For tonight's social, he's dressed in white polyester pants, a bolo tie, a beige leather jacket with brown leather shoulders, and a cowboy hat. Arturo records every minute of the trip on his Tablet's video function and then replays clips over breakfast.

As the tour bus pulls into the dirt parking lot of Mango's, Dave cries out in his cheerio English, "Allllllrrrrrrighty gents! Pace yourself. This is about endurance. Don't let conversations go too deep too soon," he says, as if such were possible between people who don't speak the same language. "Move, flow. They'll all have the same names. You'll meet ten Luisas and twenty Christinas. So get phone numbers and e-mails and Web site IDs, if possible. And remember, when you're walking away from a table after getting contact info, rip the sheets out of your little book so the next girl doesn't know she's actually twenty-third on your list!"

Bart—who has chosen black dancing shoes, gray slacks, and a white tuxedo shirt open at the chest—is incredulous, his mouth open in giddy disbelief like a twelve-year-old being told about porn for the first time. "Good luck hunting, guys! We wish you all the best!"

The inside of Mango's looks like a Western-themed bar. It's as if a Hard Rock Café merged with Hooters, Johnny Rockets, and a rodeo. Clint Eastwood posters adorn the wall. Red-and-white-striped manne-quin legs hang from the ceiling. Urinals are shaped like Rolling Stones lips. In the entrance, by the registration table, stands a three-foot midget. The registration table ensures that the women who enter the social are authenticated Amo Latina users, not simply passersby looking for a night of free food and drink.

The women trickle in, wearing jeans or minidresses, blouses, and high heels. Colombia's females are staggeringly beautiful, the product of a transnational genetic slosh that includes mestizo, Spanish, Italian, Por-tuguese, German, and African heritage. Even the least attractive girls are curvy. Botero didn't lie. Much of the beauty is natural. Some of it is engineered. In addition to romance tourism, Colombia specializes in vanity tourism, attracting American and European travelers in search of cut-rate deals on liposuction, rhinoplasty, wrinkle removal, and breast and buttocks augmentation.

Steve, a skeletally svelte accountant from Sacramento, stands by the bar holding his umbrella like a beat stick. He's becoming visibly upset over a scheduling glitch. "Look," Steve says, glaring at the door. "Look at this. It's going to take at least an hour for them to get all the girls in. So you lose an hour right there." Steve is drinking a six-dollar can of Red Bull, a noncomplimentary item. He's been on Amo Latina tours several times before, and has a few tips. "Listen, if you sit down at a table with a group of girls, and you wind up liking one of them, you can't just ask for her phone number and not ask the friends. So what you do is you leave and then send over one of the translators to ask the one you like to come to a table with just you. But don't be too obvious about it, because that's just wrong."

At the translator table, ten college-aged women, most of them more conservatively dressed than the other women in the room, chat with each other, drink soda, and wait to be deployed.

"People ask a lot of standard questions," says Valentina, a twenty-year-old translator majoring in international business at the local university. "They both want to know if the other has been married and if the other has kids. That's the first thing. Then they want to know about the person's expectations for the future. The guy wants to know why she's interested in an American man, and she wants to know why he's interested in a Colombian woman."

"It's weird," adds Juanita, a brainy twenty-one-year-old who's majoring in physics and fashion and has a cat named Aristotle. "As translators we have to, like, channel the emotions back and forth. It's not just words. If you're doing it well, it's also expressions and gestures. Like we flirt for them. But if the conversation doesn't go well, it's hard for you to go well. This is like an internal joke we have between the translators."

Mango's is now full, with well over one hundred Colombianas present for perusal by seventeen gringos. To get things started, two Colombian Chippendales—shirtless, oiled-up beefcakes—do some choreographed bumping up on stage. The midget from reception, who is now dressed like a construction worker, dances inside a cage, swinging stiff-limbed from the top bars. Tony, the ER doc, joins two bikini-clad dancing girls on a high railing.

Dave says that most of the clients who come on tour are surprised by the possibilities for age gaps: twenty years is nothing; thirty years is not unusual. But these tour clients seem to be plenty aware. In their profiles, Andy, fifty-two, says he's looking for women twenty to thirty-five; while Arturo, fifty, wants to find a woman between eighteen and twenty-eight. Rod, a fifty-six-year-old Japanese Canadian architect from Vancouver, says that no matter how old he gets he still goes for the twenty-three-year-olds. "Where I live," he says, "that's just not possible anymore. The girls up there, they have certain what they call mores."

This is the real selling point of premium international online dating. Like fine leather bucket seats or truffles on pasta, you'll pay a little extra, go a little farther, for the tonics of youth and beauty. Anastasia emphasizes the health benefits that accrue to men who marry younger women. They cite a 2009 study by Germany's Max Planck Institute, which found that a man's chances of dying early are reduced by 20 percent if his bride is between fifteen and seventeen years younger. The study found that men who marry older women are more likely to die early.*

That marriage, as an institution, is on the rocks back home is not in doubt: In America, the average marriage age is rising while the marriage rate plummets. But in places like Moscow and Medellin, where tradition reigns, it's still frowned upon for a woman to be single past her midtwenties.

On the tour the men talk of fleeing gold diggers up North, a legal system whose alimony rules unfairly favor women, and/or a misguided culture of feminism. But the gold-digger rationale falls apart under the lightest scrutiny. The men are in Colombia to meet women who are interested in them for no other reason than what they can provide. And yet, for most of the romance tourists, squaring this incongruity requires little effort. He is here to meet women who both value the controlling, masculine gender role that he enacts and embrace the servile, "family-oriented" femininity without which his own role would not make sense to him. His desire to be captain of his own ship finds validation in an image that is necessarily vague: the beautiful but unstable Colombiana who deserves better than her circumstances provide. It's not that she's so poor, nor her options so limited, that she's willing to sell her youth to a man more than twice her age. A parity of power must be assumed. This is why the neat geopolitical overlay—i.e., the obvious fact that the power hierarchy between these two gender roles happens to conform with the hierarchy that binds developing nations to the industrialized world, so long as they agree to adopt their benefactors' ideas about democracy, or capitalism, or family—proves not to be a popular subject of conversation for the romance tourists, when brought up. The view among the Amo Latina reps, a view that filters down to its clients, is that it's all about enjoying oneself,

---

* Women don't experience the same benefits, reports the Max Planck Institute. Women with husbands older or younger by between seven and nine years *increase* their chances of dying early by 20 percent.

seeing what happens. You're the man. Be assertive. Take control. But don't stress.

"You won't find a more open-hearted place," Dave says. "All these Colombian girls want to do is have a good time. Medellin is called the City of Eternal Spring for a reason. Men come here and have years added to their lives. That's not bullshit."*

Late that night, back in the lobby of the Dann Carlton, Bart and Andy are new men. "To pull off something like that!" Bart says. "To have a bar where they supplied *all* the booze and *all* the food and *all* the girls. Boy, it was like . . . you can't do that at home! The possibility of romance was in the air for all those women. You could see it in their eyes."

For Andy's part, he's no longer carping over the twenty-year-old who blew him off. His mind is fixed on Paola, a twenty-four-year-old he met at Mango's and spent all evening speaking to via interpreter. "I tell you, we just clicked," Andy says. "I asked her at the very beginning: 'I'm fifty-two, do you have a problem with that?' You see, I was trying to shoot her down. But she didn't see the problem. She asked if I could cook, 'cause she doesn't. I said I make a really good spaghetti, a couple Mexican dishes, and a champagne brunch."

"You think she was running a game on you?" Bart asks. "You never know in these third world countries, when you're out at these places meeting girls."

"Nope," says Andy. "I don't think so. I said to the translator, 'This girl seems very special,' and I asked the translator for her feedback, and she said, 'You know, I think you've found the one. She's very simple, very affectionate, and very caring.' And then I said to the translator that I would consider selling everything I have and moving down here, instead of taking her up to Florida and turning her into a fucking gold digger."

———

* Medellin is called the City of Eternal Spring because its moderate mountain climate and proximity to the equator mean the temperature hovers around 77 degrees Fahrenheit all year round.

In the eighteenth century, Bogotá—Colombia's capital—was the cultural and political center of the Spanish empire, a territory that comprised what today are Colombia, Panama, Ecuador, and Venezuela. Three centuries later, Colombia has South America's second-most unequal distribution of wealth after Paraguay. Structurally it has one of the most stratified social systems in the world. It is split into six "stratos." Strato one is the poorest, six the richest. Only people from stratos four, five, and six pay taxes. Most of the women who register with bridal agencies are from either strato two or three. As with the women of Eastern Europe and the men of the West, the women of Colombia who turn to bridal agencies have a standard narrative too: A third world economy combined with Colombia's machismo culture, its drug wars, and *la violencia* have depleted the supply of eligible males.

So when Amo Latina tour clients praise "the beautiful simplicity of these women," they are speaking really of grinding poverty, of the narrow aims and provincial ambitions imposed by a life that has never known anything beyond Medellin. After all, there's no gene for "traditional family values," or "femininity." Rather, they are norms and expectations engendered by culture and circumstance, including class structure, race, ethnicity, nationality, and other aspects of identity that determine who people are and what they want. Through this lens, one understands better how the eyes of a Colombiana could go bright at the sight of, say, Nick, a thirty-four-year-old machinist from small-town Indiana who says almost nothing, except when he's high on painkillers, and then he says things like, "My brother's married to a Jew, so he thinks he's got to get everything half price and then sell it back to the family at three times what he paid for it."

Norma Ramos, the executive director of the Coalition Against Trafficking in Women, suspects that many Colombianas do not understand the degree to which they'll be dependent on their husbands for support and social integration. "What about their precarious legal status in the States?" she says. "Or the possibility of violence and exploitation?"

To what extent does our very modern ideal of marriage as a nonfinancial arrangement account for the natural revulsion we feel when we think of American men descending on the world's final frontiers of development to search for that perfectly young and beautiful and submissive wife, the one who will never ask for more than she gets, who will never doubt his command, will never leave him when he's old and sick, and will certainly never drag him over the coals and take all his money like that evil ex-wife? When we turn our noses up, what are we feeling? Do we mock what we don't understand? Or do we mock what we understand all too well: lonely/desperate/horny people trying to be less lonely/desperate/horny?

Anastasia and A Foreign Affair have been successful companies, and are becoming more so, because they meet a demand that they help create. How different is their stigma from the one that once attached to Gary Kremen's Match.com? Given the social iniquities and power dynamics on display in Colombia, one could argue that the two stigmas are sufficiently different. So a big question is whether increased access and availability, along with more widespread use among younger people, will, over time, be enough to change how these cross-border relationships are perceived.

Premium international online dating? Mail-order brides? Sex tourism? Human trafficking? "There is nothing that indicates they are mutually exclusive explanations," writes Ericka Johnson in *Dreaming of a Mail-Order Husband*, "and I think it is quite possible that the industry is made up of consenting adults who know what they are doing at the same time as the international framework of inequitably distributed wealth and migration regulations are influencing the options available to these 'consenting' adults."

The potential influence that Steve or Nathan or Bart or Andy could have on these women's lives might, to the women, seem trivial compared with the dismalness of what awaits at home. But when this view is presented to Norma Ramos, she insists that trading one vulnerability for another makes premium international online dating no different from any other form of human trafficking: "It's about those with power and choices shopping around for those without power and choices."

The second social takes the form of a beauty pageant. In order to document the event, and drum up publicity, Amo Latina has invited journalists and film crews to Museo El Castillo, a renovated castle on a hill in the center of Medellin. Pageant contestants have been invited from all over Colombia, though how closely tied to Amo Latina they are is in question: According to several sources, the best-looking ladies are professional models who've been paid by Amo Latina to participate in the pageant. This is standard operating procedure. In the States, Anastasia pays Dasha Astafieva, *Playboy* magazine's fifty-fifth anniversary playmate, to tout the company in interviews and photo shoots.

Tonight's judging panel is comprised of four Amo Latina tour clients and a local television celebrity named Patrizia, whose body has been biomechanically engineered to distract the male eye. The freckled blonde to my left touches my arm. Such is my state of mind after a few days of romance touring that I simply assume she wants me, or wants something from me. "*Qué lástima,*" she says, shaking her head. *What a shame.* I see her Telemundo press credential. She, like me, is here to cover the event.

The contestants first traipse around in dresses and then in swimwear. Andrea is studying economics. Karina hopes to become a veterinarian. The men's faces melt into smiles.*

The pageant's winner is a nineteen-year-old model from Bogotá. The Telemundo reporter rushes onstage with her film crew. "You have many more choices now," the reporter tells the winner in Spanish. "What are you looking for? What do you want?"

"*Como todo el mundo,*" the winner responds, "*yo estoy buscando el amor de mi vida.*" ("Like everyone, I'm looking for my true love.")

Love can emerge anywhere. Anastasia says 20 percent of its tour clients find a long-term relationship—about half of those are marriages; the other half are nonmarried relationships lasting over four years. But the situations in Medellin share themes of disillusion and hopelessness.

---

* Colombia prizes the beauty of its women. In addition to the Miss Independence pageant and the Miss Colombia pageant, juries award many lesser titles: Miss Plantain; Miss Coal. Cellblocks in a Bogotá women's prison have their own pageants. One town in northern Colombia puts makeup and wigs on its donkeys and parades them for the annual Miss Burro celebration.

Take fifty-three-year-old Marc Bovet, another Amo Latina poster boy, whose forthcoming marriage to a Colombiana is being used as a promotional tool for the company, plastered across billboards and television. Bovet, who says he was a former mercenary in the Middle East, came to Colombia because he had to declare bankruptcy in the United States after his properties were foreclosed on. He says he owes his ex-wife a million dollars he doesn't have. He says one of his cousins invented Velcro and that another cousin is a well-known Wall Street mogul, but that no one in his family will help him financially. He says that having his face on the Amo Latina ads has made him a kidnapping target in Colombia. He regrets leaving his gun collection in Oregon. An alcoholic with a seething, hostile energy, Bovet comes across as a psychopath even to the tour's more fringe figures. And yet Bovet's marriage to a woman who cannot understand a word he says is Amo Latina's biggest success story.

An American video crew is now interviewing the Telemundo reporter. "What makes the women sign up?" she's asked.

"*Mucho dinero*," she says, rubbing her fingers together in the universal sign for money. "I think eighty percent of girls want travel, money, clothes. Not love."

Andy is falling in love with Paola. She's from strato two and has diabetes, he's discovered. "But she seems like she would be the type of girl, when she falls in love, that will be there at my bed in the nursing home when I die, and not just take my money and run off with another guy," he speculates. "And you know, that's an issue I have." On the back of Andy's white denim button-down, with the sleeves torn off, an American eagle wrapped in stars and stripes flies above the words RIGHTEOUS RULER.

Nearby, Juanita the translator has been facilitating a conversation between Bart and a Colombiana, which she describes as strange: "He said that for every child she has, he would give her one plastic surgery," Juanita reports. "I don't know if he was making a joke. I've never heard that one before. I just told her he said she was very pretty."

Tony, the ER doc, bought his fiancée new shoes and a dress for the social. But he ignores her and flirts with other women. One wonders whether Tony intends, at the subconscious level, to see how poorly he can treat his fiancée, and for how long, until she leaves him, an outcome that would confirm his view of himself as a no-good shmuck. He is telling a group of people about his new Corvette when his fiancée walks by. "Tony," she whines, "I no enjoy alone. I no enjoy alone."

Over cocktails, Marc Bovet and his fiancée are meeting with a real estate agent about buying a condo in Cartagena, the beachside town where, in a few months, several of President Obama's Secret Service agents will clash with Colombia's legalized prostitution industry.

A Colombian camera crew has been told I'm a journalist. The producer asks me to do an interview with Patrizia, the television personality with the mechanically enhanced figure. Since neither her English nor my Spanish are good enough for the camera, we agree that she will speak in Spanish and I will reply in English, having been told beforehand what the questions will be. The camera rolls. Patrizia reels off something in Spanish that I know means, "Why did the American men come to Medellin? And what have they found here?"

I could say I've been sent to Medellin as a corporate shill, to report on what will likely become known as the love junket. I can say it's good or I can say it's bad. I can say whatever. ("We expect that whatever you write will fall somewhere between neutral and positive," I was told by an Anastasia rep during the journalistic negotiation that preceded the trip.) It's not that they don't care what I say. Rather, it's that they care more that I say *something*. The point is not: This is good or this is bad. The point is: *This is happening.* Whatever Anastasia actually believes about the relationships it facilitates, the company believes strongly, and based on the numbers, justifiably, in the allure of its product to overcome a little societal disapproval.

I could say that, for the time being, this particular technology seems to be satisfying the needs of tough cases, but that for all I know, in five or fifteen years there could be tours of Ivy League graduates coming here to date the daughters of strato six families. As for Western women, well, they don't use international online-dating sites yet. But they can be seen paying for sex and companionship in the Caribbean. As the financial status of Western women continues to improve in a local relationship market that resembles, increasingly, the competitively favorable situations of successful African American men and in-demand Chinese women, who's to say they won't be shipping back commitment-minded husbands from somewhere like Tibet, a historically polyandrous country* whose males are said to be found attractive by Western women.

I could mention that Anastasia and its ilk are merely brands in an undifferentiated communications industry, and that in the course of research I met several middle-aged Western men who, by simply changing the zip code on their searches, use traditional online-dating sites to date women in other countries. On one such Match-facilitated journey from London to Manila, George, a forty-three-year-old architect, was stood up, so he salvaged the trip with a couple days of scuba diving in Boracay. I could say it's no big deal. That, as shocking as it all seems, the rise of international online dating is just another slide toward the end of a long-vanishing moral arc in the West, where the rule of sexual conduct by authority has been dissolving for one hundred years. If history is any lesson, a new set of guiding conventions will come along soon, just in time to be overthrown once again, antiquated before they can ossify. All that is holy is profaned. All that is solid melts into air.

The shift is happening now. Neither Anastasia nor its main competitor, the Arizona-based A Foreign Affair, will divulge its profits or registration numbers. However, in the six years between 2005 and 2011, Anastasia says the number of Russian and Ukrainian women joining its site has tripled, while the number of Western men signing up has more than quadrupled. A Foreign Affair says its business has grown by an average of 25 percent a year over the last decade. Both companies say male clients are skewing younger.

In places where international online dating operates, it's powerful enough to recruit high-quality talent on the ground to run the agencies, maintain the Web sites, and host the tours—even in a place like Ukraine, where the local stigma that attaches to the business is so strong that staff members are embarrassed to tell their friends and family they work in

---

* Women have two or more male partners.

the bridal industry; if pushed, they're likely to explain that the hopeless women they broker abroad are from a different Ukraine. Natalia Pankova, a Ukrainian woman who works for a Kiev-based bridal agency named Charming Brides, never admits where she works. "They have a very negative view that we are selling girls to rich foreign men," she says. "But there is no buying or selling. And it is not mail-order brides. You can't pack a girl and send her. It's just another way of meeting people."

ALEXIS, PART VI

↓

A Searing Chronicle

WHEN A PTER ASKS ALEXIS WHETHER SHE'S WORRIED THAT BEN might find out about his role in her second life and exact retribution, she writes: "Yes, but you guys would probably love me more for all the lulz if a random boy came to air dirty laundry/pics, and at least I would see his true colors."

In fact, he does know. Shortly after Ben met Alexis, a friend of his, who happened to check out Phantasy Tour from time to time, forwarded Ben the link to one of Alexis's threads about online dating, because he knew Ben was on Match. Even though PTers post under handles like Wonderbrah and McFly, it was clear to Ben, from the details provided, that he was dating the person who was leading these conversations. It struck him as a bizarre coincidence, until he thought about it. The Internet had expanded his social circle, but perhaps not as much as he imagined. The kinds of people he met online were similar in their tastes and background to the friends he had.

Ben was amused by Alexis's habit. Her sharing compulsion wasn't atypical. Every day he watched his friends on Facebook broadcast all kinds of information about their families, relationships, marriages, and children. But then Alexis's reports become increasingly revealing. "I am seeing him on Friday and Saturday," she writes on Phantasy Tour, "making for dates 4 . . . and 5!"

It's uncomfortable to see his private life broadcast like this, even if he is kept anonymous. Alexis, he feels, is crossing some boundary of loyalty or trust. This goes beyond Facebook-style sharing. What bothers him is that she seems to be prioritizing this public persona over their actual relationship. It also bothers him that her reports stray from the facts. They already slept together, on the third date. Why not tell like it like it happens? Then again, he wasn't being entirely honest when he told Alexis that he'd been on Match for one only month prior to meeting her. In fact, he'd been on Match before, and also had an account on OkCupid.

Casually, Ben mentions to her that one of his friends follows chat room discussions on a site called Phantasy Tour, and that the friend recently sent him a thread discussing online dating. "Do you ever read that site?"

Alexis blushes, says yes, she loves Phantasy Tour, and may have even participated in some of those threads about online dating.

The next day she relates this coincidence on Phantasy Tour. "He does not have a handle," she writes, "but his friend sends him funny threads occasionally. Including, he told me, a thread entitled 'Match .com.' That. Is. Crazy."

"Epic!" writes a PTer, in a comment typical of many others expressing giddy dismay.

"And a bit embarrassing," Alexis writes. "Not to mention that he could very well be reading this, which is scary."

When Ben sees this, it becomes impossible for him to take the relationship seriously. Who is he dating? The Alexis of an online-dating profile? The woman he's spent a few dates with? Or the Phantasy Tour persona? Is there a difference? He cancels the fifth date and never calls back to reschedule.

Alexis is distressed, but briefly. A week later she's back on Phantasy Tour, posting enthusiastically about another potential boyfriend from Match. "I had a really fun first date last weekend," she writes. "Delicious dinner/drinks, fun conversation, ordered 3 desserts ... quite tipsy by the end. He called my bluff about singing, so we went around the corner to a karaoke bar, got more drinks, raged it. Super fun. He asked for another date yesterday."

"This isn't the one who originally inspired these threads, is it?"

"No, a freshie."

"What happened to the first guy?"

"I just got a case of the meh. I think he did too, or he sensed it, because we both stopped making the effort."

"Poundtown?"

"I slept with him," she writes. "It was a lackluster experience though. Felt totally disconnected."

Alexis's opinion of online dating soon cools, when the second guy from Match stands her up. "When I texted to confirm," she writes on PT, "he cancelled, said he was sick. Then no call back. Very perplexing. But I've been flirting with my date for tomorrow and he's a stud." After a first-date hookup, that guy disappears as well.

On PT Alexis announces she's quitting Match.

"What happened?" asks a PTer. "Didn't like what you were finding?"

"It was an entertaining venture," she explains, "but it always seemed forced. Mostly it was an experiment and a way to get me out of the house during winter. I also needed the confidence boost. But I'm feeling better now. The weather is getting nicer and it will be easier to meet people out and about. Sundresses get me farther than Internet profiles." She continues: "I've decided to stop trying in the life partner department. If it happens, it happens. But focusing on it too much is draining and that energy should be put toward my career right now."

"Someone should make a weekly Internet dating thread so we can all continue to discuss/share experiences," writes a PTer. "I used a lot of helpful tips in here."

For Alexis, too, the sharing compulsion remains strong. "I'm considering starting an anonymous personal blog," she writes, "a searing chronicle of my dating life. I just started writing the first entry."

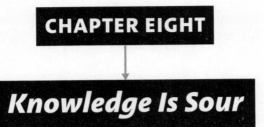

CHAPTER EIGHT

Knowledge Is Sour

HOW TOO MUCH INFORMATION
TURNS US INTO *THAT KIND* OF GIRLFRIEND

Online relationships are vulnerable to a "boom and bust" phenomenon. . . . Relationships can get quite intense quite quickly.

> —"Romance in Cyberspace:
> Understanding Online Attraction"

There is an optimal pace at which intimacy develops, and too great
a change might have the effect of undermining the relationship.

> —"A Second Chance to Make a First Impression: Factors
> Affecting the Longevity of Online Dating Relationships"

When Trish McDermott was hired to market the first iteration of Match, she wrote an advice column called Tell It
To Trish. One female online dater wrote to Trish with a
problem. The woman had always operated on a "five-
date rule"—no sex till date number five. She found it took the pressure
off getting to know the other person, and also helped build some antici-
pation if things were going well. On the first date with someone she met
through Match, she told him about her five-date rule.

Okay, he told her, the rule's been satisfied.

Huh?

Well, he explained, they'd exchanged two e-mails apiece on the site and spoken on the phone twice. Since those conversations had been at least as revealing as face-to-face dates would've been, their first date was, in theory, their fifth date, and therefore they should sleep together.

"Even as rudimentary as the service was back then," McDermott recalls, "it felt like we were living in a Wild West of technology. No one knew what the rules were."

This new way of meeting someone surely meant new behavior online. But should it also alter the way you conducted yourself offline? What was a woman to do? "So many people had this problem," says McDermott. "It was hard to know what to say, except to remind them that behind the technology they were dealing with real people."

For centuries, relationship-advice givers have debated how much "togetherness" is the right amount. In a twelfth-century advice manual, *Treatise on Love and its Remedies*, Andreas Capellanus warned that too many opportunities to see or chat with the beloved diminishes love, another way of saying absence makes the heart grow fonder. Today's technology means more communication. But online dating adds a new wrinkle: What *is* togetherness? Do e-mail and text messages count? How about interaction on social networks? What happens when the opportunities to see or chat with the beloved are commitment-free, nonexclusive opportunities to see or chat not with the beloved per se, but with the beloved's self-extension, or simply to watch the beloved chat with the self-extension of some other person?

Internet-mediated relationships aren't just about pheromones giving way to CMC, or competing algorithms, or the splintering of PXRs into SEOs and PMXs. It's also about an entirely new set of rules and signaling in a digital world that enables not only more communication but also a new broadcasting capability, which can be disastrous for things like intimacy and trust.

Fifteen years after online dating first subjected the five-date rule to scrutiny, the spread of dating sites and social media have accelerated connection and sharing. Today's togetherness is often instantaneous, and then constant. You begin dating someone you met online, or off, and in a matter of days you are Facebook friends who also follow each other's Twitter feed and show up on each other's Tumblr dash and chat throughout the day via IM and text. By midday you've opened ten tabs on your browser, and on five of them the avatar of your paramour is blinking and winking and typing and poking and accepting and liking and smiling and frowning and inviting.

In the first months of Facebook, the site established a new system of signals for students at Harvard. "Now," wrote David Kirkpatrick in *The Facebook Effect*, "if a girl met a guy at a frat party, an elaborate set of electronic rituals was set in motion. They took on even more significance if you had already hooked up. The first key question was whether the guy immediately friended you. . . . If he didn't, that was a disastrous sign."

Similar rituals occur with online dating. "The first thing you do when you meet someone online," explains Dara, a twenty-eight-year-old documentary filmmaker in San Francisco, "is exchange a couple messages through the dating site. Then you send texts and e-mails to coordinate the first date. Then, after the first date, if things go well, there's the question of who's going to add who first on Facebook. Then you look at each other's pictures and all their stuff. You Google them, read their résumé, maybe an essay written ten years ago. It feels intimate, but also really distant. You have a ton of information, but you've only met them once. Maybe just thirty minutes for coffee. So there's a huge disconnect between what you think you know about each other and what you've actually established in real life."

San Francisco's proximity to Silicon Valley has resulted in a particularly gadget-crazed, heavily connected culture that seems to dovetail perfectly with online dating. It's always been one of OkCupid's best markets. "There are more techies, more early adopters than anywhere else," says Sam Yagan.

A self-described tomboy with a chilled-out California vibe, Dara sticks to a simple philosophy of life: Don't blame people for being the way they are; but if they're really stupid, then go ahead and blame them. She moved to the Bay Area from San Diego. "I'd just been through that one devastating breakup that everyone goes through. I had this big plan for my life, and then the bottom dropped out."

In San Francisco, Dara found a group of friends, but no one she was interested in romantically. So she had a choice: remain single or go on-line. "Everyone in San Francisco is too busy to date. But everyone owns an iPhone. So dating becomes one more thing you access through an app. I have one app to get my music, another to suggest movies, another for news, another to keep up with friends, one to show me where a good bar is, and another app to help me find a date to go to that bar with. I used to think of dating as this special thing. Now it's mixed in with all these other things. In a way, dating is easier. It's definitely more efficient. But it's also really confusing."

Through Match, Dara went on a few lackluster dates, and then she met someone she liked. She thought, "Well, he's still on Match. So I guess we're not exclusive?" They dated for a couple of months before hitting what Dara calls "the Great American Drop-Off." They would hang out from time to time, with long gaps in between.

But then the relationship picked up again. She looked on Match and saw that his profile had been taken down. So she quit Match too. She figured they were an item, even though no one had said anything. "It was based on what I guess you might call appearances."

Over the holidays, while Dara was visiting her parents, she noticed he'd popped up on Match again. That's when she found herself monitoring him on Facebook, puzzling over the identity of new female "adds," and trying to deduce the nature of the relationships he had with the Facebook friends who posted on his wall. Why hadn't she met these people or heard about them before? Were they other women from Match, or just friends? Was he trying to make her jealous? Did she need to do the same?

Dara thought she was alone in her confusion until one night when, after several glasses of wine, she and her girlfriends began discussing Facebook stalking. They noticed a cycle to San Francisco's dating scene:

meet online; go on a few dates; then try to decide whether a relationship exists by checking back at the dating site and monitoring Facebook behavior. Less than ideal, but there it was.

The ladies' wine-fueled chat was itself a mating tradition. "To guard against deception, women spend hours discussing with their friends the details of interactions they have had with their mates or with potential mates," writes David Buss in *The Evolution of Desire.** In the past, the girlfriend consultants might've had some previous knowledge of the guy whose intentions were being scrutinized. The special modern problem faced by Dara and her friends, all of whom used online dating, was that they often had no idea of the guy being discussed. Thanks to technology, their social circle lacked coherence. Often guys were referred to by their professions, or just by their online-dating screen names. Everyone was meeting everyone, it seemed, and yet no one knew anyone. They discussed every man in San Francisco, it seemed, and no one at all.

The solution, they decided, was to cultivate a Facebook presence of what they called hot-and-wanted. This entailed posting pictures of yourself doing fun things, featuring flirtatious comments on your wall from guys, and generally exuding the image of a fantastic life. Hot-and-wanted: This was their hypothesis. A little immature, they all agreed. But desperate times called for desperate measures.

"Humans," says Gian Gonzaga, the director of eHarmony's relationship lab, "evolved in tightly interwoven groups, where everyone knew each other's business. So you could argue that today's hyperconnectedness is actually a lot more natural than what we've gone through over the last hundred years, with the geographic dispersal and breakup of families. On the other hand, there is something quite different about the social interweaving of today. We have so many more people in our social network, and our brains aren't all that big."

The next day, before Dara could implement the hot-and-wanted strategy, her paramour texted her a picture of himself standing on a golf

---

* "Men," writes Buss, "are significantly less inclined to devote effort to this problem of assessment."

course, wearing a pair of silly plaid pants that she'd encouraged him to buy. She felt the special bond of an inside joke. When Dara logged onto Facebook she saw that he'd posted the same picture. She watched while other women plastered his Facebook wall with flirtatious comments about how great he looked in the silly plaid pants.

"But I'm the one who told him to wear those pants!" Dara fumed.

Her girlfriends told her she had a right to feel hurt. Her male friends said he probably hadn't even considered it. He was trying to seem hot and wanted too.

If a third of American singles are meeting through Web sites that are explicitly for dating, how does the rest of one's online presence complement or complicate relationships? In the past, certain things were only shared with your lover, while some details of your relationship may have been shared with a few friends. But now it's natural to broadcast every encounter to a group of strangers.

Technology, writes Sherry Turkle in *Alone Together: Why We Expect More from Technology and Less from Each Other*, "supports an emotional style in which feelings are not fully experienced until they are communicated.... [T]here is every opportunity to form a thought by sending out for comments." Turkle finds teenagers who send text messages to friends all day and wait, with palpable anxiety, for a response to validate the feeling. "We are stimulated by connectivity itself," she writes. "We learn to require it, even as it depletes us."

Each person's social network—whether Dara's Facebook or Alexis's Phantasy Tour—becomes a kind of Greek chorus sounding off on the dramatic action of her life. When word escaped on Facebook that Jennifer, a twenty-seven-year-old fashion designer, had left a physically abusive relationship, her ex's Facebook friends booed him down publicly after he posted about the breakup on his wall. On 4chan.org, the message board called /b/ is where young hackers come to collude, trade n00dz (porn), and discuss how to prank pedos (pedophiles). In her 2012 book, *We Are Anonymous*, about a famous hacking organization, Parmy Olson observed that even while constant insults between posters on /b/

create a "throbbing mass of negativity," beneath it all there is a supportive side. In so-called bawww threads, hackers appeal to the sympathetic side of 4chan with titles such as "gf just dumped me, bawww thread please?" This is the rare instance when users offer sincere advice, comfort, or funny pictures to cheer each other up, converting the social network into a self-help network.

Perhaps Phantasy Tour members suffer from no classifiable disease or pathology. They're not overcoming any psychic trauma, like Mothers Against Drunk Driving. Nor are they committing to a course of improvement, like Jenny Craig or Weight Watchers. But they are coming of age in a world where relationships are discovered, initiated, and maintained in ways that are starkly different not only from their parents' era, but from all of human history.

"We're not married and we're not having kids," Dara says. "But we're still trying to make the same kinds of connections our parents made when they were our age and perhaps had already had us."

Dara went back to monitoring her paramour's online behavior, as if more Facebook stalking was the answer to incomplete information on Facebook. A couple of days later he deleted the silly pants picture with the flirtatious comments beneath it. This made her happy. But then she got to thinking: "Did he delete the picture as a gesture of care toward me? Or was he trying to hide something?" Was his profile meant to speak to Dara, individually, or to his five-hundred-plus Facebook friends?

Second-order information, writes communications professor Ilana Gershon, is the meaning of a message beyond its explicit terms, "the information that can guide you into understanding how particular words and statements should be interpreted." Linguistic anthropologists refer to this as metapragmatics. In *The Breakup 2.0*, Gershon's 2011 book about how things like Facebook and text messaging complicate relationships, she gives the following examples of second-order information. A woman refuses to e-mail her ex-husband's personal e-mail account, sending all correspondence to his work e-mail instead. Translation: *I mean to emphasize my wish that the relationship remain over*. In another case, a twenty-one-year-old doesn't know if her boyfriend is serious when he breaks up with her, because he did it via text message. During the relationship they'd used texting only to send jokes. The exact same message, sent via e-mail, would've been clearer. The second-order information conveyed by the medium—this is a text, therefore this is a joke—was at odds with the message. Texting, Gershon's female interviewees say, is a medium men use, because it's so low stakes.

Facebook is a rabbit hole of second-order information. Take Dara's paramour's willingness to flirt with other women on his wall. Did that communicate second-order information that he was interested in them? Uninterested in her? Unwilling to commit? Very likely, but who knows. She wouldn't have been wrong to take it that way. Public signals, writes David Buss, are one of the foremost indications of a man's intent to commit.

The Facebook effect ripples across cultures. In *Tales from Facebook*, digital anthropologist Daniel Miller's study of Facebook's impact in Trinidad, we learn that Facebook is called *Fasbook*. The name is less a variation on pronunciation than meaning: In Trinidad, to be *fas* is to try to get to know someone too quickly. *Fas* is likely derived from *facile*, which means shallow, simplistic, superficial. And yet Trinidadians believe that the truth of another person is more readily discerned on *Fasbook* than in real life. The shield of the screen means people talk more openly and reveal unintended truths. Trinidadians believe in "truth by construction": The labor a person puts into crafting her *Fasbook* profile is more suggestive of her truth than concrete facts could ever convey.

Research indicates that when it comes to building trust and nurturing romantic relationships, Facebook, along with other social portals that link lovers in a nonprivate forum, often play a negative role, particularly for those who try to balance risk and commitment in their relationships by evaluating Facebook profiles for signs of infidelity. The problem with Facebook-as-relationship-facilitator is that it simultaneously offers *too much* information and *not enough*. Facebook, writes Gershon, promotes a "contextless promiscuity." In *The Breakup 2.0*, one of Gershon's male interviewees says his girlfriend gets upset when his

Facebook friends post pictures of him with other women. He tries to appease her by "untagging" (deleting) his name from the picture. But it does no good. She can still see the picture on Facebook, and see that he's untagged himself. Then that looks even worse.

Young women tell Gershon that the ease of monitoring their boyfriends on Facebook changed them, "made them into *that kind of girlfriend*, the one who is ever suspicious and constantly asking her boyfriend to prove he only thinks of her."

A journal paper published in *CyberPsychology & Behavior*, entitled "More Information Than You Ever Wanted: Does Facebook Bring Out the Green-Eyed Monster of Jealousy," explains the vicious cycle that is Facebook-stalking:

> With the vast majority of our sample reporting that their partners have unknown individuals and past romantic and sexual partners as friends on Facebook, the potential for jealousy in this environment is evident. The qualitative data we collected indicates that participants recognize that increased exposure to information on Facebook without proper context can increase their experience of jealousy. What is perhaps more puzzling is that despite this knowledge, many of these same participants also engage in a high degree of personal disclosure on Facebook.

Total information versus total control: This has been the tension driving Facebook's business model, and the recipe for its seemingly limitless growth potential. "The problem Facebook is solving is this one paradox," a twenty-one-year-old Mark Zuckerberg told *The New Yorker* magazine. "People want access to all the information around them, but they also want complete control over their own information. Those two things are at odds with each other." In an article entitled "Saving Facebook," New York University law school professor James Grimmelmann phrased the paradox in terms of socializing: "There's a deep, probably irreconcilable tension between the desire for reliable control over one's information and the desire for unplanned social interaction."

As Zuckerberg made the previous comment, in 2006, he was planning a major change to the architecture of his site, one that would shift the user experience further toward total information exposure, endowing her with a kind of social omniscience that was as addicting as it was anxiety inducing. Facebook introduced a feature called "News Feeds." Upon logging into Facebook, the user would now see a cascade of his friends' latest entries—comments, photographs, news about new Facebook friendships, etc. Prior to News Feeds, Dara would've had to visit her paramour's Facebook page to see that he'd posted the plaid-pants photo. With News Feeds, the plaid-pants photo would be the first thing she'd see upon logging in. Facebook would inundate her with every move her lover made on Facebook, plus every move made by anyone else— whether she knew that person or not—that referred to him.

The problem with News Feeds, writes social-media anthropologist Danah Boyd, is that it collapses "disparate social contexts" into one. "How one behaves in a pub differs from how one behaves in a family park, even though both are ostensibly public," Boyd writes. "Social convergence requires people to handle disparate audiences simultaneously without a social script."

For Gershon's Facebook-addicted women, the only way out was to call it quits, delete their profiles, and walk away, but this was harder than it sounds. Humans have evolved to express proprietary attitudes toward their mates. Men have had more success using public markings. Women tend to rely more on vigilance, through which they detect signs of defection and send their mate the message that consequences await.

"You're left feeling a little shameful," says Dara. "You don't know how you're supposed to interpret these things. We can obviously choose to communicate better than we do. But there's no protocol. It's not like it's been written down in a Jane Austen novel."

A novel no, a blog yes. At How About We, bloggers Chiara Atik and Scott Alden have written extensively on how to prevent technology from capsizing a relationship. Atik provides the woman's perspective on subjects such as things you shouldn't do until you're exclusive (friend each other's friends on Facebook), the crazy things women do on Facebook ("They will continuously monitor your Facebook page. If another girl writes on a guy's wall that girl will also get stalked."), and how to properly manage a Facebook relationship so you don't annoy your friends (don't write personal messages on a public space; limit the amount of "together" photos and the number of partner-focused status updates). Alden proposes reasons why Facebook might be ruining your dating life (keeping you in touch with old flames; public flirting), when it's appropriate to become Facebook friends with someone you're casually dating ("Talking on the phone as opposed to texting is a step. Gchatting is a step. And Facebook *is* a step."), the crazy things guys do on Facebook (purposely pissing off the boyfriend that she's too good for by, say, "posting a clip from last night's Rachel Maddow on her wall, which you know will lead to like 14 comments back and forth between you and her, and a decision to get coffee soon to discuss it further, but nothing from the boyfriend, cause he's more a *Big Bang Theory* kind of guy, you know?"), and why Gmail's instant-messaging function, Gchat, is terrible for new relationships: "brb" is hardly the language of love.

In her 2006 book, *The Joy of Text*, Kristina Grish lays out the elements of digital style, urging her readers to think carefully about punctuation, grammar, spelling, and the signals they send. For example:

> **Exclamation points:** Assign yourself a quota of two exclamation points per message. . . . If six out of seven of your sentences end with this overzealous punctuation mark, most guys will assume they don't have the energy to keep up with your cheery attitude. NEVER (yes, I'm screaming) use more than one in a row unless you want the reader to think you're on some really good crack.

> I had such a great time last night. I've never seen the original King Kong, but I'm so glad you made me watch it. Next time, I'll call shotgun on movie rentals. It's only fair . . . Talk soon!

All this code seems downright explicit compared with some of the texting schemes reported in 2011 by the *Wall Street Journal*. Following fights with her husband, a wife sends him blank text messages to create an air of mystery and score a callback. Other power plays include replying, "who is this?" when you receive a text from someone you know, and having a friend text you repeatedly while on a date in order to paint a picture of popularity. A twenty-three-year-old woman writes texts to new boyfriends while pretending to be drunk. She writes something honest, such as "I really like hanging out with you," but spells words wrong and mentions her drunkenness. If the guy responds in a gentlemanly fashion ("I like you, too. Why don't we talk tomorrow?"), he's proved himself. If he writes something inappropriate, he's dead. The *Journal* coined such behavior bluffting.

To which a frustrated *WSJ* reader responded: "I don't know who thinks that they're going to start a successful relationship by trying to mess with someone's head."

But to live as a single adult in today's postrules world of techno-relating is to play a nonstop game of puzzle-and-parse. To derive meaning from an abstract web of ambiguous connections. To look for clues and relevance in effortless gestures, such as an offer of inclusion in one's social network. To interpret the meaning of a four-hour lag in e-mail response versus a one-day lag versus a one-week lag and so on. To read romantic intent into the late hour of a text message or flirtatiousness in an abbreviated salutation. To glean entire emotional states from messages hammered out in text-speak, punctuated with emoticons, all nuance rendered down to *me happy, me sad*.

Or . . .

:O (me surprised), :S (me confused), >_< (me angry), =_= (me bored), -_- (me annoyed), -_-' (me nervous), ¬_¬ (me suspicious), O_O (me shocked), ._. (me intimidated), =^_^= (me blushing).

Yet all the Facebook stalking and bluffting in the world won't change the fact that while new relationships can be discovered online, trust and loyalty are established IRL, based not on how well or poorly someone manipulates text and images on a screen but on how he or she behaves offline.

Before leaving town for a work trip, Dara erased the lengthy paragraphs in her OkCupid profile and wrote simply: "I'm sick of online dating. Let's just meet in a Laundromat."

When she returned home she had a message from a guy named Chris. He was tall, blond, into rock climbing, and had photos of himself on camping trips. "Want to go for pizza at 7:30 on Wednesday?" he wrote. "If so, send me your phone number and I'll give you a call."

"He actually called!" Dara says. "No one had ever taken the reins like that."

It turned out they had several friends in common, but probably wouldn't have run into each other had it not been for online dating. Pizza lasted several hours, and then became dessert, then a drink, and then a weekend date that lasted all day.

She was never planning to put her relationship status on Facebook, but he asked her early on to be his girlfriend. No one had ever been so direct. Boundaries had never been set. But they had dated enough people online to know what they didn't want. He'd also had communication problems in past relationships, in part because online dating had been the catalyst. They both wanted to trust someone, establish a connection, and then say, "That's it, we're done looking."

By the time they moved onto Facebook, Dara couldn't have cared less what he did on Facebook.

ALEXIS, PART VII

↓

The Battle of Least Interested

ALEXIS OPENS UP A NEW ACCOUNT ON TUMBLR, THE BLOGGING site, and begins writing a searing chronicle of her dating life in New York City. The first entry details her relationship with the law student, their intimate moments, their fights and escapades, and what she learned about the dangers of dating a person for his money. She writes another entry about the forty-year-old, and then posts a link to the blog on Phantasy Tour, expecting it to give her fellow PTers lulz. Their responses surprise her.

"That story kind of makes you seem like a bitch," one writes.

"I'm no expert (that's a lie)," writes another, "but I think you should work on making yourself a more likable and reliable narrator. You sound like a total gold digger."

"I am sorry about your dad," writes another, "I really am," implying that Alexis's dating problems might be tied to unresolved issues with her father, the straight-edge tax attorney who seems to be a model for some of the men Alexis pursues.

These comments are hurtful. "Hmm???" she replies. "My dad's the man." She begins writing more, but then decides to delete the whole thing.

During the summer Alexis begins dating a guy she meets through a music industry connection. He introduces her to his friends and family. A few months into the relationship his birthday arrives. She makes him a mix of her favorite music and prepares dinner. When he shows up he says they shouldn't see each other anymore. He travels too much for work, he says, and he doesn't have time for a relationship right now. It sounds like he just doesn't like her enough to work through these obstacles.

"Happened literally minutes ago," she writes on Phantasy Tour—starting a new thread under the title "And I just got dumped"—"and I needed to tell someone, somewhere."

As the short ribs and gnocchi cool in the kitchen, she continues: "I feel just awful. I am sure he sniffed that I liked him more than he liked me, and that he'd rather just be alone than feel obliged. I wish I knew how to play hard to get. I blow off everyone I'm not into but if I want to tap it I tiger pounce with all my loving. Now I lost the battle of least interested and I'm paying for it." While Alexis posts about the breakup on PT, she watches online porn and gets drunk on the wine she bought for supper.

A week later she posts a new dating profile on OkCupid. "At least the Internet is always there for a confidence boost via messages, or some quick dates to get out of a slump in my single times," she thinks.

She's heard rumors that guys think it's weird when women message them first, that it makes the woman seem desperate or somehow less desirable, so she waits to be contacted. Several messages per day come in, some from kind-seeming suitors and some from repulsive slimeballs.

"Your general pretentiousness is quite irritating," writes one suitor on OkCupid, "but I think I'd enjoy pounding you senseless. Up for a drink? I'd even consider taking you somewhere exclusive."

"The idea of even having a conversation with you makes my skin crawl," Alexis responds. "Why don't you stick with Craigslist hookers and gold digger sluts. Maybe they'd be impressed by 'somewhere exclusive.' Fuck off and die you arrogant little prick."

Another message comes in from mw_01: "How are you? My wife and I saw your page and thought we'd say hi since you were really attractive. Hope that's not super weird. Sorry we don't have any pictures up—our friends don't know we are into other women—but we can send some. Anyway, how is your weekend going? Do anything fun for the holidays? Hope all is well!"

A PT colleague starts a new thread, "How to get laid online," and writes: "How does this shit work? The most I got was a couple dates from chicks who were lame or fat. The last chick I met left after 5 minutes, claiming she got a phone call and her friend was having her wisdom teeth removed so she had to go pick her up."

"That's 5 minutes longer than my date lasted last night," replies a female PTer. "Guy hits me up and we chat a bit, trade some pics. He asks me out. I go to meet the guy. He gets there and abruptly tells me he changed his mind on the drive over, but he came to meet me anyway because he didn't want to be a dick. Then he left. WTF?!?!"

"Post your pics," someone tells the original poster.

"Let's just say I've been told on several occasions that I look like Jake Gyllenhaal," the OP replies.

"If you looked like Jake Gyllenhaal you would not be resorting to online dating. Someone lied to you."

The OP posts his Plenty of Fish profile.

"You look like a fucking pedophile in your picture and your profile is boring as shit," someone advises.

"For God's sake shave that chode stash!"

"There is some really trite language on there," writes another. " 'I am always seeking the next level!!' What does that even mean?"

"I'm fucking crying over here."

"Switch to OkCupid. They have all these questions girls answer. You can specifically view questions about sex. It's easy to tell if you're going to have your dick sucked within an hour of meeting them."

"My wife and I split up back in September. She recently told me she joined OkCupid and went on a horrible date. I of course got jealous and joined. Who does it match me up with? HER!!! Like a 95% match or something. If this was a paid site I'd be demanding my money back. My female friends are saying it's a sign we are meant for each other and need to get back together . . . FUCK that."

Alexis contributes some suggestions for the OP: "Don't tell her she's cute. It's creepy. Also don't list your salary. It just makes you look like an asshole. Short, funny, and positive. Casual is the way to go. Don't plead your case or ask for a date right off the bat. I ignore almost all those messages. There needs to be a little banter and buildup before you ask someone out. Just point out a common interest and ask a follow-up question."

Over the next two months, Alexis goes on what she calls an Ok-Cupid bender. These dates seem strange after a while. Each time out feels like "a performance of herself," she says, acting out the qualities that she thinks the guys expect her to have based on her profile—bubbly, sarcastic, funny.

"I've gone out with like 10 dudes," she writes. "Nice guys. Lots of entertainment. I'd like to meet a guy who's into Phish, but I feel like a lot of guys keep that off their profiles."

One day, her most recent ex, who recently joined OkCupid, pops up on the site. Turns out they're a 90% match. It's painful for Alexis, but also reassuring. At least she knows the system works.

CHAPTER NINE

Let's Keep This Fucker Coming Back

WHEN A HAPPY CUSTOMER IS BAD FOR BUSINESS

If you succeed, you lose.

—Aaron Schildkrout, chief executive officer, How About We

Dating sites, like the behaviors and matches they facilitate, don't come out of nowhere. There is a geek behind the technology. That geek has a vision. That vision is shaped by his unique geek background.

Although Gary Kremen was born in the sixties and became one of the Web's earliest entrepreneurs, a tech pioneer in every sense, he came of age in the print era, during the eighties, when newspaper personals were enjoying a resurgence. Kremen's dating site, Match.com, reflected those classifieds: anonymous profiles with a checklist approach. The eHarmony of Dr. Neil Clark Warren adapted the paternalistic, hands-on approach of the midcentury marriage-guidance movement that produced Warren. The White Label Dating of Ross Williams grew out of his belief in the efficiency gains of targeting niche networks. With Plenty of Fish, Markus Frind stood on simplicity: Make it easy; make it free. Plenty of Fish became the Costco of the date-o-sphere, the place where other name-brand sites advertise to the masses. Before OkCupid, Chris Coyne and Sam Yagan made their name by putting information on the Web, in the form of study guides. They came to online dating with a particular geek sensibility—that data was king.

Despite their differences, these innovators have been successful for the same fundamental reason: They made profitable businesses out of the search for love and companionship.

The rise of online dating as the dominant way to meet people means that many of the economic principles we've long applied to dating, in a theoretical way, are now *actually* applicable. It used to be that by living in a certain place and moving in a certain crowd we participated in "a relationship market" that operated on scarcity and demand. Now that market is owned and managed by people with a profit motive, people whose interests might diverge from ours. To varying degrees, they want satisfied daters. But they also spend their days focused on maximizing nonromantic metrics, such as "customer acquisition," "conversion rates," and "lifetime value."

Is a conflict of interest inevitable?

Explaining the mentality of a typical dating executive, Justin Parfitt, a British dating entrepreneur, puts the matter bluntly: "They're thinking, 'Let's keep this fucker coming back to the site as often as we can, and let's not worry about whether he's successful.' There's this massive tension between what would actually work for you, the user, and what works for us, the shareholders. It's amazing, when you think about it. In what other industry is a happy customer bad for business?"*

Indeed, getting daters to come back to the site is a point of pride at Match. Virtually every Match CEO, including former CEO Greg Blatt and current CEO Mandy Ginsberg, have on multiple occasions boasted to the media that most of their users are return customers. It's a PR talking point meant to suggest customer satisfaction, sort of like tracking the number of hamburgers sold nationwide. Even back in 2003, then-CEO Tim Sullivan told the *New York Times* that although his subscribers tended to leave Match after about five months—having either found a

---

* Psychiatry? The weapons trade? Plastic surgery? Pharmaceuticals?

mate or had no luck—many of them come back to the site. Sullivan, who now heads the genealogy juggernaut Ancestry.com, said 40 percent of Match subscribers are returnees. "Match.com," observed the *Times*, "does not necessarily benefit if its users pair off for good."

As the first mass-market site, Match established the industry's business-model prototype. It's a bizarre, inherently conflicted system of incentives that's been more or less replicated by every pay-based site to succeed Match in the last fifteen years. Outwardly, the industry sells a promise of customer satisfaction. Inwardly, it understands that profits can be inversely proportional to that satisfaction guarantee. The faster the user makes the site work for him, the faster he finds a mate, the faster he deletes his profile, ends his subscription, and walks away.

"We can sum up the paid dating industry pretty easily," wrote Markus Frind on his blog. "Screw your customers . . . and extract as much money as you can."

The success of free dating sites between 2005 and 2010 sparked a new debate in the industry. When daters are not being charged, when sites get paid by advertisers instead of users, are the interests of the daters and the business more closely aligned? Did the free business model therefore mean a more effective site for users?

To understand what the debate over free versus paid means for dating, it's necessary to know a little about the business itself. Most paid sites let people post a profile and search the site for free. These people are called "free users," or simply "registrations." The business of running a paid dating site therefore depends entirely on what the industry calls "conversions": convert the free user into a paying subscriber, and then maximize his "lifetime value" by getting him to come back to the site as often as possible.

Conversion rates for most paid sites dwell in the low single digits. A paid site will spend perhaps $120 in advertising to acquire one paying subscriber. That subscriber then pays the site anywhere from $20 to $60 per month. The site must keep him on long enough to recoup the original $120 investment required to get him—two to seven months, on average. Every subscription month beyond that is profit. It's a cycle: The site needs to get the original investment back as fast as possible so that the money can be funneled back into advertising to get more subscribers.

So the question becomes: What's fair in love and business? What tactics should a paid dating site use to convert its free users?

Until 2001, Match took a generous approach with its free users: If the free user received a message from a paying subscriber, he could open the message and respond to it without subscribing himself. He didn't have to put down a credit card until he wanted to initiate contact with someone. If he had a good experience messaging with a subscriber, then he might be convinced that the site worked, that there were good people on it, and it was worth subscribing himself. This business model, called "pay-to-initiate," removed a barrier to meeting for all of Match's users—paying and free—but it did so at the expense of the bottom line.

So Match instituted a new model called "pay-to-respond." Now when the free user received a message from a paying subscriber, he would get an e-mail alerting him that he had a message in his Match in-box from a wonderful woman who was eager to meet him. To read the message, and respond to it, he'd need to pay up.

The pay-to-respond model can create headaches for Match's paying customers. If they send a message to the profile of a free user, there's a slim chance they'll get a response. Yet it's often difficult to tell who's paid and who isn't. According to several former Match employees, the majority of "new profiles" seen by users in their search results belong to people who haven't paid and therefore cannot respond.

But when asked about the typical balance between free and paid users in the search results, Match's current head of product, Sharmistha Dubey, says she doesn't know. "It's not something we measure or keep track of," she says. Although she adds that "close to 80 percent" of messages exchanged on Match are sent to subscribers, and that "the bulk" of Match's users are not looking at inactive profiles.

"In our experimentation around conversion rates," Dubey explains, "we've found that it doesn't pay very well to manipulate subscription status. Instead, we've found it's more beneficial to play with factors like relevance, recency, and freshness." Dubey defines "relevance" as how well a profile fits with the searcher's stated criteria and browsing habits, "recency" as how active a profile is on the site, and "freshness" as how new a profile is, and/or when it was last updated. "We've found that emphasizing these factors [in determining search results] increases message initiation and response rates," she says. "Fortunately for us, we've found these factors to be good for monetization, too. If it hadn't worked out that way, then, well, it would've been a much more contentious thing of balancing monetization with user success."

However the economics work out, online dating is a give-and-take: In order to access a big network of potential mates, the user helps the company build an ever larger network of potential mates.

It's difficult to know exactly how any online-dating company drives conversion rates and manages the tricky balance between the success of its business and the success of its users. But it's clearly an issue. A 2011 industry report, published by *Subscription Site Insider*, found that nearly 90 percent of U.S. dating executives polled were "highly concerned" about unethical practices: "Dating sites rely heavily on personalized e-mails—supposedly triggered by individual profile activity—to convert free registered users into paying members," the report explains. "We say 'supposedly' because many in the industry suspect that some sites send non-genuine e-mails. For example, a new registered user may receive several e-mails from the site indicating women are interested in his profile, when no women actually have responded to the profile yet."

Match's former head of marketing, Trish McDermott, says that while Match's business model may be skewed in favor of Match, and against its users, there's nothing wrong with that. "I don't think there's anything illegal or unethical about pay-to-respond," says McDermott. "It just makes the barrier to connecting a lot higher. It becomes much more common to not get responses to your messages."

McDermott says Match's database is padded with the profiles of people who are no longer active on the site. In industry-speak, these profiles are called "date bait." Match makes it difficult to delete profiles, she says, because the more profiles left on the site, the more messages get sent. The more messages get sent, the longer you remain on the site. Mc-

Dermott says Match never posted fake profiles when she was there. "The sense that Match is loaded with fake profiles"—profiles representing nonexistent people—"grows out of the experience many users have of sending lots of messages and not getting replies."

But Match's CEO differs. "The truth," says Mandy Ginsburg, "is that a lot of the people who don't respond to your messages *are* paid users. They got your message. They didn't respond because they're not interested in you. Unfortunately, we can't come out and say that."

The online dating business can run afoul of its users in other ways. In the Brooklyn offices of How About We, CEO Aaron Schildkrout combs his site for scammers, people who post fake profiles in order to con real daters out of money in romance scams. Some clues? They often come in through a Google search, have registered under a Yahoo or Hotmail e-mail account (never Gmail), and use particular words and phrases that most genuine daters would find peculiar in an introductory message: blessing; companion; wife; sincere; open-minded; I am; you look gorgeous; God; children; caring; love.

Schildkrout stops at the profile of a man claiming to be from Brooklyn. He posted what appears to be a stock photo of a golfer in midswing. He calls himself a Christian conservative and writes form messages along the following lines: "Hello: I am looking for someone who I can love and will love me back, someone to support me in all my endeavors and dreams. I am a caring man with a college degree who is looking for a wife and children. I abstain from smoking and drinking."

Another likely scammer has posted a picture of a busty and seductive Latin woman. The scammer has written fifteen form messages that say: "Hi, I am Shantel. Single and ready to mingle. I want you to know that you look gorgeous. If you want a real relationship and are serious about meeting, holla!"

"Every time I throw a scammer off the site I lose money," says Schildkrout. "Not only do I lose the scammer's subscription, but I lose the subscriptions of the free users the scammer would've duped into converting."

In theory, scammers could be helpful to a dating site, by luring in real users and getting them to convert to subscribers. But I found no evidence of dating sites turning a blind eye to scammers. Many of the execs I met were obsessed with ridding their sites of scammers. "A clean site, with no scammers, is always a better long-term business proposition," says Schildkrout. Match says it spends millions on antifraud efforts.

Still, romance scams are rampant. Dotti Gale is a Chicago-based woman who helps operate sites such as Scamwarners.com and 419eater .com, where victims of romance scams come to commiserate with each other and seek support. Gale says that a single scamming outfit in Nigeria might operate up to fifty thousand dollars worth of online-dating memberships at one time. Scammers harvest information from online forums, chat rooms, dating sites, and social-networking sites. They use software designed to spot keywords that betray vulnerability ("lonely"), wealth (the name of an expensive car), depression, and old age.

In the typical West African scam, the scammer poses as a charming, affectionate, but down on his luck lover. There's also Vlads, short for Vladimir, the scamming world's nickname for scammers who target men looking for Russian brides. The newest is the Soldier at War scam, wherein the scammer poses as a U.S. soldier in need of a laptop, a plane ticket, or money for an operation the military won't pay for.

Here's how the standard scam works: The scammer strikes up a steamy online relationship, pulling the victim close and gaining his or her trust. Men are lured with sex, women with love. If the scammer is good, Gale says, he'll put in some extra time to "whiplash" his victim, alternating between hot and cold. The scammer might use a stolen credit card to send flowers, as if to say he can't possibly be a scammer, because he's spending money. Meanwhile, he's now confirmed the victim's mailing address, through which he can find out more information, plus get a fairly accurate sense of his victim's net worth.*

Once a victim has been lured in, he or she is often passed up a chain of seniority within the scamming organization, sort of like buying a car. Over the course of a fraudulent online relationship, the scammer's writ-

---

* If you own property, put your address into Google to see how much a stranger could learn about you.

ing often magically improves. In the typical case, the scammer broaches the money issue by asking for a large sum to finance a fictive life-or-death medical operation for his son or mother, or to complete a crucial business deal that will allow the two of them to finally be together. He might direct the victim to a bank account, alleging that he's owed money and simply needs a temporary loan.

In 2009, a fifty-eight-year-old man in Britain threw himself under a train after losing nearly one hundred thousand euros to a Nigerian woman. In 2010, a fifty-two-year-old woman in rural England was scammed out of three hundred thousand euros by a prolific Ghanian romance fraudster named Maurice Asola Fadola, who posed as a strapping sergeant serving in Iraq. When Britain's Serious Organised Crime Agency, working with local Ghanian authorities, caught up with the thirty-one-year-old Fadola, he was living in a gold-plated, marble villa on the outskirts of Accra, complete with a gym, a pool, and Rottweilers as guard dogs. In 2012, a Nigerian man and an Argentine woman were nabbed for separating fifteen Americans from more than five hundred thousand dollars in romance scams. Several victims, including a sixty-nine-year-old woman in Minnesota, were taken on Match. Jim Arlt, an agent with the Minnesota Department of Public Safety, said, "We all have a need to have somebody in our life, and these suspects prey upon that."

Like an aspiring politician, any innovator seeking to disrupt an industry must choose an injustice sufficient to hang his ambitions on. For Sam Yagan and his OkCupid team, it was paid dating.

Free sites, led by Plenty of Fish and OkCupid, began eating up market share in 2007, eventually coming to own about a third of the U.S. online-dating market. In 2008, Match offered $175 million for Plenty of Fish, but Frind turned it down. At iDate 2009, Frind won the Darth Vader Award, suggesting his site was the Dark Star crippling paid sites like Match and eHarmony. Still, paid sites insisted on their superiority, defaulting to the female-friendly argument that willingness to purchase access to a dating database is a proxy for commitment. Men who pay are more likely to stay.

"Paid sites signal fundamental seriousness and mate value," says Jim Talbott, a Match strategist. "I don't know how you replicate that on a free site."

It's the velvet rope theory, and proponents of free call its logic absurd. A dater's intent, say the Frinds and Yagans, can be measured only from within the relationship. If willingness to buy access to a dating pool signals anything, it signals naiveté and/or desperation.

"Match does a fundamentally bad job of matching people up," said Yagan at iDate 2011. "They just show you every person you want to see, based entirely on looks, even if that person doesn't want to see you. All they care about is that their paid users send lots of messages to free users so that the free user signs up. Most of the people they show you aren't even active on the site anymore. They waste everyone's time."

In 2010, OkCupid's blog published a well-read article, written by Christian Rudder, entitled "Why You Should Never Pay for Online Dating." It made an argument that Coyne, Rudder, and Yagan had been refining for years: Paid dating sites—Match and eHarmony being the best examples—misrepresent the size of their memberships, bamboozle their subscribers, and have "a unique incentive to profit from their customers' disappointment." Using public information about eHarmony and Match, Rudder concluded: 1) 96 percent of eHarmony's twenty million profiles are "dead"; 2) 6 percent of eHarmony's users get married; 3) the odds that a Match profile is active are 7 percent; and 4) Match collects $137,000 in user fees for each marriage it produces.

The hatchet job hit a vein of populist outrage in the online-dating user community. A couple of weeks before iDate 2011, Match was sued in its home state of Texas by people claiming the site uses deceptive practices to separate online daters from their money. The plaintiffs claimed that Match "takes virtually no action to remove" inactive profiles and that, "with regard to the thousands of fake or fraudulent profiles, Match likewise makes little to no effort to vet, police, or remove these profiles and thereby permits, condones, and acquiesces in their posting." After iDate, another deceptive trade practices suit was filed against Match in California, alleging similar improprieties.

The cases, which were consolidated, were thrown out by a Dallas federal court in 2012. The language in Match's user agreement, wrote U.S. district judge Sam Lindsay, "in no way requires Match.com to police, vet, update the Web site content, verify the accuracy of all profiles submitted and contained on the Web site, or to undertake any of the actions that Plaintiffs allege Match.com failed to do. . . . There is nothing in the Agreement that obligates Match.com to conduct its services using only current or 'active' profiles."

In other words, it's a jungle out there. Buyer beware.

The theory of free dating goes like this: Since free sites make a vastly smaller marginal profit off each user, they can't afford the massive marketing initiatives of sites like Match and eHarmony. Therefore, free sites rely on word-of-mouth advertising, which incentivizes them to focus entirely on user satisfaction rather than conversion rates and date baiting. On a free site the user pays with his time and information, which the site then catalogs, analyzes, and sells to marketers that, theoretically, will pay a premium for targeted marketing opportunities.

Online dating should be an advertiser's dream. Sexual orientation, religion, politics, food and drink preferences, travel habits, pop culture and media consumption—it's all there. Yet despite OkCupid's success at iDate, Yagan found the advertising market a tough nut to crack. "Yes," he says, "we know whether you smoke and how many hours a week you play video games. We know everything. But when it comes to businesses like ours, businesses that have historically carried a stigma, advertisers are risk averse. Their opinions lag behind the population at large. The chief marketing officer of Coke is probably fifty. He doesn't get it. And if you're the ad agency, then your job is to get approval from the CMO. So you've got to be even more risk-averse than he is."*

---

* Any dating-site partner—whether advertiser or investor—must also be more risk-averse than the credit-card companies, which label all dating sites as "adult services." For paid sites, this means that in "charge-back" situations—when a consumer contests a billing, arguing, for instance, that he thought he had canceled his subscription—the dating site is given no leverage, no credit, in the dispute. Charge

At present, the Cokes and Nikes of the world have no interest in associating their brands with a Web site that queries its users on everything from their preferences regarding oral sex to their thoughts about threesomes, strap-ons, masturbation, pornography, and how they'd feel if asked to play out someone else's rape fantasy. What gained OkCupid a loyal following and made it one of the industry's most admired sites also capped its upside. As a result, the biggest advertisers in the online-dating industry are not Coke or Nike, but rather *other online-dating companies.*

Two weeks after iDate 2011, OkCupid announced it was selling itself to Match for $90 million, an astounding figure for an advertising-based business that had good but not great traffic and brought in little more than $4 million per year in revenue. "We know that many people who start out on advertising-based sites ultimately develop an appetite for the broader feature set and more committed community" of subscription sites, explained Greg Blatt, CEO of Match parent IAC.

During the deal negotiations at OkCupid's Manhattan headquarters, Yagan brought up the infamous article, "Why You Should Never Pay for Online Dating," that gave fuel to the lawsuits against Match. Blatt, the man Yagan was trying to convince to pull out his checkbook, unloaded with a stream of sentiment that you wouldn't exactly call collegial. Outside the conference room, OkCupid's employees suddenly took a great interest in their keyboards. Who was this person keelhauling their fearless leader? It was their new boss, Barry Diller's right-hand man, and it was just business, nothing personal.

On the day the deal was announced, Yagan removed the piece from OkCupid's site. When asked about the capitulation, he back treaded. "I chose to take that down," he said. "Match didn't ask." The article's claims—that Match profits by duping its customers—were pieced together from public information, he said. Some of the assumptions made, he'd since learned, were untrue. "It's a common sense thing to do," Yagan

---

backs are the bane of the dating business. Pretty much any charge can be disputed successfully by a customer.

added. "We're joining a bunch of new colleagues; there's no need to have that post." Why ruffle more feathers? In due time Blatt will appoint Yagan, now thirty-five, head of Match Inc., where he'll oversee IAC's entire online-dating operation, paid and free—nearly $500 million of business, a quarter of the North American market.

So maybe free versus paid wasn't such an important distinction after all. Don't free sites want you coming back as often as possible too? Isn't "socializing" the product being sold and guaranteed by all social-media portals, regardless of their profit model? The message is always: *Come back! Hang out! Find someone new!*

In 2011, as dating sites came under pressure from the government to improve security, a high-profile rape allegation turned the issue into national news. A fifty-three-year-old woman in Los Angeles alleged that she'd been raped by a man she met on Match who turned out to be a convicted sex offender. Days after she filed a lawsuit against Match, demanding that it screen its database for sex offenders, Match announced that it would be checking all members against the national sex offender register. Match hoped the announcement would mollify politicians and stave off legislation; the added expense of statewide regulations, it worried, would gouge profits. A few months later, California's attorney general issued "a joint statement of business principles" that was signed by Match, eHarmony, and Spark Networks, which operates Jdate. The companies promised "to help protect members from identity theft, financial scams and sexual predators" and "to proactively educate members about safe online dating practices."

"The whole thing was pathetic," recalls Brian Bowman. "All these sites had to do was bring in the social graph"—the rest of one's online identity. "But that'd mean the end of anonymity in online dating, which would mean risking hundreds of millions of dollars for a business model change that's probably inevitable anyway."

Bowman is a particularly well-pedigreed geek. He majored in math and art at Purdue University. In the early nineties, he started his career in the world of computer-generated visual effects. He handled Internet products at the Cartoon Network, the Disney Channel, and ABC. After his stint as head of product strategy at Match, in the early 2000s, he worked for Yahoo! and a search engine called InfoSpace, where he tried to improve online search results by blending everyone's results together. In 2012, Bowman returned to the dating industry with a new idea that caught the attention of many.

For Bowman, the next phase of online dating is not about free versus paid but about open versus anonymous. Based on Bowman's experience at Match, he claims that "about 97% of the profiles" on Match belong either to free users—people who've posted a profile, are searching the site, but haven't paid yet and therefore can't send messages or respond to messages—or to former users, people who never removed their profile when they discontinued membership. According to Bowman, Match never goes out of its way to signal to users which 3 percent of profiles belong to paying subscribers. In fact, he says, Match doesn't go out of its way to authenticate much of anything about its users, and for a good reason: While user success thrives on efficiency, business success requires some inefficiency.

In the early years, he explains, promising anonymity was crucial for dating sites. It was not until later that the industry realized how important anonymity was to a paid business model that relies on message volume: keeping profiles anonymous meant a lower response-rate to messages sent. A lower response-rate to messages sent meant . . . *more messages sent.* Meanwhile, for the user, anonymity works to her detriment. While anonymity assures privacy (your boss will never find out you date online, unless he too is on the site and sees your picture), it also theoretically *diminishes* security and efficiency by withholding what Bowman calls "badges of authenticity." *Are you really not a criminal? Are you really not married?* By failing to distinguish between free users and subscribers, sites can also represent much larger membership numbers. A site that claims a membership of ten million might actually have only three hundred thousand active subscribers.

For a 2012 segment about the online-dating industry, CNBC's Amy Robach interviewed eHarmony's Dr. Gian Gonzaga. "Just how big is eHarmony's haystack?" Robach asks in a voiceover. "The company told us forty million—until we got specific." The interview continues with Robach asking Gonzaga how many daters are currently using the site.

"I'm not quite sure how to answer that question," Gonzaga replies after an awkward pause.

Later, when Robach asks if it's possible that eHarmony matches paying subscribers with non-paying subscribers, Gonzaga says, "It is possible they're not a subscriber and would have to subscribe in order to communicate with you."

In all cases, says Bowman, the concealment of your true identity becomes the site's main asset. Bowman would eventually marry. Ten years later, his Match profile was still on the site. Those who looked at it could discern only that he hadn't been active on Match in the past three weeks.

In the early days of Match, social media was not yet big. Privacy on the Web was taken much more seriously than it is now. Then Facebook came along. On Facebook, the presumption is that you go by your real name, and even provide an e-mail address and phone number. This is the opposite of most dating sites, where a few photos accompany generic, heavily edited, anonymous profiles. Bowman argued for "lifting the veil": dating sites would be more authentic, and therefore more effective, if they became more social by, for instance, encouraging users to post more pictures and information, and even perhaps linking their dating profile to the rest of their online identity. What would it take to move users in this direction?

As Facebook and other social-networks pushed society past its privacy concerns, some dating entrepreneurs wondered how they could leverage more of a user's online identity to make dating more like meeting in the real world, and move away from the old model of a private transaction between anonymous avatars. While the online-dating stigma still existed, online dating seemed neither novel nor extreme to a generation raised online, nurturing networks and watching each other's lives play out in a cascade of Facebook status updates. Privacy was something old people fussed over. *Who cares if your boss finds out?*

To the extent that Facebook is used for dating, it's the biggest dating site in the world. Dating-minded Facebookers will browse through the friends of their Facebook friends, letting interesting profiles lead to others. This way of dating was the main draw of Friendster, a Facebook predecessor. In 2003, after Friendster amassed 1.5 million members in just three months, the *New York Times* described it like this: "users sign up and post a picture and a list of interests. They also provide e-mail addresses of friends, who are invited to join. Users can search the service for their friends, then contact their friends' friends for dating or simply socializing." This "is more reflective of reality," said Friendster founder Jonathan Abrams, who also claimed to be chasing Match's market share: A friend of a friend felt less anonymous, more safe; the implication was that he or she had been vetted by someone you knew. This is precisely the argument that Bowman makes today. Though his timing may be more auspicious.

Friendster would fumble the ball, getting overtaken by MySpace, which in turn gave way to Facebook. These social-networking sites stole a significant chunk of online dating's market. Between 1998 and 2005, the online-dating industry grew at an average rate of 9 percent a year by revenue. Over the following six years, from 2006 to 2011, year-on-year growth slowed to less than 3 percent. At the same time, however, social-networking sites helped online dating by chipping away at privacy concerns.

Bowman hoped to leverage some of that behavioral evolution for dating when he started theComplete.me in 2012. On theComplete.me, the user clicks a button and his information gets sent over from Facebook. (If your relationship status on Facebook is "married," then you're not allowed on the site.) The user begins anonymously, in his "second skin." Then he can pull back that second skin as much as he wants. This might mean minor additions to his identity, such as posting more pictures. Or it might mean major reveals, such as linking to his LinkedIn page. As on Facebook, users control who sees what. Maybe every dater who is one degree removed from him on Facebook is permitted to see his complete online identity.

Rather than a static profile, theComplete.me hopes to "tap into the sites that consumers use every day"—such as Netflix and Amazon—to create "a more dynamic interest graph." In Bowman's unique geek vision, as Internet use rises, and people define themselves increasingly by where they go, who they talk to, and what they post and buy—*online*— their dating profile will evolve with them.

"The first version of the Internet," he says, "was based around 'It'—an index of linked Web sites, like Yahoo directories. Web 2.0 was based around 'We'—me and my human relationships, my social graph. Facebook won that round. The next iteration will be about 'Me'—who I am, my interests at this time, based not on what I say but on what I do. Mate selection will no longer be driven by looks. The average-looking person could become a great person, because you see the complete package."

There's a paid element to theComplete.me, making it a "freemium" site. Like Google, users can pay small amounts for premium placement in search results. Otherwise, the site is free, sort of: You pay with your privacy. Through a reward system—referred to as "gamification"— Bowman induces his free users to do what he wants them to do by giving them the tools to do what they want to do. For instance, a new user may be allowed five free messages after he transfers his profile from Facebook and fills out some basic information. If he proves himself to be a quality user—by, say, not sending overtly sexual messages—Bowman might offer him another ten free messages, but only if he posts two more photos or sends invitations to ten Facebook friends. Bowman compares it to frequent flyer miles.

Bowman's innovations caught the industry's attention, in part because many sense that, given the friction created by anonymity, something has to give. His early investors included Plenty of Fish's Markus Frind and Intel Capital, the investment arm of the semiconductor maker.

Mark Brooks, the dating industry consultant, is helping Bowman get the word out. "There are a lot of social norms that need busting," says Brooks, who moonlights as an "antiprivacy advocate." "Look at me, I've got nothing in the way of secrets. It's a nice, stress-free way to live." Leading by example, Brooks posts his credit-card transactions to a Web site called Blippy. When the *Times* ran a front-page story about Blippy in 2010, Brooks was featured in the lead: "Mark Brooks wants the whole Web to know that he spent $41 on an iPad case at an Apple store, $24 eating at an Applebee's, and $6,450 at a Florida plastic surgery clinic for nose work."

Like Badoo—whose stated goal is simply to maximize real-world interactions, whether for dating or some other purpose—Bowman and Brooks, among many others in the business, also believe online dating will get consumed by a broader world of social discovery. By taking the pink hearts off the homepage and rebranding the industry, dating execs expect to have an easier time reeling in not only Madison Avenue and investors, but users as well.

"There's still so much more social data that could be included in these algorithms to make them smarter," says Amarnath Thombre, Match's algorithm geek. "I'm sure the world will be more open in a few years from now."

By encouraging transparency—"mutually assured disclosure"—the innovators in online dating are blazing a path toward ever greater accuracy and choice. These innovators are not so much refining some science of compatibility as they are optimizing the Internet's supreme asset: search and discovery. Which is to say, the ability to combine several kinds of technology into one, the same virtue that captivated Barry Diller when he stood on the selling floor of his home-shopping network twenty years ago.

"What's cool about the social Web is that, unlike old dating sites, you're not trying to be a generically perfect person," says Bowman. "You're just living your life, in a fairly transparent manner, while looking for someone who is looking for someone like you. The goal, of course, remains the same: finding great first dates as efficiently as possible."

It's unrealistic, however, to believe that the openness of the social Web will cure all online-dating ills, particularly the problems of fraud and deception.

The need to connect deeply with others is a "fundamental human motivation." Whether subscription- or advertising-based, anonymous or authenticated, online dating or social discovery, any technology claiming to offer an antidote to solitude will always present opportunities for misdealing.

On Facebook, Rose, a multilingual artist in Switzerland, was contacted by a profile that appeared to belong to an olive-skinned forty-four-year-old Hispanic man living in New York.

"Hello," he wrote, "you look gorgeous. There is a saying that a picture is worth a thousand words, but when I saw yours I was speechless. Well my name is Dean Morris. I will be glad to communicate with you. Maybe we can chat."

Rose heard a voice counseling prudence. At fifty-two, she'd never been married and had attracted a string of guys who'd been interested only in "superficial relationships, bed stories."

Rose recalls: "The message was weird. But I thought it was interesting and fun to be in touch with someone from abroad. It felt like an escape from my life at home, which hadn't been going too well."

She sent a tepid response. Dean Morris said he was married for fourteen years, then widowed; and had an eleven-year-old son, a fact that appeared to be corroborated by his profile photos.

"You must be a fake," she wrote. "You can't be real."

But within a week, Rose and Dean Morris were calling each other "dear" and wishing one another sweet dreams. He expressed interest in Rose's artwork. No one had ever done that. Her weight never came up. He would ask: "Did you sleep well?" "How was your day?" "Take care," he would sign off at night, "and God bless your heart."

After two months, Dean Morris sent Rose a bank-account number. He asked her to log into the account so she could see that the bank owed him money. In the meantime, he needed a temporary loan to complete a crucial business deal in Africa. The money he would make on the deal would allow him to come see her in Switzerland. She should wire the loan via Western Union, or MoneyGram, her choice.

In the end, Rose gave Dean Morris—an identity concocted by an organized-crime organization in Nigeria—a total of eight thousand dollars. After she wired the money to the account in Africa, Dean Morris said his son needed a kidney transplant in Hungary. That's when she said enough. He got angry. Her last word to him was: "Fake."

It's tempting to shake one's head at Rose's fiasco. What was she *thinking*? But this isn't about education or IQ. It's about the power of loneliness, and the unthinkable ways we'll delude ourselves when offered even the thinnest hope of beating it.

In 2012, Ralph Gagliardi, a state policeman in Colorado who heads the identity fraud unit, led a bust of two American women, a mother-daughter team, who helped a Nigerian organized-crime organization run romance scams around the world. Through dating and social networking sites, the defendants helped defraud 374 people, mostly women, out of $1.4 million. That money, accumulated in one year, went to a single scamming "cell" in Nigeria. Gagliardi estimates that one scamming enterprise, comprised of dozens of cells, could bring in $50 million a year through romance scams.

"No one has any idea how much money flows out of the country every year in these scams," Gagliardi says. "It's massive, and there's not a lot dating sites can do about it. The Internet is so vast. When people go looking for love and companionship online, it almost seems like some disappointment is the price to be paid for opening you up to so much, and much of it great. There's always going to be something that cancels something else out."

ALEXIS, PART VIII

↓

In Terms of Sheer Numbers

IT'S MIDSUMMER 2012, AND MONTHS HAVE PASSED SINCE ALEXIS last posted on Phantasy Tour.

In the previous year she's worked as a set and costume designer on several films and advertisements, and is ascending in the business. Her twenty-sixth birthday is a month away, and she's in her longest relationship ever: For six months she's been seeing a thirty-year-old comedy writer who works at the production company where she works. They flirted for a long time at the office, while she scoured every post on his Facebook wall to figure out which women he'd slept with. Finally he gave her his cell number and casually suggested that she send him a text sometime.

"WHEN ARE WE HANGING OUT?" she texted immediately.

Now, over a glass of sangria, Alexis reflects on her first years in the city. "My past relationships had this one-foot-in-one-foot-out kind of thing," she says. "I never set any boundaries. I'd sit in my apartment clutching my cell phone and waiting for whoever the guy was to call or text. We'd sleep together, hang out, and it would never progress." She continues: "This relationship"—with the comedy writer—"developed more organically. I never had to set boundaries with him because nothing was rushed. He came right out and said, 'I really like you.' And I was like, 'Oh yeah. This is how it's supposed to be. I'm not supposed to have to chase you down and wonder if you're going to call.'"

Alexis realized that music isn't as important as she thought. "I don't even spend much time listening to music," she says. Her boyfriend has been sober seven years, so Alexis doesn't take him to concerts because the temptation is too much. "When it comes to guys, I think temperament is more important." She likes that he's a creative type, like herself, and works hard at what he does. "I don't know why I didn't realize until now that this is the kind of person I should be with."

Alexis recently moved to Brooklyn, where he lives. She hopes their respective living situations—they both share apartments with multiple roommates—will be incentive for them to get a place of their own. "I think we could be engaged within a year," she says, "if we can get our shit together."

The sticking point seems to be Alexis's past. He's concerned that she's been with too many guys in too many quick relationships.

"Our sexual histories, in terms of sheer numbers, are comparable," she explains, frustrated. "But when we get in arguments, or he's angry, he'll often lash out and say something like, 'Well I'm just another one of your boyfriends, and pretty soon you'll move on anyway.' I know I'm supposed to soothe his worries, but I get defensive. I mean, it worries *me* that he's had two long-term relationships, lived with one of them, and had butt sex with another, and *we* haven't reached that level of intimacy yet. The fact is, there's no such thing as perfect compatibility, and there is no perfect person for you, whom when your powers combine will make a totally effort-free relationship. If you've got a good thing going, with love and respect, where you treat each other well, you stay and make it work."

Alexis thinks there's more good than bad. Still, it's hard to discuss the problems without uncertainty creeping in. "I want someone stable and he needs someone who understands his demons," she says. "And what do I find myself doing sometimes? Itching to get back on OkC, to see who's there this time around. Of course it's good to know that if it falls apart it's not like it's the end of my whole romantic existence. The thought/fear/curiosity of someone better around the corner is always there, Internet or not, especially when you live in a big city. But I try not to let these thoughts bother me."

EPILOGUE

Dating Starts Here

I n the heyday of Operation Match, Jeff Tarr appeared on a CBS game show called *To Tell the Truth*, where he and two other young men—all claiming to be Jeff Tarr, for purposes of the show—faced a table of judges. The judges asked questions, then guessed which one was the real Jeff Tarr.

"I guess number two," said the female judge. "Because he looks like the kind of boy that would want to take all the romance and the mystery and the uncertainty out of dating!"

Whether Tarr looked like that kind of boy was up for debate. But she guessed correctly.

Tarr had big plans for Operation Match. He opened offices across the country and hired more staff. Colleges looking to match freshmen room-mates, he predicted, as well as businesses looking to optimize hiring would provide the next markets for Tarr's matching service. His com-petitor, David Dewan, had similar ambitions for Contact. In the end, both men would make their fortunes elsewhere. Shortly after Tarr and Dewan left Harvard in the midsixties, as the sexual revolution was gaining steam, they abandoned their companies. "It was easier when we had a captive audience, people at single-sex colleges with time on their hands and high hormone levels," an Operation Match employee recalled. "We all felt it was time to go find real careers."

Tarr and his partners set up an office in New York, but struggled. Tarr sold Operation Match to a student marketing company, then headed for Wall Street, where he pioneered the use of computers in stock arbitrage. Optimistic as Dewan was about the future of computers, he folded Contact, cut up his credit cards, and embarked on a two-and-a-half-year journey around the world, eventually returning home to a very lucrative career as a software entrepreneur, selling two companies in deals worth over a billion dollars combined.

Two of Tarr's Operation Match partners found success in the law. Returning to Texas, David Crump became a law professor, politician, poet, novelist, and online-dating success story. A few years ago he met his wife, a German, on Match. He was in Houston. She was in Hamburg. Douglas Ginsburg became a federal judge. In 1987, Ronald Reagan nominated him to the Supreme Court, but Ginsburg withdrew the nomination from consideration after admitting to smoking pot.

There was a third fellow, however, who couldn't leave the dating business behind.

In the sixties, a Yale student named Chris Walker helped Tarr advertise Operation Match around the country. Among Walker's PR gambits: He convinced a nineteen-year-old model named Shelley Hack to pose as an Operation Match user in photos taken for Gene Shalit's *Look* article. Hack later became the face of Revlon and appeared in the TV show *Charlie's Angels* and in the Woody Allen film *Annie Hall*.

Walker's interests in matchmaking extended to the laboratory as well. In his senior year, Walker wrote a psychology thesis entitled "An Experimental Investigation of Heterosexual First-Impressions." Walker's paper, a study of attraction, drew a conclusion that would inform the rest of his life: "Each person approaches others from an essentially exploitive angle," he wrote, "and judges others according to an inflexible self-centered set of standards."

After Yale, Walker picked up law and business degrees from Harvard, then became a real estate mogul in the D.C. area. He also tinkered on the side, inventing EXSYS, a hydraulic fitness machine. Politically, Walker became a prominent libertarian who championed environmental causes. As for relationships, he kept the lab going, entering into an open marriage with the same woman for forty years.

It is late October 2010, when Walker arrives in the restaurant of the Tribeca Grand Hotel. He wears a blue suit, an iPhone around his neck, and is dragging a suitcase behind him. He settles into the leather banquette, splaying his arms and legs like a fighter down on the ropes. He has a leading chin, a small underbite, huge ears, and the sort of tumescent lips that don't always notice when specks of food stick to them. A broad forehead and high cheekbones carve out of Walker's face a look of permanent bemusement. The deep-set ocular structure makes it seem as though his eyes are always searching. When a scantily clad cocktail waitress walks by, he cracks a crooked smile, and says: "Cappuccino."

"I believe in the European tradition," Walker explains. "There's marriage, and then relationships on the side. Here, in the States, most women, if they get wind that you're even laying eyes on a third person, they go ballistic. My wife and I decided a long time ago that there are certain things not worth fighting about. She doesn't say, 'Who have you slept with recently?' And I don't say, 'Where did you spend that last bit of money I gave you?' Most people fight over sex and money. If you can get those two things out of the way, there's nothing left to fight about. You save so much time."

Walker often travels abroad alone, using newspaper personals and online-dating sites, including Craigslist, to meet women near and far, including Rio de Janeiro and Tokyo. "I've recently had a string of successes with Japanese women," he says. "I love the Japanese culture. They're the most uninhibited about sex, and they have the most sex. Japan pioneered the love hotel."

At sixty-six, Walker is stooped, yet moves with the cricked wiriness of a man who carries on vigorous exercise without regard to stasis. In fact, he's very sick: Walker was diagnosed with leukemia and told he had five years to live. That was six years ago. It was after diagnosis that Walker decided his last business venture would entail a return to what he calls the "digitally intermediated introductions business." He hired consultant Mark Brooks to help him execute his idea for a site called Dating Starts Here.

This is why Walker is in New York. He's meeting with one of Brooks's consultants, Eric Resnik, to discuss the site launch. Resnik is a thirty-three-year-old red-haired man who used to handle public relations for the tomato industry, once worked for Match and eHarmony, and now runs a service that helps online daters polish their profiles.

On an iPad, Resnik shows Walker the test version of Dating Starts Here. Walker wants Dating Starts Here to be an aggregator of dating sites. In the same way that Kayak.com makes it possible to search airfares from the Web sites of several different airlines, Dating Starts Here (slogan: "We Cover the Field") aims to be the umbrella site of dating sites, offering users the ability to search scores of sites at once before deciding which one to join. The red-and-white homepage looks pretty much like any other dating site, with a picture of a couple laughing and having a good time, but Walker likes what he sees.

"It'll be like a dating choose-your-own-adventure!" he says, and then asks Resnik: "Did you add the feature we discussed?"

"Nope," Resnik responds, a little annoyed, "didn't add that one. Come on, Chris. We agreed we weren't going to discuss this anymore."

For weeks, Brooks and Resnik have been trying to dissuade Walker from his idea that Dating Starts Here should ask female users to measure their clitoris, in order to improve matching. "I just read," says Resnik, eager to change topics, "that Japan is so worried about the low birth rate that they're doing a government-sponsored matching service."

"We've got to talk to those guys!"

As with some other dating entrepreneurs, it is difficult to tell where Walker's sexual prerogatives end and his business interests begin. Well versed in the literature of evolutionary biology, he believes humans are closer to bonobos—a famously nonmonogamous species—than they are to gorillas and orangutans. He peppers his language with phrases like "mixed reproductive strategy," "diversification," and "mating in peer populations."

"Ornithologists used to think birds were monogamous," Walker says. "But then they started doing DNA studies on bird eggs, and they found that these supposedly monogamous female birds had mated in peer populations. You spread your risks. What if the guy turns out to have a genetic defect or gets killed? Most of the animal world works like that: You have a main squeeze, but it turns out that, medically, from an evolutionary point of view, it's more stable to mate around."

Much of the human world finds Walker's views distasteful, or at least impractical—including, it seems, the waitress, who overhears Walker's monologue and votes with her feet.

Whatever one thinks about the lifestyle Chris Walker promotes, some version of his libertarian sexual morality is gaining ground in America. The change happens so quickly that official declarations of right and wrong fade shortly after they're enshrined. In 1986, when considering whether the Constitution protected sodomy, the Supreme Court laughed off the notion, concluding that a right to engage in such conduct was "facetious." To hold otherwise, sneered Chief Justice Warren Burger in his concurring opinion, "would be to cast aside a millennia of moral teaching." Just seventeen years later, in 2003, the Court pulled an about-face in *Lawrence v. Texas.* Now the Constitution did protect sodomy.

In *Lawrence*, the Court's scrappiest member threw a fit over the ruling. If, fumed Justice Antonin Scalia in dissent, promoting Texas's "majoritarian sexual morality is not even a *legitimate* state interest," then criminal laws against bigamy, incest, and bestiality could also fail constitutional challenge. Justice Scalia exaggerated in order to make his point, that the Court was killing off all possibility for "laws based on moral choices."

But the Court's opinion in *Lawrence* contained a subtler message: Sexual norms evolve. It makes no sense to speak of some collective American mating tradition, because there is none. Modern conceptions of sexuality are far removed from the categories through which earlier generations made sense of their urges and behavior. The concept of the homosexual as a distinct category of person, the majority in *Lawrence* pointed out, did not even emerge until the nineteenth century.

The evolution of computer dating, and then online dating, coincided with a period of great change in American mating norms. The trends are disparate, of course: There was no more a link between Jeff Tarr's Operation Match and Supreme Court decisions that constitutionalized contraception than there was a link between Chris Walker's lifestyle and the cheating site Ashley Madison. But we do know that the technology developed in unison with, and abetted some of, this rapidly changing value system.

At present, gay marriage is winding through the courts and will likely be embraced fully in due course. What will the next legal battle be over? Does it matter?

Surely legal recognition of lifestyles—of moral choices—matters to the interest groups backing them. But the idea that judges or politicians control who has sex with whom, and how, is, in this connective age, as facetious as Justice Burger's millennia of moral teachings. To the extent moral legislation ever regulated sexual conduct, that regulatory torch is now passing, increasingly, to technology. This is partly why I've tried to resist value judgments about online dating, even though I believe strongly in it. Any technology that helps people find companionship, helps them not be alone, *offline*, is something to be thankful for. Though I can't be more specific than that. Online dating is so ubiquitous, and is being used in so many ways, that to talk about any one iteration as good or bad would be like talking about "sex" or "marriage" as good or bad. It works great for some people, less well for others. My goal, instead, has been to chronicle how, in a time when technology seems to define social norms, our conceptions of meeting, mating, and love are adapting to the new choice and control provided by these revolutionary means.

And since I've been looking at relationships through the lens of how online dating changes them, I've also tried to avoid passing judgment on all the many behaviors, new and old, facilitated by the date-o-sphere. Again, this is not because I don't have feelings about infidelity, commitment, monogamous marriage, or diaper fetishes. But rather because the technology is neutral, largely undifferentiated, and therefore it's only how people use it that matters.

I wouldn't use Tai Lopez's or Brandon Wade's sugar-daddy/sugar-baby Web sites, and I don't agree with Wade's view that all relationships are exchanges of beauty for money. But it doesn't really matter what I think, nor even what Justice Scalia thinks. All that matters is that Wade is offering a channel and people are connecting through it.

"I'd like to think of myself," says Wade, "as a telecommunications service provider more than enabling a specific lifestyle." It's a false distinction. He's doing both. But point taken. Like his colleagues, Wade does little more than slap a brand on a universal communications network.

Universality, and the advancement of a common good, were two of the Internet's founding principles. In 1980, a physicist named Tim Berners-Lee, working in a cabin near the French-Swiss border, wrote a computer program for organizing information. Entitled ENQUIRE—short for "Enquire Within Upon Everything"—Berners-Lee's project would, ten years later, become the World Wide Web, the most popular application for the Internet.

In *The Master Switch*, Tim Wu explains the genesis of WWW:

> Accessed through a browser, the Web was originally just an agreement to store information in a common format (HTML), coupled with a means of connecting pieces of information by so-called hyperlinks. The supreme value of the Web was, and is, its *universality*. The idea, as Tim Berners-Lee told me, was that "the Web has to work on everything: any hardware, any software, every language, all kinds of different media, any quality level of data, be accessible to people with disabilities, and work with any culture. Not just different languages, but different cultures."

In Berners-Lee's utopic vision, the Web would be a place where personal identity could flourish, unconstrained by monopolists or regulators but directed by "a firm sense of some common good." Wikipedia, YouTube, Facebook: All were founded on some collaborative endeavor, whether it be connection, knowledge, or entertainment. "Even Google," writes Wu, "can be understood, particularly in its inception, as a consequence of the Web's natural evolution, a faster way of getting around when the terrain became too vast to be navigated by human faculties alone."

Among these tech giants, Facebook is perhaps closest to the Internet's original vision. During its rise to prominence, Mark Zuckerberg shunned buyout offers from many media conglomerates because he intuited a difference between those "media" companies and Facebook, which he thought of as simply a "technology" company. The difference was one of control. Facebook didn't produce content or make assumptions about what people ought to be interested in. It didn't offer to get you married or arrange a fling. It was nothing more than the collective actions of its users. It was agnostic, like a public utility, but even more so. Tearing down anonymity on the Web by encouraging as much openness and sharing as possible—this was the mission.

Brian Bowman's idea for theComplete.me, in which users sign up through Facebook and their dating profile encompasses part or all of their online identity, may not become a big success. But he's on to something. Judging from recent history, transparency in the "social graph" appears to be the final destination for online dating, or social discovery. But whatever label we use to describe the process of meeting new people online, introducing more openness will be at least as important as the switch to mobile. Taking the long view, anything that inhibits efficiency is likely to lose out.

In the summer of 2011, as Dating Starts Here is preparing to go live, Chris Walker receives an invitation to the Harvard Club in New York.

Jeff Tarr and his wife are throwing a dinner party. There's no special occasion, other than that Tarr has recently reconnected with a couple of his old Operation Match partners, Professor David Crump and Judge Douglas Ginsburg; and also that the Tarrs' daughter, Jennie (Harvard '99), is eight months pregnant with her second child. In a twist, Jennie married Harvard classmate and OkCupid cofounder Chris Coyne, whose interest in the dating business predated his relationship with Jennie. His father-in-law stays out of operations.

The old guard sits at one table, the new at another. Jennie Tarr and Chris Coyne sit with Coyne's business partners, including OkTrends blogger Christian Rudder. Also present is the journalist Nick Paumgarten, who last week published a story about online dating in *The New Yorker*.

Walker, severely stooped now and walking with a cane, hobbles over to Coyne in the middle of dinner. Coyne stands; his father-in-law introduces them. Walker denounces OkCupid and the rest of the industry, insisting that there's no algorithm or "black box" that can forecast compatibility. The best a dating site can do, he says, is provide its users with as many choices as possible.

"I'm going to shake things up with my new site," Walker promises, and Coyne nods respectfully.

Walker's philosophy of matching is not entirely out of sync with industry thinking. Still, no one quite understands how Walker's site can be successful. Even if Dating Starts Here "scrapes" the profiles of hundreds or thousands of dating sites, there would be no "reciprocal indication" of the user's matches: The searcher might be able to see everyone on fifty dating sites who lives within twenty-five miles and fits his criteria, but he'd have no idea whether those people wanted to see him. Even Walker's own consultants are doubtful that a dating-site aggregator will work. The sites that are aggregated would need to agree to be included. Only a couple have expressed interest.

After dinner, Tarr, Crump, and Walker, along with a few other dinner guests, head to the Harvard Club's bar for beers and coffees. It's the first time the three of them have been together since their undergraduate days, over four decades ago. The gathering feels like a warm but awkward date between men who once shared very memorable experiences.

Tarr peels off. Crump and his wife hail a cab. Walker stays to discuss a book called *Sex at Dawn: The Prehistoric Origins of Modern Sexuality*. One of many recently published books that attacks monogamy, *Sex at Dawn* argues its case via evolutionary biology. "In the West," Walker says, paraphrasing the book, "we inflate the value of sex by restricting supply. The illusion of scarcity is what makes us so possessive and jealous. We're not naturally that way." *Sex at Dawn* suggests that, given the relaxation of social codes—from hook-up culture to sexting to recognition of legal rights for gay couples—the arc of history seems "to be flowing back toward a hunter-gatherer casualness," assuming, of course, that hunter-gatherers were casual in their approach to mating, which is a matter of scientific debate.

And yet for those who believe that technology might carry us away from the monogamous ideal, recall not the dawn of sex but the dawn of the information industry. Like religion, which aims to overcome human suffering through togetherness, a similar ennobling ethos accompanied the rise of broadcast technology: It was thought that social interconnectedness would free man "from his baser unmediated impulses," that connection itself would have some kind of civilizing effect.

Well, yes and no. As the world adjusts to the new reality that technology provides, many traditions and taboos surrounding meeting and mating are on their way out, and more will likely fall, replaced by whichever new theories of relationship happiness win out in a marketplace of possibilities that never in history has been so vast. Monogamy is not going away, and neither is infidelity. Rather, it is the way we make sense of these behaviors, the values and labels and portent we place on them, that will evolve.

"The way I work my marriage," Walker explains, "is that my wife always gets first shot at everything. You want to attend a political convention? You want to go around the world? And if she doesn't, then I either go by myself or I take someone else. But you've got to have your priorities straight when you're in a marriage."

The lifestyle that Chris Walker pursued was extreme, or ahead of its time, or both. At the Harvard Club, Walker bids his audience good night. Clinging to a brass rail for assistance, he heads toward the elevator. In two months, Walker will succumb. Dating Starts Here will die with him.

ACKNOWLEGMENTS

My gratitude to Mickey Rapkin, formerly of *GQ*, for suggesting that a book be done, and to my friend and mentor Farley Chase, of the Chase Literary Agency, for making it happen.

At Current I thank Adrian Zackheim and Will Weisser for their sponsorship, as well as Julia Batavia, Jackie Burke, Tiffany Liao, Bria Sandford, and Margot Stamas for their faithful cheer and hard work on this book's behalf. Rachel Burd put a mean copyedit on the manuscript, and Joe Perez turned out a banging design. Deepest thanks to my peerless editor, Brooke Carey, for enriching *Algorithms* with her prodigious talents and unswerving sensibilities; from start to finish Brooke's enthusiasm and insight nourished my own. Any flaws are the author's entirely.

The construction of *Algorithms* relied on cooperation from the men and women of the online-dating industry, as well as the daters who spoke so frankly about their personal lives. I am also indebted, in the most fundamental of ways, to Jeff Tarr and David Dewan, and to the examples of fortitude set by my parents—all people without whom this book would not exist.

Many thanks to the editors, journalists, lawyers, and other teachers around town who've made the world of writing a friendly place to toil: Jess Bravin, Jason Feifer, Jennifer Forsyth, Vanessa Grigoriadis, Jamie

Heller, Neil Janowitz, Ashby Jones, Yvette Kantrow, Nathan Koppel, Patty Larson, Peter Lattman, David Marcus, Bethany McLean, Joe Nocera, Katie Pollet, Laurie Sandell, Dawn Schneider, Summer Shirey, Andrew Simon, Andrew Ross Sorkin, Bob Teitelman, Binky Urban, William Wallace, Jesse Wegman, Lizzie Widdicombe, Dick Winfield, and Elizabeth Wurtzel.

I've found refuge in some wonderful places. I'm especially thankful for all my families, adopted and biological, past and present, in Minnesota, on both coasts, and abroad, including but not limited to the Afshars, Bakers, Heaneys, Hunters, Mellons, Ryders, Shelskys, Simmonses, and Speerts. To think I might've never been lost and found in a Canadian snowdrift, hunted for morels in Cannon Falls, cast for trout on the Deschutes, enjoyed mutton on a stick in Abruzzo, defaced a pig's head in Park Slope, or known that the best secondhand items in Connecticut are found at Furniture on Consignment, located in Westport, where you should always ask for Jim Klinko and he'll treat you right.

To the Herbert-Kostyra-Plimpton-Stewart clan for giving me the most important gift of all, my Sophie: thank you.

NOTES

Introduction: Liquidity in the Market

Page

vii **"The Internet did not develop":** Monica T. Whitty and Adrian N. Carr, *Cyberspace Romance: The Psychology of Online Relationships* (Basingstoke, UK; New York: Palgrave Macmillan, 2006).

1 **"needs about 3.8 dates":** Frind's 2009 appearance can be viewed here: http://www.youtube.com/watch?v=YjU4nE3K-To.

2 **His look:** Maryam Sanati, "The Vancouverite behind Plenty of Fish," *The Globe and Mail*, Aug. 25, 2011.

2 **reached $2 billion in North America:** Mark Brooks, "Online Dating in the U.S.," *IBISWorld* (Dec. 2011). Brooks, who tracks the industry for *Online Personals Watch*, confirms that U.S. revenues hover around $2 billion, with about another $2 billion being made abroad.

2 **service thirty million of America's ninety million single adults:** Ibid.

2 **the Facebook-led rise of social networks:** "Market Share of Monthly U.S. Visits Among All Sites," *Experian Hitwise* (November 2010).

2 **the science behind their algorithms is bunk:** Finkel, J., P. Eastwick, et al. "Online Dating: A Critical Analysis From the Perspective of Psychological Science." *Psychological Science in the Public Interest* XX (2012): 1–64.

3 **a graduate of Harvard and Stanford Business School:** Don Aucoin, "Digital Man: Eight years out of Harvard, Sam Yagan has helped build two online companies and he says he's not done yet," *Boston Globe*, Sept. 5, 2007.

3 **a Canadian who comes from German-farmer stock:** Max Chafkin, "And the Money Comes Rolling In," *Inc.*, Jan. 1, 2009.

3 **Frind owns 20 percent of the world's online-dating traffic:** May 2012 data on market-share by visits from *Experian Hitwise*, reported by Irena Brooks at the online-dating consultancy Courtland Brooks.

10 **With around 1.5 million paying subscribers:** Julia Boorstin, "The Big Business of Online-Dating," CNBC, Feb. 12, 2010.

10 **OkCupid makes less than $5 million:** "Inc. 5000," *Inc.*, Jan. 2011. Available online at: http://www.inc.com/inc5000/profile/okcupidcom.

11 **"We don't know anything about dating":** Aucoin, "Digital Man."

Chapter One: Your Pleasure Is Our Business

13 **"It is clearly the most unusual entry":** Philip Shenon, "Nominee Left College to be Matchmaker," *New York Times*, Oct. 30, 1987. A spokesman told the *Times* that Ginsburg was a twenty-year-old vice president of Operation Match, which once had offices in New York; Cambridge, MA; Chicago; and Los Angeles. The *Times* reported that Ginsburg was a founder, and his initial investment was about eight hundred dollars.

13 **Shalit, then twenty-nine years old, to investigate:** Some of what I know about the development of computer dating at Harvard comes from Gene Shalit's article for *Look*, "New Dating Craze Sweeps the Campus" (Feb. 1966). The rest comes from a series of interviews I did between 2010 and 2012 with Jeff Tarr, David Crump, Chris Walker, and David Dewan; as well as other media reports from the era, all cited below. To a limited extent, some of the material in Chapter 1 appeared previously in an article I wrote for *GQ*, "The Social Network: The Prequel" (Jan. 2011).

13–14 **In 1959, two Stanford engineering students:** C. Stewart Gillmore, "Computers in Love: Stanford and the First Trials of Computer Date Matching," 26, nos. 2–3, *Sandstone & Tile* (Summer/Fall 2002). Available online at http://www.mgb67.com/computersinlove.htm.

14 **In the early sixties, some colleges used computers to optimize:** Erin Rosacker, "Before Internet Dating . . . ," *Time*, Feb. 15, 2008. See also "216 Meets 14," *Time*, Oct. 25, 1963.

14 **Harvard had owned computers since 1944:** IBM's online archives, available at http://www-03.ibm.com/ibm/history/reference/faq_0000000011.html, describes the Automatic Sequence Controlled Calculator, known as the Harvard Mark I, "as the first operating machine that could execute long computations automatically . . . the industry's largest electromechanical calculator."

15 **In sixty-three, a Defense Department employee:** J. C. R. Licklider, "Memorandum for Members and Affiliates of the Intergalactic Computer Network." Apr. 23, 1963. Available at http://www.kurzweilai.net/memorandum-for-members-and-affiliates-of-the-intergalactic-computer-network.

15 **raised $1,250 in start-up capital:** Timothy Leland, "2 Harvard Men Replacing Cupid With Computer," *Boston Globe*, Mar. 14, 1965.

16 **In March, just weeks before the official launch:** The scene in Tarr's dorm room was re-created using both Leland's *Globe* article and Tarr's recollection of events.

17 **"A computer-dating service?" laughed Ginsburg:** Douglas Ginsburg, now a federal judge in Washington, D.C., declined my interview requests. The limited information about Judge Ginsburg that appears in Chapter 1, and later in the epilogue, was gleaned from public records as well as from interviews with Tarr and Chris Walker.

17–18 **"I approve of it as a way to meet people":** Shalit, "New Dating Craze Sweeps the Campus."

18 **"We're not trying to take the love out of love":** Ibid.

18 **from any given geographical area:** Interview with Jeff Tarr.

18 **Having followed the success of Operation:** Roger Doughty, "He Programs Futures of Young People," *Times-News* (Hendersonville, NC), Mar. 17, 1969.

18 **Over the summer he drafted his own dating questionnaire:** Interview with David Dewan.

18 **Dewan played the part:** "Young Man Rides Crest of Computerized Life," *Sarasota Journal*, Mar. 13, 1969.

19 **Operation Match's questionnaire was "less sophisticated":** "University Police Eject Man from Winthrop House," *Harvard Crimson*, Sept. 30, 1965.

20 **"If there's some chick I'm dying to go out with":** Shalit, "New Dating Craze Sweeps the Campus."

20 **"Funny," an Operation Match employee later recalled:** The employee was a Yale student, Chris Walker, whom I interviewed three times between 2010 and 2012. He remains nameless here because he doesn't reappear in the book until the epilogue.

20 **"The way I envision things":** *Sarasota Journal*, "Young Man Rides Crest of Computerized Life."

20 **Going back to the Newtonians:** Walter Lippmann, *A Preface to Morals* (Piscataway, NJ: Transaction, 1982), 241.

20 **"Back then I was going out with a girl from Wellesley":** Interview with Dewan.

20 **Meanwhile, on campus, a political science major named Gerry:** The correspondence between Nancy and Gerry was quoted directly from the author's trove of letters between them, which includes a copy of Gerry's completed Contact questionnaire and the Contact sheet he received with Nancy's name on it. All other information about the young lovers was gleaned from a lifetime of being their son.

23 **In urban areas across the country:** John D'Emilio and Estelle B. Friedman, *Intimate Matters: A History of Sexuality in America* (Chicago: University of Chicago Press, 1988), 304–5.

23 **one of the first bars that "respectable" single women could visit alone:** Nick Paumgarten, "Looking for Someone," *The New Yorker*, July 4, 2011.

24 **In some ways this world of urban nightlife:** My understanding of the sexual revolution of the 1920s, and how technology affected courtship then, came from many great books, including: Beth L. Bailey, *From Front Porch to Back Seat: Courtship in Twentieth Century America* (Baltimore: Johns Hopkins University Press, 1988); Paula S. Fass, *The Damned and the Beautiful: American Youth in the 1920s* (New York: Oxford University Press, 1977); Ellen K. Rothman, *Hands and Hearts: A History of Courtship in America* (Cambridge, MA: Harvard University Press, 1984); E. S. Turner, *A History of Courting* (New York: Ballantine, 1954); Frederick Lewis Allen, *Only Yesterday: An Informal History of the 1920s* (New York: Harper & Row, 1931); Ben B. Lindsey and Wainright Evans, *The Revolt of Modern Youth* (Garden City, NY: Doubleday, 1925); and Robert S. Lynd and Helen Merrell Lynd, *Middletown: A Study in Modern American Culture* (New York: Harcourt Brace Jovanovich, 1929).

24 **"had elicited pity, scorn or fear":** D'Emilio and Friedman, *Intimate Matters*.

24 **a "privileged, spotlighted, envied group":** Ibid.

25 **billed as "one of England's most reputable marriage counselors":** Eustace Chesser, *Love Without Fear: How to Achieve Sex Happiness in Marriage* (New York: Signet, 1962).

25 **a "right to privacy" could be divined:** The relevant text of Douglas's opinion in *Griswold*: "[S]pecific guarantees in the Bill of Rights have penumbras, formed by emanations from those guarantees that help give them life and substance. . . . Various guarantees create zones of privacy. The right of association contained in the penumbra of the First Amendment is one, as we have seen. The Third Amendment, in its prohibition against the quartering of soldiers 'in any house' in time of peace without the consent of the owner, is another facet of that privacy. The Fourth Amendment explicitly affirms the 'right of the people to be secure in their persons, houses, papers, and effects, against unreasonable searches and seizures.' The Fifth Amendment, in its Self-Incrimination Clause, enables the citizen to create a zone of privacy which government may not force him to surrender to his detriment."

26 **when men showed off their assets:** Bailey, *From Front Porch to Back Seat.*

26 **desire for security in an uncertain world:** Ibid.

26 **to act as if they were already married:** Ibid., p. 49.

26 **"was further breaking down":** Ibid., p. 52.

26 **"Through at least the first two-thirds of the twentieth century":** Ibid., p. 25.

27 **"great and mysterious motive force in human life":** *Roth v. U.S.*, 354 U.S. 476.

27 **Judge Lindsey held heart-to-heart meetings:** Turner, *A History of Courting*, pp. 184–85.

28 **The youth of past generations didn't have the same economic independence:** Lindsey and Wainright, *The Revolt of Modern Youth*, pp. 158–59.

28 **Before dating there had been "calling":** Bailey, *From Front Porch to Back Seat*, pp. 13–16.

29 **The idea was that women:** Rothman, *Hands and Hearts*, pp. 188–89.

29 **Henry Ford and his ilk believed:** Turner, 208-213. See also Lynd and Lynd, Middletown, *258*: "Here again the automobile appears to some as an 'enemy' of the home and society."

29 **In 1919 the country had seven million registered cars:** Allen, *Only Yesterday*, p. 6.

29 **which furnished girls with the school's rules:** Bailey, *From Front Porch to Back Seat*, p.19.

30 **The etiquette expert Emily Post wondered:** Emily Post, *Etiquette: In Society, In Business, In Politics and At Home* (Funk & Wagnalls Company: New York, 1922), p. 293.

30 **"With the old order of things":** Allen, *Only Yesterday*, p. 100.

30 **"the rule for young couples was conversation in pairs":** Duncan Aikman, "Amazons of Freedom," *Harper's* (June 1926).

30 **"A growing emphasis on personality":** Rothman, *Hands and Hearts*, p. 225.

30 **"were separated from their parents":** Ibid., p. 289.

30 **no amount of fast driving could outrun:** Allen, *Only Yesterday*, p. 97: "A time of revolution, however, is an uneasy time to live in. It is easier to tear down a code than to put up a new one in its place.... People who have been brought up to think that is sinful for women to smoke or drink, and scandalous for sex to be discussed across the luncheon table, and unthinkable for a young girl to countenance strictly dishonorable attentions from a man, cannot all at once forget the admonitions of her childhood."

31 **The trending divorce rate of today:** Ibid., p. 95. As the divorce rate continued increasing, wrote Allen in 1931, there "was a corresponding decline in the amount of disgrace accompanying divorce. In the urban communities men and women who had been divorced were not socially accepted without question; indeed there was often about the divorced person just enough of an air of unconventionality, just enough of a touch of scarlet, to be considered rather dashing and desirable." (See also Lynd and Lynd, Middletown, p. 121: From Muncie, Indiana, the Lynds reported a much higher divorce rate—in 1909, there were twenty-five divorces for each one hundred marriage licenses. That rate increased to forty-two in 1924.)

31 **That "they should distrust the new freedom":** Lippmann, *A Preface to Morals*, p. 17.

31 **"The inexperienced":** Ibid., p. 300.

Chapter 2: Delivering More Love than Jesus

35 **"We are the most important search engine on the Web":** Nick Paumgarten, "Looking for Someone," *The New Yorker*, July 4, 2011.

35 **As a youngster in Skokie, Illinois:** The facts of Match's history and Gary Kremen's background were taken from an interview I did with Kremen; a keynote address he gave at the 2012 iDate conference in Miami; a series of

interviews I did with his first publicist at Match, Trish McDermott; and the following articles, listed in order of their value to this book: Ron Jackson, "Be Careful What You Wish For: The Continuing Saga of Gary Kremen and Sex .com," *DN Journal*, Mar. 31, 2008; Todd Krieger, "Love and Money," *Wired* (Sept. 1995); Julia Angwin, "Love's Labor Lost: Online matchmaker still seeks love, money," *San Francisco Chronicle*, Feb. 12, 1998; David Gelles, "Inside Match.com," *Financial Times*, July 29, 2011; and Jeff Kauflin, "How Match .com's Founder Created the World's Biggest Dating Website—And Walked Away With Just $50,000," *Business Insider*, Dec. 16, 2011.

36 **Over in France:** I learned of the Minitel and early French dating chat rooms from an interview I did in Paris with the present CEO of Meetic, Marc Simoncini's successor, Philippe Chainieux.

37 **The BBS revolution began:** Peter Zelchenko, "Jack Rickard, editor of Boardwatch magazine, saw it coming," *Chicago Tribune*, Oct. 30, 1998.

37 **Early BBSs would be used by clubs and communities:** Dwight Silverman, "Once the forums of computer devotees, bulletin board systems are dwindling as the graphical, global appeal of the Net's World Wide Web lures away the faithful," *Houston Chronicle*, Sept. 29, 1996.

38 **"We had some awful press coverage":** Andrea Orr, *Meeting, Mating, and Cheating: Sex, Love, and the New World of Online Dating* (Upper Saddle River, NJ: Reuters Prentice Hall, 2004), p. 28.

38 **The Matchmaker network grew into a nationwide chain:** Jeff Corydon, "Computerized Singles Scene," *Tampa Bay Times*, July 20, 1992.

39 **In the early seventies, James Schur:** Jim Schur passed away in 2010. My knowledge of Phase II comes from an interview I did with his wife and business partner, Iris. Iris and Jim met in 1967 through a Boston-based computer dating service called Data Mate, while Jim was doing research for his own dating service.

39 **referenced computer dating in his debut novel:** Don DeLillo, *Americana* (New York: Houghton Mifflin Harcourt, 1971), p. 5.

39 **Dating services had a reputation for drawing losers:** Bruce McCabe, "Who's Dating By Computer?" *Boston Globe*, Jan. 18, 1970.

40 **compiled letters sent to computer-dating services:** Bill Adler, ed., *Dear Dating Computer* (New York: Signet, 1968).

40 **In 1976, Jeffrey Ullman, a handsome young techie:** My understanding of video dating comes from two interviews I did with Jeff Ullman and the following articles, listed in order of importance: Amy Wallace, "Love God from Hell: The Man Who Brought You Video Dating Hates to Date, Loves to Taunt and Has Himself Been Unlucky in Love. Would You Buy a Relationship from Jeffrey Ullman?," *Los Angeles Times*, Jan. 16, 1994; Washington Post Service, "'Great Expectations' Fulfilled by Videotape," *Tri City Herald*, April 30, 1976; Barry Siegel, "Videotape Takes Blind Out of Dating," *Milwaukee Sentinel*, Apr. 26, 1976; Associated Press, "Who You Callin' Zero?" *Times Daily*, Sept. 27,

1990; Dan Dorfman, "Love, Not Burgers, Is Latest Franchise Item," *Lakeland Ledger*, June 24, 1984.

41 **montage viewable:** Available at http://www.youtube.com/watch?v=0bom kgXeDkE.

41 **the sketch-comedy:** The clips can be seen at http://www.youtube.com/ watch?v=FTBObmbe83A.

41 **He organized a demonstration:** Associated Press, "Who You Callin' Zero?"

41 **when TV talk-show host Montel Williams:** Wallace, "Love God from Hell."

42 **In 1690 in Britain:** H. G. Cocks, *Classified: The Secret History of the Personal Column* (New York: Random House, 2009).

43 **in Plato's ancient Greece:** Turner, *A History of Courting*, p. 16.

43 **The first known dating agency:** Cocks, *Classified*.

43 **It was not until the middle of the eighteenth century:** Aaron Ahuvia, Mara Adelman, and Elif Izberk-Bilgin, "Commercial Channels for Mate Seeking," *Encyclopedia of Human Relationships* (2009).

43 **"Everybody was letting it all hang out in other ways":** Patricia Morissroe, "Strictly Personals: Romance in the Want Ads," *New York Magazine*, Mar. 19, 1984.

44 **In 2011, *The New Yorker* observed:** Paumgarten, "Looking for Someone"; Marshall Sella, "iBone," *GQ*, (October 2011).

44 **Instead, we heat seek via search engine:** Eli Pariser, *The Filter Bubble: What the Internet Is Hiding from You* (New York: Penguin, 2011).

45 **he came to his first television interview:** Kauflin, "How Match.com's Founder Created the World's Biggest Dating Website."

46 **The Internet, writes communications historian:** Tim Wu, *The Master Switch: The Rise and Fall of Information Empires* (New York: Vintage, 2010), p. 266.

46 **Kremen's girlfriend met someone else:** Gelles, "Inside Match.com."

47 **remembers hearing about a couple who met online:** Lois Smith Brady, "The Vows at 20," *New York Times*, May 18, 2012.

47 **"It's really a bummer":** Angwin, "Love's Labor Lost."

48 **while standing on the selling floor of QVC:** Frank Rose, "Barry Diller Has No Vision for the Future of the Internet," *Wired* (November 2004).

48–49 **the young lawyer who:** Joy W. Wang, "Greg Blatt: A Perfect Match," *Columbia Law School Magazine*, (Winter 2010).

49 **average marriage age was twenty-three for men and twenty for women:** See "Median Age at First Marriage, 1890–2010." Available at: http://www.infoplease.com/ipa/A0005061.html.

49 **By 2011:** Anne Holland, "Dating & Matchmaking Site Benchmark Report" (Anne Holland: 2011), p. 15.

50 **attitudes toward online dating become more positive:** Doan, T. T. and S. A. Meyers. *Online dating: Determining the presence of a stigma.* Poster session presented at the meeting of Midwest Psychological Association, Chicago, IL.

Cited in Finkel, E. J. et al, "Online Dating: A Critical Analysis From the Perspective of Psychological Science," *Psychological Science in the Public Interest* (Feb. 2012).

50 **In 2010, nearly 33 percent of people between forty-six and sixty-four were divorced:** I-Fen Lin and Susan Brown, "Unmarried Boomers Confront Old Age: A National Portrait" 52(2), *The Gerontologist*, 1-13, Jan. 31, 2012. Available at http://www.documentcloud.org/documents/322105 -baby-boomers-confront-old-age.html. This study was cited in Rachel L. Swarns, "More Americans Rejecting Marriage in 50s and Beyond," *New York Times*, Mar. 1, 2012.

50 **accounting for 21 percent of the market:** "Dating & Matchmaking Site Benchmark Report," p. 15.

50 **The press release cited:** "IAC, Operator of Match.com and Other Popular Dating Sites, Unveils New Online Dating Site for Singles 50-Plus," *PR Newswire*, May 10, 2011.

50 **The top ten players:** Statistics for top visited dating sites comes from Irena Brooks at the online-dating consultancy Courtland Brooks, which aggregated data from *Experian Hitwise* for the month May 2012.

51 **one in five committed relationships originated online:** "Match.com and Chadwick Martin Bailey 2009—2010 Studies: Recent Trends: Online Dating Research Study." Available at http://cp.match.com/cppp/media/CMB_ Study.pdf

Chapter Three: The New Serendipity

59 **Back at Harvard, a math geek from Maine:** The foundation story of OkCupid was cobbled together from a series of conversations I had with Sam Yagan, Chris Coyne, and Christian Rudder, together and separately, between 2011 and 2012. The following news articles were also helpful: "A brief history of SparkNotes," available at http://www.sparknotes.com/about/ history; Catherine A. Zielinski, "15 Questions with Sam A. Yagan '99," *Harvard Crimson*, Feb. 11, 2009; Paumgarten, "Looking for Someone"; Aucoin, "Digital Man"; Lingbo Li, "Site Makes Matches with Math," *Harvard Crimson*, Jan. 31, 2008.

62 **OkCupid is premised on the idea:** See http://www.okcupid.com/help/ match-percentages for Coyne's overview of how the OkCupid algorithm works.

63 **researchers observed 109 "attraction tactics":** David M. Buss, *The Evolution of Desire: Strategies of Human Mating* (New York: Basic Books, 2003), pp. 103, 117.

64 **defines pheromones as:** Ibid, 244–48.

64 **scientists believed that because nonverbal cues:** Joseph B. Walther, "Computer-Mediated Communication: Impersonal, Interpersonal and Hyperpersonal Interaction" 23, no. 1, *Communication Research* (Feb. 1996).

65 **Potter's approach:** My interview with Potter was supplemented by Jordan Ellenberg, "The Netflix Challenge," *Wired* (March 2008).

68 **Dissonance, a popular concept in social psychology:** See Eastwick, P. W. and E. J. Finkel. "Sex Differences in Mate Preferences Revisited: Do People Know What They Initially Desire in a Romantic Partner?" 94, no. 2 *Journal of Personality and Social Psychology* (2008), pp. 245–64. Markus Frind, of Plenty of Fish, takes credit for introducing the concept of dissonance into online dating. In a rare 2007 appearance on the *Today* show, Frind said: "What people say they want and what they actually want are two completely different things. On my site, if someone is searching for clean-cut guys, but they really are messaging all the bad boys, I'll show them more bad boys than good guys." http://www.youtube.com/watch?v=3_eniyhXUZw.

68 **"If I had laid out criteria for what I was looking for":** Gelles, "Inside Match .com."

74 **"When I walk down the street":** Robert Andrews, "Google's Schmidt: Autonomous, Fast Search Is 'Our New Definition,'" *paidContent*, Sept. 7, 2010.

74 **Badoo was invented in 2006:** David Roman, "How Badoo Built a Billion-Pound Social Network," *Wired*, April 25, 2011.

74 **"It's no coincidence that Badoo was built in Spain":** Dan Slater, "How Badoo Bridges the Gap Between Online Dating Profiles and Real-Life Attraction," *Fast Company*, June 18, 2012.

75 **"Any site that can be used for flirting will be":** Jenna Wortham, "New Apps Connect to Friends Nearby," *New York Times*, Mar. 8, 2012. Through a spokeswoman, Parker denied several requests to be interviewed for this book.

75 **which was bought by Facebook:** Stacey Higginbotham, "Facebook buys Glancee in another mobile play," *GigaOM*, May 4, 2012.

75 **"We are thinking more about ourselves as simply a dating site":** Meghan Walsh, "Dating Sites Aim for a Novel Idea: Actual Dates," *Bloomberg Businessweek*, July 27, 2012.

76 **Airtime, Parker told CNN:** YouTube video, "Sean Parker explains how 'Airtime' works," available at http://www.youtube.com/watch?v=LeVzvu1GB4U.

76 **The word "dating" appeared nowhere:** Jenna Wortham, "Airtime Adds to a Growing Choice of Video Chat Services," *New York Times*, June 6, 2012.

76 **found that the "natural equilibrium mechanism":** Hitsch G.. J., A. Hortacsu, and D. Ariely. "Matching and Sorting in Online Dating," *American Economic Review* (2010), p. 1,

Chapter Four: It Knows My Anal Preferences?

81 **"No one knows what chemistry is at work":** Reuters, "Erk! Eek! Bloop! He Loves You," *Washington Post*, Sept. 12, 1973.

81 **In an early scene:** Gary Shteyngart, *Super Sad True Love Story* (New York: Random House, 2011), p. 89.

82 **"People are going to have to have a device":** David Kirkpatrick, *The Face-book Effect* (New York: Simon & Schuster, 2010), p. 314.

83 **"There was a lot of randomness to it":** Interview with Dewan.

84 **Born in 1934, Warren was:** Warren's background and the foundation of eHarmony were gleaned from media reports, marketing materials, books, and radio interviews, many of which were cited in a 2006 unpublished dissertation by Stephanie Blake, entitled "A Virtual Love Triangle: Mainstream online dating sites, the companies that own them and women subscribers." The original source materials, in order of importance, are: Rebecca Traister, "My date with Mr. eHarmony," Salon.com, June 10, 2005; Neil Clark Warren, interview by Terry Gross, *Fresh Air*, National Public Radio: Aug. 17, 2005; Janet Kornblum, "eHarmony: Heart and Soul," *USA Today*, May 19, 2005; Valerie Reitman, "We Clicked," *Los Angeles Times*, Apr. 26, 2004.

86 **"We came to the conclusion":** Interview by Terry Gross.

89 **In 2012, a team of five psychology professors:** Finkel, "Online Dating: A Critical Analysis from the Perspective of Psychological Science," 2012. The Finkel paper, published halfway through the writing of this book, was instrumental in helping me synthesize the results of my own research into how online dating affects relationships. My summary of the paper, which distills the material on pages 38 to 44, captures the heart of the authors' argument.

89 **made famous in:** Malcom Gladwell, *Blink: The Power of Thinking Without Thinking* (New York: Back Bay Books, 2005), pp. 21–22.

91 **"A very anxious person":** "Is there a science to compatibility?" *Psychologies* (May 2012).

92 **Chemistry ran competing TV ads:** Paul Farhi, "They Met Online, but Definitely Didn't Click," *Washington Post*, May 13, 2007.

93 **Between 2007 and 2010, personality-profiling sites:** "Dating & Matchmaking Site Benchmark Report," p. 15.

95 **two pioneering sex surveys:** D'Emilio and Friedman, *Intimate Matters*, pp. 55, 171. See also Christopher Turner, *Adventures in the Orgasmatron: How the Sexual Revolution Came to America* (New York: Farrar, Strauss and Giroux, 2012), pps. 215–17. Much of Davis's work was used for political ends. The information she gathered while running the Laboratory of Social Hygiene, an annex to a women's reformatory in Bedford Hills, New York, supported the eugenics campaign led by John D. Rockefeller Jr. Over the next four decades, Rockefeller would direct nearly $6 million into sex research. Beneficiaries included the Planned Parenthood project of Margaret Sanger, who would become involved in the research that led to the development of the Pill.

95 **predicted that Kinsey's studies:** *Look*, Dec. 7, 1947, pp. 106–7, as cited in D'Emilio and Friedman, *Intimate Matters*, p. 286.

95 **their write-up of a ten-year study of sexual physiology:** Mary Roach, *Bonk: The Curious Coupling of Science and Sex* (New York: W. W. Norton & Co., 2008), pp. 42–43.

96 **He started writing a corporate blog called OkTrends:** I've cherry-picked findings from OkTrends posts that appeared between September 2009 and April 2011, all available at http://blog.okcupid.com. In chronological order: "Online Dating Advice: Optimum Message Length"; "Exactly What to Say in a First Message"; "How Races and Religions Match in Online Dating"; "How Your Race Affects the Messages You Get"; "Your Looks and Your Inbox"; "The 4 Big Myths of Profile Pictures"; "The Case for an Older Woman"; "What Is *Your* Best Profile Picture"; "The Big Lies People Tell in Online Dating"; "Don't Be Ugly by Accident!"; "The REAL 'Stuff White People Like'"; "Gay Sex vs. Straight Sex"; "The Mathematics of Beauty"; "The Best Questions for a First Date."

97 **Black women reply to messages at the greatest rate:** This appears to be a reflection of the offline reality that college-educated black women are twice as likely as their white counterparts to wind up alone. See Ralph Richard Banks, *Is Marriage for White People? Why the African American Marriage Decline Affects Everyone* (New York: Dutton, 2012). Banks, a black professor at Stanford Law School, argues that the decline in black marriages is due to a tangle of factors, including: 1) black women's outperformance of black men in high school and college; 2) high rates of incarceration among black men; and 3) the tendency of economically successful black men to forego commitment and maintain several concurrent relationships with black women and/or to marry outside the race, trading their professional status for the higher racial status of a white wife. Black women, Banks argues, should respond to the black marriage crisis by dating outside the race. But doesn't this conflict with Rudder's finding that black women are ignored by white men online? No, says Banks. But he explains that the truth about why black women are far less likely to date outside the race than black men is more complex than the OkCupid stat implies. For one thing, on OkCupid, Latino, Middle Eastern, Indian, and Native American men all responded to black women at rates substantially higher than did white men. Also, studies tend to understate black women's options because black women are a numerical minority—13 percent of the female population—while nonblack men account for roughly 87 percent of the male population. So even if two thirds of nonblack men refuse to date a black woman, there would still be at least two or three times as many nonblack men willing to date black women as there are black women. Banks argues that the dating pools of black women are limited more by their own racial preferences than by those of nonblack men. Academic research suggests Banks is correct: A study of online mate selection showed that the same-race preferences of women are more pronounced than the same-race preferences of men.

99 **Online daters are, on average, two inches shorter:** In a separate study, social scientists found that the average deception for weight in online dating is 5.5 percent of actual weight. They also found the average deception for

height to be 2 percent of actual height, and the average deception for age to be 1.4 percent of actual age. C. L. Toma, J. T. Hancock, and N. B. Ellison, "Separating Fact from Fiction: An Examination of Deceptive Self-Presentation in Online-Dating Profiles" 34 *Personality and Social Psychology Bulletin* (2008), p. 1032.

102 **"Vast digital trails of social interaction":** Jon Kleinberg, "What Can Huge Data Sets Teach Us About Society and Ourselves?" in Max Brockman, ed., *Future Science: Essays from the Cutting Edge,* (New York: Vintage, 2011), p. 80.

102 **Masters and Johnson relied on somewhat cruder instruments:** Roach, *Bonk*, p. 48.

102 **In 2010, the OkTrends blog served as fodder:** Scott James, "In the Calculations of Online Dating, Love Can Be Cruel," *New York Times*, Feb. 12, 2010; Jenna Wortham, "Looking for a Date? A Site Suggests You Check the Data," *New York Times*, Feb. 12, 2010; Jenna Wortham, "Three Steps to Demystifying Online Dating," *New York Times Bits blog*, Feb. 13. 2010; Catherine Rampell, "What We're Reading . . ." *New York Times Economix blog*, April 6, 2010; David Colman, "Me, Myself and iPhone," *New York Times*, June 30, 2010; Rob Walker, "Stats Appeal," *New York Times Magazine*, Nov. 5, 2010.

102 **the rights to Rudder's forthcoming book:** Rachel Deahl, "London Book Fair 2012: Crown Nabs Book by OkCupid Co-founder in Rumored 7 Fig Deal," *Publishers Weekly*, Apr.17, 2012.

Chapter Five: Better Relationships but More Divorce

108 **"If you were standing in front of a group of business school students":** E. B. Boyd, "Match.com Boss, Now Head of IAC: 'There's No Recession in Love,'" *Fast Company*, Dec. 20, 2010.

109 **To say that his roots are small-town:** The background of Markus Frind and the foundation of Plenty of Fish comes from two interviews I did with him in 2011 and 2012, his corporate blog, and the definitive magazine profile by Max Chafkin, "And the Money Comes Rolling In," *Inc.*, Jan. 1, 2009.

113 **that you have no control:** Barry Schwartz, *The Paradox of Choice: Why More is Less* (New York: Harper Perennial, 2004), p. 103. Schwartz cites M. E. P. Seligman, *Helplessness: On Depression, Development, and Death* (New York: W. H. Freeman, 1975); and C. Peterson, S. F. Maier, and M. E. P. Seligman, *Learned Helplessness: A Theory for the Age of Personal Control* (New York: Oxford University Press, 1993).

113 **It's thought that the "brain pain" of lost love:** Louann Brizendine, MD, *The Female Brain* (New York: Broadway Books, 2006), pp. 75–76, citing Eisenberger, N. I. and M. D. Lieberman. "Why rejection hurts: A common neural alarm system for physical and social pain," *Trends in Cognitive Science* 8 (7), 294–300. See also Eisenberger, N. I., "Why rejection hurts" in Max Brockman, ed., *Future Science: Essays From the Cutting Edge* (New York: Vintage, 2011). "Social connection," writes Eisenberger, "may have been so important

for survival that the painful feelings associated with physical injury were co-opted to ensure that social separation was equally distressing—that individuals would be motivated by such feelings to avoid social disconnection and maintain closeness with others." Eisenberger argues that the dorsal portion of the anterior cingulate cortex, or ACC, registers the distressing aspect of physical (sensory) *and* social (distress) pain. Chronic pain patients who've undergone cingulatomies—the removal of the ACC—say they can still *feel* the pain, i.e., experience its felt aspect, but that it no longer bothers them, is no longer unpleasant. During episodes of rejection, heightened activity in the ACC correlated with self-reports of distress. In another study, Tylenol was found to reduce sensitivity to social rejection by reducing activity in the ACC. It's not yet been determined whether online dating's enhanced access to partners functions as natural Tylenol in the event of breakup.

115 **adopted by their peers in the face of "hook-up culture":** Kat Stoeffel, "Meet Your Gaggle: Crowd-sourced Love is Ready for Rom Com," *New York Observer*, May 31, 2011.

115 **each of whom fulfills a specific role:** Jessica Massa, *The Gaggle: How the Guys You Know Will Help You Find the Love You Want* (New York: Simon & Schuster, 2012).

117 **Abraham Maslow's Human Potential Movement:** Barbara Ehrenreich, *The Hearts of Men: American Dreams and the Flight from Commitment* (New York: Anchor Books, 1983).

118 **ten varieties of casual-but-emotional-sex:** Scott Alden, "The 10 Types of Non-Casual Sex," Aug. 12, 2011. Available at: http://www.howaboutwe .com/date-report/1633-the-10-types-of-non-casual-sex/#.

118 **any one of nine "pre-exclusive relationships":** Scott Alden, "The 9 Types of Pre-Exclusive Relationships," Dec. 29, 2011. Available at: http://www.how aboutwe.com/date-report/1402-the-9-types-of-pre-exclusive-relationships.

119 **elevates activity in brain regions associated:** Finkel et al., "Online Dating: A Critical Analysis from the Perspective of Psychological Science," p. 32.

119 **mate seekers are liable to become "cognitively overwhelmed":** Ibid., p. 33; see also Schwartz, *The Paradox of Choice.*

119 **three ingredients determine the strength of relationship commitment:** Le, B., and C. R. Agnew, "Commitment and its theorized determinants: A meta-analysis of the Investment Model," 10 *Personal Relationships* (2003), pp. 37–57.

126 **people will often overinvest:** Shin, J., and D. Ariely, "Keeping Doors Open: The Effect of Unavailability on Incentives to Keep Options Viable" 50 no. 5, *Management Science* (May 2004).

126 **have faced at least three constraints:** Buss, D. M., and D. P. Schmitt. "Sexual Strategies Theory: An Evolutionary Perspective on Human Mating" 100 no. 2, *Psychological Review* (1993), p. 207.

126 **change us by changing our perception of the world:** Marshall McLuhan, *Understanding Media: The Extensions of Man* (Berkeley, CA: Ginko Press, 2003).

Chapter Six: Diaper Daddies and Lonely Stoners

132 **founded in 1974 by John Broussard:** Lisa Belkin, "The Mail-Order Bride Business," *New York Times*, May 11, 1986. See also Melinda Henneberger, "Well, the Ukraine Girls Really Knock Them Out," *New York Times*, Nov. 15, 1992; and Christine S. Y. Chun, "The Mail-Order Bride Industry: The Perpetuation of Transnational Economic Inequalities and Stereotypes" 17 *University of Pennsylvania Journal of International Economic Law*, p. 4.

132 **his country had "become a real shopping market":** Kathleen Callo, "Philippine Mail Order Brides Are Booming Export," Reuters, Sept. 28, 1987.

133 **"There is a difference":** Wu, *The Master Switch*, p. 213.

138 **Wade, a Chinese American:** Marlow Stern, "Brandon Wade: The Man Behind 'Sugar Daddy' Web sites Miss Travel and Seeking Arrangement," *Daily Beast*, May 10, 2012.

142 **Simkhai released a smartphone application:** Background on Simkhai comes from my conversations with him, as well as Marshall Sella, "iBone," *GQ* (Oct. 2011); and Matt Kapp, "Grindr: Welcome to the World's Biggest, Scariest Gay Bar," *Vanity Fair* (May 2011).

143 **melted down:** Keir Mudie, "Gay app Grindr crashes as Olympic athletes arrive in London," *The People*, July 22, 2012.

144 **"Unlike a traditional dating site":** "Ashley Madison's Noel Biderman on the Profitability of Infidelity," *BlackBook*, Dec. 11, 2011. I interviewed Biderman in 2012. I was unable to unearth the article he refers to.

145 **particularly for primetime television slots like the Super Bowl:** Steve McClellan, "Fox Rejects AshleyMadison's Super Bowl Ad," *Adweek*, Jan. 20, 2011. The allegedly banned ad, which wound up running in Texas, depicts a beautiful woman celebrating her anniversary with her husband while he ignores her and ogles the waitress. The voice-over: "Have you ever been on a really bad blind date? Imagine that date lasting the rest of your life. Isn't it time for AshleyMadison.com?" And the tagline: "When divorce isn't an option."

146 **prompted a record number:** "Swedish 'Have an Affair' Ad Sets Complaint Record," *The Local*, Mar. 18, 2011.

146 **"the fastest growing community when it comes to infidelity":** "Ashley Madison.com Says Hispanics Are 'Fastest Growing Community When It Comes to Infidelity,'" *Huffington Post*, Nov. 11, 2011.

146 **Washington, D.C., was Ashley Madison's biggest market:** Brian Browde, "Washington, D.C. best city for cheating, online dating service finds," *New York Daily News*, Feb. 25, 2012.

148 **reviewed a bunch of books about life online:** Adam Gopnik, "The Information: How the Internet gets inside us," *The New Yorker*, Feb. 14, 2011.

Chapter Seven: Like Everyone, I'm Looking for My True Love

149 **"I like women from countries":** "Behold: Julian Assange's profile on Ok-Cupid," *Reddit*, posted Dec. 12, 2010. Available at http://www.reddit.com/r/politics/comments/ekgvz.

150 **had reached $2 billion:** Jessica Pilot and Julie Cohn, "Service With a Smile," *The Daily*, Apr. 23, 2012.

151 **New York–based Scanna International:** Melinda Henneberger, "From Warm Letters to Cold Warring, Romance Fades," *New York Times*, Oct. 28, 1992.

151 **only one of the hopeful mail-order brides:** Ericka Johnson, *Dreaming of a Mail-Order Husband: Russian-American Internet Romance* (Durham, NC: Duke University Press, 2007).

152 **"venturing abroad for love":** "The Mail-Order Bride Trade Is Flourishing," *Bloomberg Businessweek*, Jan. 6, 2011.

153 **When Western men use the Internet to meet women in China:** My understanding of the Chinese mail-order bride market comes from interviews I did with various members of Anastasia's staff.

159 **Medellin's "rich and beautiful come to show off":** *Colombia* (London: Lonely Planet, 2009), p. 213.

162 **Colombia specializes in vanity tourism:** Sergio de Leon, "Tourists Heading to Colombia for Plastic Surgery," *USA Today*, Mar. 14, 2006.

164 **which found that a man's chances of dying early:** Press Release, "Marriage and Life Expectancy," The Max Planck Institute, May 12, 2010.

166 **South America's second-most unequal distribution of wealth:** Simon Romero, "Dueling Beauty Pageants Put Income Gap on View," *New York Times*, Nov. 30, 2010, citing Center for Economic Development Studies in Bogotá.

167 **"There is nothing that indicates they are mutually exclusive explanations":** Johnson, *Dreaming of a Mail-Order Husband*, p. 154.

168 **to tout the company:** "AnastasiaDate Signs Playmate Dasha Astafieva as Spokeswoman," *Market Wire*, Oct. 7, 2011.

168 **juries award many lesser titles:** Romero, "Dueling Beauty Pageants Put Income Gap on View."

170 **will clash with Colombia's legalized prostitution:** Jackie Calmes and Matt Flegenheimer, "Secret Service Agents Accused of Misconduct," *New York Times*, Apr. 14, 2012.

171 **who's to say they won't be shipping back:** Mail-order grooms would not be unprecedented. In the mideightiess, Susie Carter, a woman who ran a daycare center in Anchorage, Alaska, noticed a surplus of single dads picking up their children. So Carter founded a catalog that became known as "Alaska Men USA." Several others followed, including "Bachelor Book." See Henneberger, "Well, the Ukraine Girls Really Knock Them Out," *New York Times*. This market, however, was purely domestic, and it was still expected that the woman would be the one to move.

171 **the number of Russian and Ukrainian women joining its site has tripled:** Amanda Walker, "Western Men Look East For Internet Brides," *Sky News*, Sept. 20, 2011. Although Anastasia is not cited in Walker's article, I was told by the company that they provided her with those numbers.

Chapter Eight: Knowledge Is Sour

176 **"Online relationships are vulnerable":** Cooper, A. and L. Sportolari, "Romance in cyberspace: Understanding online attraction," 22 no. 1 *Journal of Sex Education and Therapy* (1997).

176 **"There is an optimal pace at which intimacy develops":** Taylor, L. S., Fiore, A. T., Mendelsohn, G. A. and Cheshire, C. "A Second Chance to Make a First Impression: Factors Affecting the Longevity of Online Dating Relationships," Poster Paper. *Proceedings of the International Conference on Weblogs and Social Media*, 2010, p.4.

177 **In a twelfth-century advice manual:** Cited in Laura Kipnis, *Against Love: A Polemic* (New York: Pantheon, 2003), p. 60.

178 **the site established a new system of signals:** Kirkpatrick, *The Facebook Effect*, p. 91.

178 **"There are more techies":** David Weird, "SF Home to Next Generation of Online Dating Services, but Algorithm for Love Remains Elusive," *7x7SF*, Feb. 10, 2011.

180 **"To guard against deception":** Buss, *The Evolution of Desire*, p. 155.

181 **"supports an emotional style":** Sherry Turkle, *Alone Together: Why We Expect More from Technology and Less from Each Other* (New York: Basic Books, 2011), p. 175.

181 **Turkle finds teenagers:** Ibid, p. 176.

181 **constant insults between posters on /b/:** Parmy Olson, *We Are Anonymous: Inside the Hacker World of LulzSec, Anonymous, and the Global Cyber Insurgency* (New York: Little, Brown and Company, 2012), p. 30. See also pp. 34, 35, and 38.

182 **Second-order information:** Ilana Gershon, *The Breakup 2.0: Disconnecting Over New Media* (Ithaca, NY: Cornell University Press, 2010), p. 18.

182 **A woman refuses to e-mail:** Ibid.

183 **doesn't know if her boyfriend is serious:** Ibid., p. 19.

183 **is a medium men use:** Ibid., p. 109.

183 **are one of the foremost indications of a man's intent:** Buss, *The Evolution of Desire*, p. 135.

183 **Trinidadians believe that the truth of another person:** Daniel Miller, *Tales From Facebook* (Cambridge, UK: Polity, 2012), p. 50.

183 **his girlfriend gets upset:** Gershon, *The Breakup 2.0*, p. 87.

184 **"made them into *that kind of girlfriend*":** Ibid., p. 83.

184 **explains the vicious cycle:** Muise A., E. Christofides, S. Desmarais. "More Information than You Ever Wanted: Does Facebook Bring Out the Green-Eyed Monster of Jealousy?" 12 no. 4 *CyberPsychology & Behavior* (2009).

184 **"The problem Facebook is solving":** John Cassidy, "Me Media: How hanging out on the Internet became big business," *The New Yorker,* May 15, 2006.

184 **"There's a deep, probably irreconcilable tension":** James Grimmelmann, "Saving Facebook," 94 *Iowa Law Review* (2009) p. 1137.

185 **"How one behaves in a pub":** Danah Boyd, "Facebook's Privacy Trainwreck: Exposure, Invasion, Social Convergence" 14 no. 1 *Convergence: The International Journal of Research into New Media Technologies* (2008), p. 18.

186 **things you shouldn't do:** Available at http://www.howaboutwe.com/date -report/1543-10-things-you-shouldn-t-do-until-you-re-exclusive.

186 **the crazy things women do:** Available at http://www.howaboutwe.com/ date-report/1361-the-crazy-things-women-do-on-facebook-true-or-false.

186 **why Facebook might be ruining:** Available at http://www.howaboutwe .com/date-report/1603-5-ways-facebook-is-ruining-your-dating-life.

186 **the crazy things guys do:** Available at http://www.howaboutwe.com/date -report/1375-the-crazy-things-guys-do-on-facebook.

186 **terrible for new relationships:** Available at http://www.howaboutwe.com/ date-report/1172-the-worst-thing-you-can-do-in-a-new-relationship-gchat.

186 **the elements of digital style:** Kristina Grish, *The Joy of Text: Mating, Dating, and Techno-Relating* (New York: Simon Spotlight Entertainment, 2006), pp. 54–58.

187 **coined such behavior bluffting:** Elizabeth Bernstein, "Why Texting Turns Us Back Into Teenagers," *Wall Street Journal,* Nov. 1, 2011.

Chapter Nine: Let's Keep This Fucker Coming Back

193 **"If you succeed":** Anand Giridharadas, "Dating Site for Married Couples," *New York Times,* Mar. 9, 2012.

194 **then-CEO Tim Sullivan told:** Bob Tedeschi, "E-commerce Report; In quest for financial payoff, online dating services are expanding to do more than find you the love of your life," *New York Times,* Aug. 11, 2003.

197 **"highly concerned" about unethical practices:** "Dating & Matchmaking Site Benchmark Report," p. 92.

200 **In 2009, a fifty-eight-year-old man:** See Jonathan Leake, "Police target lonely hearts fraudsters," *The Sunday Times* (London), Nov. 27, 2011; Jim Dubreuil, Gerry Wagschal, and Rena LaFaille, "Online Dating Nightmare: N.Y. Woman Scammed Out of Thousands by Soldier," *ABC News,* June 22, 2011; Bill Tyson, "Smart Consumer: The lonely heart mum who lost €300,000 in an internet scam," *The Independent,* May 27, 2010; Harriet Alexander, "Police arrest suspected romance fraudster who posed as US soldier," *The Telegraph,* May 1, 2010; Harriet Alexander, "British victim of 'romance fraud' tells of ordeal," *The Telegraph,* May 2, 2010.

200 **including a sixty-nine-year-old woman in Minnesota:** Tad Vezner, "Love at first scam? Rice County woman defrauded on Match.com," *Pioneer Press,* Feb. 28, 2012.

201 **"Why You Should Never Pay for Online Dating"**: The article is no longer available on the OkCupid site, but it's available here: http://www.scribd .com/doc/48916912/Why-You-Should-Never-Pay-For-Online-Dating-%C2 %AB-OkTrends.

201 **Match was sued in its home state of Texas:** "Customers sue Match.com," *Dallas Business Journal*, Jan. 4, 2011; Robert Wilonsky, "Yet Another Federal Deceptive Trade Practices Suit Filed Against Match.com. Wink!" *Dallas Observer*, June 22, 2011.

202 **The language in Match's user agreement:** See *Robinson, et al. v. Match.com, LLC*, U.S. District Court for the Northern District of Texas, 10-cv-02651, pp. 15–16.

203 **OkCupid announced it was selling itself to Match for $90 million:** "IAC's Match.com Acquires OkCupid," *IAC Media Room*, Feb. 2, 2011. The stated acquisition price was $50 million. Several sources informed me that the actual price, including payouts, was $90 million.

203 **he back treaded:** Brenna Ehrlich, "OkCupid CEO: We Will Not Charge Users Following Match.com Acquisition," *Mashable*, Feb. 2, 2011. See also Adrianne Jeffries, "OKCupid: We Didn't Censor Our Match.com-Bashing Blog Post," *New York Observer*, Feb. 2, 2011: "I know everyone wants to make a big deal out of this," Yagan said. "They didn't tell us take it down. I wanted to do it . . . We obviously believe in a free model but there are also paid models and I didn't think [the post's] continued existence served much of a purpose. People will say, 'Oh my God, they've sold out and they're censoring it,' that's fine. When we put our next blog post next week and keep being awesome and the product keeps being awesome and free, people will just realize they're overreacting." He added: "In general the totality of data that we have become exposed to leads us to believe that yes, the subscription sites are probably more successful than the post made them out to be."

204 **alleged that she'd been raped:** Rachel Quigley, "Tired of hiding: Match.com 'rape victim speaks out about ordeal at the hands of convicted sex offender she met on dating site,'" *Daily Mail*, Apr. 19, 2011.

204 **Match announced that it would be checking:** Leon Watson, "'If I save one woman I'm happy': Sex attack victim drops case after Match.com agrees to screen its members," *Daily Mail*, Aug. 24, 2011.

204 **"a joint statement of business principles":** Press Release, "Attorney General Kamala D. Harris Announces Agreement to Strengthen Consumer Protections for Users of Online Dating Web sites," State of California Department of Justice Office of Attorney General, Mar. 20, 2012. Available at http://oag .ca.gov/news/press-releases/attorney-general-kamala-d-harris-announces -agreement-strengthen-consumer.

204 **In due time:** "IAC Announces Management Changes at Its Match Segment," PRNewswire, Oct. 23, 2012.

205 **interviewed eHarmony's Dr. Gian Gonzaga:** "Love at First Byte: The Secret Science of Online Dating," CNBC, Feb. 9, 2012.

207 **described it like this:** Tedeschi, "E-commerce Report; In quest for financial payoff, online dating services are expanding to do more than find you the love of your life," 2003.

207 **Between 1998 and 2005:** Revenue growth statistics come from *IBISWorld*.

209 **The need to connect deeply:** Baumeister, R. F., and M. R. Leary. "The need to belong: Desire for interpersonal attachments as a fundamental human motivation," 117 *Psychological Bulletin* (1995), pp. 497–529.

211 **led a bust of two American women:** Jessica Fender, "Brighton mom-daughter team accused of $1 million online dating scam," *Denver Post*, June 19, 2012. Available at http://www.denverpost.com/recommended/ci_20892031, indictment attached.

Epilogue: Dating Starts Here

215 **a CBS game show:** Clip is available here: http://www.youtube.com/watch?v=lmIC7VFyE4M.

216 **Ginsburg withdrew the nomination:** Steven V. Roberts, "Ginsburg Withdraws Name as Supreme Court Nominee, Citing Marijuana 'Clamor,'" *New York Times*, Nov. 8, 1987.

218 **"that Japan is so worried about the low birth rate":** Aki Ito, "Japan's Government Plays Matchmaker," *Bloomberg Businessweek*, Aug. 26, 2010.

219 **a right to engage in such conduct was "facetious":** See Justice Byron White's majority opinion in *Bowers* here: http://www.law.cornell.edu/supct/html/historics/USSC_CR_0478_0186_ZO.html.

219 **To hold otherwise:** See Chief Justice Warren's concurrence in *Bowers* here: http://www.law.cornell.edu/supct/html/historics/USSC_CR_0478_0186_ZC.html.

219 **Now the Constitution did protect sodomy:** See Justice Kennedy's opinion in *Lawrence* here: http://www.law.cornell.edu/supct/html/02-102.ZO.html.

219 **the Court's scrappiest member threw a fit:** See Justice Scalia's dissent in *Lawrence* here: http://www.law.cornell.edu/supct/html/02-102.ZD.html.

221 **"I'd like to think of myself":** Stern, "Brandon Wade."

221 **explains the genesis of WWW:** Wu, *The Master Switch*, p. 282.

224 **"The illusion of scarcity is what makes us so possessive and jealous":** See Ryan, C., and C. Jetha. *Sex at Dawn: How We Mate, Why We Stray, and What It Means for Modern Relationships* (New York: Harper Perennial, 2010), see, e.g., p. 145: "For most human beings, reality is pretty much what we're told it is. Like practically everything else, jealousy reflects social modification and can clearly be reduced to little more than a minor irritant if consensus deems it so."

224 **"from his baser unmediated impulses":** Wu, *The Master Switch*, p. 38.

INDEX